Elizabeth Hanford Dole

Speaking from the Heart

MOLLY MEIJER WERTHEIMER AND NICHOLA D. GUTGOLD

FOREWORD BY KERRY TYMCHUK

Praeger Series in Political Communication

Westport, Connecticut
London

Library of Congress Cataloging-in-Publication Data

Wertheimer, Molly Meijer.
    Elizabeth Hanford Dole : speaking from the heart / Molly Meijer Wertheimer and
Nichola D. Gutgold ; foreword by Kerry Tymchuk.
      p. cm. — (Praeger series in political communication, ISSN 1062–5623)
    Includes bibliographical references and index.
    ISBN 0–275–98378–1 (alk. paper)
      1. Dole, Elizabeth Hanford.   2. Women legislators—United States—Biography.
3. Legislators—United States—Biography.   4. United States. Congress. Senate—
Biography. 5. Women cabinet officers—United States—Biography.   6. Cabinet officers—
United States—Biography.   7. American Red Cross—Biography.   I. Gutgold, Nichola
D. II. Title. III. Series.
    E840.8.D63W47 2004
    328.73′092—dc22   2004011906

British Library Cataloguing in Publication Data is available.

Library of Congress Catalog Card Number: 2004011906
ISBN: 0–275–98378–1
ISSN: 1062–5623

First published in 2004

Praeger Publishers, 88 Post Road West, Westport, CT 06881
An imprint of Greenwood Publishing Group, Inc.
www.praeger.com

Printed in the United States of America

The paper used in this book complies with the
Permanent Paper Standard issued by the National
Information Standards Organization (Z39.48–1984).

10 9 8 7 6 5 4 3 2 1

To Richard B. Gregg, who would have been delighted by this book.

Contents

Series Foreword

Those of us from the discipline of communication studies have long believed that communication is prior to all other fields of inquiry. In several other forums I have argued that the essence of politics is "talk" or human interaction.[1] Such interaction may be formal or informal, verbal or nonverbal, public or private, but it is always persuasive, forcing us consciously or subconsciously to interpret, to evaluate, and to act. Communication is the vehicle for human action.

From this perspective, it is not surprising that Aristotle recognized the natural kinship of politics and communication in his writings *Politics* and *Rhetoric*. In the former, he established that humans are "political beings [who] alone of the animals [are] furnished with the faculty of language."[2] In the latter, he began his systematic analysis of discourse by proclaiming that "rhetorical study, in its strict sense, is concerned with the modes of persuasion."[3] Thus, it was recognized over twenty-three hundred years ago that politics and communication go hand in hand because they are essential parts of human nature.

In 1981, Dan Nimmo and Keith Sanders proclaimed that political communication was an emerging field.[4] Although its origin, as noted, dates back centuries, a "self-consciously cross-disciplinary" focus began in the late 1950s. Thousands of books and articles later, colleges and universities offer a variety of graduate and undergraduate coursework in the area in such diverse departments as communication, mass communication, journalism, political science, and sociology.[5] In Nimmo and Sanders's early assessment, the "key areas of inquiry" included rhetorical analysis, propaganda analysis, attitude change studies, voting studies, government and the news media, functional and systems analyses, technological changes, media technologies, campaign techniques, and research techniques.[6] In a survey of the state of the field in 1983, the same authors and Lynda Kaid found additional, more specific areas of concern such as the presidency, political polls, public opinion, debates, and advertising.[7] Since the first study, they have also noted a shift away from the rather strict behavioral approach.

A decade later, Dan Nimmo and David Swanson argued that "political communication has developed some identity as a more or less distinct domain of scholarly work."[8] The scope and concerns of the area have further expanded to include critical theories and cultural studies. Although there is no precise definition, method, or disciplinary home of the area of inquiry, its primary domain is the role, processes, and effects of communication within the context of politics broadly defined.

In 1985, the editors of *Political Communication Yearbook: 1984* noted that "more things are happening in the study, teaching, and practice of political communication than can be captured within the space limitations of the relatively few publications available."[9] In addition, they argued, that the backgrounds of "those involved in the field [are] so varied and pluralist in outlook and approach, . . . it [is] a mistake to adhere slavishly to any set format in shaping the content."[10] More recently, Nimmo and Swanson have called for "ways of overcoming the unhappy consequences of fragmentation within a framework that respects, encourages, and benefits from diverse scholarly commitments, agendas, and approaches."[11]

In agreement with these assessments of the area and with gentle encouragement, in 1988 Praeger established the series entitled "Praeger Series in Political Communication." The series is open to all qualitative and quantitative methodologies as well as contemporary and historical studies. The key to characterizing the studies in the series is the focus on communication variables or activities within a political context or dimension. As of this writing, 80 volumes have been published and numerous impressive works are forthcoming. Scholars from the disciplines of communication, history, journalism, political science, and sociology have participated in the series.

I am, without shame or modesty, a fan of the series. The joy of serving as its editor is in participating in the dialogue of the field of political communication and in reading the contributors' works. I invite you to join me.

Robert E. Denton, Jr.

NOTES

1. See Robert E. Denton, Jr., *The Symbolic Dimensions of the American Presidency* (Prospect Heights, IL: Waveland Press, 1982); Robert E. Denton, Jr., and Gary Woodward, *Political Communication in America* (New York: Praeger, 1985; 2d ed.,

1990); Robert E. Denton, Jr., and Dan Hahn, *Presidential Communication* (New York: Praeger, 1986); and Robert E. Denton, Jr., *The Primetime Presidency of Ronald Reagan* (New York: Praeger, 1988).

2. Aristotle, *The Politics of Aristotle*, trans. Ernest Barker (New York: Oxford University Press, 1970), p. 5.

3. Aristotle, *Rhetoric*, trans. W. Rhys Roberts (New York: The Modern Library, 1954), p. 22.

4. Dan Nimmo and Keith Sanders, "Introduction: The Emergence of Political Communication as a Field," in *Handbook of Political Communication*, eds. Dan Nimmo and Keith Sanders (Beverly Hills, CA: Sage, 1981), pp. 11–36.

5. Ibid., p. 15.

6. Ibid., pp. 17–27.

7. Keith Sanders, Lynda Kaid, and Dan Nimmo, eds. *Political Communication Yearbook: 1984* (Carbondale: Southern Illinois University Press, 1985), pp. 283–308.

8. Dan Nimmo and David Swanson, "The Field of Political Communication: Beyond the Voter Persuasion Paradigm," in *New Directions in Political Communication*, eds. David Swanson and Dan Nimmo (Beverly Hills, CA: Sage, 1990), p. 8.

9. Sanders, Kaid, and Nimmo, *Political Communication Yearbook: 1984*, p. xiv.

10. Ibid.

11. Nimmo and Swanson, "The Field of Political Communication, " p. 11.

Foreword

Over the course of the past three decades, few Americans have achieved more "firsts" than Elizabeth Hanford Dole. She was one of the first women to serve on the Federal Trade Commission and as secretary of labor. She was the first woman to serve as secretary of transportation and the first woman since Clara Barton to serve as president of the American Red Cross. She was one of the first women to run for the presidency of the United States. And she is the first woman ever to serve as a U.S. senator from North Carolina.

There are many qualities that have helped propel Elizabeth Dole to this remarkable career, including a keen intelligence, unquestioned integrity, and a never-ending commitment to helping those most in need. There can be no doubt, however, that her success is due in no small part to her remarkable public speaking abilities.

Elizabeth Dole cemented her reputation as one of America's most eloquent and sought-after speakers at the 1996 Republican National Convention, when she left the podium and delivered a thirty-minute tribute to her husband—presidential candidate Robert Dole—as she walked among the convention delegates, speaking, as she said, "from the heart," and without notes or a teleprompter. It was a tour de force that had television commentators tripping over themselves with superlatives.

It has been my privilege to serve for nearly fifteen years as a speechwriter, consultant, and friend to Mrs. Dole. In that time, I have seen her give literally hundreds of speeches to an endless variety of audiences. I have yet to see her deliver a speech that wasn't first-rate.

Even in this time where it seems that e-mail and instant messaging have rendered rhetoric obsolete, Elizabeth Dole's success is proof that the art of public speaking remains critical to success in business and in life.

Indeed, by speaking so often and so well, Senator Dole has effectively presented a model of rhetorical excellence for women who may follow in her path and create their own "firsts" in the years to come.

Speaking of "firsts," Nichola Gutgold and Molly Meijer Wertheimer are to be congratulated for this book, which is the first-ever rhetorical biography of the speeches and career of Elizabeth Dole. Their study was greatly assisted by the fact that they were able to personally interview Senator Dole on several occasions, gaining firsthand insight into the care and attention she devotes to the art of public speaking.

In one of Elizabeth Dole's favorite quotations, Oliver Wendell Holmes Jr. described the events that shaped his generation by saying, "In our youth, it was our great good fortune to have our hearts touched by fire." I am confident that those who learn more about the life and words of Elizabeth Dole by reading this book will better understand what propels her to such passionate service for the good of others and will likely have their hearts warmed by her example.

Kerry Tymchuk
Beaverton, Oregon

Preface

> You go out there and talk about things you care about, it's from the
> heart.
>
> —Elizabeth Dole (Interview, July 8, 2003)

Speeches are a vital part of public life. Often what a politician says is as
important as what he or she does, and is remembered longer. Who can
forget such memorable lines as Abraham Lincoln's: "government of the
people . . . by the people . . . for the people . . . shall not perish from the
earth," or John F. Kennedy's: "Ask not what your country can do for you,
ask what you can do for your country," or, about civil rights, Martin
Luther King Jr.'s: "we will not be satisfied until justice rolls down like
waters and righteousness like a mighty stream," or, about women's rights,
Susan B. Anthony's: "Failure is impossible." The speeches in which these
lines were uttered have long ago become defining documents of the
American character and spirit. Children memorize the lines at school, well
before they understand their meaning. One such line Elizabeth Dole may
have learned when she was growing up and later quoted in her own
speeches is by George Washington: "Of all the dispositions and habits
which lead to political prosperity, religion and morality are indispensable
supports." During her career as a public speaker, Dole has quoted many
memorable lines from American authors and speakers, and she has uttered
a substantial number of her own.

This book presents a rhetorical biography of Elizabeth Hanford Dole,
a seasoned Washington, D.C., insider with the genteel charm of a socialite,
whose combination of political skills and elegance have earned her nick-
names such as the "Steel Magnolia." Of particular focus are the speeches

she delivered in the primary roles she has played—as a public servant dedicated to making a difference by influencing government policy, as a humanitarian meeting the needs of people who face dire circumstances, and as an advocate for political candidates, including her husband and herself. Each of the following chapters discusses many of her major speeches and provides contextual material to help the reader understand her purposes, as well as the circumstances she was in when she presented them.

The introduction, "Her Words Paint the Portrait," provides an overview of Dole's life and sketches her special traits as a public speaker. Chapter 2, "Advocate for Public Policy," explores Dole's career in public service, detailing the positions she has held, and how she used her rhetorical communication skills to achieve legislative and humanitarian goals. Chapter 3, "Advocate for Religious, Patriotic, and Humanitarian Values," traces the impact of Dole's religious faith and patriotism on her career and speech making. Chapter 4, "Advocate for Women's Rights," examines Dole's subtle feminism, especially her career choices and her record on improving the working conditions for women and minorities. Chapter 5, "Advocate for Her Husband, the Republican Party, and Herself," describes Dole's skill and activity as a campaigner, first helping others achieve elective office and then campaigning for herself. The conclusion, "A Leader 'A Long Way from the Twilight,'" highlights the areas of speech making in which Dole excels and provides a summary of what this study contributes to an understanding of contemporary women speakers in the public/political arena. The appendix includes full texts of Elizabeth Dole's most significant and representative speeches, given during the years 1987–2003.

Writing a book of any kind requires the knowledge, experience, and patience of many persons, and this book is no exception. We would like to acknowledge several administrators from Pennsylvania State University who provided us with encouragement and the necessary travel funds to attend professional conferences where many of the ideas in this book were critiqued by colleagues. From Berks/Lehigh Valley College, Dr. Gene Slaski, former CEO at the Lehigh Valley campus; Dr. Kenneth Fifer, division head of humanities, arts, and sciences; and Dr. Carl Lovitt, associate dean, all showed their confidence in the project by approving university support for Nikki [author Nichola D. Gutgold]. From Commonwealth College, Dr. Monica E. Gregory and Mrs. Deidre Jago, respectively director and assistant director of academic affairs at the Hazleton campus; Dr. Priscilla F. Clement, division head of arts and humanities; and Dr. Sandra E. Gleason, associate dean of faculty and research, provided leadership and goodwill, as well as released time from teaching for Molly [author Molly Meijer Wertheimer], including a sabbatical leave in the spring of 2001.

From Praeger Publishers, we are grateful to Hilary Claggett, senior editor of politics, international affairs, legal studies, and current events and Robert E. Denton Jr., political communication series editor, both of whom saw merit in our prospectus. Hilary's sound advice and editorial recommendations helped us through the publication process; she answered our questions with surprising speed, even on the weekend.

Our sincerest gratitude goes to Kerry Tymchuk, a gifted speechwriter with a great sense of humor, who oriented Nikki at the beginning of the project and supplied her with copies of many of the speeches in the appendix. His belief in the value of the project and his willingness to write the foreword for this volume are greatly appreciated. We are also very grateful to Senator Bob Dole, who granted us a memorable and lengthy interview. He answered our questions about his most eloquent wife fully and with humor, enlightening us with behind-the-scenes stories.

Elizabeth Dole couldn't have been more gracious when Nikki interviewed her in 1998, and again when both of us met with her during the summer of 2003. She gave us key insights into her career as a public speaker, especially into the evolution of her campaigning style, which has become more extemporaneous—and impromptu—especially when she ran for a U.S. Senate seat from North Carolina. She generously gave us permission to include texts of her speeches in the appendix, and we have quoted from them liberally in our chapters. Her staff members, including Carol Maltman, Janelle Carter, Mary Brewer Brown, and Gia Colambraro, provided material that greatly improved the quality of the book.

A word should also be said about the origin and development of the project. The initial inspiration came one August evening in 1996, when Nikki, a PhD student in speech communication at the time, saw Elizabeth Dole on television descending the platform stairs in high heels at the Republican National Convention. Dole's exquisite performance proved an irresistible subject for Nikki's dissertation, which began under the direction of Dick Gregg, to whom this book is dedicated. With Dick's passing, Molly helped Nikki finish her dissertation and in the process became impressed with Elizabeth Dole's contributions to public policy, especially her work on the glass ceiling. From those beginnings, a new work has grown as we researched biographies, asked questions during interviews, and downloaded as many newspaper and magazine articles as we could find through search engines such as Lexus/Nexus and Proquest.

Throughout the writing process, both of our families have been enormously helpful. Nikki's son, Ian, helped her with citations and recorded speeches, while daughter Emily Ann motivated her to keep the project alive for the next generation of women leaders. Molly's son, Aaron, and his friend, Blake, organized a huge stack of miscellaneous newspaper and magazine articles by date, and Aaron scanned in some of the speeches that are included in the appendix. Nikki's husband, Geoff, forwarded many useful articles to her in-box and drove her to Salisbury, North Carolina, to see Elizabeth Dole's birthplace. Molly's husband, Frits, prepared image files of the photos used in this book, and assembled the final manuscript into a well-formatted document.

Finally, we would like to acknowledge the help we have given each other. Nikki's passion for the subject provided the impetus for the project. Her perseverance in collecting (and transcribing) speech manuscripts and in setting up interviews generated vital material for us to use in writing the chapters. Her insight into Senator Dole's platform presence, charisma, and exceptional agility as a speaker gave us our central themes. Molly's expertise in the fields of rhetoric and women's studies moved the project from dream to reality. Her passion for research provided contextual material to deepen our understanding of Dole's motivation, purposes, and contributions. Her gift at assimilating bits of material gave the chapters their logic and the book its coherence. Her lucid writing and skill as an editor gave the volume clarity and precision.

Both of us hope this book will make a contribution to the literature on women's political rhetoric and that others will continue to study Elizabeth Dole as an American spokeswoman who blazed a trail for herself and other women leading to the Oval Office—all the while fending off flak with grace and humor.

Chapter 1

Introduction:
Her Words Paint the Portrait

> Now, you know, tradition is that speakers at the Republican National
> Convention remain at this very imposing podium. But tonight I'd like
> to break with tradition for two reasons—one, I'm going to be speak-
> ing to friends, and secondly, I'm going to be speaking about the man
> I love. And it's just a lot more comfortable for me to do that down
> here with you.[1]

In August 1996, Elizabeth Dole captured the attention of the nation when
she daringly descended the platform stairs at the Republican National
Convention clad in three-inch spike heels. She broke with tradition to
deliver her Oprah-like campaign speech about "the man I love," her husband and candidate for the presidency, Bob Dole. During this widely televised speech, she conveyed the impression of being not only a political
virtuoso in her own right, but also the devoted helpmate of her candidate
husband. Relying on her ability to tell cogent stories throughout her
speech, she presented his bravery and altruism, often turning to witnesses
placed throughout the convention floor for corroboration. Her goal was
to demonstrate how her husband, who was seen by some as "the nation's
mortician" and a hatchet man for the Republican Party, was instead the
"strongest, most compassionate man" she had ever known and why he
was without question the best choice for election as the next president of
the United States.

Her publicly acclaimed convention speech may have seemed like a
grand finale for Dole, who began campaigning for her husband for the
vice presidency in 1976, and who had participated in his many unsuccessful attempts for the presidency across a twenty-year span. At the same

Elizabeth Dole actively campaigning for the presidency. (Photo courtesy of Elizabeth Dole for President Campaign)

time, this top-ranking Republican woman had served in appointed offices under six presidents—from Democratic Lyndon Baines Johnson to Republican George Herbert Walker Bush. Twice she had served in presidential cabinets, as secretary of transportation during the Reagan administration and as secretary of labor during the Bush administration. She had served as well as an ardent spokeswoman for the Republican Party, chairing the Republican National Convention in 1988, where she presented a rousing speech to persuade the women of America to vote Republican—not an easy task at that time.[2] A year earlier, in 1987, she had delivered the keynote address at the National Prayer Breakfast meeting, disclosing the twists and turns of her own spiritual journey to a huge audience of Washington, D.C., leaders.[3] Through these and other speaking events, Dole gained a reputation as an articulate, thoughtful, and captivating public speaker, who was always well prepared to engage with her audience. By the time she presented her conspicuous spouse speech in 1996, her reputation had grown nationally through her speech making and media coverage as she performed the duties of president of the American Red Cross, a huge philanthropic organization with resources comparable to a Fortune

500 company. But anyone who has followed her career since that time, including her run for the presidency during Campaign 2000, and her bid for a U.S. Senate seat in 2002, knows that Dole is always moving forward. Rather than being a finale, her grand 1996 campaign speech may have been only a mid-career point for the ambitious North Carolinian whose mother lived to see her hundredth birthday, and whose grandmother lived to within two weeks of hers.

On January 4, 1999, camera crews descended upon the historic Board of Governors Hall in anticipation of Dole's resignation from the American Red Cross. In what was called the "Political Play of the Week," the media and public anxiously awaited word of whether she would announce her decision to run for the presidency in 2000. Wearing a bright watermelon red tailed suit, she appeared at the podium and warmly greeted her audience, telling them about all the hard thinking she had done about the future during the Christmas holidays. She reviewed the sorry condition of several Red Cross operations when she took over as the president, and she told all assembled before her and her vast television audience how the Red Cross was now as "solid as a rock." She bid farewell as their president, coyly suggesting that she would soon "begin considering new paths." Shortly thereafter, she set up an exploratory committee, and then launched her campaign for the U.S. presidency. She stumped all across the country, this time campaigning for herself in places such as Melrose High School in Boston, where she outlined her plan for restoring U.S. education to its former quality and at the U.S. Naval Academy, where she talked about updating U.S. military equipment and sound foreign policy. Months later, a sign went up at her headquarters that read: "We made history." Not having the funds to continue, Dole withdrew from the race—but her visibility on the American political scene had been greatly enhanced.

Two years later, at her victory celebration after winning a U.S. Senate seat from North Carolina, a jubilant Elizabeth Dole stepped up to the podium to address her cheering supporters. With the theme of Rocky III playing in the background, she declared: "O Wow! What a Night!" and "We'll never forget this night, will we?" This was the thrilling culmination of months of campaigning back and forth across one hundred counties of the state. She relished the opportunity to speak to prospective constituents about the economy and education. President George W. Bush and First Lady Laura Bush, eager to see her win, flew into her home state to help with fund-raising. She debated her opponent, Democrat Erskine B. Bowles, forcefully asserting her positions on how she could help make life better for the people of North Carolina. She responded directly to pointed questions about how she would deal with terrorists and with the impending war with Iraq. This campaign proved Dole to be a formidable politician in her own right. Any mistakes she may have made during her bid for the presidency were not to be repeated in this race. True to her campaign promises, she presented her maiden speech to the Senate on June 5, 2003, requesting relief for the hungry people of North Carolina and throughout the United States through legislative action that would reward businesses and volunteers for recycling farmers' surpluses into sustenance for those who desperately need it.

During her lengthy career, Dole has garnered much media attention, some of it critical, most of it favorable. Although she received much media coverage when she served in the cabinets of Ronald Reagan and George H. W. Bush, her success on the campaign trail stumping for her husband first propelled her to national visibility, prompting journalists to raise the question in 1988: "Is the Right Dole Running for the Presidency?" Her husband humorously acknowledged her popularity, saying he withdrew from the race when Elizabeth passed him in the polls. Her campaign speeches were not substantially different from his, but her passionate delivery, her gracious Southern style, and her apparent ease with public speaking impressed nearly all who had heard her. She was described by the press as a "glamorous, worldly woman, and one half of the capital's premier couple."[4] After her famous 1996 Republican National Convention speech, the press raved about her "Oprah-like" stroll among the delegates, calling the speech a "smash hit with viewers." An article in *USA Today* described her as "likely to be the most agile TV campaigner of the new Republican ticket,"[5] while a headline in the *New York Daily News* described the aftermath of her performance as a "Liddy Lovefest."[6]

On the other hand, some commentators faulted her for some of the very traits for which others praised her, including her femininity and her gracious Southern self-presentation. When she worked on Capitol Hill, for example, Democrats called her "sugar lips," a name coined by a frustrated senator one day after she had disarmed a group of his colleagues at what was supposed to have been a tough hearing. Feminists, too, have been suspicious of her silky smoothness of speech, preferring women leaders to speak more directly and robustly—with less storytelling, dialogue, and personal anecdotes.[7] Their comments indicate the difficulty women politicians face with regard to their gender identity, that is, their personal style or self-presentation. Criticisms were especially evident when Elizabeth Dole ran for the presidency. Some journalists scrutinized her in ways different from her male counterparts. For example, they wrote more about her youthful good looks and her fashionable hairstyle, dress, and accessories than on what she had to say. A study produced by the White House Project,[8] a national nonpartisan organization dedicated to increasing the number of women in elective office, found Dole to be the victim of a double standard. In one case, after she had given a speech in New York City, a newspaper columnist found fault with her choice of dress; she was criticized for wearing bright blue, rather than the expected black. Exasperated, Dole commented about this to another reporter: "Did he report on the speech? No, he did not. He reported on the blue dress."[9]

Exploring the challenges faced by a significant contemporary female politician is only one of the reasons why Elizabeth Dole makes a fascinating subject to understand. Throughout her lengthy career, women in leadership positions especially have praised her record as an advocate for women and minorities working inside a male-dominated system. Yet, time and again, she chose to give up high-powered positions to honor her spousal obligation to promote her husband's career. She took a leave of absence from the Federal Trade Commission (FTC) in 1976, when Gerald Ford invited her husband to run as his vice president. She stepped down from the FTC in 1979, when Bob Dole ran for president. She resigned her position as secretary of transportation in 1987, to help her husband campaign for the Republican nomination for the presidency, and she took a leave of absence from the Red Cross in 1996, when Bob ran for president against Bill Clinton. Every time she "put her career on hold," as some commentators expressed it, she received criticisms. For example, Peter Jennings began the *ABC Evening News* on September 15, 1987, by announcing: "One of the most important women in government has given up her job for a man," while syndicated columnist Ellen Goodman quipped: Dole "is leaving Washington to become—heaven help her—a frequent flier in the presidential campaign of her husband, Robert."[10] Journalist Richard Cohen accused her of selling out: "For a long time Liddy Dole had occupied the fault line between feminism and traditional womanhood . . . [The] real conflict of interest was never between Bob Dole's campaign and her cabinet post, but between traditional views about women's role and the one Liddy Dole forged for herself. In the end, she didn't just resign, she sold out."[11] Balancing the competing demands of her political and spousal roles makes the study of Elizabeth Dole absolutely germane for anyone interested in the struggles of today's women. Journalist Ann Grimes put her finger on this point when she commented about a speech Dole made during the 1988 campaign: "You could hardly find a more telling image of America's befuddlement over sex and work and marriage in the eighties—a candidate's wife spending perhaps a third of her precious personal campaign stop arguing that she had a right to be there at all."[12] From Dole's perspective, her husband's career was fundamentally important to her, but she also gained national visibility and valuable speaking experience that allowed her to run independent campaigns of her own.

To understand her career choices more fully, it is necessary to view her against the culture in which she was raised—Salisbury, North Carolina, in the 1950s.

BACKGROUND OF A TRAILBLAZER

Mary Elizabeth Alexander Hanford was born on July 29, 1936, the only daughter of John and Mary Hanford.[13] Her brother, John, had been born thirteen years earlier. By the time she was two, Elizabeth had given herself the nickname "Liddy," a name that stuck with her throughout her childhood and most of her Washington career. She grew up in Salisbury, North Carolina, into a Southern belle type of genteel life, where the most important quality a young girl could learn was to be a gracious young lady. Her father built considerable family wealth as a floral wholesaler, and her mother, who had given up the opportunity to study music at Juilliard for marriage, volunteered for many church and community activities.

Elizabeth grew up in a family of overachievers. When she was three, she ran for and was chosen to be the mascot of her brother's graduating class. She was elected president of her third grade bird club, and she also established a book club and named herself president one summer, when she had read forty books. She was a serious child who worked very hard on her grades. Her parents provided her with many lessons—such as tap, ballet, piano, horseback riding, and more. The family took exciting trips by train all over the United States and Canada, and Elizabeth collected dolls from different countries, sent to her by her brother, John, when he served in the navy. All of this hard work and a rich cultural life contributed to her knowledge and sparked a desire in her to see and do more.

In high school, Elizabeth was active in student government and made an unsuccessful bid for its presidency when she was a senior. In a campaign speech, she forecasted her own political future in a bold declaration: "more and more the modern world is giving women a big part to play. Women must keep pace with the rest of the world." Despite her unsuccessful bid, Elizabeth's classmates voted her "most likely to succeed."

After she graduated from high school, she attended Duke University. At the time, the campus was divided into male (West Campus) and female (East Campus) halves. Students only crossed paths with the opposite gender on their way to classes that were not offered on their home campuses. The separation of the sexes was enforced with screens dividing the classrooms, and the girls' dormitory windows were painted over so that neither sex could look in or out at the other. Rules about behavior were very strict; alcohol use, tobacco, and jeans were prohibited, and Elizabeth's curfew was 10:30 P.M. A freshman handbook set forth the prevailing criteria for academic success for women: "A Duchess should have the tact and good judgment to know when the occasion requires her to be serious and when to be gay, when to dress up and when to be casual. Everything she does is in good taste and up to the highest standards."[14]

While at college, Elizabeth dated and attended social functions, but her interests were more academic. She studied government, and was one of only a few women to take political science courses, in which she majored. Importantly, she won the Political Science Department's highest honors upon graduation. Elizabeth also practiced politics. As a freshman, she ran for class representative, and in a campaign speech she encouraged classmates "to take a more active interest in politics." "I did the unpolitical thing of comparing them to Rip Van Winkle," she said, and the students woke up in time to defeat her campaign.[15] In 1957, she was elected president of the women's student government. Serving in that position allowed her to develop her communication skills such as parliamentary procedure and negotiation. In 1958, her senior year, she was selected "Leader of the Year" by both the men's and women's campuses; her performance as a campus leader earned her glowing reviews in the campus newspaper. She was also elected May Queen and came out as a debutante in Raleigh.

When Elizabeth Hanford graduated from Duke University, Phi Beta Kappa, she was unsure of her career plans. At the time, most of her female friends were ready for marriage and motherhood,[16] just as her male friends were expected to develop successful careers and provide for their families. Instead, she chose a different path. After applying for and failing to get a position as a journalist for the *Charlotte Observer*, she found a job as secretary to the head librarian at Harvard Law School, who must have been impressed by her academic credentials because she did not know shorthand and was only a novice typist. She also enrolled in a Master of Arts degree program in Harvard University's School of Education, with a dual major in government. As a student teacher, she was talented and innovative, but she decided that teaching was not the field in which she was most interested. Nonetheless, she completed the degree program in 1960.

Elizabeth made significant use of her summers. She went to Oxford University in England in 1959, to study history and government, and her curiosity prompted her to continue her travel to Russia. During the summer of 1960, she found a secretarial position working in Washington, D.C., in the office of North Carolina senator B. Everett Jordon, a Democrat. While there, she visited successful women to ask them for advice about entering a career in government. Senator Margaret Chase Smith, appointed originally to complete her deceased husband's term of office before winning a Senate seat on her own, advised her to get a law degree. Elizabeth also volunteered to help Lyndon B. Johnson campaign for the vice presidency on the ticket with John F. Kennedy, and traveled in the South on his campaign train. She spent the summers of 1961 and 1962 in New York, working at the United Nations as a tour guide.

In 1962, Elizabeth entered Harvard Law School. The climate for female students at that time was far from hospitable to the twenty-four women in a class of 550. Women were required to wear dresses or skirts, stockings, and heels to class; they were forbidden from eating in Lincoln's Dining Hall, and they were not encouraged to speak in class except on Ladies Day, when the permissible topics of discussion were frivolous.[17] It was not until 1966, the year after she graduated from Harvard, that women began protesting the conditions at the Law School. Elizabeth and her female peers were willing to put up with whatever was required to get their degrees. They bonded together and helped each other get through even the most trying circumstances such as the "Ladies Day Inquisition" and the dinner party for new students at Dean Erwin Griswold's, where each female student was asked, "Why are you at Harvard Law School, taking the place of a man?" Pat Schroeder, a year ahead of Elizabeth and a former U.S. congresswoman, has said about her experience at Harvard Law School: "There's something about being totally surrounded that causes you to bond. . . . It was more like a foxhole mentality than your normal educational experience."[18]

Elizabeth moved to Washington, D.C., after her graduation from Harvard Law School. Then twenty-nine years old, she found a temporary position with Health, Education, and Welfare (HEW), organizing a deaf education conference. She also passed the Washington, D.C., bar exam and when her position at HEW was completed, she turned her attention to trial law, learning the skills of public defender in night court. Her next position was with the Johnson administration, working for the White House Office of Consumer Affairs under the direction of Betty Furness, a commercial spokeswoman superstar who had turned her attention to consumer protection. At the time, Elizabeth was registered as a Democrat and was excited about working as a consumer advocate. Consumer protection was popular; watchdog agencies were being established all around the country.

After Johnson declined to run for reelection, Richard Milhouse Nixon won the presidency in 1968. Even though Nixon was a Republican, Elizabeth kept her position, but her boss, Betty Furness, was replaced by Virginia Knauer, who had been head of the Pennsylvania Consumer

Protection Bureau. Elizabeth was subsequently promoted to deputy in the office, which was renamed the President's Committee on Consumer Interests. This agency had no real power to resolve consumer complaints, referring them to other agencies such as the Federal Trade Commission and the Consumer Product Safety Commission. However, the committee did effect positive changes: they had labels put on food and other products to reveal their contents, and they had expiration dates put on food and drugs. Fighting for consumers became a crusade for Elizabeth. She was frequently asked to fill in for Knauer, which often meant giving speeches.

Elizabeth applied for a position on the Federal Trade Commission in 1973, and after a great degree of lobbying, she was confirmed as one of five commissioners. For years, the FTC had been a commission with little power to cause change. It was a guardian agency set up to protect the consumer from big business. When she joined the FTC, it was undergoing transformation, being given more power. Some of the initiatives that occurred during her tenure include cracking down on fraudulent merchants and careless nursing home operators and informing single women of their right to borrow money.

In 1972, Virginia Knauer introduced Elizabeth to Robert Dole. At the time, he was serving as the national chairman of the Republican Party. The two women went to his office to petition him to put a consumer plank in the Republic Party platform before the next presidential election. Elizabeth and Dole did not start dating until several months later, and then they dated for several years before they were married. She was a wealthy woman from the South, and a belle of the Washington social scene,[19] while Robert Dole was a busy senator from Kansas, thirteen years her senior. They married on December 5, 1975; he was fifty-two, and she was thirty-nine.

In August 1976, Gerald Ford, who had become president in 1974 when Nixon resigned, invited Bob Dole to serve as his vice presidential running mate. Dole accepted, and Elizabeth's life changed dramatically. She wasn't sure whether she could keep her position at the Federal Trade Commission and campaign for her husband at the same time. She resolved the potential problem by taking a leave of absence, but she still received criticism over whether she would have a conflict of interest when she resumed her work, if her husband was elected. She also received questions from reporters about why she interrupted her own career for the sake of her husband's. The Ford-Dole ticket lost to the Democratic ticket of Jimmy Carter and Walter Mondale.

In 1979, Bob Dole announced that he would be a candidate for the presidency in the 1980 election. Elizabeth's role in his campaign became a subject of debate among her friends and in the press. "Her feminist friends begged her not to step down from the FTC, arguing that the move would send the wrong message to professional women everywhere," according to biographer Kozar.[20] She chose, nonetheless, to relinquish her position and concentrate on her husband's campaign. She did quite a bit of campaigning for him, to the point that some people thought she was running for office. Bob was too busy in the Senate and had to restrict the amount of time he could spend on the campaign trail. He dropped out of the race in the spring of 1980, saying with humor, "at about the time Elizabeth passed me in the polls."[21] Elizabeth continued to campaign for Ronald Reagan and his running mate, George H. W. Bush. When Reagan was elected, he appointed her head of the Office of Public Liaison, a position that required her to marshal grass roots and organization support for the president's policies. In 1983, Reagan invited her to serve as secretary of transportation, a cabinet position responsible for 100,000 employees nationwide with a budget of $27 billion. She served four years in that position before stepping down to campaign for her husband for the presidency in the 1988 election. Once again, her decision to put her career on hold was questioned by feminists and others. Once Bush received the Republican nomination, both Elizabeth and Bob were rumored to be on the short list of possible vice presidential running mates, but the position went instead to a young senator from Indiana, Dan Quayle.

Once elected, Bush invited Elizabeth to serve as secretary of labor, and she began to fulfill the duties of the position in early 1989. During her eighteen months of service in that position, she targeted work-related issues of at-risk youth, women, and minorities. She left the position to become president of the American Red Cross in 1991, in order to devote her attention to dire human needs on a full-time basis. She was thrilled to head the Red Cross, because it filled her "with a sense of mission." In 1995, however, Dole took an unpaid leave of absence for fourteen months to help her husband campaign for the presidency in the 1996 election. This time, he received the Republican nomination, but lost the election to incumbent, Bill Clinton.

After the 1996 election, Elizabeth seemed well positioned for her own run for the presidency or vice presidency. The White House Project conducted a study that identified women who could be president, and Elizabeth Dole was one of those named.[22] As we have seen, when she stepped down as American Red Cross president on January 5, 1999, she only hinted at a possible run. This may have been partially because she was uncertain about whether she would be able to raise the money needed— about $25 million. In late January, her advisers opened up an unofficial headquarters, but it wasn't until mid-March that she announced the formation of an exploratory committee. Dole continued to test the waters by giving speeches in a number of different locations. By October, however, she withdrew from the race, citing a lack of funding as the main reason. Nevertheless, in 2002, she ran and won a U.S. Senate seat in North Carolina, held for thirty years by Republican Jesse Helms, who retired.

For Dole to perform the duties associated with the positions she has held required that she use her communication skills, which were developed fully by her long career in government service. One of the reasons she was so successful in politics was undoubtedly her consummate speaking ability. A hallmark characteristic of her public speaking is her ability to accomplish more than one goal at a time in her speeches—a phenomenon we have dubbed "rhetorical multitasking." Her public speaking has also kept pace with the mediated age of politics. She has learned well that cultivating her image and getting her message across via the television medium are both important goals a political speaker must master.

THE PUBLIC SPEAKING PROWESS OF
ELIZABETH HANFORD DOLE

Journalist Jeanne F. Brooks dubbed Elizabeth Dole the "second Great Communicator" after Ronald Reagan, in recognition of her skill as a public speaker.[23] Former first lady Betty Ford went further when she called Dole "the finest speaker I have ever seen or heard and a kind and gracious person."[24] Represented by the Washington Bureau, Dole is a highly sought after speaker, and accepts approximately one hundred fifty speaking engagements a year. She possesses "high wattage," which is the ability to light up a room and stop conversation just by entering.[25] She also possesses negotiating, consulting, and fund-raising skills, as discussed in the following chapters. Suffice it to say, there seems to be no area of communication in which Elizabeth Dole does not excel, although during her run for the presidency she was faulted by some commentators for seeming overly rehearsed. Her "movie star" quality, glamour, charisma, tenacity, and more—have all contributed to her effectiveness. The question is: How did she become so accomplished?

Experience the Best Teacher

When Elizabeth Dole was a student at Duke University, she took a one-semester course on public speaking. Years later, when she was back in Durham presenting a speech, she noticed a man standing by himself way up in the back of the auditorium. After she finished, he came over to talk to her; it was her public speaking teacher from fifteen years before. She asked him for feedback on her performance and he praised her voice projection, but told her to use more examples in her speaking and to shift her weight front to back, not side to side.[26] She also participated in Peter Lowe seminars: "My press secretary came with me to one of these things and he said, 'I can't make myself go out there in front of all of those people.' And I said, 'but you just have a conversation, you go out there and talk about things you care about, it's from the heart.'" Dole never hired a communication coach or consultant, but for the most part she learned to speak effectively through experience.[27]

She knew early on that she had natural talent as a public speaker. One evening, when her dad overhead her preparing for a speech, he told her how much he liked hearing her voice. Knowing her father to be a man of few compliments, she took his comments to heart. She began giving speeches in high school and then in college, when she ran for office and at other times. As president of the student government of the Women's College at Duke, she learned parliamentary procedure and gained experience moving an agenda forward. Her early positions, including public defender and consumer advocate, required that she stand up in front of audiences and speak to them. Experience was her best teacher, she said, "By public speaking so often throughout my life, I gained skill at it. Like anything, when I first began to speak, I was not as comfortable doing it as I am now and that certainly is reflected in my speeches over the years. A good speaker is a combination of innate ability and experience."[28]

Elizabeth Dole's career has included many high-powered positions in Washington, D.C., and each required her to use communication in a variety of ways. She also performed a number of roles; most significantly, she promoted both her own career as a public servant and her husband's career. Her marriage to Bob Dole in 1975 presented her with unique communication challenges. For example, she criss-crossed the country for more than two decades, campaigning for her husband and for other Republican candidates. On the road, she gained valuable experience speaking to different kinds of audiences. In addition, she faced criticism when she stepped down from positions and gained experience defending her choices. She has also made the transition from advocating for someone else who is running for office to advocating for herself. For example, she introduced herself to the public during many campaign speeches for her husband, and the public exposure helped her launch her own bid for the presidency in 2000. Both she and Hillary Clinton projected the role of helpmate during the election of 1996, but as the century turned, both women worked in earnest, speaking in the first person, to launch their own political careers, including their successful runs for the U.S. Senate.

Characteristics of Her Public Speaking

Over the years, Elizabeth Dole has developed an uncanny ability to address more than one purpose in the same speech. She has a savvy eye for public relations in that she offends no one in her speeches, and she cultivates future relationships as she moves her agenda forward—both in the short run and the long term. For example, in her 1988 Republican National Convention speech, her explicit purpose was to speak for the rights of women, which put her in a "feminist" light, but also to tout the past successes of the Reagan administration in this area and to insist that women would be better off during the next four years under the leadership of George H. W. Bush. She also had an opportunity to reach a wide national audience, perhaps cultivating a relationship with them so the next time she or her husband ran for elective office, each would be better known. Another example of the phenomenon occurred in 1990, when she helped celebrate the seventieth anniversary of the Department of Labor's Women's Bureau, a federal agency, representing the needs of women who work in public policy. As secretary of labor, she told the group that she was speaking for two reasons: to help them celebrate their seventieth anniversary, and to help sketch the future direction the bureau should take. But she also did some politicking for her boss, George H. W. Bush, when she made the comment: "I might add that I am proud to work for a president who has appointed more women to senior positions than any other president in history," and for herself: "and I am delighted that 62% of my senior staff are women and minorities." This was also a "good-bye" speech, since the following day she would announce her resignation from the Department of Labor. A third example is her "America We Can Be" speech, presented at many locations, including Lancaster, Pennsylvania, where she was booked by the local chamber of commerce to present an after-dinner speech at their annual banquet. She successfully amused her audience with humorous stories of the kinds of things that happened to her when she first went to Washington, D.C. She told about how she had experienced prejudice because of her gender. By turning those experiences into humorous stories, she showed her audience that she did not carry a grudge, that she was for women's rights, and that she recognized how much things have changed for women for the better. At the same time, she presented her resume by detailing the positions she has held in the nation's capital, told about how important her husband was to her

("I would do anything for Bob Dole"), and outlined her conservative agenda for the rebirth of America. She impressed the audience as a highly talented and personable political force—a great American woman leader and perhaps someone to watch—and support—in the future.

"Multitasking" is only one of the characteristics of Elizabeth Dole as a public speaker; there are others, such as her graciousness and femininity. Part of the reason why her appearance on the *Tonight Show*, October 1, 1996, dressed in a black leather jacket emblazoned with the words "Bikers for Bob" worked so well was because of the contrast it made with how she otherwise presented herself. One of her friends from the South described her as a "genteel Southern woman through and through." Speaking about some of the negative reactions Dole has received for her "niceness," her friend further explained how her manners were just "inbred" in natives of Salisbury, who were raised to be charming and gracious. They were taught that you "can get more bees with honey." They were raised to be ladies. With Elizabeth Dole, however, there was quite a bit more: "You have this brilliant, talented woman who is still a woman. She is very feminine. But she can outthink and outwork a man any day of the week. It's a unique package."[29]

During an interview, Carl Anthony, an expert on American first ladies, said that Dole's "Southerness" helps to define her as a public figure. And, further, that she uses that quality to protect her from rude attacks, much as did Lady Bird Johnson, who traveled through the South campaigning for her husband's pro-Civil Rights position. Dole "wears" her Southerness, according to Anthony, "like a suit of armor." "For her, everything is wonderful and she is happy to see every person. But this seems to be her way of steeling herself against anyone who wants to probe beneath the surface."[30] This trait must have been useful, working with those who would have been threatened by her ability; concealing her inner strength and ambition behind her Southern femininity must have been an effective rhetorical strategy as she rose through the ranks—and it was a happy accident that she was raised to be that way.

A quotation attributed to Elizabeth Dole in an exhibit on American women in the Hoover Library in Stanford reads: "Women have had to be over achievers to succeed. We worked twice as hard as men to be considered as good." Her comment indicates two other, related characteristics she has as a public speaker—her perfectionism and her penchant for preparation. Dole does not, or at least did not, enjoy speaking impromptu or off the cuff. Whenever possible, she prepares her speeches by working closely with her speechwriters, editing again and again until she is comfortable and satisfied with the finished product.[31] According to biographer Carolyn Mulford, this perfectionism goes back to her childhood. She tells of an incident when Liddy was a toddler. She was a flower girl in a wedding, who tried her very best to space the flowers perfectly as she walked down the isle. She demonstrated the same trait as a college student when she studied Robert's Rules of Order so that she could preside over student government meetings without making mistakes. In an interview in *Vanity Fair*, her brother, John, commented on her perfectionism: "Oh, man was she thorough . . . thorough in planning, thorough in execution, and thorough in wrap up."[32] Her husband also described her perfectionism as a well-ingrained family trait: "She's disciplined . . . her mother's disciplined . . . her brother's disciplined, I think her father was disciplined. That's the family. They're very careful, they don't like making mistakes, and they're always searching for the answer to a problem or a question."[33]

Related to her perfectionism is her thorough preparation. Her husband has said: "She is much more disciplined [than I am]. I hear a voice coming out of the bedroom, and it is Elizabeth rehearsing her speech. She probably gave it twenty times already, but she is giving it the next day and she just wants to rehearse it twice."[34] Early in her career, in 1953, Elizabeth ran for president of Boydin High School and lost. She said it was because she wasn't well prepared. When she ran for president of the Women's Student Government at Duke University, she was so well prepared and articulate that even her opponent voted for her. One of her speechwriters, Kerry Tymchuk, commented on how her insistence on being well prepared has helped her excel in her positions. One example he cited was when she asked him to draft her some toasts, just in case she would need them on her upcoming trip to Poland.[35] She rehearsed those toasts and, sure enough, she was asked to give toasts at every dinner she attended. "The male secretaries were over there stumbling through their remarks, and she has these beautiful toasts memorized. People were crying when she was finished."[36] She has even been said to rehearse important phone calls with her staff before she makes them.[37] During her run for the presidency, Dole's degree of preparation and unwillingness to stray from her prepared remarks caused journalists and others to compare her to a martinet. Maureen Dowd, for example, referred to her as "Little Miss Perfect," and she was caricatured in "Doonesbury" as an automaton who needed to be rebooted. Commenting on that line of press coverage, Dole called it "overplayed." She said she can speak impromptu about issues she has worked on whenever called upon to do so, but when she knows about an event in advance and it is important, she considers her remarks more carefully to make sure her ideas flow. True to her word, she displayed much more spontaneity during her run for a U.S. Senate seat in 2002. Her stump speeches developed from a list of talking points that were adapted to audiences as she interacted with them.[38]

Another trait of Elizabeth Dole as a public speaker is her political prag-
matism. She prides herself on being able to work with members of both
the Republican and Democratic parties—a claim born out by her stint as
secretary of labor, when her work was praised by union leaders. Her own
party affiliation has changed over the years, and that might be a key to
her ability to work with others who serve on opposite sides of the aisle.
One of the first positions she held was that of secretary in 1960, in the
Washington, D.C., office of U.S. senator B. Everett Jordon, a Democrat from
her home state of North Carolina. She volunteered that same summer to
accompany Lyndon B. Johnson as he campaigned for the vice presidency
in the South. After her graduation from Harvard Law School, she took a
position in the Johnson administration's White House Office of Consumer
Affairs. During all of these years, she was a registered Democrat. In 1968,
when Richard Nixon was elected to the presidency, she retained her position in the Republican White House, working under the direction of
Virginia Knauer. She retained this position until 1973, when she changed
her affiliation to Independent and lobbied for a seat on the Federal Trade
Commission. In 1975, she married lifelong Republican senator Bob Dole
and changed her affiliation once again to Republican. This ideological
"flexibility" or "nimbleness," might cast her as a shallow opportunist. But
anyone who studies her life—her pattern of choices and the ideas she
expresses—knows that her faith is most important to her, and the core
values to which it gives rise. Above all else, her commitment is to the
public good.

Invention

Dole's faith-based core values are the ultimate spring of her rhetorical
invention—the source from which she generates ideas to use in her
speeches. She has said: "I am a person of faith with a strong belief in God
which makes a difference." When asked what she thought was the best
way for anyone to make a difference, she said: "the person has to feel
passionately [about] what they do. They have to feel a sense of mission.
The work they do has to come from the heart."[39] For her, faith must be
practiced—it must be put into service, acted upon. Typical themes that
occur in her speeches include a call to public service and to aid the community and neighbors. Her core religious values give rise to her patriotism and to her promotion of diversity, including a kind of feminism that
works for the rights and opportunities of women and minorities. Her interest in the moral climate of America is also an important theme much
repeated in her speeches. And throughout the past quarter century, since
her marriage to Bob Dole, she has spoken often about the conservative

approach to solving national problems by promoting GOP (Grand Old Party—Republican) candidates. Her faith-based values make it difficult to pigeonhole her with a label, because the goals or "ends" are consistent with both Republican and Democratic tenants. However, the "means" or policies she chooses to achieve those ends have varied as she moved from one political stance to another.

Disposition

Dole often organizes her ideas, especially in her policy speeches, by identifying a problem and providing a solution. A key to deciphering her typical speech organization is the way she arranges the introductory material—what she says before she discusses the problem. She usually begins her speeches in an upbeat, gracious, and welcoming way. Often, to establish credibility and goodwill, she discloses a portion of her resume and illustrates experiences that happened to her or others by telling amusing stories. Her stories lead to her main thesis, which is usually the identification of a problem, which she follows by recommending what type of attitude and actions can help resolve it. For example, she used this pattern in her "America We Can Be" speech. She began by telling humorous stories of what it was like for her as a woman attending Harvard Law School and serving in Washington, D.C., during the early 1970s. These stories performed many functions for her, and they led to the main topic of the speech, which was about the declining moral climate in America. She talked about aspects of the country's problems, such as a lack of public involvement in government. And she pointed to a solution, which was a renewal by Americans of their faith and participation in government. She stressed the feasibility of this solution by testifying to the generosity and goodness of the American people. As president of the American Red Cross, she had witnessed countless acts of kindness. She wanted Americans to extend their goodness to civic engagement.

Style

Elizabeth Dole's typical use of language in her speeches—her rhetorical style—has several characteristics, including her use of the active voice and vivid word choice, personal and inclusive pronouns, quotations and storytelling, humor, and involvement of the audience. Whenever she gives a speech, she always uses the active voice and her words carry a sense of passion and energy. For example, in a speech to the American Federation of Labor-Congress of Industrial Organizations (AFL-CIO), she said: "What seized my attention when I came to the Department of Labor was the fact that we are on the brink of some revolutionary changes in American Business and in the American workforce . . . They are challenges that are ill-served by short-term, quick fixes that can tend to grab attention."[40] Interesting phrases she uses in her speeches include "so long as books are kept open, then minds can never be closed"[41] and "the 'Me Decade' has been replaced by the 'We Decade.'"[42] She also uses a great deal of personal and inclusive pronouns. For example, in her "America We Can Be" speech, she said "I" sixteen times in the three stories she related at the beginning. A good example of her preference for inclusive pronouns may be found in her editorial marks handwritten on a draft of a speech that she gave in 1995, to the Charlotte World Affairs Council. She changed a sentence that began with: "The members of the Charlotte World Affairs Council understand that" to "As members of the Charlotte World Affairs Council, you understand that." The difference between the two sentences is telling and is vintage Dole.

Another hallmark of her style is her use of quotations and storytelling. She often uses quotations that are geared to the audience she is addressing, such as when she quoted Virginian Woodrow Wilson during a speech to the graduating class at the University of Virginia. She quoted his line: "We should not only use all the brains we have, but all that we can borrow."[43] When she uses storytelling in her speeches, her typical pattern is to draw lessons from her experience that she believes will both entertain and instruct her audience. She tells stories about herself, her husband, and others, often making them into main characters of her speeches. The best example of her telling stories about her husband is her 1996 Republican National Convention speech, when she told several stories to convince her audience that he would make a great president. She included the following story about herself in her Mothers Against Drunk Drivers speech and elsewhere: "I can still vividly recall the Sunday afternoons I spent in 'Mom' Cathey's living room, munching on cookies, and drinking lemonade as she told us stories from Scripture. It was Mom Cathey's deep faith that helped her persevere through a tragedy shared by three of today's honorees, and by thousands more across the country—the loss of a child to a drunk driver."[44] She continued the story, talking about how Mom Cathey used the proceeds from her son Vernon's life insurance policy to build a wing on a hospital in Pakistan.

Often, Dole acts out these stories with dialogue. For example, in her "America We Can Be" speech, she acted out the dialogue between herself and a doorman who refused to allow her to enter the Metropolitan Club in Washington, D.C. "As I rushed by him," she said, "the doorman yelled 'Stop! You can't go in there, lady! Women are not permitted in this club!' I told him that there must be some misunderstanding. 'My name is Elizabeth Hanford . . . and I work at the White House and I have a meeting on the 4th floor with some business people from Cleveland.' 'I'm sorry,' he said. 'If you were Queen Elizabeth, you still couldn't go in.'" By using dialogue, she enlivens her speech, making them more dynamic and entertaining for her audience.

Some of her stories are about others. She often tells a story about Ronald Reagan and the way he learned to deal with the pressures of the Oval Office. Quoting Reagan, she said: "'Each morning began' he says, 'with someone standing before my desk describing yet another disaster. The feeling of stress became unbearable. I had the urge to look over my shoulder for someone I could pass the problem to. One day it came to me that I was looking in the wrong direction. I looked up instead of back. I'm still looking up. I couldn't face one day in that office if I didn't know I could ask God's help.'"[45] Another favorite story of hers is about Oliver Wendall Holmes, which she often uses during commencement addresses: "There is a famous story about Justice Oliver Wendall Holmes, who once found himself on a train, but couldn't locate his ticket. While the conductor watched, smiling, the ninety-nine-year-old Justice Holmes searched through all of his pockets without success. Of course, the conductor recognized the distinguished justice, so he said: 'Mr. Holmes, don't worry. You don't need your ticket. You will probably find it when you get off the train and I'm sure the Pennsylvania Railroad will trust you to mail it back later.' The justice looked up at the conductor with some irritation and said, 'My dear man, that is not the problem at all. The problem is not, where is my ticket. The problem is, where am I going?'"[46]

Bringing out the humorous side of her experiences and stories is certainly a characteristic of Dole's communication style. She is fond of using humor because it helps her break the ice and allows the audience to get to know her and her to get to know them through their reactions.[47] Using a self-deprecating humor, for example, she poked fun of herself in a speech she gave in May 1999, when she said: "Some pundits say I'm scripted . . . but according to my notes, that is not true."[48] Another example is when she spoke at a business luncheon in 1997. She talked about strategic planning, customer service, financial systems, and more as required by the occasion. But because her speech was given at a luncheon, she began her speech by telling a number of humorous stories about her experiences on the campaign trail. After much laughter by her audience, she leaned over the podium and asked them: "What do you think, should I write a book?" Her audience responded with an enthusiastic "Yes," and they gave her a standing ovation.[49]

Questioning her audience from the podium is one of the ways Dole involves her audience in her speeches. Another technique she uses is to ask members of the audience to give themselves a round of applause or to stand up and be acknowledged. For example, in her U.S. Senate Kick-Off Campaign speech in North Carolina, she said to her audience: "I know some of our veterans are with us today, and I promise you that one of my top priorities is to stand up for you and our men and women in uniform. Now, would all of you please stand up, so we can show our appreciation for your service and your sacrifice?" Another example is when she involved members of the Red Cross in her resignation speech: "So, I'd like to start out the New Year by asking you to join me in giving all of you a well-deserved pat on the back and a big round of applause. Shall we? (Clapping begins.) This is for you. (Sustained applause) What a team. What a great team." By including her audience in her speeches, she is able to create a sociable atmosphere of mutual respect and support.

Delivery

One of the most significant aspects of Dole's public speaking is her nearly flawless speech delivery. To begin with, her appearance at the podium and in other venues is impressive. She is a beautiful woman, who appears years younger than her age. Of medium height and trim physique, her brown hair is always neat, her blue eyes sparkle, and her clear skin displays freckles, giving her an almost girlish appearance even though she is in her sixties. Always impeccably dressed, usually in brightly colored, two-piece skirted suits, she frequently accents her dress with a prominent gold necklace and earrings. She has not adopted the subdued neutral tone of dress of many women leaders, such as Hillary Clinton who uttered the unforgettable line during her acceptance speech when she won a U.S. Senate seat from New York: "sixty-two counties, sixteen months, three debates, two opponents, and six black pantsuits later, because of you, here we are."[50] The contrast of her dress to other women leaders might be one of the reasons why the press often writes about what Dole is wearing when she gives a speech. During her presidential bid, for example, she favored wearing a bright red suit and is pictured in many photographs in that outfit. What those static photos do not reveal, however, is how dynamic her voice is when she delivers her words. For example, when Dole won her U.S. Senate seat from North Carolina, she exclaimed to her supporters: "Oh, wow, what a night! I'm so proud to be a North Carolinian! I'm just as thrilled as you are! We'll never forget this night, will we?" Her jubilance carried in her voice.

Elizabeth Dole has a dignified and graceful posture, yet is very energetic as she speaks, moving around, smiling and gesturing frequently. In a public speaking situation, she views the podium as a barrier; she prefers to move around the audience, sometimes feeling fettered even by a microphone. She enjoys saying hello and shaking hands with audience members while her speech is in progress. This is especially true of her campaign speeches. Sometimes, she injects a greeting to a special member of the audience, as she did during the 1996 Republican National Convention, when she quipped casually: "Governor, how are you doing tonight?" to California governor Pete Wilson as she was delivering her speech. A consummate politician, her handshake makes the recipient feel special; she looks the person in the eye while holding on just a few seconds longer to insure the bond is created. During an interview, she explained how well walking around the audience works for her.[51] Commenting on speeches she gave when she was the American Red Cross president, she highlighted how important it was to create a bond with her audience of one or more, especially with victims and their families or when she had to ask them to make donations of time, money, or their blood: "If I could get close to them—if I could talk to them like it was a conversation, it worked much better."[52] Her ability to connect with people is effective when she is in front of an audience, onstage and off.

Memoria

Lastly, Elizabeth Dole's command of her material—rhetorical *memoria*—is equally impressive. Her penchant for preparation and practice helps her to be a polished speaker. Her clever conversational delivery usually sounds spontaneous, yet, until her recent run for the U.S. Senate, when she relied mostly on talking points instead of finished texts,[53] she rarely leaves anything to chance. Sometimes she speaks with no notes at all or if she has a speech text in front of her, she typically does not refer to it because she has in fact memorized what she wants to say. She keeps the prepared text with her, she says: "in order not to miss important points which I feel compelled to cover in the speech."[54] There is no evidence in speeches we have seen her give in person or on videotape that she ever forgot a part of her speech or needed to refer to her notes. Kerry Tymchuk, one of her speechwriters who worked on her 1996 Republican National Convention speech, noted that he had a written copy in front of him as he listened to her deliver the speech and she did not miss a single word.[55] Because she strolled through the audience as she gave this speech, use of

a teleprompter was not possible. The astounding part is how spontaneous her speeches can sound, especially when the audience has not heard
the story before. This semblance of spontaneity is a gift for any politician
because it serves the purpose of enabling her to sound well prepared for
just that audience. For example, while giving the 1996 Republican National Convention speech she segues: "And that reminds me of the time,"
which suggests that she only just thought of the example at that moment.
In fact, she used the same example in many other campaign speeches that
season. Looking through the texts of the speeches contained in the appendix, it is obvious that she tells many of the same stories in different
speeches. This repetition has the advantage of helping her polish her delivery, so the anecdotes are delivered smoothly and are well timed. She
is also able to test audience reaction to them and to continue using those
stories to which audiences respond favorably. Importantly, she can also
use those stories as the occasion demands; for example, she said she likes
to "tailor each speech to meet the needs of the audience," so she will often
"depart from her prepared text at specific points and tell humorous stories
or anecdotes."[56] Having a stockpile of anecdotes to pop into a speech
when they are needed is another trait of an accomplished speaker. The
only downside is when the same journalists cover her speeches, then regardless of how spontaneously she delivers them, hearing the same stories
repeatedly does lead to the conclusion that she is "overly scripted," even
though this is not a factor for audience members hearing her remarks for
the first time.

Public speaking is a means to an end, and the following chapters detail Dole's use of speech to advocate for public policy; religious, patriotic,
and humanitarian values; women's rights; and for her husband, fellow
Republicans, and herself as candidates for office. She has used her voice
throughout her life for causes important to her, and during those years
she has become a consummate contemporary woman rhetorician well
worth studying, not only for the techniques she uses in her speeches, but
also and more importantly for the ideas she espouses.

Chapter 2

Advocate for Public Policy

If there is an overriding theme to my thirty-plus years in service to the public, it lies in placing service over politics and consensus over confrontation.[1]

With her smooth North Carolina drawl, Elizabeth Hanford Dole has repeatedly noted that she chose to work for the public good because she wanted to "make a difference in the lives of others." That has been her primary goal since her career in public service began in 1965, with her arrival in Washington, D.C., a twenty-nine-year-old graduate fresh from Harvard Law School. Returning to her home in Salisbury, North Carolina, was out of the question for this ambitious, well-educated daughter of the South, who had set her sights on a more cosmopolitan life. During summers, while she was in graduate school, she had worked in New York City, as a tour guide at the United Nations, and also in Washington, D.C., as a secretary in the Peace Corps office. She had tasted public service and life in big cities and was attracted to what they offered.

Dole, then Hanford, became convinced that she wanted to work in government service after her graduation from Harvard Law School. Biographer Carolyn Mulford quotes Dole, after she had interviewed with several major law firms, as saying: "I think that's when I became absolutely convinced this is not really right, not my cup of tea. It's public service work."[2] Since her family did not favor a move to New York City for safety reasons, Washington, D.C., closer to her home, with its opportunity to work in government, "drew her like a magnet."[3] From that time forward, Dole held many government positions, including service under six presidents—from Lyndon B. Johnson through George Herbert Walker

Portait of Elizabeth Dole as Secretary of Transportation.
(Photo courtesy of Elizabeth Dole)

Bush. Presently, she serves as a U.S. senator from her home state of North
Carolina.

LOBBYING FOR POSITIONS

One of the first positions Elizabeth Hanford held in Washington, D.C.,
was at the Department of Health, Education, and Welfare (HEW). The
atmosphere in the city at that time was progressive. John F. Kennedy and
Lyndon B. Johnson promoted antipoverty programs, including Head Start
and the Job Corps. Many interest groups advocated for civil rights,
women's rights, and against the war in Vietnam. Hanford's entry-level
position fit into this atmosphere; she was hired to plan a conference for
the National Advisory Committee on Education of the Deaf and then
oversee publication of the proceedings.[4] This position required a great deal

of interpersonal communication skill, as well as skills in planning and organization. According to Charlotte Coffield, Hanford carried out her assignment with intelligence and grace. She drew up seating charts to help those who attended the meetings identify speakers and discussants easily, even though they had never met each other. Coffield told biographer Mulford that Hanford "dealt with people in a very smooth and gracious manner. She had a way of making people feel very comfortable in her presence. . . . She was flexible, and she could handle things and smooth them out in an easy way—a very tactful person. . . . She was always a lady."[5]

The completion of Elizabeth Hanford's position at Health, Education, and Welfare gave her an opportunity to learn about the criminal court system. She passed the bar exam in Washington, D.C., in 1966, but had no experience with trial law. She began to attend night court, and after several evenings, the presiding judge assigned her clients to defend. This experience was an eye-opener; she learned about criminal behaviors from which she had been sheltered her whole life: "It was such a way to open your eyes to the problems of the inner city. I was fearless. . . . I would pick up witnesses and ride them around in my car and drive into areas at night, you really shouldn't, a women alone, to pick up somebody."

Hanford relied on her determination and used her interpersonal communication skills to find her next position, which began in April 1968, in the White House Office of Consumer Affairs. She was awarded the position as a consumer advocate because she was able to persuade the head of the Food and Drug Administration to put her on the payroll and to transfer this slot to the Consumer Affairs Office in the White House. Her official title was "deputy assistant for legislative affairs" and her duties included lobbying Congress to approve administration policies to protect the consumer. Lyndon B. Johnson was president at the time, and consumer advocacy groups were springing up all over the United States. Their purpose was to protect consumers from "deceptive advertising, inferior and dangerous products, and companies' refusal to take responsibility for broken or harmful products."[6]

A year later, Republican Richard M. Nixon entered the White House, and the office where Hanford worked was renamed the President's Committee on Consumer Interests. She retained her position, once again largely because of her interpersonal communication skills. Her new boss, Virginia Knauer, a Republican from Pennsylvania who had headed that state's Consumer Protection Agency, agreed to keep her on after Elizabeth reminded Knauer that she would have to testify on the department's budget not long after her arrival. When Hanford offered to help, Knauer not only accepted the offer, but also advanced her position two grades.[7]

Knauer and Hanford formed a good working relationship. Hanford was often asked to stand in for Knauer at meetings, and to give speeches in her place. Mary Hanford, Elizabeth's mother, told biographer Carolyn Mulford: "When Mrs. Knauer was scheduled for a speech and something came up that was really important, she just handed it to Elizabeth and said, 'Go give this speech.' She would work on it until she got there and gave the speech."[8] Over time, Hanford gained a reputation as a good speaker. Once again, her mother told Mulford that Elizabeth had a special talent or gift for public speaking and enjoyed doing it. However, one of her coworkers at the time said that Hanford wasn't a totally comfortable speaker, but with practice she became more at ease.[9] Some of the speeches she gave included testifying before Congress.

Hanford worked on other consumer issues, including a government clearinghouse for information, which was later established by executive order and called the Consumer Information Center, Pueblo, Colorado.[10] She also helped design curriculum on consumerism, targeted for children in grades K–12. She traveled across the country lobbying for these courses and others designed for college and law school students. This work became a personal crusade for her—as she struggled to help the underdog. She was a registered Democrat at the time, but changed her affiliation to Independent. Unfortunately, the President's Committee on Consumer Interests had no real power. Cases were passed to other agencies such as the Federal Trade Commission (FTC) and the Consumer Product Safety Commission. It is not surprising, therefore, to learn that in 1973, she lobbied for a position on the FTC, which was responsible for investigating "violations of antitrust laws and preventing business from using unfair methods of competition."[11] This was not an easy appointment to get for political reasons,[12] requiring once again much face-to-face and telephone persuasion.[13]

Hanford joined the FTC at a time when it was undergoing change. Originally, the commission had been set up to protect consumers by working on unfair practices of companies, but it had little power to cause change, investigating abuses one company at a time. In 1974, legislation was passed to allow the FTC to write regulations that would affect entire industries. The commission began their work by cleaning up their own act—rescinding 145 of their own rules.

Hanford saw the commission's work as an extension of what she had been doing to defend consumers who were "victimized by discrimination or economic abuse."[14] She worked on enforcing the Equal Credit Opportunity Act, which was written to help women who were divorced or separated get credit. She also worked on issues concerning health care of the elderly, especially the poor. She investigated deceptive claims regarding nursing home services and contractual disclaimers that relieved nursing homes of their responsibilities for patients' health, safety, and property. She saw her work at the FTC as "a chance to bring about lower prices for consumers, to insure better-quality goods and services, and to expand the choices available in a free, competitive marketplace."[15] She remained at the FTC until March 1979, when she stepped down to help her new husband, Bob Dole campaign for the presidency.

When Ronald Reagan won the presidential election in 1980, Elizabeth Hanford Dole was invited to head the White House Office of Public Liaison, devoted to building grassroots support for presidential policies. She led a staff of thirty-two people and reported to Jim Baker, Reagan's chief of staff, but she also had access to the president himself.[16] Dole described the position this way: "If the White House were a business, Public Liaison would be the marketing and sales division. Our job was to make sure the West Wing's ivory-tower types stayed in contact with the world beyond the gates, that organized groups had their views heard and considered, and that once official policy was determined it was supported. Failing this, we hoped to neutralize opposition at the grass-roots level."[17]

Her office orchestrated more than two thousand meetings between the president and special interest groups such as the Hispanic Chamber of Commerce, Hadassah, and so on. Outside of the office, Dole gave more than two hundred speeches on behalf of presidential policies.[18] She and her staff also marshaled public support with grassroots letter and telephone campaigns through which recalcitrant congresspeople would be targeted in an effort to gain their support. During the first year of the Reagan presidency, this work was directed at approval of Reagan's economic policies. Dole and her team were so successful that in July 1981, "more than a million messages demanding enactment of the President's three-year, 25% tax cut inundated Capitol Hill." According to Dole, Tip O'Neill called it "a telephone blitz like this nation had never seen."[19]

DOLE'S CAREER "TAKES OFF"

In 1983, President Reagan invited Elizabeth Dole to join his cabinet as secretary of transportation. On February 7, her position was confirmed by a Senate vote of 97 to 0, and she was sworn in by Justice Sandra Day O'Connor. This was quite a challenging position for several reasons, not the least of which was that Dole would be the first woman to hold the position. Both the nature of the position and its scope were challenging. The Department of Transportation (DOT) had 100,000 employees and a budget of $27 billion; the secretary was in charge of giving out billions of dollars to highway, airport, and mass-transit systems. In *Unlimited*

Partners, Dole described DOT's jurisdiction as an agency that: "channels highway funds to the states, regulates the movement of hazardous materials and inspects commercial and private aircraft. It wages war on illicit drugs at sea through the Coast Guard and campaigns against drunk drivers on land. Promoting commercial development of outer space, DOT is one branch of the government for which the sky is the limit."[20]

The position was also challenging because of the political atmosphere in which Dole would work, as well as the complexity of the issues. According to Dole, her years as secretary coincided "with a dramatic period of transition, as industries accustomed to four decades of Washington's economic oversight were forced to adjust to a freer, more competitive climate."[21] Privatization and deregulation were hallmarks of the Reagan White House. Key players in the transportation industry—such as auto and insurance executives, railroad union leaders, and government officials—would have to adjust to the new atmosphere. Another complication was that Dole followed Drew Lewis, who had resigned after two years. From his tenure, she inherited a major piece of legislation—the Surface Transportation Assistance Act—that was designed to provide aid for road and bridge repair with money raised from gasoline and other taxes. The truckers' industry opposed this measure, and during her first week in office, she faced a truckers' strike. It was Dole's responsibility to enforce the legislation without being part of the debates and compromises that led to its passage.[22] By the time the truckers went back to work, Dole claimed she needed "to implement complex legislation doubling federal funds that assist states in repairing highways and transit systems."[23] This is just one of the many complex policy issues Dole inherited as head of DOT.

As secretary of transportation, Dole was able to prioritize which issues she wanted to work on, but some problems she was forced to deal with. A day after her appointment was confirmed, an editorial in the *Washington Post* detailed the kinds of issues she would have to tackle, such as "improving highways, training air traffic controllers, and making cars safer."[24] Dole saw that a common theme, "safety," cut across all of these areas, and she made that the chief emphasis of her administration.

One way to improve the safety record of all transportation areas was to make sure the employees did not work when they were under the influence of alcohol or drugs. During her tenure, Dole began testing employees after accidents and discovered that about 5.1 percent had traces of alcohol or drugs in their blood. This discovery convinced her to make DOT "the first civilian department to undertake . . . random drug testing."[25] She and her senior staff, as well as others in safety or security positions, such as air traffic controllers and railroad inspectors, were part of the thirty thousand people who were tested. Dole was criticized for her decision, but she was certain that random testing was the right thing to do: "Public safety is a public trust. If you work in a cockpit or engine room, you are responsible for the lives of your passengers. . . . I had to be able to look people in the eye and assure them I'd done everything possible to give them what they expect and deserve—a drug-free transportation system."[26]

Dole made automobile safety one of her early and important priorities. She began by examining "what was on the drawing board and in the research labs." She discovered "promising highway safety ideas," one of which was to mount an additional break light at the base of the car's rear window. The lights had been successfully tested for five years in taxis and police cars. Since the cost to consumers would be less than $20 and the potential reduction of rear-end accidents approximately 900,000 a year, Dole did not hesitate to require that all 1986 cars have this light.[27] Another automobile problem she tackled, however, was not as easy.

Dole was in favor of requiring automobile manufacturers to install airbags and/or passive restraint devices in new cars. However, she had inherited a history of controversy between officials in government and in the automobile and insurance industries that went back to the Carter administration, which had passed Rule 208 in favor of these devices. The Reagan administration, however, had rescinded the rule, taking the matter to the Supreme Court, which supported Reagan and called for additional research. When Dole inherited this problem, she felt "it was time once and for all to settle the issue." She said: "For twenty years, while the lawyers argued and the politicians debated, people had been dying on the highways."[28] She and her staff reworked Rule 208, which she claimed was the "toughest policy issue I have ever encountered." They designed the rule to foster competition between consumer groups that advocated airbags and passive restraints on the one hand and automobile manufacturers, which advocated strict state safety belt laws on the other. According to Dole, the compromise worked, and she felt more proud of what she had accomplished in auto safety than anything else she had done in twenty-five years of government.[29] Through 1994, she estimated that 65,290 lives had been saved by safety belt laws, and more than 1.5 million injuries prevented.[30]

Dole also worked on automobile safety by waging a war on drunk drivers. She had been struck by a drunk driver and hospitalized herself.[31] Young people were especially at risk, because they were driving across borders to states with lower minimum drinking ages. She and President Reagan encouraged all fifty states to raise the minimum drinking age to twenty-one, and they were successful. She worked with groups such as Mothers Against Drunk Driving (MADD) to foster a national climate of zero tolerance to drunk driving.[32] In her foreword to *Alcohol in America: Taking Action to Prevent Abuse*, she advised "parents, teachers, students, legislators, community organizers, government officials" to "take action."[33]

Dole worked on airline safety, an area of transportation that was experiencing explosive growth and suffering from concomitant problems such as delays, lost luggage, and so on. She was given the task of implementing a $9 billion modernization of the air traffic control system.[34] One of Dole's first actions was to order an additional 1,400 inspections of 374 airlines, to examine general aviation practices, and to study the Federal Aviation Association (FAA). She established a Safety Review Task Force, which she instructed: "Tell us what we need to do differently, what we need to do better."[35] As a result of these studies, the FAA was changed drastically, beginning with a "massive overhaul of the FAA's system of inspecting aircraft." They rewrote the manuals, which hadn't been updated in twenty-eight years, they rotated inspectors, and they changed the way inspectors were hired. They fined airlines for noncompliance. In a speech given in 1986 to the Aviation-Space Writers Association Conference, Dole said, "where safety is concerned it is not business as usual at the FAA." Before Dole had become the head of DOT, the largest fine for airline safety violations had been $500,000 in 1979, when an American Airlines DC-10 lost an engine during takeoff. In 1985, under Dole's leadership, American Airlines was fined $1.5 million and in May 1986, Eastern Airlines was fined $9.5 million.[36] Money from the fines would be put to good use. In a speech given in January 1987 in Charlotte, North Carolina, Dole spoke about the FAA budget, saying it "would be increased by 20% or about $1 billion dollars, and the money would be used to hire 225 additional air traffic controllers and 178 aviation inspectors."[37]

One of the reasons Dole favored reforms of the U.S. aviation system was because more people were traveling than ever before, and the airlines were struggling to keep up with the demand. In *Unlimited Partners*, she explained, "the economy was just coming out of recession . . . fuel costs dropped, and airline deregulation . . . realized its promise . . . Millions of people who never thought that they would have the money to fly were taking advantage of lower fares."[38] Safety was becoming a public issue and demand. The public was tired of canceled or delayed flights and lost baggage; they were also beginning to fear flying. Two events occurred in 1985, which brought the airline industry national media attention. One incident was the hijacking of TWA Flight 847 by Shiite terrorists, who insisted that Israel release 735 political prisoners ("detainees"). Bombs had been placed at airports in major American cities, and travelers were too frightened to fly. Dole was interviewed on the *MacNeil Lehrer News Hour*.[39]

Before she spoke, the program featured journalists who had described the hijacking, travelers who had attested to their fear of flying, and commentators who had talked about new security measures such as using sky marshals on planes. Dole stressed ground safety and training, "very, very extensive training." She said she couldn't discuss DOT's plans to improve safety in detail because that would render them ineffective.

This incident came on the heels of another airline disaster, the downing of a KAL jumbo jet by Soviet warplanes that killed 269 people. In November 1985, the United States, Soviet Union, and Japan signed the Pacific Air Safety Agreement, detailing the protocol all should follow in dealing with aviation emergencies in their airspaces. Commenting upon the agreement, Dole said it was "an important step in advancing the cause of safety and international cooperation in civil aviation. . . . For the first time, we will have standard procedures for dealing with emergency aviation situations that may occur in airspace of vital concern to our three nations."[40]

Even though the public was in favor of changes in aviation procedures, members of Congress and special interest groups slowed down or halted Dole's progress. Some members of Congress resisted her drug testing policy because they thought it was a violation of workers' rights. Special interest groups resisted her proposed initiatives to change the flight patterns of small aircraft. In *Unlimited Partners*, she described the letters that poured in when a special interest group ran full-page ads in newspapers to voice its disapproval.[41]

Despite the criticism, Dole wrote in *Unlimited Partners* that the last three years she served as head of DOT were the safest in aviation history. She brought a consumer protection perspective to the position, and it is evident in a new rule her investigations spawned, which she called a "truth in scheduling rule." This required airlines to report their "on-time" and "baggage complaint" record to the public,[42] information she thought would enable the public to promote more efficiency through their consumer power.

Deregulation and privatization were key themes of the Reagan administration, and Dole promoted them in her role as head of DOT. She followed these principles with the sale of Conrail, reforms in the trucking industry, and with legislation governing private satellite launches. The sale of Conrail was a responsibility Dole inherited when she accepted the position at DOT. Conrail was a federally chartered company that had been created in the 1970s from several failed smaller companies. During the first four years of its operation, it ran up a $1.6 billion loss. Congress agreed to sell the company to the highest bidder before Dole had been appointed. After aggressively marketing the company, Dole found a buyer in 1985 who agreed to abide by a number of protective covenants she thought necessary. Congress had to approve the sale, but she ran into difficulty with some members of the House of Representatives. Eventually, when all of Congress was pressured to take measures to reduce the federal deficit, a committee proposed selling stock in the railroad to the public. Eventually, Conrail was sold and Dole was able to reduce the deficit by $2 billion dollars. She was also successful in moving the two airports in Washington, D.C., Dulles and National, into the hands of an independent regional authority. She helped with deregulation of the trucking industry, whose regulations were like a "crazy quilt," and with an initiative that would allow private companies to launch satellites into space.

When Dole became the secretary of DOT, the National Aeronautics and Space Administration (NASA) was launching satellites for the government as well as for private industries. Dole felt that this was unfair because the government was giving private companies discounted rates to launch their satellites and private launching companies could not compete for the business. When the *Challenger* space shuttle exploded in 1986, the government stopped sending satellites into space and companies that wanted to put satellites into orbit had to go outside the United States. The idea of a private company to launch satellites gained favor by 1987, and Dole was able to approve a preliminary launch by a private company.[43] She also moved forward with renovations to Union Station.

After serving as secretary of transportation for four and a half years, longer than anyone else, Dole resigned to help her husband campaign for the presidency. Her farewell address to the employees of DOT usefully summarized all of the initiatives they had worked on together. Their record of accomplishments under her leadership was impressive.[44] Her speech is noteworthy because of the personal tone she took as she thanked all of her coworkers for their dedication. The first lines she uttered set the tone of the speech: "I can't tell you how it touches my heart to look out at this audience and know it's the last time I'll address you . . . as Secretary of Transportation." She admitted that the decision to leave DOT was "a bit of a wrenching experience." Waxing patriotic, she ended her speech by praising her staff for all of the work they had done together: "I think any country must be great that can inspire people like you to devote your lives to service."

A VOICE FOR THE WORKING PUBLIC

President George H. W. Bush phoned Elizabeth Dole on December 22, 1988, and invited her to join his cabinet as secretary of labor to lead a large department with a budget of $31 billion and a staff of approximately

18,500 employees.[45] At that time in her life, Dole wanted more than any-thing to help the unfortunate and to encourage others to give through volunteer efforts. She wanted to be a "point of light," and wasn't certain how best she could serve others. When she received Bush's call, she told him she would think about his offer. She wrote in *Unlimited Partners*, "It didn't take me long to decide that the Department of Labor offered a wealth of opportunities to affect people's lives for the better."[46] President Bush faxed her material to study, and she was impressed with what she read. "Originally founded in 1913," she wrote, "the Labor Department was meant to be a voice for America's workingmen and women. Its many re-sponsibilities included workforce training, workplace safety, promotion of good labor-management relations, and oversight of pension plans." Dole recognized the opportunities she would have to help the American worker: "young Americans just entering the workplace, adult Americans already in the workforce, and Americans seeking security in their golden years."

Dole's nomination as secretary of labor received little opposition dur-ing the Confirmation Hearing before the Senate Committee on Labor and Human Resources. The entire proceedings took just over an hour. Dur-ing the hearing, many of the senators communicated what they consid-ered to be the most important priorities for labor—minimum wage, parental leave, child and elderly care, OSHA (Occupational Safety and Health Administration) and MSHA (Mine Safety and Health Administra-tion) regulations, pension plans, health care, and so on. Dole was asked whether she would work on these problems, what her priorities would be, and whether she would be willing to work across party lines. Dole probably recognized how tricky the position would be—acting as an ad-vocate for labor in a Republican administration that was traditionally on the side of business. Dole emphasized her "agreement with the president's position that the government should encourage, not require, businesses to offer such benefits as health insurance, child care, and parental leave."[47] She made this point in her prepared statement: "The mission of the Labor Department must be to coordinate a strategy of 'growth plus,' policies to help those for whom the jobs of the future are now out of reach because of a skills gap, family pressures, or because of a lack of supportive policies."[48]

As secretary of labor, Dole worked on skills training, safety, and secu-rity issues, as well as maintaining a good relationship with labor. Indeed, the president of the American Federation of Labor-Congress of Industrial Organizations Lane Kirkland, viewed her appointment positively; her record as an advocate for the consumer and public must have been attrac-tive to labor. As it turned out, his confidence in her was justified, since she became an activist secretary at a time when labor in the United States was waking up after eight years of the Reagan administration's anti-union stance.

Skills Training

When Dole became the head of the Department of Labor (DOL), the economy was struggling, companies were downsizing, and workers who were laid off were having a difficult time finding new jobs they could perform. One of Dole's top priorities was skills training. She focused on workers who were in the marketplace, as well as those who would be joining it in the future. She saw the position as an opportunity to make sure that all Americans could have jobs and the skills needed to perform them. She expressed this idea eloquently by using a refrain in her speeches, "everybody counts," that is, everyone deserves the opportunity to make a decent living.[49]

Dole knew that the workplace of the 1990s and beyond required an educated workforce, with people who could "read complex manuals, operate computers, analyze data, organize information and make difficult judgments."[50] In her "State of the Workforce Address," delivered to the State Teachers and Principals of the Year Award winners on October 26, 1989, she expressed her strong feelings about the quality of the American workforce and the need for a top-quality education system. However, she told her audience that the training students received in schools was not adequate, and many were dropping out before graduation. She spoke similarly during a speech given at the "Urban League." Many young people, she said, do not "make the connection between success in school and success in the real world. There is a link—a profound link—between the two . . . they can be assured of a good job, a fulfilling job, if they stick in there and get a good education."[51]

Dole targeted different populations of at-risk youth as one of her top priorities. She appointed "a blue-ribbon commission," chaired by former secretary of labor Bill Brock and charged it "with developing national competency guidelines that reflect work readiness and . . . can be used by schools for curriculum development." She visited Department of Labor offices in ten cities, where she discovered many successful programs and met young people whose lives had been turned around by the training and counseling they had received.[52] Later, she would use these students' stories in her speeches as examples of how effective government programs can be.

Dole worked on the problem created by students who enter the marketplace for the first time without adequate preparation.[53] She promoted school-to-work programs, including work-based apprenticeship programs to make sure students would have the skills businesses wanted. She sponsored "the first-ever national conference on the 'school-to-work' population."[54] She called on business leaders to encourage their employees to mentor at-risk students. She targeted especially the most disadvantaged and least skilled. To help them, she refocused the Job Training Partnership, providing not just training for a job, but basic skills such as literacy and remedial education.[55]

Dole targeted the homeless: "We must help the homeless find a permanent solution, so they do not continue spinning through the revolving door of emergency assistance." She worked out an arrangement with the secretary of housing and urban development to provide housing for the homeless while she provided the training, which included literacy skills as well as counseling for drug and alcohol addiction.[56] In an article in *Industry Week*, May 15, 1989, Dole was said to be working with Health and Human Services' Louis Sullivan and Education Secretary Lauro Cavazos to make policy about human resources on a government-wide basis. Their mission was to tie together elements of job training with other goals such as welfare reform and vocational education.[57]

Two Cabinet Positions, the Same Mission: Safety

As part of her work at DOL, Dole became involved in safety issues. She solicited President Bush and Congress to increase funding to OSHA for several initiatives. She and her staff worked on legislation to help workers avoid injuries from repetitive movements. She proposed a regulation designed "to protect 5.4 million workers against blood-borne pathogens, such as AIDS and Hepatitis B." According to Dole, this was "the first time in history that OSHA had proposed rules to deal with a biological hazard of infectious disease."[58] She made underage workers a priority and enforced laws that were already on the books. She organized a crackdown, but discovered that the fourteen- to sixteen-year-olds who were flipping burgers really were doing it to earn money for clothes and cars. She thought the teenagers should be spending more time on their educations.[59] She also requested that all employees of private industries wear their seat belts and motor cycle helmets.[60]

Dole instigated a crackdown on safety violations. During the Reagan administration, OSHA was virtually dormant. In an article that appeared in *Industry Week* magazine, "'Rip van OSHA' No Longer Sleeping," Dole was credited with establishing a new level of activity. She was committed to uncovering violations of health and safety standards and visiting corporations to check on them. Early on, she levied a fine of $1.5 million on a construction company and engineering firm when a tunnel exploded, killing a worker, and another fine of $100,000 for a trucking accident.[61] She levied a record fine of $500,000 against Pyro Mining Company for 121 violations, which were uncovered after a terrible methane explosion killed ten miners. Dole issued a statement that demonstrated her commitment to worker safety: "The fine we are levying today is the largest penalty in history to result from a single mine accident. It signifies the gravity of the violations and the commitment of the department to see that our nation's miners work under safe conditions."[62]

Workers' Security a Priority

Dole took on several workers' security initiatives, from minimum wage to pension plans. Workers economic security confronted her soon after her confirmation hearing in the form of a controversy about minimum wage. During the eight years of the Reagan administration, minimum wage remained at $3.35 an hour—a stalemate between Reagan and organized labor. With the change of administration, Democrats were eager to raise minimum wage to $4.65 an hour, phased in over three years. The Bush administration, however, threatened to veto such an increase, recommending instead a raise to $4.25, with a provision for instituting a lower "training wage," which new employees would receive during their first six months on the job. Dole helped negotiate a compromise with Lane Kirkland, AFL-CIO president.[63] Many criticized the Bush administration's stance, including the National Women's Political Caucus, which argued that women workers, who were twice as likely to work for minimum wage, were victims of the low wages. Even when working a forty-hour week, Caucus members claimed, a person making minimum wage would remain below the poverty level, if she had to support a family of three. In the end, the Bush bill passed, probably because it was an improvement and the Bush administration was not willing to support a higher wage.

The issue of pension security emerged at the end of Dole's first year as secretary of labor in the form of a disagreement between the Pittston Coal Company and the United Mine Workers Association (UMWA). An article in *Business Week* reported that miners accused the coal company of wanting to break a forty-year-old industry-wide agreement to pay full benefits for those who had worked for the company for twenty years— including retired miners.[64] Workers were struggling to retain these benefits and demanding higher wages,[65] while the company was reeling from "increases in the cost of health benefits." Dole helped resolve the conflict by inviting the two leaders, Paul Douglas of Pittston Coal and Rich Trumka of the UMWA, to her office for a meeting on October 14, 1989.

They had not talked directly since June 7.[66] She served them lunch, and by the end of the meal, they agreed to accept the help of a supermediator, whom Dole would appoint. That agreement led to the resolution of the strike on December 31, 1989. This episode was significant because the issue contested transcended the one coal company. Seventeen hundred workers were involved at Pittston, but during the course of the strike, 46,000 miners in ten states also staged "sympathy strikes,"[67] and the agreements reached by Pittston Coal and the UMWA set standards for the entire coal industry. It was also a victory for the collective bargaining process, claimed UMWA president Trumka.[68] According to biographer Mulford, the associated press ran an article that was widely distributed in U.S. papers saying, "Labor Secretary Elizabeth Dole may have made a philosophical homecoming when she put aside a decade of Republican labor doctrine and intervened in the Pittston coal strike."[69]

Once the Pittston strike was settled, Dole faced public expectations for greater federal activism from her department. She had created a special commission that was charged with examining problems in the coal industry, such as financing the skyrocketing health and pension benefits. Quickly, a Department of Labor spokesperson, Johanna Schneider, clarified that the creation of the commission was "not meant to be a precursor for a broader policy outside the coal industry. . . . Those are perhaps the hopes and desires of those outside of the federal government but not necessarily within it."[70] Some had hoped that Dole would intervene as well in the Eastern Airlines strike. However, she felt this was more the bailiwick of the Department of Transportation.

Working Fair: Equal Opportunity at Home and Abroad

Having experienced gender bias firsthand when she was a student at Harvard Law School and later as she entered the male-dominated field of government service, Dole worked on equitable employment opportunities for women and minorities during her tenure as secretary of labor, a subject treated in more depth in Chapter 4. She began with her own department, establishing a senior staff that consisted of more than two-thirds women and minorities. She said she chose the best people, hoping corporate America was taking notes. One of her objectives, she said, "was to serve as a catalyst for change in removing every last vestige of discrimination from the workplace, and ensuring that women and minorities have equal access to senior management employment opportunities."[71]

In a speech she gave to the National Urban League, Dole talked about the shortage of traditional white male workers, claiming this would help women and minorities find positions. She said: "Those who have been outside looking in—many women, members of minorities, the disadvantaged, the disabled—will have unprecedented opportunities for productive work . . . every man and woman who wants a job can have a job—if they have the skills."[72] She stated her views unequivocally, "I firmly believe that we will not totally eliminate discrimination from our society until we have stamped it out of our economy."

Dole was not in favor of using a quota system to redress the problem, which had become known as the "glass ceiling," but she did intend to use her position "as a 'bully pulpit' to tell business in no uncertain terms that if they effectively block[ed] half of their employees from reaching their full potential, then they . . . [were] also hurting themselves."[73] Dole called this problem a "top priority" that is "a matter of fairness and equity, borne out of personal experience."[74] She had the support of her husband, who was working in the Senate to pass legislation establishing a "National Commission on the Glass Ceiling."[75] Both Doles, according to Elizabeth, hoped the glass ceiling would meet "the same fate as the Berlin Wall."[76] How much the Bush administration supported her work is not known.

In discussing Dole's work on the glass ceiling, biographer Mulford says in this context: "Mrs. Dole was not always able to get administration support for programs she wanted to sponsor." Dole herself said: "The president has such a broad array of interests to be concerned about that you may fight for something internally that you think is very important. But as he looks at the overall picture, the timing isn't right for one reason or another. Something else is going on that's going to conflict with that. I think you have to be willing to say, 'Okay, I am part of a bigger team here.' You may not always get approval for everything you want to do at the moment."[77]

In November 1990, after announcing her plans to resign from the Department of Labor, she announced a multifaceted initiative to help women gain access to the skilled trades that paid well, including jobs that had traditionally been reserved for men—electrician, machinist, carpenter, auto mechanic, painter, and so on. Dole said:

> Although the number of women has increased significantly over the past 20 years and is expected to increase further, 80 percent of working women are in traditionally female jobs, many of which are low paying. . . . These skilled trades jobs have the potential for greatly improving the economic status of women—higher wages, better fringe benefits, a wider variety of work schedules, greater job security and more opportunities for advancement. For some women, it means the difference between being on welfare and being economically self-sufficient.[78]

As part of this initiative, Dole worked on the recruitment and retention of women apprentices. She enlisted the aid of other agencies—the Bureau of Apprenticeship and Training (BAT), the Office of Federal Contract Compliance Programs (OFCCP), and the Women's Bureau to implement outreach and educational programs.

As secretary of labor, Dole worked on issues of international labor. Many Eastern Block countries were changing from communist to free societies. After years of their leaders telling them what to do, the shift to self-determination was not an easy one for workers to make. Dole traveled to Poland, one of the countries establishing a market economy, with private ownership and little governmental control.[79] She was part of a team whose purpose it was to "provide training in business management and craft skills, set up an unemployment insurance system, and gather statistical information." Dole met with Lech Walesa, an electrician and leader of the labor union, Solidarity. Later, he became the president of Poland. Dole provided experts to help with technical advice; especially noteworthy was the program cosponsored with the AFL-CIO to establish a construction training cite in Warsaw.[80] It must have been the human needs Dole witnessed there and when she and her husband visited earthquake victims in Armenia that motivated her to accept the position of American Red Cross president. After her trip to Poland, Dole tried to raise money to help the Polish people, but she was told she couldn't do it legally in her position as head of DOL.

Dole was hesitant to accept the position as president of the American Red Cross until its board was about to hire someone else. She consulted with President Bush, and when her departure from DOL became public knowledge through a leak, she and the president held a news conference where she stressed the positive—all of the things she could do to help the really unfortunate. President Bush said he was sorry to see her go, but understood how much the American public respected her. She also answered reporters' questions about her motivation for leaving, saying she didn't plan to run for any office. She denied allegations that she was leaving because of White House resistance to her initiatives: "We were right in there on all the issues," Dole said. "The president was supportive of all the initiatives I wanted to go forward with. There was never a, 'No, we don't want to do that,' or 'Put that on hold.'"[81]

Dole explained her motivations for resigning to her staff and the public in her "Everybody Counts" speech, presented on October 24, 1990. She began by saying how proud she had been to accept the position two years earlier: "I stood before you in this very hall to take the oath of office. . . . It was one of the proudest moments in my twenty-five year career in public service." Calling DOL "the people's department," Dole said she accepted the position to make a difference, "a positive difference—in people's lives." She told them how much she thought they had succeeding in improving the safety and security of the American workforce. She said that she had moved forward all of the programs that were important to her, either completing them or taking them far enough for others to finish. She concluded the speech by mentioning her legacy: "And if I could write my own legacy for our time here, it would simply be . . . , "They did their best to ensure that everybody counts." Lynn Martin, her successor, worked with Bob Dole on the Glass Ceiling Initiative, but when she was first appointed, Martin did not mention it as one of her priorities for DOL.

LEADING AN ARMY OF HUMANITARIANS

When Elizabeth Dole became president of the American Red Cross on February 1, 1991, she was taking the reins of one of the leading humanitarian organizations in the world. She was joining "an army" of 22,000 employees with more than a million volunteers and a yearly budget as large as that of a Fortune 500. For Dole, this position was different from all of her previous work, which had been in government service. What attracted her to the Red Cross was the opportunity to appeal to the generosity of the American people, asking them to help the victims of natural and man-made disasters—those most vulnerable and in greatest need: "The Red Cross's mission," she said, "is meeting dire human needs on a full-time basis. . . . It's what we do day in and day out."[82]

As with her other positions, this one had its challenges, including problems with the quality of the blood supply, a slow response time to natural disasters, and fiscal/bureaucratic mismanagement. In addition, the situation in the Middle East was tense; there were fears of war, and the soldiers and victims would need blood and other forms of humanitarian aid. Already the Red Cross had set up operations to supply 7,000 units of blood a week, and 150 disaster workers and medical personnel were scheduled to depart for Saudi Arabia.[83] Money was an issue, too, because of the slow economy and a scandal at the United Way,[84] which caused consumers to look more closely at the spending patterns of nonprofit agencies. Dole presented her "Tradition of Trust" speech to an audience of about fifteen hundred employees and volunteers on February 4, 1991, pledging to take aggressive action on all of these measures.

Dole wanted to accomplish several goals with this speech. She wanted to introduce herself and reassure the group that she was committed to working with them. This was important because she had been in government service all of her life and the position of Red Cross president had to be apolitical. She also wanted to provide an overview of the special challenges the organization faced and to outline the initiatives she planned to take during her tenure as president. Finally, she wanted to ask the audience to work with her; she wanted—needed—their experience, wisdom, and support.

Dole worked on her credibility with her listeners by praising all of the volunteers who made up the organization and telling them that she was about to join their ranks. She told them she wanted "to earn the patch on my sleeve. During my first year as President," she said, "I will accept no salary. I, too, will be a volunteer." This decision was widely reported in the press,[85] and it dispelled rumors that she was leaving her $99,500 a year position as secretary of labor for a $200,000 a year position as president of the American Red Cross.[86] Dole promised to visit members of the staff: "In the next few weeks, as I find my way through the tunnel, I hope to drop by as many offices as I can, so we can become better acquainted."

There was plenty of work to do at the American Red Cross. Dole highlighted her priorities during the "Tradition of Trust" speech, explaining that she understood the fiscal challenges the organization was under: "When the search committee first approached me about coming here, they told me of the great challenges facing this organization—about an organization struggling mightily to preserve that tradition of trust. The Red Cross is challenged because the country is challenged." She talked about the increased needs of the military and the challenge of finding ways to "pay for them." "But let there be no doubt," she said, "we will find ways to live up to this trust." She talked about "the blood of life we distribute to hospitals, and now to men and women in the Gulf," and pledged to take "every step possible to ensure that the blood supply is as safe as we can make it." She also talked about the hope Red Crossers bring to the victims of disasters and pledged to improve disaster services to bring volunteers and supplies more quickly and efficiently to those who need them. Lastly, she promised to honor the trust and generosity of the American people who provide the funds for the Red Cross by taking measures to insure "complete fiscal accountability, integrity, and just plain good sense when it comes to spending each and every dime."

Each of the challenges Dole faced as president of the American Red Cross had one thing in common: all required money to solve the problems. She learned quickly that the American Red Cross operated differently than any of her other positions. When she worked for government agencies, she simply submitted a budget for funds she needed and fought for it on Capitol Hill. At the Red Cross, however, she had to raise the money she needed by asking American businesses and people to contribute. Dole became a successful fund-raiser, delivering speeches across the country and using the media to bring attention to the needs of the military and natural disaster victims. She also chose board members wisely, and instituted procedures to insure fiscal accountability. During her eight years as president, she helped raise $3.4 billion.[87] Some of the money came from her private speaking engagements and from the salary she declined during her first year. The funds raised were used to solve problems such as decreasing the Red Cross's disaster response time and making sure the United States blood supply remained pathogen free.

Even before Dole joined the American Red Cross, the organization had been faulted because of its slow response time, for example, with Hurricane Hugo and the earthquake in Loma Prieta (1989). Dole made "a quick response" one of her priorities as president. In *Unlimited Partners*, she wrote about how she had launched "a multi-million dollar disaster service revitalization effort," which opened "a war room—a National Disaster Operations Center." The center was "open twenty-four hours a day, 365 days a year," and it was used to "monitor ongoing disasters and impending threats, mobilize relief efforts, and move . . . people and equipment wherever they are needed." Under her leadership, the Red Cross also "quadrupled to sixteen-thousand the number of those trained to handle national catastrophic disasters, and positioned millions of dollars' worth of state-of-the art communications equipment and resources in strategic locations most vulnerable to the ravages of nature."[88] Most amazing about these accomplishments was that the Disaster Relief Fund was projected to be in the red by $30 million when Dole took over the reins at the Red Cross, but it was $100 million in the black when she left.

Another priority for which Dole raised funds was the national blood supply. Congress and the American public were critical of the blood supply. An article appearing in *USA Today*, for example, asked members of the public: "Are you concerned about the safety of the nation's blood supply?" People interviewed answered, "Yes, I am." "Very much so." "Extremely." "Definitely." Many were afraid of contracting AIDS/HIV, Hepatitis A and B, and one respondent mentioned parasites from Desert Storm. They feared both giving blood and receiving it through transfusions.[89] In reality, only a small number of persons had contracted AIDS from tainted blood, but the Red Cross at that time was simply not able to test the blood they collected thoroughly enough before using it. The Red Cross was also accused of not keeping adequate records.[90]

Dole announced sweeping plans to upgrade the entire blood collection, testing, and distribution systems at a Red Cross Convention on May 20, 1991, in San Diego.[91] She announced that the Red Cross would "transform its Blood Operations into a state-of-the-art system that would quickly incorporate medical advances and new technology as they evolve."[92] The system would have the world's largest database of information about blood. The quality assurance systems would be "unsurpassed." Fifty-three aging and independent labs would be replaced with nine state-of-the art centers, using cutting-edge testing procedures. One computer system would be used to replace twenty-eight outmoded ones, and it would be able to link together all of the Red Cross operations. A training center would be built to deliver the latest techniques to staff members. During Dole's tenure as president, the Red Cross accomplished all of these improvements. She was deeply praised by Secretary of Health and Human Services Donna Shalala, who called Dole's efforts "extraordinary." The cost of the improvements was supposed to be $120 million, but the upgrade actually cost closer to $162 million. Dole was 80 percent finished with the upgrade when she took her leave of absence to help her husband campaign for the presidency; she completed the project after her return.

Dole raised large sums of money and she spent them to meet Red Cross challenges. With sizeable amounts of money coming in and going out, she felt it incumbent on her to update the Red Cross's system of financial management and accountability. During a speech she gave to the Forum Club in Houston, she said: "When it comes to managing money, good intentions are no longer good enough."[93] She explained that the Red Cross needed to overhaul its financial systems. By the time she stepped down as president, she had accomplished much in this area.

> I instituted a series of strict financial controls aimed at making donations to the Red Cross go further. As a result, we were able to achieve a $20 million reduction in overhead at the national level. These economies in turn allowed me to reduce local chapter dues by 20 percent. Nearly 93 cents of every Red Cross dollar is spent on programs and resources. I am very proud that we have the highest possible rating from the National Charities Information Bureau, the Council of Better Business Bureau's Philanthropic Advisory Services and numerous other charity watchdog organizations.[94]

No one could institute that many changes in the Red Cross without receiving some degree of criticism, and Dole was no exception. She was criticized on a number of fronts—for not getting relief to victims quickly enough and because of the burden of training caused by her update of the blood systems.[95] The area in which she received most criticism, however, was her approach to the job: she made it one of fund-raising, and ran a public relations oriented administration. For example, during a National Health and Safety Conference in October 1994, Dole spoke to the group, saying the American Red Cross had to become more market oriented. She spoke about other initiatives—updated apparel, younger volunteers, more services to seniors—to help influence more Americans to make donations.[96] Dole was reported to have hired three of Bob Dole's presidential advisors for six-figure salaries as consultants. They worked on and off for the Red Cross and for Bob Dole. One woman, Melinda Ferris, worked for the Red Cross until March 1996, and again in October 1996. In between, she acted as a consultant, helping Elizabeth craft a graceful image as she campaigned for her husband for the presidency, even helping with the Republican National Convention speech. Although the consultants said they were able to keep their Red Cross work separate from their campaign work, expressions of doubt surfaced. A law professor from the University of Miami was quoted in the *Houston Chronicle* as saying: "if these people prove to be the nucleus of a future Dole campaign, how is anyone to distinguish what they are doing for the Red Cross from what they're doing for Elizabeth Dole as a presidential candidate?"[97] Along similar lines, Dole was criticized for filling a number of the top positions at the Red Cross with former Reagan supporters and some who worked for the Doles in her husband's campaign.[98] She also raised millions of dollars from American corporations to help the Red Cross; some hinted that the money might have influenced Bob Dole's policies, but there was no evidence that the donations ever influenced any of his decisions.[99] Still another accusation was that funds were mismanaged; this came from a study that was commissioned by Gene Dyson, acting president of the Red Cross, when Dole took a leave of absence to campaign for her husband. It found that the organization was not running as efficiently as it should be and recommended creating two new positions, one for planning and one for finances.[100]

Just as there were critics of Dole's performance as Red Cross president, so were there admirers who recognized all she had done in that role. In a January 25, 1999 issue of *Business Week*, two journalists gave her a "report card" in which she received an A in public relations. Others were generous with their praise, such as journalist Frank Greve, who credits her with raising a great deal of money for the Red Cross.[101] Dole summed up her own achievements in a speech she gave to her staff and volunteers when stepping down from her position as president.

Elizabeth Dole addressed a large and diverse audience on January 4, 1999, to give what has become known as her American Red Cross Resignation speech. After eight years of service, Dole decided it was time for a change. The day before her announcement, aides had "leaked" word to the press that she might be considering a bid for the U.S. presidency in 2000. These leaks drew significant media coverage of the speech; for example, camera crews from *CNN* and *C-Span* were on hand to broadcast her message, and all of the major networks carried clips on their evening news broadcasts. This speaking situation became quite a media event.

Dole's speech was designed to accomplish several goals. First and foremost, she wanted to address the Red Cross staff and volunteers and tell them officially that she was resigning as their president. She wanted to thank them for all they had accomplished together, presenting herself as someone who appreciated their help—learned from their wisdom and example. She wanted the country to know what a dedicated group of people made up the organization, and how they use to best advantage all the donations they are given. She also wanted everyone to understand the challenges she faced when she became the president of the American Red Cross, and the accomplishments the organization had made under her leadership. There had been criticisms of her, and she wanted to show that the "big picture" of her accomplishments far outweighed any minor problems the organization may have encountered. In addition, Dole was considering a run for the presidency and she needed to position herself as the kind of experienced leader who could step in and handle the challenges of that kind of office.

During the speech, Dole reviewed all the Red Cross had been able to accomplish under her leadership. She said: "I love the Red Cross. But the Red Cross is now solid as a rock, and at this important time in our national life, I believe that there may be another way for me to serve our country. The Red Cross has been a glorious mission field, but I believe there may be other duties left to fulfill." Dole drew the speech to a conclusion by saying that she had "not made definite plans" about what she would do next, but she would soon "begin considering new paths and there are exciting possibilities." Then followed her customary ending: "Thank you one and all. God bless you, and God bless the American Red Cross." In retrospect, we know she was thinking about the presidency because shortly after this speech—in March 1999—she officially threw her hat into the ring. Though she would not be successful in her bid for the presidency in 2000, she would be victorious in her bid for a U.S. Senate seat from North Carolina. The policy initiatives she will undertake in her role as senator remain to be seen.

This chapter has traced Elizabeth Dole's record as a public servant, both in government and in humanitarian positions. She has worked hard in all of the positions she has held, using public speaking and other communication skills to champion the needs of consumers, the administrations she served, the traveling and working public, and victims of war and natural disaster. Throughout the course of her career, she has accepted positions based on her deep-seated and abiding interest in the well-being of others.

Studying her activity as a public servant makes it clear that she developed and then used her voice to make a difference in others' lives. As discussed in the next chapter, she has continually deepened her interest in serving others by daily renewing her faith in cherished religious and patriotic values.

Chapter 3

Advocate for Religious, Patriotic, and Humanitarian Values

We've been blessed to be a blessing. We've received that we may give.[1]

The race for the presidency in 2000 saw front-runners from both parties engaging in talk that described their core belief systems more forcefully than candidates in previous presidential races. The most urgent reason, according to political analysts, was that Americans were particularly weary of White House scandal, and candidates sought explicit ways to signal their trustworthiness to preside from the Oval Office. Although presidential candidates have always made a point of having themselves photographed while leaving church on Sunday, during Campaign 2000 they moved way beyond that.[2] Republican nominee George W. Bush, for example, speaking in a Houston church, described his decision to recommit his life to Jesus Christ. Vice President Al Gore, at a convention of black Baptists, declared himself to be a person of strong faith and "a child of the Kingdom." Presidential hopeful Elizabeth Dole attested to her faith at a prayer breakfast in Philadelphia. She repeated almost verbatim a speech she had given more than a decade before, describing the renewal of her commitment to the religious values she had grown up with in North Carolina. In other speeches, Dole identified a lack of spiritual and civic values in contemporary media culture and called for a similar, but grander, "rebirth" or "renewal" of America. This chapter explores the continuum of her religious, patriotic, and humanitarian values as expressed in her speeches and demonstrated in her public actions.

Elizabeth Dole's house at 712 South Fulton Street, Salisbury, North Carolina. (Photo by Nichola Gutgold)

ORIGIN OF DOLE'S CORE VALUES

Elizabeth Dole's spirituality may be traced to her life as a child in Salisbury, North Carolina, where her parents and grandparents on both sides of her family practiced a living faith. On the Hanford side, both her grandfather and father had built a flower business, supplying roses all over the South. Escaping the hardships of the Depression, Elizabeth's father helped others by controlling the rent he charged to those who were not as fortunate. She described her father's altruism in *Unlimited Partners*: "It was dad's expression of a practical faith that regarded every man as his brother's keeper."[3] She praised her mother's service, too. Mary Hanford was an active volunteer, devoting her life to her church and to other activities, such as raising funds for the historic preservation of the town. According to Elizabeth, her mother's acts of "constant service to others were daily expressions of her faith."[4] Mary Hanford told her daughter how fulfilling her volunteer work for the Red Cross had been: "Elizabeth, nothing I ever did made me feel so important."[5]

Dole's maternal grandparents, "Mom" and "Pop" Cathey, lived just two houses away, and young Elizabeth spent many of her days with Mom

Cathey "munching on cookies and drinking lemonade." She listened to Bible stories and witnessed her grandmother's faith. Mom Cathey was a faithful reader of the Bible, who kept a radio next to her bed tuned to religious broadcasts. Dole was deeply influenced by her grandmother: "Through her I was encouraged to have a vital, living faith," she wrote, and "religion was about doing things for other people." In a speech she delivered in 1997 while serving as president of the American Red Cross, Dole told about how her grandmother dealt with the death of a son to a drunk driver: "My grandmother was not a wealthy woman, but because she was concerned that Vernon [her son] had never had a chance to make his contribution in life, she took the money from his life insurance and built a new wing for a mission hospital in far-off Pakistan."[6] Another story Dole told about Mom Cathey was how her grandmother viewed the prospect of entering a nursing home. "There might be some people there who don't know the Lord," she said, "and I can read the Bible to them."[7] Reflecting on her early family life, Dole said as an adult: "Truth be told, I can't imagine a more loving environment in which to raise a child."[8]

Raised as a Methodist, Dole's religious values informed the decisions she made as a college student and early in her career. When she was a student at Duke University, she attended parties for underprivileged children in Durham, and as a member of Delta Delta Delta sorority, she helped raise scholarship money for poor women.[9] One summer, she worked in the Peace Corps headquarters in Washington, D.C., writing years later in *Unlimited Partners* how the agency "reflected a missionary impulse" and praising the individuals who served in that program.[10] After receiving her law degree, Dole took public service positions where she could help those in need or the "underdog." She helped organize a conference on deaf education before working as a public defender and consumer advocate. The years she spent on the Federal Trade Commission were devoted to protecting the rights of citizens who often faced unfair and sometimes harmful practices of business and industry. When she accepted the position in the White House Office of Public Liaison in the Reagan administration, she relied on her faith to help her through difficulties. The position was stressful and, at the time, her husband suffered a painful bout with kidney stones.[11]

Dole's commitment to her White House position at Public Liaison and her ambition began to overwhelm other aspects of her life. She experienced a spiritual crisis, when the practice of her religion became "ritualistic." In 1984, she told a women's group at the Salisbury First United Church that her life seemed "threatened with spiritual starvation."[12] Praying about this, she was led to people who could help her reclaim her spiritual center. She joined a spiritual growth group that met once a week at the Foundry Methodist Church in Washington, D.C., under the direction of Minister Edward Bauman. This group helped Dole draw strength from "the power that comes from above."[13] She returned to the faith of her grandmother that she had known as a little girl and began to refocus her attention less on what she wanted to do in life and more on what God wanted to do through her.[14] Speaking at a Billy Graham crusade in 1983, she gave testimony to the power of Christ, saying that as a child, the "Gospel was as much a part of our lives as fried chicken and azaleas in the spring."[15] Asked about this period of her life by Barbara Walters on *20/20* during her husband's presidential bid in 1996, Elizabeth denied that she had a "spiritual rebirth," choosing instead to regard her experience as "a reordering of priorities." She said, "It was a matter of feeling that my career had become all-consuming and that I really wanted to shift my priorities back to the way things were as I was growing up in a family where faith is the center of your life and all else sort of flowed from that." When President Reagan invited her to join his cabinet as secretary of transportation, she discussed the prospect with her spiritual growth group, and they encouraged her to take it. One of the members pointed out how much good she could do for women: she would be the first woman to serve in Ronald Reagan's cabinet and the first to lead the Department of Transportation.

Dole's faith informed her speeches and public actions throughout the years she was secretary of transportation. She drew upon biblical imagery, stories, and language in her speeches, and closed many of them with "God bless you," "Godspeed," or "God bless each and every one of you." In a 1991 speech given to staff and volunteers of the American Red Cross, for example, she told the group: "And, as we set about our work, we will follow the principle of Noah, that first great proponent of disaster preparedness: 'No more prizes for predicting rain. Prizes only for building arks.'"[16] Her maiden speech to the U.S. Senate on July 5, 2003 also made direct reference to passages from the Book of Ruth and Leviticus in the Bible. She recommended the wisdom of initiating a contemporary form of "gleaning" to feed the poor. In many of her speeches, she also reminded her listeners how blessed they were and asked them to be a blessing to others. In her 1997 "Business with a Heart" speech, she told her guests, "As you in this room recognize, we have been blessed to be a blessing. We've received that we may give." And in 1999, while campaigning in New Hampshire, she said to her listeners: "Look how blessed we are. . . . We take a lot for granted, don't we? I believe that we have been blessed, that we might be a blessing. We have received that we might give."[17]

DOLE'S PRAYER BREAKFAST SPEECH

Without question, Dole's single most passionately religious speech was her 1987 National Prayer Breakfast keynote address, which she gave after she had been working closely with Ronald Reagan from the time of his election as president in 1980. Dole was deeply impressed by Reagan's frequent invocations of faith in his speeches, especially after the 1981 attempt on his life, when he became increasingly ready to share his faith with those around him.[18] Still, Dole's account of her religious life in her Prayer Breakfast speech was personal to a degree not often seen in that forum, certainly more so than the keynote speech Reagan had given the year before when he called for joy in the face of tragedy, which was fitting given the tragic explosion of the *Challenger* space shuttle only days before he spoke. In contrast, Dole talked about her childhood faith, her lapse during the years when she lived a fast-paced, career-focused life in Washington, D.C., and her spiritual renewal. This is true about the speech she gave in 1987, and two of the other times she presented it—on July 6, 1997, at the Farhills Baptist Church in Dayton, Ohio, and in May 1999, in Philadelphia, Pennsylvania, when she was a candidate for president. When she spoke in 1987, she was the secretary of transportation and her boss, Ronald Reagan, and his vice president, George H. W. Bush, were in the audience, along with many members of Congress and other prominent Washingtonians.

Dole's purpose in the Prayer Breakfast speech was simply to share her own spiritual story with an audience of people she worked with; she wanted to act as a witness to the power of religious ideals and tell how much they have affected her public and private life. Without question, there is some celebrity attached to being chosen as the Prayer Breakfast speaker. By speaking, Dole was given the opportunity to raise her profile as a moral agent and servant of the public. She began her speech by stating her purpose: "I consider it one of the greatest possible privileges to be invited to share this morning with fellow travelers a little of my own spiritual journey. Like most of us, I am just one person struggling to relate faith to life, but I am grateful that members of the congressional prayer group have asked me to speak from the heart about the difference Jesus Christ has made in my life."

She told her audience that her "spiritual journey began many years ago in a Carolina home where Sunday was the Lord's Day, reserved for acts of mercy and necessity." She traced her spiritual roots to her family, especially the example of her grandmother, Mom Cathey. She described how her ambition came to dominate her life: "From an early age I was active in the church. But as we move along, how often in our busy lives something seems to get in the way of a more than ritualistic faith. It may be money, or power, or prestige. In my case, it was career." And she explained how her perfectionism with regard to her career began to dominate her life. It became "pretty demanding," she said, "when you're trying to foresee every difficulty and realize every opportunity." She had little time to "be a friend to friends, let alone to the friendless." She stopped appreciating all the blessings she had, and Sunday became "just another day of the week." She said: "I had God neatly compartmentalized, crammed into a crowded file drawer of my life somewhere between 'gardening' and 'government.'" She needed to find a way out of this "spiritual starvation," and prayer led her to join a spiritual growth group at the Foundry Methodist Church. She also studied the Bible with other Senate wives.

The biblical story of Queen Esther is a very prominent part of Dole's Prayer Breakfast speech. Overall, approximately 75 percent of the speech relates the story of this Hebrew heroine, drawing lessons from her life, and applying those lessons to Dole's own situation. She extracted three lessons from the story of Esther: predicament, privilege, and Providence. Esther's *predicament* was that she lived well as the wife of a king, but her cousin, Mordecai, reminded her that as a Jew, her life would not be spared if Jewish people were to be condemned. Mordecai asked Esther for her help, even though it meant risking her life. Applying this to Dole's own life, she said that she, too, lived "the comfortable life," and like Esther, she felt called upon to make a total commitment to her faith. Further, Dole explained that Esther was given the *privilege* of helping her people, but God had others to choose from if she turned away. Likewise, Dole felt that she had been given the privilege of serving others and she, too, could be replaced if she failed to act on her faith. Finally, for Esther, God had given her a unique assignment when He chose her to fulfill His mission. In a similar way, Dole felt her life was guided by *Providence* in that "a Sovereign God" called her to serve those within her own sphere of influence. "We've been blessed to be a blessing," she said, "we've received that we might give." She told her audience that "the challenges Esther needed to hear were challenges I needed to hear, and continually need to hear: the call is total commitment."

According to Helen Thorpe, Dole was inspired to use the Bible story of Esther during a visit to her nephew, John Van Hanford III, who was at seminary. There she heard a sermon preached about Queen Esther—how she chose to speak out for her people even if it meant her downfall: "If I perish, I perish." Parallels between Queen Esther's experience and Dole's were evident to her. Thorpe writes, "whenever her views were at odds with senior White House staff, she could speak up only at the risk of losing her position."[19] She didn't often feel like an interloper in the company of men, but she did comment in *Unlimited Partners* about the "locker room" atmosphere in the Reagan White House: "There is a jackets-off, loose tie informality that goes with the long hours, the high pressure and the slangy irreverence of the political fraternity." Describing the language as "colorful and to the point," Dole said one day she was shocked to see thirty-two men in the Roosevelt Room for an eight o'clock staff meeting and she was the lone woman.[20]

Near the end of her speech, Dole emphasized that the real meaning of the Esther story is one of dependence. She said she had to learn that "dependence is a good thing, that when I've used up my own resources, when I can't control things and make them come out my way, when I'm willing to trust God with the outcome, when I'm weak, then I am strong." This was a hard lesson for her to learn. She said: "What God had to teach me was this: it is not what I do that matters, but what a sovereign God chooses to do through me."

> God doesn't want worldly successes. He wants me. He wants my heart in submission to him. Life is not just a few years to spend on self-indulgence and career advancement. It's a privilege, a responsibility, a stewardship to be lived according to a much higher calling, God's calling. This alone gives true meaning to life.

Like Esther, Dole called on her fellow Washingtonians to submit themselves to divine guidance:

> It has struck me that this is really our purpose in gathering together this morning at this, the Annual National Prayer Breakfast. We have come to humbly acknowledge our dependence on God. We have come, as our invitations to this event state: To seek the Lord's guidance and strength in our individual lives and in the governing of our nation, with the hope that the power of Christ may deepen our fellowship with one another.

She reminded her audience that self-interest is limiting and asked her colleagues to adopt Esther's humility and dependence. She closed her speech by indicating that "total commitment to Christ is a high and difficult calling. And one I will struggle with the rest of my days." Perhaps Dole was thinking about her grandmother when she said this, for earlier in the speech she had talked about one of her most prized possessions— her grandmother's Bible. She drew attention to one of the marginal notes next to Psalm 139: "'Search me O God, and know my heart—try me and know my thoughts. And see if there be any wicked way in me, and lead me in the way everlasting.'" The entry was dated May 22, 1952, 1:00 A.M.

Dole's forty-five-minute Prayer Breakfast speech was uniquely personal. A conservative Republican, Dole had been described as a "very private, public person," yet she shared her autobiography of faith with a large audience. Her nephew, John Van Hanford III, said Dole was "very courageous" to present her speech in such personal terms: "It was a very bold thing for her to be that vulnerable." In addition, although she was married to Senator Robert Dole at the time, she did not refer to him at all, choosing instead to keep the audience's focus on herself. This further increased the personal nature of her remarks as did her many uses of the pronoun "I" during her speech. Above all, she made it clear that service to others was and would continue to be at the center of her life. Her former aide, Kerry Tymchuk, has said that in all of her transitions from one government position to another, her outlook remained steadfast: "She views public service as a mission."[21] Indeed, throughout her career, the language of "missions" has appeared in many of her speeches.

FROM RELIGIOUS TO PATRIOTIC VALUES

Dole gave versions of her 1987 Prayer Breakfast speech in local and national venues. When she hit the campaign trail, especially during her own run for the presidency, she gave speeches in which her religious values melded seamlessly in a continuum with her patriotic values. An abiding theme in many of her speeches was patriotism, which for Dole was simply faith applied to society and community. In her speech to the graduating seniors at Duke University in 2000, for example, Dole presented her equation of faith and service, claiming she had derived her beliefs from her small-town rearing: "Religion was about doing things for people," she said, and "our faith taught us that service came before self." In several of her speeches, Dole made political activism an application of faith to community and society.

Dole turned not only to her family background to connect religious and patriotic values, but also to the historical roots of the country. "Long before there was an American dream," she said in her Republican National Convention speech in 2000, "there was a dream of America as liberty's home and refuge." Speaking to graduating seniors more than a decade earlier at the University of Virginia, Dole told the students that our values set us apart from other nations. Faith-based values were extolled by the founding fathers from the beginning of the country, she said: "The record of the Constitutional Convention leaves no doubt that our nation's founders were sustained by their faith in God." Describing the men "who invented America" in her 1998 "An America We Can Be" speech, she said they were not "wide-eyed rabble rousers," rather they were men "with a firm reliance on the protection of the Divine Providence," who "pledged to each other their lives, their fortunes, their sacred honor." Quoting

George Washington in another speech, she said: "'Of all the dispositions and habits which lead to political prosperity, religion and morality are indispensable supports.'"[22] In that same speech, she also spoke about Thomas Jefferson and other men who attended the Constitutional Convention in Philadelphia. For Jefferson, the nation would only be successful as long as the citizens could "distinguish good from bad ideas." She expressed this notion in a memorable line: "so long as books remain open, minds will never be closed." She also quoted Benjamin Franklin, who spoke about the challenge of "'being a free people.'" His words "have not lost their resonance," she said.

Dole spoke at length about the Constitution in a speech she delivered at a Department of Transportation Awards Ceremony on September 16, 1987. "The bicentennial year of the Constitution," she said, "offers the opportunity to ponder the meaning of that sacred document." She told her audience that the "idea behind the document" gave "we the people" the opportunity to "rule ourselves." "The signers of the Constitution," she said, "believed implicitly in the ability of seemingly ordinary people—people like you and me—to accomplish extraordinary things." She reminded her audience of the special challenge posed by that charter: the only way a democratic form of government can survive is by enlisting "the energies and the devotion of the people themselves." She encouraged her audience to participate in service activities, saying that the Constitution "calls each of us, in our own way, to service." Rather than merely granting us rights, it "reminds us of our responsibilities to each other and to America."[23] During her Republican National Convention speech in 2000, she reiterated a similar thought when she told her vast audience: "the values on which this great nation was founded are just as vital today as they were 200 years ago."

In other speeches, Dole cited contemporary Americans who exemplified her ideal of faithful service to others. Particularly noteworthy for Dole was the Reverend Dr. Martin Luther King Jr., whom she lauded for giving his life to the highest cause of racial justice. During a speech presented at Duke University in 2000, Dole described King's sacrifice in the same terms as that of the early American Revolutionary heroes who gave their lives for freedom while battling against a foreign power. She referred to "the modern civil rights revolution" as unfolding "on a wave of Biblical teaching, African-American spirituals, and a courage reminiscent of the early martyrs." She praised the "believers of all stripes" who "have regarded society's imperfections as a call to duty, not as an excuse for bitterness." She predicated a time of full racial equality and compared America to "Joseph's many-colored coat." "In our diversity," she said, "lies our strength." She quoted Martin Luther King's words again in the speech she gave at the Republican National Convention in 2000, saying we have a responsibility to make "'justice roll down like waters and righteousness like a mighty stream.'"

Dole's religious and patriotic values also stand behind her commitment to women's rights. For her, the dream of America is just as meaningful for women as it is for other minorities. During her Prayer Breakfast speech, she demonstrated the central role women can play in bringing about freedom when she described in detail the predicament Queen Esther found herself in and how she risked her life to save her people. In Dole's "America We Can Be" speech, she praised the men and women who sacrificed their lives for freedom throughout our history, including when the country was first founded. She also insisted: "if the [Constitutional] Convention was held today, there'd not only be men representing the colonies, but women as well."

THE COUNTRY AS SHE FOUND IT

Not long after Dole had given her Prayer Breakfast speech in 1987, she spoke to a University of Virginia commencement audience about the moral condition she perceived in the country. She described to the graduating seniors the world they would soon enter: a "land in the throes of national renewal—an America born again . . . in need of leaders whose character is matched by their commitment." She praised the people of America for beginning to think less about themselves and more about others: "The 'Me Decade' has been replaced by the 'We Decade,'" she said. Of course, this "grassroots revival of fundamental principles" that occurred during the Reagan years lost ground, according to Dole, once Bill Clinton took office in 1992, and during the years of his presidency.

In her "America We Can Be" speech, given on different occasions during the late 1990s, Dole talked about how reluctant Americans have become to participate in civic affairs. For her, too many have grown disenchanted with government. "Qualified people," she said, "are being discouraged from entering government service." She said that Americans no longer trust the government to do the right thing, and she said the reason they feel that way is simply that government is "too big, too complex, too bureaucratic." For her, the solution was for more decisions to be made at the local level by "we the people," "you and me."

In 2000, Dole spoke about similar problems in the country, during a commencement speech she presented at Duke University. She described the isolated lives most Americans lead and the negative effects of today's media culture, wherein people have difficulty telling where "life begins and entertainment leaves off." She continued: "Controversies are made by and for television; politics are reduced to fodder for late night comics." And Washington itself reflects a "society coarsened by tabloid values" where candidates "without ideas hire consultants without convictions to run campaigns without substance."[24]

Dole claimed that the solution to the problems of the country might be found in the fundamental values that make up our individual and national character. She developed this point by calling for a return to personal responsibility. In her view, we have tried to legislate morality: "We have campus speech codes to keep us civil. We apply harassment rules to schoolyard kisses. Drug policies have become so tied in knots we can no longer distinguish between aspirin and crack. And edicts from our courts now protect the freedom of molesters and stalkers and abusers so well that America's children and daughters and wives no longer trust society to keep them safe." The solution for Dole was not to pass government regulations, but for individuals to take personal responsibility for their actions.[25]

Dole presented her views on character in several speeches. In 1991, speaking at a Commencement at Albion College, she called character, "a voice inside us" that "calls us to our better nature, that motivates us to help those in dire human need, that tells us there are causes greater than ourselves."[26] In her speech at Duke University in 2000, she said that character is defined and tested "through the practical application of faith." Who a person is depends on what he or she believes, and "acting upon those beliefs is the essence of a personal life." An illustration of what she meant was how she spoke about her husband in 1996, when he ran against Bill Clinton for the presidency. Dole talked about the values that contributed to her husband's character—"values such as honesty, decency, respect, personal responsibility, hard work, love of God, love of family, patriotism."[27] Those same values, she said, enabled her husband "to risk his life on the battlefields of Italy," and sustained him while he was recuperating for three years from his near-fatal injuries.

Dole spoke about values similarly during Campaign 2000 for the presidency. In March 1999, while campaigning in New Hampshire, she said: "There is a yearning to make us a better nation. We need to get back to basic values: personal responsibility, honesty, integrity . . . cooperation over conflict. . . . Haven't we been blessed?"[28] When George W. Bush received the Republican nomination, she called on all Americans in her August 2000 Republican National Convention speech to continue to become more involved. Using religious language, she said: "For one day, each of us will be held to account not for the money we made, but for the difference we made. Not for the worldly status we may have enjoyed, but for the stewardship we provided." Dole claimed that "millions of

Americans—of both parties and no party—are seeking a politics of purpose." She told her audience how she had seen "the extraordinary power of the American heart," during her tenure as president of the American Red Cross. Saying how she was often "uplifted . . . by those armies of compassion," she praised Americans "who are willing to go cross town or cross the globe to minister to those they've never met and will never see again." Kindness of this type, for Dole, came from "faith, neighborliness, and yes, occasionally, saintliness." She said: "you don't have to be a missionary to be filled with a sense of mission." These ideas became more prominent in the speeches she gave after the terrorist attacks of September 11, 2001. She said: "Since September 11, we have experienced a sense of universal fraternity—love of country, love of community, love of neighbor."

Dole, herself, raised the question about whether her faith-based form of service blurred the domains that rightfully belong to the church and those that rightfully belong to the state. She addressed this issue in her Duke University Commencement speech, when she talked about the faith of the founding fathers. She said they were very faithful to an established church, but what they could not accept was a compulsory faith. In her view, "They never insisted on government hostility toward faith itself."

Thus, Dole's religious and patriotic values meld seamlessly in a continuum. She learned from her family that faith, to be authentic, must be applied. Further back in her family, her ancestors had established an early church, the Cathey Meeting House, outside of Salisbury. And patriots from Rowan County, North Carolina, including a distant relative, had signed the Rowan Resolves, a document that is similar to the Declaration of Independence, only it was written one year earlier in 1775.[29] Dole's pride in her religious and patriotic ancestry further reinforced the association between the two. The belief that service came before self was deeply rooted in her.

DOLE'S PRACTICAL APPLICATION OF FAITH

Elizabeth Dole's career, when examined from the perspective of public service, shows an unmistakable dedication to the well-being of others. She has repeatedly noted in her speeches that she chose to work in public service because she wanted to make a difference in people's lives. From her first positions in Washington, D.C., organizing a conference on deaf education and learning the practice of a public defender, she demonstrated that helping people would be the center of her life. As a consumer advocate, Dole continued to fight for the underdog when she worked in the White House Office of Consumer Affairs and on the Federal Trade Com mission. She and her colleagues took on different kinds of challenges, including setting fat limits in hot dogs, dating supermarket items for freshness, and designing a government clearinghouse for consumer information. They worked on credit for women, on protecting the elderly from nursing home abuses, and on getting better quality products to consumers for lower prices. All of these projects were very much people-oriented.

As head of the Office of Public Liaison, Dole's position required her to deliver grassroots support for Reagan's policies. There is some evidence that she didn't always agree with those policies, but her position was not to ask questions, but to build support among various constituencies. She may have had to give up her support of the Equal Rights Amendment, and she may not have been sympathetic with some of Reagan's cost-cutting policies because of the impact of his budget trimming on the poor, but he was her boss and she was loyal and hardworking. During these years, she experienced her spiritual crises. Perhaps part of the crises occurred because she was not working directly enough in the service of people who needed her. When she accepted the Department of Transportation (DOT) position, she was better able to protect and save people's lives.

Holding a copy of her grandmother's Bible, Dole was sworn in as secretary of transportation in February 1983. Above all, she was committed to public safety in different areas of transportation. One of her first initiatives was requiring rear break lights, but she tackled harder policy issues, such as the legislation concerning automobile passive restraint systems. She was in favor of them, even though her predecessor, Drew Lewis, had gone to the Supreme Court to prevent their requirement in new cars. Observers saw this issue as a challenge for Dole and wondered whether she would follow her conscience. Consumer advocate Ralph Nader said that the way she handled the issue would either "confirm the impression that Elizabeth Dole is not willing to stand up for victims against power or it will make Elizabeth Dole the most courageous Cabinet secretary in the Reagan administration." Dole worked hard on a compromise that Reagan would approve. She said: "It was the toughest policy issue I've ever dealt with."[30] In consequence of her efforts, many lives have been saved. In the early 1990s, she said she was very proud of what she had achieved and proud as well to receive the 1989 National Safety Council's Distinguished Service to Safety Award.

While head of DOT, she worked on other safety issues. Another unpopular initiative she worked on was guaranteeing that all DOT employees were drug-free. Her mandatory drug testing initiative met with much resistance. "Hardly anyone supported me," she said, but "I felt very strongly that if an air traffic controller or a person inspecting the railroad is on drugs, then that is absolutely intolerable." She was convinced—with a heartfelt certainty—that it was the right thing to do. She said, "No matter how many people oppose me on this, when people are directing traffic in the air and literally hundreds of people could be killed if their judgment is off, no one can tell me it isn't right to test." After the program went into effect and became accepted, she said: "It's such a wonderful feeling when I'm on the side of the angels. . . . when you have that kind of feeling, it's a wonderful inspiration to drive forward."[31]

The efforts by Dole and Reagan to rid the roads of drunk drivers also show how she was willing to push forward unpopular ideas when she knew they were the right things to do. In a speech she gave years later as president of the American Red Cross, she said, "making a change in both the laws and the attitudes involving drunk driving was on top of my agenda when I became Secretary of Transportation."[32] The blood borders between the states that had a lower drinking age and those that had a higher drinking age were claiming too many lives. She was convinced that raising the drinking age to twenty-one in all states would eliminate the sacrifice of young people.

During the Christmas vacation of 1988, Dole pondered what she really wanted to do next in her life. She had stepped down from her Transportation post to campaign for her husband. In *Unlimited Partners*, she wrote that she had spent twenty-three years of her life in government service and maybe there was another way to make a difference in people's lives. She was surprised when she learned that Americans give only about 2 percent of their incomes to charity, and she wondered whether they could be persuaded to give more. She and her nephew, John, began to investigate whether they could convince Americans to contribute more. Just a 1 percent increase, she wrote, "would mean an additional $62 billion for those who need it."[33] She hoped to raise the money by "uniting churches, philanthropies and leaders from the worlds of government, advertising, business, sports and entertainment." Though the foundation she envisioned would not come to pass as she had originally foreseen it, she certainly did unite such different sources of philanthropy when she became head of the American Red Cross. But an invitation from George H. W. Bush, elected president in November 1988, to become secretary of labor promised too many ways to help others—especially women and minorities, at-risk youth, the elderly, in fact, all Americans—for her to turn down that opportunity.

Dole worked on skills, safety, and security when she was head of the Department of Labor (DOL), targeting especially the most vulnerable members of society, such as at-risk youth and the homeless. She instituted a number of programs to help these constituencies and others, such as women and minorities. She worked on skills training, raising the minimum wage, the "glass ceiling," child labor laws, and the prevention of injury to workers. Dole summarized her achievements in a speech she gave when stepping down from DOL. Her "Everybody Counts" speech is significant because it expresses her values and shows how they influenced her decisions and actions at that time in her life.

Dole traced the idea of "everyone counts" to the words Thomas Jefferson wrote in the Constitution: "that we're each endowed with certain inalienable rights, including 'life, liberty and the pursuit of happiness.'" She explained what these rights mean: "that the government would work to ensure that everyone has a chance at a good education, a decent job, and a secure retirement." In return, Dole continued, "all citizens would accept a responsibility to work hard, provide for their family, and obey the law." She referred to this set of mutual obligations as a "social contract," saying that it "has served as the glue that holds our society together." Traveling across the United States during her tenure as secretary of labor, she said in her speech that she met many individuals who were not benefiting from this contract; they "have been left behind." She closed her speech by saying that "the world has changed many times . . . in the past two centuries, as the torch has been passed from generation to generation. But our mission remains the same." Speaking for herself and for those she worked with at the Department of Labor, she said: "And if I could write my own legacy for our time here, it would simply be, 'They did their best to keep the contract intact. They did their best to ensure that everybody counts.' Thank you and God bless you."

During her speech, Dole used narratives and storytelling to describe the people she met, how they needed the programs she instituted, and how much they benefited from them. She quoted a young man from Brooklyn, Tim Douglas, whose life had been turned around by a job-training program. He subsequently gave testimony to senators during a hearing that he had been "evil" before the program gave his life meaning. Dole found the plight of young people like him to be especially compelling. For them, she felt, the "social contract" was "in tatters." She believed that through "policies and programs" the Labor Department, "the people's department," could make a difference in their lives.

In the same speech, Dole also praised the people of Poland, who were just beginning to live according to democratic tenants. While she was secretary of labor, Poland and other Eastern European countries were trying to set up market economies, private ownership, and limited government regulations.[34] She traveled to Poland and met with Lech Walesa, an electrician and leader of the Solidarity union, who would later become president of Poland. Dole was deeply impressed when he told her a metaphor for what it meant to labor under communism: "'100 workers standing around a single shovel.' Then he said, 'What Poland needs is 100 shovels.'"[35]

She presented two emotionally moving toasts[36] during her mission to Poland. One of them attested to the friendship between the people of the United States and Poland. She told them that their friends in the United States were eager to help the Polish people reach "the shores of freedom." In her second toast, she compared the sacrifices of the men who had signed the Declaration of Independence two hundred years ago with the present-day sacrifices made by the leaders of Poland. She recounted the losses of the founding fathers: "Of the fifty-six patriots who signed, nine were killed in action, five died as prisoners of war, twelve had their homes burned, several lost sons, one man's wife died in prison, and seventeen—including Thomas Jefferson—went broke." She quoted Thomas Paine, who said: "'Those who expect to reap the blessings of freedom must undergo the fatigue of supporting it.'" She drew a comparison with the leaders of Poland: "Over the past decade, many courageous Poles have sacrificed much, and have experienced fatigue in the hopes that one day, Poland would reap the blessings of freedom." Now is the time, she told them, to reap the benefits of your sacrifices.

When Dole returned to the United States, she wanted to raise money for the people of Poland. She and her husband had also witnessed the dire needs of earthquake victims when they traveled to Armenia in 1989, to deliver needed supplies.[37] Lawyers from the Department of Labor, however, felt she could not approach persons or corporations to ask for funds because of her position. According to biographer Carolyn Mulford, Dole initially was unaware of these restraints and began to raise money for infant formula. When she became aware of them, she asked her husband to stand in for her as cochair of a bipartisan effort.[38] It was this kind of activity that attracted the attention of the American Red Cross; their leadership began a campaign lasting several months to persuade Dole to become their president. Even though it meant leaving "the people's department," the prospect of bringing humanitarian aid to those in dire need on a daily basis was too vital a mission for Dole to turn down. She accepted the offer and took the reins of the leading humanitarian organization in the world.

Nowhere can Dole's practical application of faith be seen more clearly than in the eight years she serviced the American Red Cross as their president. The position demanded all of her communication, organizational, and public relations skills as well as her intelligence, wisdom, experience, and charm. From her first day as president, she began to build a working relationship with her staff and volunteers. In her "A Tradition of Trust" speech, she told the hundreds of people in her audience: "We are united in a common mission—a mission of making a difference for people." She wanted her fellow workers to understand what the Red Cross meant to her in personal terms. She said:

> For me, the most rewarding times in my public service career were not spent in smoke filled rooms exchanging political gossip. Rather, they were in classrooms, listening to at risk youth and teen mothers who were turning their lives around; in fields, meeting with migrant workers who needed a voice; deep in coal mines, meeting with miners concerned about their safety; in businesses, ensuring full compliance with child labor laws; and in far flung corners of the world where people needed help.

She told them: "The opportunity to devote myself to these causes on a full time basis is what drove me to the Red Cross." The mission of the organization was utterly consistent with her religious and patriotic values.

Dole told the group during this speech how the organization had touched her life through members of her family. "When my brother was stationed in the Pacific during World War II, his load was made lighter by the presence of Red Cross volunteers. . . . my mother was a Red Cross volunteer, telling me that 'she couldn't remember when she felt so important.'" Her husband as well was touched by the Red Cross: "when Bob Dole was wounded, the Red Cross was there with kind words and support, every step of the way." She said she was a member of the Senate wives' Red Cross unit and pledged to earn the volunteer's badge on her sleeve by not accepting a salary during her first year of service. Significantly, she also donated about half a million dollars from her public speaking fees to the organization.

During the eight years she worked for the Red Cross, Dole engaged in humanitarian relief efforts both at home and abroad. As early as February 1991, she began to raise money to help with humanitarian efforts in the Persian Gulf. In a letter she wrote to the American public and published in *Compass* magazine, she asked for help: "I would like to say to the American public that we appreciate all the support and help we have gotten so far. I think that a grateful nation certainly owes it to our troops, their families and certainly to the victims of war to do what we can to provide humanitarian assistance. The ecological damage is just sickening. . . . We have a lot to do here."[39]

After the war, Dole traveled to Kuwait to deliver supplies and to take stock of what else the soldiers, staff, and victims might need. She visited refugee camps and talked to displaced people. She surveyed burning oil fields by helicopter. One of the institutions she visited was a hospital for physically and mentally handicapped children. She described the conditions there as "nightmarish." One hundred seventy of the children had died, and another three hundred were being cared for by only twenty-two staff members. She pledged to send fifty doctors, nurses, and physical therapists to help. Even before she left Kuwait for home, she was on the phone, soliciting volunteers. In *Unlimited Partners*, she praised the "courageous doctors and nurses from across the nation [who] answered our call for help." She also praised the "generosity of the American people," who over time contributed $26 million to help the Red Cross meet its challenges in the Gulf. Flying home from Kuwait, Dole said she realized after only one month as president of the American Red Cross how right the position was for her: "I had found a job that filled me with a sense of mission like I had never known."[40]

In *Unlimited Partners*, Dole wrote about other trips she had made abroad to help international efforts during both natural and man-made disasters. Without doubt, these experiences provided some of the most heart-wrenching moments of her service in the Red Cross. She traveled to war-torn areas such as Somalia, Croatia, and Bosnia. She visited refugee camps set up for the Rwandans in Goma, Zaire. She described, for example, a little boy she fed during a trip to Somalia. At first the boy looked dead, but his brother sat him up, and Dole realized that he was alive, but severely malnourished and diseased. As she put her arm around his back to support him as she fed him a cup of goat's milk, she could feel "the little bones almost piercing through his flesh." Her overwhelming feeling was that the "horror of starvation" became real "when she touched it."[41] There seemed to be no end to the suffering, and she drew inspiration from the example of Mother Theresa, who, when asked, "how she could do the same heartbreaking work day after day in the streets of Calcutta," answered: "'God did not call me to be successful, he called me to be faithful.'"[42] What Dole witnessed during this trip and others would haunt her for the rest of her life, and she would describe what she had witnessed in speeches she gave after she had stepped down from the American Red Cross, for example, in her maiden Senate speech, where she issued a plea to congressional leadership to help eradicate world hunger.

During her years with the American Red Cross, there were a record number of destructive and expensive natural disasters. In *Unlimited Partners*, Dole described her experience in 1992, when Hurricane Andrew devastated parts of Florida.[43] She witnessed much destruction as she drove through the region and flew above it in a Blackhawk helicopter. To meet the dire needs she witnessed, she used an effective strategy to elicit the media to help her raise money. As she visited areas of devastation, the television cameras went with her. Broadcast from Florida, she appeared on national programs such as *Good Morning America* and *Nightline*, where she detailed the devastation, praised the work of the American Red Cross volunteers, and asked the American people for help. On *ABC News*, for example, Dole explained the extent of the disaster: "This is, of course, probably the largest natural disaster in the history of the United States." And she praised the efforts of the Red Cross volunteers: "We are a volunteer organization, we're totally dependent on charitable contributions, we're not funded by the government," she said. Volunteers are "providing services, food, clothing, medical supplies, and shelter." Then she asked for help: "Obviously, if we're going to be here in the future, we're going to have to raise the funds, because our disaster relief fund is depleted."[44] Viewers responded sympathetically; one donor who saw Dole on television called her and pledged one million dollars. Dole responded similarly to other natural disasters such as floods in the Midwest in 1993, earthquakes in Los Angeles, wildfires in California, tropical storms in Alberta, and floods in Houston in 1994.

When Dole stepped down from her position with the Red Cross, she told the audience during her resignation speech that the presidency of that organization was "more than a job" to her, "the Red Cross was a mission . . . with the goal . . . of making a difference in the lives of those in dire human need."[45] She said: "I love the Red Cross," adding that it was now as "solid as a rock." She described her experiences with the Red Cross in speeches she delivered after her departure. In her Republican National Convention speech in 2000, for example, she talked about all of the volunteers she had met and how kind and generous they were to strangers both in the United States and abroad. Giving to others in this way was noteworthy for Dole, because it exemplified how individuals put their religious and patriotic values into practice. She told her audience: "you don't have to be a missionary to have a sense of mission," all you need is to have a politics of purpose.

Dole was able to express her faith more explicitly in the speeches she gave during her successful run for a U.S. Senate seat from North Carolina. During a recent interview, she called North Carolina the "buckle on the Bible belt," and explained how she felt more comfortable expressing her ideas in religious terms because she shared beliefs with her Southern audience. When she kicked off her campaign, she pledged: "With God's help, I will run a positive campaign worthy of you—the people I serve."

Dole's maiden speech to the Senate in July 2003 used religious imagery and language as she presented her case to eradicate hunger. She eloquently demonstrated her commitment to the well-being of her constituents in North Carolina, throughout the United States, and around the globe. She began her speech by telling the audience that she wanted to share her thoughts "on a matter that weighs heavily on . . . [her] mind." That matter was hunger: "Hunger is the silent enemy lurking within too many American homes," she said. Dole claimed that the number of hungry Americans was increasing, especially in North Carolina. One of her goals was to persuade her colleagues to work with her on several initiatives to eradicate hunger: "In my lifetime," she told her audience, "I have seen Americans split the atom, abolish Jim Crow, eliminate the scourge of polio, win the Cold War, plant our flag on the surface of the moon, map the human genetic code and belatedly recognize the talents of women, minorities, the disabled and others once relegated to the shadows." She invited her colleagues to join her in "eradicating hunger."

In her speech, Dole presented a strategy derived from the Bible to help feed the hungry—that of gleaning. Dole told her audience about the discussion of gleaning in the book of Ruth in the Old Testament: "She gleaned in the fields so that her family could eat. You see, Mr. President, in Biblical times, farmers were encouraged to leave crops in their fields for the poor and for the travelers." Dole cited another passage from Leviticus, chapter 19, which made a similar point about leaving some of the grapes in the vineyard for the hungry. She said that "gleaning was long a custom in Biblical days . . . a command by God to help those in need." She provided a contemporary example of gleaning by describing an organization in North Carolina, the Society of Saint Andrew, that is having a great deal of success. They glean "excess crops that would otherwise be thrown out" and take them "from farms, packing houses, and warehouses" for distribution "to the needy." She recommended gleaning as a model to use throughout the country, and she proposed tax cuts to encourage small businesses to donate food and to transport the food for distribution to the hungry. She concluded her speech by assuring her audience that they could make a difference, if they worked together.

Since Dole presented her maiden speech to the Senate, her reputation as a humanitarian has continued to grow. When an earthquake struck Iran in December 2003, President George W. Bush invited Elizabeth to lead a mission to Bam in southeast Iran. The mission never materialized because Iranian leaders did not trust the overture as humanitarian in intent, viewing it instead as a way to insinuate renewed diplomatic relations. Nonetheless, her invitation from Bush showed how much respect he has for her as a humanitarian. Given her track record as president of the American Red Cross, Dole's motives of making a difference to those in dire need were authentic. She has served the public since the late 1960s in a variety of roles, and her motivation has remained the same: to be a blessing to others, to live her life with purpose. As she continues to serve in the U.S. Senate, it will be interesting to follow what humanitarian efforts she takes up next.

Chapter 4

Advocate for Women's Rights

[T]he progress of women in public life is like climbing trees . . . too many of the branches seem just out of reach. But the last few years have been especially good for women in American government. More and more, we're gaining the confidence to reach out, grab the branches, and pull ourselves up.[1]

In May 1997, Elizabeth Dole ended her Economic Summit for Women speech[2] by telling her audience that it is time for a new fairy tale about women. Many women have read stories when they were children about princesses who had to be rescued by princes in order to live a happy life. "That was the pattern in *Cinderella*, *Snow White*, and *Sleeping Beauty*," Dole said. She called for an updated story:

A fairy tale about a young girl—or even a mature woman—who isn't a princess. A woman who sees there are things that need to be changed to make life better for herself and others. A woman who is not a victim of life or circumstances, and who doesn't need a rescuer. A woman who believes in herself and knows she can succeed and can pass that success on to others. We need a tale about a woman who motivates, inspires, and builds.

She praised the members of her audience for living that new fairly tale, and although Dole did not include herself among them, it is obvious that she is living it, too.

Elizabeth Dole sketched her heroine only in general terms. Nowhere did she say the heroine had to be a silky traditionalist, who wears high heels and colorful form-fitting skirted suits, and who speaks by telling personal stories and anecdotes. Neither did she say the heroine should

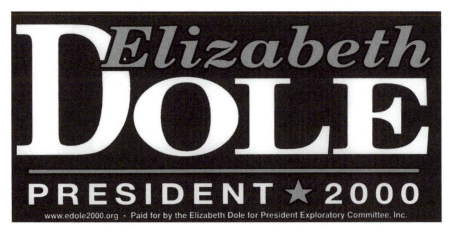

Elizabeth Dole for President 2000 bumper sticker. (Imaging by Frits Meijer Photography)

wear solid-heeled pumps, interchangeable black pantsuits, and speak by marshalling evidence in an argument. Both Elizabeth Dole and Hillary Clinton have been caricatured in these ways, respectively; they have been contrasted and compared by journalists and scholars. In a *Chicago Tribune* article, for example, Cheryl Lavin wrote: "Both are graduates of Ivy League Law schools, both are highly ambitious, successful, hard-driving women whose careers have been advanced by their husbands. Yet Elizabeth Dole does not evoke the same intense feelings as does Hillary Clinton, particularly among white men. Now she is positioning herself as the anti-Hillary. The un-Hillary. The Hillary-not."[3] Dole surely did position herself as a spouse and helpmate when Lavin's article appeared in 1996, but her resume and charismatic advocacy were compelling enough for her to be considered a candidate in her own right. Even so, as Lavin points out, the perception of her competency did not detract from her positive reception by many Americans.

Some feminist scholars who compare Dole and Clinton, however, have seemed dismayed by Dole's traditional manners and feminine style of speech. For example, when public address scholar Karlyn Kohrs Campbell compared Dole and Clinton as public speakers, she lamented the fact that audiences have sometimes rejected Clinton's messages because of her direct, no-nonsense verbal approach: "If we reject all those who lack the feminizing skills of an Elizabeth Hanford Dole, we shall deprive ourselves of a vast array of talent."[4] Comments such as this are not explicitly negative toward Dole's style, verbal and otherwise, but they do suggest a disappointment by those who seem to wish that Dole—as a successful public servant, role model, and instantiation of the new fairy tale—would enact a less traditional, utterly and stereotypically feminine style of self-presentation. The question of Elizabeth Dole's femininity and feminism is discussed later in this chapter, but first it is useful to contextualize the discussion in terms of Dole's nontraditional career and her record as an advocate for women's rights. This record shows what journalist Matt Andrews describes as a "soft but pervasive feminism" present throughout her career.[5] It shows her unique blend of qualities: her Southern belle graciousness, political activism, and nontraditional life choices.[6]

LISTENING TO HER OWN DRUMMER

Elizabeth Hanford was raised at a time when girls grew up, got married, had children, and dedicated their lives exclusively to their homes and families. Instead, she chose a life of government and humanitarian service. When asked about this in an interview, she replied: "I don't know why I listened to the beat of a different drummer. I just sort of followed my stars, so to speak."[7] Even so, she is quick to point out that her career more or less "unfolded," rather than following a strict plan: "It wasn't as if I had a carefully drawn blueprint for the future. Women in that era rarely had one; you might take a job, almost by accident, only to discover ten years out that it had turned into a career." She made a similar statement in 1976, when she said: "[I] just took the best opportunity I saw when I turned a corner. That's why I think it's important for a woman to get a good education."[8] If a woman doesn't have the skills when opportunity knocks on her door, the opportunity will go to another—a lesson taught by the biblical story of Queen Esther. Being prepared, for Dole, is a central tenet of her thinking.

Even in high school, she began to break the mold of expectations for women. Although she worked diligently on academics and was active in extracurricular activities, she was also president of the Senior Methodist Youth Fellowship Group, of the Rowan Resolves Society of the Children of the American Revolution, and of her class.[9] She ran for president of her high school, a position regarded at the time as appropriate only for a boy. In a speech she gave while campaigning, she said: "More and more the modern world is giving women a big part to play. Women must keep pace in the world."[10] Elizabeth didn't win that election, but her senior class voted her the young woman "most likely to succeed."[11]

Elizabeth Hanford attended Duke University in the 1950s. Her decision to study political science was not well received by her mother. In a speech she gave almost thirty years later at Duke University, she talked about her parents' reaction to her decision: "This revelation hit my parents like a bombshell. My mother's secret wish was that I study home economics and settle down next door to her." Her mother consulted with a neighbor who was a professor at the University of North Carolina. He told Mary Hanford to allow her daughter to major in political science. "We need women in government," he said, "and besides . . . they all get married anyway."[12]

Elizabeth's time at Duke University was spent on more than books, but it is clear where she put her priorities. She attended proms and was elected May Queen, but more important to her were her political science courses. Wanting to put what she was learning into practical use, she ran for campus offices. In her freshman year, she campaigned for class representative. In a speech she gave at the time, she said to her fellow students: "Then let us strain and strive, that we may say at set of sun, 'So much to do, but something done.'"

Although her bid for office was unsuccessful, she was not discouraged. In 1957, her junior year, she ran for president of the Women's Student Government Association. This time she was successful, and the position provided her with a great learning opportunity; she developed skills in parliamentary procedure, mediating, presiding, and especially public speaking. She also contributed to the well-being of the campus and students; for example, she helped establish a leadership training program for women.[13] In 1958, both the men's and women's campuses elected her "Leader of the Year." Some of the issues she worked on during her senior year were a campus honor code and the right of women students to wear Bermuda shorts on campus (but not to class).[14]

Elizabeth was unsure of what she should do once she graduated from Duke University. She looked for a job near her hometown of Salisbury, North Carolina. In 1958, her first interview was for a position as a journalist at the *Charlotte Observer*. She described how it went in several of her speeches and in *Unlimited Partners*: "I went in assuming that if you wore the right dress and nodded at appropriate moments your credentials would speak for you." The lesson she learned when she failed to get the position was: "You had to be a little assertive, to explain in your own words why you felt you were right for the job."[15] In *Unlimited Partners*, Dole wrote about how hard she had to lobby for some positions, such as those she held at Health, Education, and Welfare and at the Federal Trade Commission. Her first interview taught her a lesson that has proven to be valuable throughout her life.

Elizabeth Hanford had many boyfriends, but she put her romantic interests second to her career objectives. She was pinned in college, but instead of getting married when she graduated, as did her best friend, she went to Boston to work at the Harvard Law School Library. She told biographer Carolyn Mulford why she decided not to get married: "I just wasn't quite ready for that . . . there were things I wanted to do. I wasn't ready to settle down. I wanted to work; I wanted to go to graduate school."[16] But she didn't have a specific career plan at this time. "I was thinking that law might be a very good background for a career in government service. That was beginning to jell, but it wasn't yet a plan or a blueprint." She also said: "For young people, women and men, I do recommend that they map out what they want to do and plan it out . . . but I don't think many of my generation did that."[17]

Dole's position as secretary to the head of the law library was a traditional woman's job and quite a step down for a Phi Beta Kappa, especially one with her record of achievement. Nonetheless, she worked hard on her typing, often going back in the evenings to retype something she didn't do a good job on during the day. About those days, she said: "All of us start with something that is not our ideal, but you get your foot in the door and you prove yourself and go on from there into things that will be much more meaningful."[18] Indeed, she used her secretarial position as a stepping-stone, first, to get her master's degree in education and government and, second, to secure a coveted position at Harvard Law School.

Elizabeth Hanford's decision to go to Harvard Law School was unusual at that time. One of her girlhood friends, Wyndam Robertson, made this comment: "In those days, women did not go to Harvard Law School. She was something of a pioneer. I think she just wanted to do something with her life other than being a wife. There were no kinds of [role] models in those days."[19] Elizabeth's parents, too, may not have understood her decision. When her mother questioned her about being a wife, mother, hostess, and so on, the traditional roles for women at the time, Elizabeth said she wanted to be all of those things, but in time. She promised she would try the law school for only one year and if it didn't work out, she would leave. Allegedly, after they had that conversation, Elizabeth heard her mother throwing up in the bathroom.[20]

Elizabeth was twenty-six years old when she enrolled in Harvard Law School. For all students, Harvard was "like a boot camp," with the workload overwhelming and the competition fierce.[21] In her speeches, she often talks about the climate for women students. At the time, there were 550 members of the Class of 1965, only twenty-four of whom were women. The male students did not take female students seriously and neither did the professors. In *Unlimited Partners*, she wrote about a professor who had the women students recite poems on Tuesdays, and then he and the male students in class would "pelt them with questions."[22] In addition, she had to walk a fine line in terms of her self-presentation. Elizabeth did modeling on the side, which made it difficult for some of her fellow students to take her seriously. Commenting upon the situation at Harvard during those years, one of her law school roommates said: "In those days, you had to be very careful how you presented yourself. Step off that line and a female student would be considered too threatening or too unattractive."[23] In spite of everything, though, Dole did exceptionally well. She was elected president of the international law club and secretary of her class—a position she holds for life.

During those years, Elizabeth Hanford supplemented her education by studying English history and government at Oxford University in England, and traveling to Russia. She began dating a young man from North Carolina who was studying medicine at Harvard. That did not stop her from spending the summers of 1960 through 1962 working in New York and Washington, D.C. In the fall of 1962, she broke up with her boyfriend and began her study of law. She was interested in international law, traveling to the Orient after her graduation. Subsequently, she moved to Washington, D.C., to begin her life in public service. She met Senator Bob Dole when she went to his office to lobby him to put a "consumer" plank in the Republican Party platform. At the time, he was the party's national chairperson. Elizabeth was thirty-nine years old when they married on December 5, 1976.

When Elizabeth met Bob Dole in 1972, she was considered one of the most eligible women in Washington, D.C., and was dating a Mississippi congressman. Bob Dole said that wooing her was like running the Kentucky Derby.[24] Biographer Mulford wrote that Elizabeth brought many men home to meet her family, but she was not interested in getting married. One piece of advice she offers young women today based on her experience is not to let continual questioning by their families and friends pressure them into marriage. For Dole, whether single or married, "The key to happiness for a woman is to be able to stand on her own two feet and become a person in her own right."[25]

Elizabeth and Bob Dole dated for three years before marriage, and during that time, Elizabeth took him home to meet her parents. In her 1996 Republican National Convention speech,[26] she tells about the conversation Bob and her mother had about the disfigurement he had suffered during his military service in World War II; Mrs. Hanford called the disfigurement "a badge of honor." After their marriage, Elizabeth retained her maiden name, going by "Elizabeth Hanford Dole." She told a hometown reporter of the advantages of keeping one's own name, especially for a professional woman. She signed her papers with both last names, but according to biographer Mulford, the name Hanford "began to drop out when Dole was Secretary . . . of Labor."[27]

It is obvious that Dole's choices in life from her early years through her adulthood were not the typical ones made by a female, especially a Southern female educated in the 1950s and early 1960s.

ADVANCING THE CAUSE OF WOMEN

> Throughout my twenty-five years of government service, one of my goals has been to assist women both in and out of the workforce.[28]

Elizabeth Hanford's early positions in public service were in tune with her times. John F. Kennedy's New Frontier and Lyndon B. Johnson's Great Society both stressed social causes such as protection for consumers, antipoverty programs, civil rights, and equal rights for women. Women were beginning to raise public awareness about the conditions they faced in education, the workplace, the home, and more. In *Unlimited Partners*, Elizabeth gave credit to John Macy, the chief headhunter for the U.S. Civil Service Commission for helping her land the position at the White House Office of Consumer Affairs. He was determined to help women and minorities increase their numbers in the federal workforce.[29] Dole was also fortunate to work under the direction of Betty Furness in that position and Virginia Knauer in her subsequent position with the President's Committee on Consumer Interests. In Furness and Knauer, Dole found role models and mentors who supported her efforts and helped her develop her skills.

In 1968, Elizabeth became deputy assistant in Lyndon Johnson's White House Office of Consumer Affairs. A thirty-two-year-old Democrat, she worked under the direction of Betty Furness, a former television actress who became popular during the 1950s as a spokeswoman for Westinghouse.[30] Twenty years Dole's senior, Furness had earned the respect of Ralph Nader and the *Consumer Reports* magazine by her extensive travel across the country to meet with consumers and her frequent testimony to congressional committees. Furness had an open door to the Oval Office, and she in turn lobbied actively for Johnson's policies. In *Unlimited Partners*, Elizabeth described the work she did in the office as "shuttling between the EOB [Old Executive Building, where her office was] and Capitol Hill."[31]

When Richard M. Nixon became president in 1969, he renamed the office, "The President's Committee on Consumer Interests." Virginia Knauer, a Republican counselor from Philadelphia, replaced Betty Furness, a Democrat. Being new to Washington, D.C., Knauer depended upon the staff already in place, especially Elizabeth, whose position she upgraded and whose office she moved next to her own. They established an effective working relationship. Knauer described Elizabeth Hanford as "a tremendously dedicated worker," "very beautiful, always a lady,"[32] while Elizabeth described Virginia in *Unlimited Partners* as "gifted," a "great politician," "thoroughly professional," and as "someone who refused to check her conscience at the door."[33]

Knauer became for Elizabeth "both mentor and surrogate mother." The two worked closely to protect the consumers' interests. They traveled across the United States to sell Nixon administration policies. One of the first speeches Elizabeth gave was during one of these trips. She spoke before an audience of women at a seminar in Prairie Village, Kansas, where she talked about women and financial credit.[34] This was the first of many speeches she would deliver while working in that agency. As time went by, Knauer often asked Elizabeth to stand in for her. Through these experiences, Elizabeth "began to build a reputation as a good speaker."[35] Her mother told biographer Mulford that Knauer would be scheduled for a speech, and then she would get called away to another task. She would hand her speech text to Elizabeth and tell her to go and give it. Dole became quite a good speaker when she worked there. Her mother cited her natural talent, but admitted that Elizabeth "does a lot of scribbling and correcting and changing."[36]

In 1973, encouraged by Knauer, Elizabeth was appointed to one of the five seats on the Federal Trade Commission (FTC) for a seven-year term. As a commissioner, Dole was especially interested in issues affecting women such as equal access to credit cards and loans.[37] She helped enforce statutes such as the Truth in Lending Act and the Fair Credit Act.[38] In *Unlimited Partners,* she wrote about enforcing the Equal Credit Opportunity Act: "Women were especially vulnerable," she said, "divorce or separation could be a kind of fiscal death. Without a credit record of their own, women were often denied credit of any kind, while the income of working women was commonly discounted by mortgage lenders and insurance companies."[39] To resolve the problem, she worked with women from the Senate and from television and radio to create a series of commercials that were designed to help the consumer. During an interview with the authors, she spoke about one spot in particular that was aimed at women who would lose the opportunity to get credit, when they lost their husbands: "I remember one ad when the husband and wife were walking along and the husband disappears." The ad went on to explain to the female viewers: "You do have recourse."[40] Dole was committed to using federal power to stop what she regarded as scams against financially inexperienced women. She was registered as an Independent at the time; her position on women and credit and many other issues was activist and liberal.[41]

After her marriage to Bob Dole and her participation in his 1976 campaign for the presidency, Elizabeth became the first woman to be appointed to Ronald Reagan's new administration. She served as head of the White House Office of Public Liaison, a position that required her to solicit the support of special interest groups across the United States, including women's groups. Reagan administration policies, however, were difficult to sell to women leaders. His proposed budget cuts were thought to favor wealthy white men at the expense of the poor. This was when ketchup was approved as a vegetable in children's school lunches. In *Unlimited Partners*, Dole wrote, "Administration budget cuts were widely portrayed as the thin end of a wedge dividing the poor, especially poor women—from the rest of society."[42] Reagan was also against the Equal Rights Amendment (ERA), but he had pledged his support of women during his 1980 campaign. To make good on that promise, his administration established a "Legal Equity Task Force," which was a "Fifty States Project" designed to "uncover discriminatory language in federal and state statutes."[43] To further promote women, Elizabeth was named head of the White House Coordinating Council on Women, whose charge was to increase "opportunities for women both within the Administration and in the country at large, [and to do] the latter through presidential initiatives, directives and specific legislative proposals."[44]

As part of her position, Dole kept in close contact with the leaders of women's groups across the country. Some of her friends and allies were angry about Reagan's anti-ERA stance.[45] Previously, Dole had supported the ERA, but when she went to work for Reagan, she was not able to express her support for the legislation. Instead, she looked for other ways to further the cause of women, for instance, by quietly lobbying to have more women hired in the administration. Dole also promoted legislation to help women collect delinquent child support payments and to help widows collect equitable social security benefits.[46] She described these activities as "perfectly consistent" with the ERA,[47] and as another approach to achieving the same ends. At least some women leaders seemed to appreciate the position she was in; for example, Pat Reuss, director of the Women's Action League, claimed that no one could be expected to do more, given the atmosphere in the Reagan White House. Articles in *Newsweek* and *U.S. News & World Report* expressed consistent positions, saying Dole really had little power or influence.[48] She retained her position at Public Liaison until 1983, when she was offered and accepted the appointment of secretary of transportation.

Elizabeth Dole accepted this cabinet post for many reasons, one of which was the opportunities it gave her to promote the cause of women. She regarded the appointment as an attempt by Reagan to win support from women.[49] Having a woman named to the president's cabinet was already an achievement, especially since no other woman had ever served as secretary of transportation. Kathy Wilson, president of the National Women's Political Caucus, expressed enthusiasm over the appointment, hoping it would be the first of many: "We see the transportation post as a start by the President in shrinking the gender gap. . . . She [Elizabeth Dole] is our ally in the White House."[50]

As secretary of transportation, Dole knew that she could help women by initiating supportive policy and legislation. The Transportation Department (DOT) had always been a largely male stronghold. One of her goals was to increase the number of women and minorities in this workforce of 100,000 people that included truckers, railroad engineers, highway construction crews, and ship captains. According to Dole, when the department was first established in 1967, it employed 18.5 percent women. When she took over its leadership in 1983, it was 19 percent. Not much had changed. She resolved to "find ways to boost midlevel employees into senior management positions and to give women in secretarial and clerical slots a chance to broaden their professional horizons."[51] The result was her Ten Point Plan that attracted the attention of other cabinet members and the Canadian government. By 1986, she boosted the number of women in the DOT workforce from 19 percent to 23 percent,[52] and doubled the women in management positions. She also opened a day-care center and an exercise room for women.[53] In *Unlimited Partners*, she wrote: "I knew we were making progress when a pilot told me that in his approach to a major U.S. airport, he was assisted by three distinct voices over the air traffic control system—and all three were women's voices."[54]

Dole acknowledged the work she had done for the cause of women since going to work for Reagan; nonetheless, she had to admit that she had not been an active proponent of the ERA during these years. The reasons she gave for choosing not to fight for the ERA publicly were altogether pragmatic:

> My view is, that issue is . . . not moving at this time and if we . . . believe in equal rights for women, what we must do is roll up our sleeves and make sure that we've eliminated vestiges of discrimination in our laws and regulations. In other words, let's go to work and do something about it, and that is what I've been trying to do through the years of the Reagan administration. And I'll continue to do that.[55]

Dole left her cabinet post in the fall of 1987, to help her husband campaign for the presidency.

In 1988, after George Bush had been elected president, he invited Elizabeth Dole to head the Department of Labor (DOL). One of the reasons she

accepted was because she could continue to work on increasing the number of women and minorities in the workforce. The position would allow
her to work on the problem on a much larger scale, and she would also
have the opportunity to work with the Women's Bureau, a branch of the
DOL.

During the confirmation hearings, Dole spoke enthusiastically about
her desire to serve the working public. Seated at a table in the center of
the room and dressed in a bright green suit, she signaled her eagerness
nonverbally, as well as with her words. As she pledged to target family
and work-related issues that primarily affect workingwomen such as child
care and minimum wage, she reinforced her ideas by using gestures.
During her speech, she pointed upward to indicate rising percentage
points and cupped her hands to indicate a close in a number's gap. To
forecast her intention to work with the Women's Bureau, Dole adopted a
solemn tone as she eulogized Libby Koontz, a fellow North Carolinian
who had recently died and had been head of the Women's Bureau from
1969 to 1973.[56]

Dole reaffirmed her commitment to work for the benefit of women
during a speech celebrating the seventieth anniversary of the Women's
Bureau, when Eve Awards were given to businesses "who open 'their
doors wide' to minorities, women, individuals with disabilities, and veterans." She established common ground with her audience when she told
them how important the goals of the Women's Bureau were to her: "One
of the true joys of accepting this job was the prospect of overseeing the
work of the Women's Bureau," she said. "Throughout my twenty five
years of government service, one of my main goals has been to assist
women both in and out of the work force."[57]

As Dole had done previously at the Department of Transportation, she
moved quickly to transform the hiring and promotion practices at the
Department of Labor. She appointed women and minorities to serve in
more than half of the senior staff positions. She requested that a team from
the Federal Quality Institute evaluate DOT to make recommendations for
improving the climate. She asked them to give advice on "trying to change
the workplace from being the sort of rigid, authoritarian, hand-down-the-
orders to [one of] employee participation."[58] She took her staff on a retreat where they brainstormed for goals and set timelines for achieving
them.

One of Dole's most important initiatives with respect to women was
the work she did on the glass ceiling. The term "glass ceiling" was first
used in 1986 by two reporters, Carol Hymowitz and Timothy Schellhardt,
in a series of *Wall Street Journal* articles on the "Corporate Woman."[59] They
used the term to point out the invisible barriers that keep women from

being hired for executive positions. As we have seen, Elizabeth Dole was committed to seeing more women enter the workforce. That would happen without legislative intervention, she believed, because the demand for qualified workers was growing faster than the supply. In her speech to the Women's Bureau, she said: "America's workforce is growing at a rate of only 1% annually—the slowest rate in forty years. And we expect this slow growth rate to continue throughout the decade—a decade where fully two-thirds of new entrants into the work force will be women."[60] From these facts, she inferred that talented women and minorities increasingly would be hired to fill the empty positions. She said: "The bottom line is simple. If employers want to compete in today's complex global market, then they can't afford to discriminate. They can't afford to ignore the needs of working women. Employers who do will simply lose out to those who don't."[61] However, Dole did not believe that women and minorities had an equal opportunity to compete for the top positions in American corporations. She said: "Any overview or examination of the make-up of the American workforce finds women—and minorities—reaching plateaus from which they feel they cannot climb."[62] They would be hired to fill positions, but not at management level or higher.

Dole launched a "glass ceiling initiative," one phase of which was to send investigators into corporations to look at their hiring and training practices. PepsiCo was one of nine companies they studied.[63] She and her staff wanted to know who was in top management and how they got there. Investigators examined personnel files with the goal of determining how employees advanced in a corporation, whether compensation schedules were fair to women and minorities, and whether they had equal access to training programs and opportunities to learn from rotational assignments. Dole said: You look at "the kinds of things companies do to develop people for the top positions and see whether those qualified women and minorities are involved in those activities. If they are not, you've got a problem."[64] The results of the studies, she said, "were disturbing": "women and minorities—who account for half of the workforce—comprised less than 10% of top managerial positions."[65]

Dole discussed the findings from these studies and similar ones with an international audience. On November 15, 1989, she spoke to the 300 Club, a women's group in England. The occasion was the anniversary of Lady Astor's membership in the club and the presentation of awards to those who have made a difference for women in England. Lady Astor was Winston Churchill's wife and an American woman from the South. Surely, Dole's similarity of background with Lady Astor as well as her advocacy of women must have been reasons why she was selected as a speaker. Dole addressed this audience expectation in the beginning of her speech.

Recalling the summer she had spent at Oxford University, she said: "What a joy it is to return to England again." She mentioned how flattered she was to be invited to speak to a group of women who were themselves dedicated to "leaping over walls and knocking down barriers." Building identification with the audience, Dole mentioned her English heritage, saying: "had the Hanford family never left England for North Carolina, I'm confident that I would have joined the 300 Group on my own." Using storytelling, dialogue, and quotations from individuals who were esteemed by her audience, this speech is vintage Elizabeth Dole. She spoke to the group about the mission shared by the members of the 300 Club and women of the United States, which was the "equal representation for women" in all domains. And she used the occasion to summarize what she had accomplished in her role as secretary of labor, as well as presenting her goals for the future.

During the speech, Dole cited statistics to show that the salaries of women and minorities in the United States were not equal to those earned by white men doing comparable work: "In 1990," she said, "women earned only $.70 for every dollar earned by a man." She continued: "There can be little doubt that a woman, no matter how well schooled, what her age, or how thick her portfolio of credentials, enters many business organizations with limited or no hope of reaching the top." Those positions, she said, "are held primarily by men." Dole provided examples drawn from a study of the five hundred largest companies in America. "Just two out of 500," she said, "have a woman chief executive officer."[66] She cited the results of a study undertaken by *Fortune* magazine, in which the highest-paid officers of the eight hundred largest U.S. companies were ranked according to gender. Of the four thousand people studied, she said, "only nineteen were women—that's less than one-half of one percent."[67] Another study she cited was of the one thousand largest companies in the United States, which found that although women and minorities make up about half of the workforce, they account for only 5 percent of the management positions.[68]

Dole saw the function of the Department of Labor to be a catalyst for change in the sexist and racist attitudes and policies of employers. She had talked about sexist attitudes years earlier at a workshop given in 1977 for women in business, where she told her audience:

> Attitudes are still very much a part of the barrier to full equality of opportunity. Part of the change—perhaps the largest part—must come on the other side, among those—both men and women—who cling to the notions that men should dominate the society. This is an effort that requires the continuing devotion of us all, and let us recognize that many of our strongest allies in this effort are often our male counterparts.[69]

She was not in favor of using quotas to achieve equality; rather, she chose to use existing legislation to force compliance, including the Department of Labor's Office of Federal Contract Compliance (OFCC). This office was responsible for enforcing "anti-discrimination laws among contractors," including the Fortune 500 companies. "Under the leadership of the Office of Contract Compliance," Dole said, "we aim to give a wake-up call to businesses, to alert them to the fact that it is in their vested interest to insure that the 'glass ceiling' meets the same fate as the Berlin Wall."[70]

Dole enlisted the aid of the OFCC, together with other agencies, such as the Women's Bureau and the Bureau of Apprenticeship and Training, to help with another initiative to recruit and retain women apprentices in skilled trades that had been traditionally reserved for men. Jobs such as electrician, machinist, carpenter, auto mechanic, painter, and so on, offered better pay than traditional women's jobs, and Dole wanted women to enter apprenticeship programs to prepare themselves for these positions: "These skilled trade jobs have the potential for greatly improving the economic status of women—higher wages, better fringe benefits, a wider variety of work schedules, greater job security and more opportunities for advancement." She knew that "for some women, it means the difference between being on welfare and being economically sufficient."[71]

Minimum wage was another hot issue during her tenure as head of the Department of Labor. President Bush took a strong stand on what kind of legislation he would and would not sign, and Dole was obliged to support the administration's positions. She testified to a congressional committee that if the minimum wage were raised to $4.59, there would be a loss of 650,000 jobs in the country. Bush wanted the minimum wage set at $4.25, and to allow employers to pay new employees a training wage of $3.35 for six months.[72] Women's groups such as the National Women's Political Caucus complained, however, because "women were twice as likely as men to work for minimum wage, and that a woman working forty hours a week at minimum wage could not support a family of three above the poverty level."[73] One way to help such women out of poverty, she felt, was to provide them with skills training so they could compete for higher-paying jobs. When she was asked about how her views fit with Bush administration positions, she told biographer Carolyn Mulford: "The president has such a broad array of interests . . . that you may fight for something internally that you think is very important. But he looks at the overall picture . . . I think you have to be willing to say, 'Okay, I am part of a bigger team here.' You may not get approval for everything you want to do at the moment."[74]

In October 1990, Dole announced her plans to leave the Department of Labor to become president of the American Red Cross. Once in that position, she continued to hire women and minorities for management positions and as interns in offices. She was succeeded at the Department of Labor by Lynn Martin, who named "worker training and pensions" as her priorities. She declined to comment on Dole's glass ceiling initiative during an interview, but the study of hiring and promotion practices in U.S. corporations continued. Bob Dole introduced the Glass Ceiling Act of 1991 into Congress, which established a twenty-one-member commission charged with finding ways to end discrimination against women and minorities for top management positions. In December 1992, the Glass Ceiling Commission began to take testimony; the final report was issued in November 1995. In December 2001, we asked Bob Dole during an interview whether he knew what had happened since 1995. He said: "Yes, nothing. They issued a report and then nothing happened. That is typical government. But at least we pointed out the facts and statistics, which you can quote. We weren't trying to force people." Indeed, since her departure from the Department of Labor, Elizabeth has continued to speak about the glass ceiling and related issues, proving she meant what she said when she called women's issues "a special mission field" of hers.

Elizabeth Dole's post-Department of Labor speeches reveal that she stayed in touch with the issues facing women, especially their status in the workforce. In her 1997 Economic Summit speech, she presented evidence to show how well women were doing. She said that "women-owned businesses" were "the fastest growing segment of the small business economy in the U.S. . . . [They] now employ more workers than all of the Fortune 500 companies combined." Commenting on the progress made in the area of the Glass Ceiling Initiative, she said, "The latest studies show that women in top management positions have increased over the past decade, [but] . . . there is still much work to do." She made a similar point in her 1998 "America We Can Be" speech, when she commented, "while women most certainly have not reached the millennium—particularly in failing to equal the earnings of our male counterparts and in the disturbingly low increase in the number of women in top management positions—there are other signs that women are playing key roles in the revolutionary change in America's work force." One change she talked about had personal meaning for her—how times had changed at Harvard Law School.

DOLE'S PERSONAL EXPERIENCE

Part of Elizabeth Dole's commitment to helping other women must have been motivated by her experiences as a young law student and public servant. She began her career just as the second wave of U.S. feminism was beginning to gain momentum in the 1960s.[75] Making her way into the professional world largely populated by men must not have been easy. In *Unlimited Partners*, she described all of the women entering the workforce in the 1970s as "nothing less than a quiet revolution," one which was reshaping "the American workforce" and reordering "the priorities of millions of women."[76] As the ranks of workingwomen swelled, Dole wrote, so did their willingness to raise questions about opportunities and salaries. She supported the Equal Rights Amendment reintroduced in 1972. As a consumer advocate, federal trade commissioner, secretary of transportation, and secretary of labor, she worked tirelessly from within the government to improve the conditions for women. Her own experiences provided her with evidence of discrimination, and these incidents surely must have verified the statistics she and her staffs at various positions had discovered, giving them special meaning. In *Unlimited Partners* and in her speeches, Dole often used personal examples of discrimination to make her points. She also praised the mentors who helped her along the way, and suggested many ways in which she, in turn, has set about helping other women.

In a speech Dole presented at a workshop for women in business in 1977, she said: "There was a time when it was said in Washington—as in many other parts of the country—that a woman had to work twice as hard as a man in order to get half as far. Unfortunately, that's still sometimes the case. But those days are changing."[77] She made a similar point in a speech she gave on June 16, 1986, when she said: "Once, not so long ago, it was necessary for any woman aspiring to responsible positions to demonstrate levels of competence well above those expected from the typical male applicant." In the same speech, she quoted social critic Marya Mannes's comments about the "'tyranny of perfection'": "'Nobody objects to a woman being a good writer or sculptor or geneticist if, at the same time she manages to be a good wife, a good mother, good-looking, good-tempered, well-dressed, well-groomed and unaggressive.'"[78] The point she stressed was that too much was expected of the American woman.

When Dole worked for the Nixon administration, she was an attractive young woman in her thirties. She described some of the difficulties she encountered with regard to her career in *Unlimited Partners*: "As a fairly high-ranking woman in the Nixon Administration," she wrote, "I still encountered lingering resentment among those who saw women only as envelope stuffers. Oh, sure, we could type position papers, but having those papers ever reflect our own positions as candidates and officeholders was the sort of utopian vision best left to a party platform."[79]

Dole often cited examples in her speeches of prejudice that occurred when she worked in the administrations of several presidents. When she worked for the Office of Consumer Affairs in the Nixon White House, she experienced the awkward situation of having to meet with "a senior part-ner of a law firm" at the Metropolitan Club on I street in Washington, D.C. The doorman, however, would not let her in because, he said, "Women are not permitted in the club." The law partner apologized for schedul-ing the meeting there, but when Dole gave him a choice—to meet with her somewhere else (she was prepared for the meeting), or to meet with a male member of the staff who was not prepared, he choose to meet with the male. Rather than advertising this outrage in a press release, she opted to remain silent because the commotion might have prevented her and her boss, Virginia Knauer, from getting their work done.[80] Later, in her 1998 "America We Can Be" speech, she would joke about this incident, using entertaining dialogue, and making the point that times have changed. In that same speech, she reported other significant advances: "Today over 40% of students entering Harvard Law School are female. The Metropolitan Club—and many others across the country—have long since opened their doors to women."

The discrimination was not just a factor of her being a young woman; both she and Virginia Knauer experienced sexist remarks as they at-tempted to do their work. In *Unlimited Partners*, Dole wrote about one particular day when she and another woman counselor had accompanied Knauer to a congressional hearing. One of the committee members asked Knauer whether she had anything against men.[81] Another time, Knauer was called away from a hearing where she was scheduled to testify, and she asked Dole to take over for her. Dan Flood, a representative from Penn-sylvania, forgot to turn his microphone off before saying to one of his colleagues, "Are we going to let this kid take over the hearing?"[82] This was quite a comment to make about a Harvard-trained lawyer.

Aside from the countless small acts of sexism, Dole also experienced pressure to conform to various administrations' positions on issues, even when she thought and felt differently. She was quite interested in women's issues and, for many years, had been a supporter of the Equal Rights Amendment. When she joined the Reagan administration as head of Public Liaison, however, she became the lone woman in the inner circle. As a kind of compromise with circumstances, she relinquished her pub-lic support of the ERA in favor of working behind the scenes to get more women appointed. Coverage of her in a *Time* magazine article during January 1983 mentioned how she had been "muzzled" when she went to work for the Reagan administration. She was quoted as saying to guests at a dinner given in her honor, "This ain't so bad. . . . First chance I have had to open my mouth in thirteen months." Maureen Dowd also reported that Dole once quipped: "The President doesn't want any yes men and

women around him. . . . When he says no, we all say no."[83] Regardless of
these humorous remarks, behind the scenes she did influence President
Reagan. In a speech given in April 1983 at an event in her honor, she told
the assembled group of one hundred executive women that she had been
one of the people who had pushed Reagan to include statements about
women's economic and legal equality in his inaugural address.[84] Other
women in her position might have handled acts of discrimination and
pressure to conform differently. But Dole, ever the pragmatist, knew she
could accomplish more for women by working with those in power from
behind the scenes rather than letting herself be deflected by agitating
loudly for what could not be changed overnight.

In her speeches, Dole mentioned many of her mentors and other persons who had helped her as she followed her own drumbeat into government service. Early in her life, her grandmother, Mom Cathey, and her
mother, Mary Hanford, both modeled the kind of religious and humanitarian values she would learn as a child and practice as an adult. Another
role model she mentioned in *Unlimited Partners* and in her commencement
speech at Duke University in 2000 was Florence Brinkley, who had been
a professor of English literature and dean of the Women's College when
Dole attended Duke university. Elizabeth worked with Dean Brinkley
when she was elected president of the student government, and gave
Brinkley credit for encouraging her to study for a summer at Oxford University. During her Duke University speech, Dole said: "She nurtured my
interest in politics, helped me establish a campus leadership program for
women, and lent tacit support to a whole series of undergraduate reforms."[85] She also mentioned Margaret Chase Smith, whom she credited
with advising her to get a law degree, and Esther Peterson, whom she
called, "one of my most cherished friends": "I have long relied on Esther's
counsel and wisdom, and am fortunate . . . to be one of many who regard
her as a mentor and role model."[86] Of course, she learned a great deal from
Virginia Knauer, under whose direction she worked during the Nixon
administration.

Dole wanted to give to other women the same support, kindness, and
mentoring that she had received from these professional women as she
developed her career. While still working for the Nixon administration,
she took the lead in forming an organization for women called the Executive Women in Government. In her Economic Summit for Women speech,
given in May 1997, Dole explained the goals of this group: "Its purpose
was twofold: to help younger women, who wanted to follow our footsteps
into public service, with information and advice, and to provide women
in policy positions with an opportunity to relate to one another across
government."[87] Such networking, she said, "is key."[88] During a recent in-

terview, Dole said that there were "few women in policy" when they
started the organization, and they wanted to help each other as well as
to show "younger women coming along . . . some shortcuts . . . [and to]
help them avoid the pitfalls."[89] According to Dole, the group is still "going strong. They send out publications and they're doing all sorts of things,
so we're really proud of them." For the work she was doing at that time,
Elizabeth Hanford was named "Outstanding Young Woman of the Year"
in 1970.

DOLE'S FEMINISM: IS SHE OR ISN'T SHE?[90]

Given Elizabeth Dole's personal and career choices, her record of working for the benefit of women and minorities, and her commitment to improving opportunities for women through networking and the initiation
and enforcement of legislation, the question of whether we can view her
as a feminist seems to have an easy answer. But when asked recently
during an interview whether she considers herself to be a feminist, Dole
said: "To me that would mean so many different things to different people.
I certainly have not been a part of a movement nor do I have a pre-
packaged set of views that are handed down at a political correctness club.
But, if we're talking about more freedom for women, more opportunities
for women, my whole career has been part of that. It has been a part of
every single job I've had—both policy and opportunities." She mentioned
the Ten Point Program she had initiated at the Department of Transportation and the Glass Ceiling Initiative she had initiated at the Department
of Labor.[91] When Bob Dole was asked the same question during a recent
interview, he gave a similar answer about his wife's and his feminism: "I
never knew what a feminist meant," he said. "I don't think you should
pigeonhole people or characterize them," and he talked about the wisdom
of examining a person's record to see where he or she stands.[92] When it
comes to feminism, both Doles preferred to avoid labels because they can
lead to misunderstanding; they stress their records instead.

During her career, Elizabeth Dole's eloquent words have articulated the
respect she has for women. In a series of speeches, she has praised the
feminine traits that many women have learned growing up. She introduced this line of reasoning in her Economic Summit for Women speech
by saying that "a virtual tidal wave of qualified women has entered the
marketplace in the recent past . . . [and they are] . . . seeking answers to
some important questions."[93] Historically, according to Dole, women have
asked: "Why can't a woman be more like a man?" As examples, she told
her audience that Abigail Adams asked her husband why women could

not have property rights and Susan B. Anthony asked why women could not have voting rights. Essentially, both women were asking why women could not have the same rights as men. She asked that question, too, she said, when she was a new law student at Harvard, being made sometimes to feel dreadfully out of place. But, a more "relevant question . . . for the 90s," she continued, was "Why can't a woman be more like a woman?" According to Dole, once women have achieved basic rights and privileges, "they could be more like themselves in behavior." She made this point in different ways in a series of speeches she gave in the 1990s.

In 1993, Dole received the Radcliffe College Alumnae Medal for outstanding contributions to the community of women. During her acceptance speech, she praised women, as she told her Radcliffe audience: "Over the ages, we women have perfected to a high art form this trait of second-guessing ourselves. . . . Perhaps it stems from our early and constant exposure to society's message that female traits and talents are inferior, but we have to get over it." Being a woman, according to Dole, was not something to get over, but which offered a great opportunity. From experiences of grassroots organizing, women have learned to solve problems by consensus and not by fiat. "In the female style of management," Dole said, "there's more of an emphasis on negotiation and mediation. . . . I don't think women give themselves enough credit for the skills they've developed."[94]

In November 1997, she spoke to ninety women at a Women's Leadership Giving Initiative sponsored by the St. Louis United Way. She raised the same question with her audience: "Why can't a woman be more like a woman?" Here, she praised women for the many important skills they bring "to the workplace, the boardroom and to volunteer organizations," such as "listening, communicating, getting at the root of problems and a higher tolerance for ambiguity because of . . . [their] experience as homemakers and mothers."[95] She also highlighted women's special traits in a speech she gave to the Alabama Economic Summit in 1998, where she advised women who want to get ahead in business not to model men, but to listen to themselves. She said that women are good communicators, they excel at listening, and they are good at getting to the root of problems. She advised women not to rest on their laurels because there was still much to do to break down the barriers of gender.[96]

During her Economic Summit for Women speech in May 1997, she discussed in more depth what she meant by the question: "Why can't a woman be more like a woman?" She began by quoting a statement made by Rebecca McDonald, a former president of a marketing subsidiary: "She said, 'You hear a lot of talk about changing the way we teach little girls because they're taught to listen and accommodate while little boys are taught to win at all costs. I wonder if, really, we shouldn't rethink the way we're teaching boys. The rigidity that comes from expecting to win at all costs doesn't necessarily play to the new skill sets for corporate America.'" The management skills in question, Dole derived from McDonald, included the ability to mediate, negotiate, and deal with less-than-perfect information. Dole continued to quote from McDonald:

> Women have a higher tolerance for ambiguity because we're always responsible for tending to the emotional needs of others—which are very fluid. We learn to read between the lines and come up with creative solutions for accommodating people. What I'm suggesting isn't touchy-feely at all. . . . Results, results, results are still the bottom line. I'm just saying that women are especially suited to today's demands—listening, communicating, getting to the root of the problem. It's what we are trained for.

In paraphrase, Dole made the point: progress for women in the workplace of the 1990s will continue, so long as women keep developing feminine skills, because they are necessary and valuable in today's corporate society.

Dole continued, in this speech, to relate the lessons she had learned from her own experience and from the words and actions of other successful women. Her advice was to: (1) plan for the unexpected, (2) trust your instincts, (3) maintain your integrity, (4) make a commitment to those who follow, and (5) define success for yourself. She illustrated each of these points with statements and stories. For example, when developing the point "trust your own instincts," she referred to a kind of experience that is shared by many women:

> Our judgment of people, situations, and the heart of an issue is often right on target—yet sometimes we women allow ourselves to go against what our instincts are telling us. I bet we've all had the experience of sitting across the table from someone—a man, let's say—with whom we disagree. How many times, in this situation, has your reaction been to question your own perception and judgment, rather than his . . . only to find out later that you were right on the money?

She talked as well about women "second-guessing" themselves—saying "we women have perfected this trait of second-guessing ourselves to a high art form." She speculated that it may be from reading beauty magazines: "Perhaps it stems from our early and constant exposure to society's message to women—we can never quite measure up to the models on the pages of *Vogue*."

She encouraged women to listen to themselves, to have confidence in their own knowledge and experience, and then she told the story of

Debbie Fields, the cookie maven, who had a difficult time convincing bankers that her idea of selling cookies could work. "In short," said Dole, "we must take our own measurements, and use our own instincts to make choices and decisions, whether it is on the job or in our personal lives. Certainly, we need to seek input and gain support. Yes, we must look at all the facts and figures we can muster, but when it's time to make the decision, we must, quite simply, rely on our own judgment and do what we think is right." In a related point about "defining success for yourself," her advice followed her religious values: "Don't let others define success for us." To her, success was: "finding something which infuses you with a sense of mission, with a passion for your life's work; finding something that leads you to say, 'Nothing I ever did made me feel so important.'" That is a quote from her mother, who felt that way about the American Red Cross.

IT'S ALL ABOUT CHOICE

Pervasive threads of cultural and liberal feminism[97] run through Elizabeth Dole's words and actions. For her, a woman's ability to choose for herself is at the heart of the struggle for women's rights, although she did not support a woman's right to choose to terminate her pregnancy during her run for the presidency in Campaign 2000. Dole advocated for "choice" for women in a number of other ways in her speeches. She said in a speech in Charlotte, North Carolina, as early as June 16, 1986: "What is important is that every woman has the right and the privilege to choose the role she wishes for herself." A study of Dole's life choices reveals that sometimes "choosing" among alternatives was difficult, if not heart wrenching.

Dole chose on more than one occasion to step down from her government positions to campaign for her husband for public office. At times, she seemed to walk a tightrope, as she balanced her role as a high-powered government official with her role as a wife. From the time she married Senator Bob Dole in 1975, until his retirement from the Senate in 1996, he ran nearly every four years for the Republican nomination for the presidency, winning the vice presidential nomination in 1976, and the presidential nomination in 1996. Whenever her husband ran for the presidency, she was faced with the choice of keeping her position or stepping down from it—temporarily or permanently—to help her husband's campaign. What follows is a discussion of her decisions, press coverage of such, and her response.

Elizabeth Hanford married Senator Bob Dole on December 1, 1975, and her professional life became complicated. In August 1976, when Gerald

R. Ford invited Robert J. Dole to become his vice presidential running mate, she had to choose whether to keep her position on the Federal Trade Commission or give it up to help her husband campaign. Her position on the FTC required her to remain nonpartisan, and being part of her husband's campaign challenged that neutrality. Members of the FTC had never had this problem before, since no other commissioner ever had a spouse running for national office.

Dole thought deeply about what she should do in the circumstances, knowing her decision would not only affect her life, but would also set a precedent.[98] Legally, she did not have to resign her seat, but complaints began to surface about whether she would have a conflict of interest if her husband won the election.[99] John Moss, a Democrat from California and chair of the House subcommittee that oversaw regulatory agencies, alleged "a possible conflict of interest because she was in the position of directly or indirectly asking for votes and financial support from persons or corporations over whom she would later sit in judgment."[100]

Dole chose to take a leave of absence to campaign for her husband. When the Ford/Dole ticket lost the election, she went back to the FTC. However, in 1978, her husband decided to run again for the presidency in the 1980 election. Once again, Elizabeth had to choose; this time, she stepped down from her position at the FTC. Having been appointed in 1973, she had already served five years of her seven-year term. According to biographer Kozar, Elizabeth's "feminist friends begged her not to step down from the FTC, arguing that the move would send the wrong message to professional women everywhere."[101] As in 1976, she also received questions from reporters about interrupting her career. She answered them by saying: "I think my own career is a pretty good testament to my belief that women should be able to develop their full potential. Above all, they should be able to choose, whether it is a career, or the role of homemaker and mother, or both. Choice is what it is all about."[102]

In 1987, Elizabeth Dole was secretary of transportation when her husband decided to run for the presidency in Campaign 1988. Once again, she was put under a great deal of pressure both to step down from her post and to retain it. During the summer of 1987, she tried to continue her work while campaigning for her husband. According to Laura Parker, journalist for the *Washington Post*, during the month of August, Elizabeth spent twenty-one days on the campaign trail visiting primary states. Unfortunately, that month was also marked "by a major air crash, a string of near collisions involving jetliners, and a major realignment of airspace over Los Angeles."[103] *USA Today* carried a half-page ad calling for Dole's resignation. The ad was paid for by the Los Angeles Aircraft Owners and Pilots Association, which paid $22,000 for it. Another industry magazine,

Air Transport World, said Dole had outlived her usefulness, and *Traffic World* ran a piece in the September issue calling for her to "get out."[104]

Dole was also criticized because of the potential for confusion over her travel expenses. Often she would travel on Department of Transportation business, and she would use her free time to campaign for her husband. One of her staff members explained that her campaign trips were paid for by the Committee to Elect Bob Dole, and when the trip combined purposes, the Department of Transportation and the Committee to Elect Bob Dole each paid its fair share, which was calculated on a minute-by-minute basis.[105] Traveling on behalf of the DOT was always something Dole had done, but adding the fund-raisers to the trip—in effect, multitasking—was something new for which she was criticized.

Part of the reason why Elizabeth Dole did not want to step down as secretary of transportation was because she was working on tough transportation issues that she was afraid would fail if she wasn't there to oversee their progress.[106] Journalist Bernard Weinraub reported the difficulty Dole experienced: the decision was "extremely difficult," "tough . . . very tough," he wrote. Dole was quoted as saying, "I love the job I'm in—it's an extraordinarily challenging job." Yet, she was under pressure by her husband's friends and staff to help more on the campaign. When her husband suggested that she resign, she was reportedly not very happy: "Her assistant told a *Time* magazine reporter that when Bob suggested . . . that she would have to resign eventually, she was very annoyed."[107]

Eventually, on October 1, 1987 Dole left the deparament of transportation. No sooner had she done so than journalists and women's advocates began to comment negatively on her decision—some accusing her of selling out. Ellen Goodman wrote: "Elizabeth Dole is taking off ahead of schedule. This itself is a unique event in the annals of modern transportation. The woman is leaving Washington to become—heaven help her—a frequent flier in the presidential campaign of her husband, Robert."[108] Peter Jennings led the evening news two weeks earlier when she first announced her plans to resign with this statement: "One of the most important women in government has given up her job for a man." Journalist Stephen C. Fehr reported that many women were debating the pros and cons of Dole's resignation.[109] Feminists, who said that she was putting her career on hold again for her husband, questioned her decision.[110] Some said that in a two-career marriage, it is the woman who must give up her job. Irene Natividad was quoted as saying that Dole's decision was really "sexism rearing its ugly head," while other women pointed out that it was fine for a woman to have a career and contribute to the family income, but it was too difficult when her career was demanding. Ruth Mandel, director for the Center of American Women in Politics at Rutgers put the point well when she said that Dole and her decision to resign reminded her of the Roman god Janus, whose face looked both backward and forward: "The traditional spouse is the one looking behind. That spouse puts her interests aside to support the advancement of her husband. . . . the modern-day spouse has her own career and attempts to juggle her interests with those of her husband."[111] Ann Grimes's comment was: "You could hardly find a more telling image of America's befuddlement over sex and work and marriage in the eighties—a candidate's wife spending perhaps a third of a precious personal campaign stop . . . arguing that she had the right to be there. . . . [S]he had to defend herself for quitting that high echelon office and taking on the role of full-time spouse of a candidate."[112]

Not all of the comments about Dole's stepping down were negative, and of course she defended herself. Ruth Mandel made an interesting comment about Dole's decision: "We've reached a new day when a woman [Dole] is recognized as so powerful an asset that her husband can't run for president without her full-time attention . . . I can't think of another instance where a wife has been seen as such a valuable commodity."[113] From Dole's perspective, stepping down would be a sacrifice for her because of the projects she wanted to finish; however, she had already served four and a half years as secretary of transportation—longer than anyone else in that position—and would have at best another year or eighteen months until the next administration took over. Dole admitted that keeping the position and campaigning were becoming too difficult for her. She emphasized that it was her choice to step down, and her feminist critics should respect her right to choose. She also said that she was campaigning for the next leader of the free world, and that was a significant undertaking: "This is a substantial undertaking. It's not standing by his side and smiling. It's meeting the press and the public and discussing the issues and taking a role in the democratic process that will elect the leader of the Free World." She also highlighted how the experience of participating in a national campaign would be a benefit to her. She would learn new skills and get great national exposure. She said: "You don't have to have an employer paying you to have that process of moving forward. Certainly, I have not set aside my career."[114]

Bob Dole did not win the Republican nomination for the presidency. The victory went to George H. W. Bush, who went on to defeat Democrat Michael Dukakis to become the forty-first president of the United States. Bush phoned Dole and invited her to serve as secretary of labor in his administration, a position she held for two years, before becoming president of the American Red Cross. When she stepped down from the Department of Labor, there was great speculation about her motivation.

Biographer Mulford attributed much of this to the secrecy Dole maintained while negotiating for the Red Cross position. The news of her resignation leaked out only one day before her official announcement, so journalists were taken by surprise.[115] There were theories about why she left—from her interest in advancing her career to her inability to work effectively at DOL. From her perspective, she was simply excited to be working for the leading humanitarian organization in the world. During the summer of 1995, however, once again she had to choose whether to stay at the Red Cross or to help her husband try again in 1996 for the presidency. She chose to take a leave of absence.

On May 20, 1997, Dole talked about her decision to take a leave of absence from her position as president of the American Red Cross in her Economic Summit for Women speech. She told her audience that "some people did not understand her decision to support her husband." "I made the choice," she said, "not because I had to, but because I wanted to. I also planned to return to the presidency of the Red Cross, regardless of the outcome of the election. If Bob had won, I guess that would have made me the first First Lady working outside the White House." Dole stressed the importance of "choice" to women: "And isn't that what we women have been fighting for all these years—the freedom to pursue the lives we choose? The freedom to decide how best to achieve our personal fulfillment based on our own standards, our individual goals, and what's best for our families?" She defined her position in other speeches as well, such as the speech she gave later that year in St. Louis to Women Leaders of the United Way.

In 1996, Dole had been criticized for her decision to take a leave of absence from the American Red Cross, for the same reasons she had been criticized when she left other positions. With this decision, however, new lines of criticism were raised; for example, some saw her as too powerful to be in the supportive role of First Lady. In addition, Dole was criticized for leaving the Red Cross for fourteen months, when the organization was engaged in a critically important drive to purify the nation's blood supply by introducing new procedures and methods. The chairman of the Louisville blood bank was quoted as saying: "'That's pretty hard for an organization to deal with, while [its] president goes on hiatus to campaign for her husband.'"[116] Some wondered if she would be able to continue if her husband won, and if she did continue, would there be a conflict of interest?[117]

Other charges related to her marriage had been made against her throughout her career. Stepping down from high-powered positions was just one of them. The question about conflict of interest had been raised from her appointment to the Federal Trade Commission to her appointment as secretary of labor. Elizabeth Dole wrote about this in *Unlimited Partners*, where she described the tensions surrounding her appointment at Public Liaison: "In those early weeks," she said, "a lot of people inside and outside of Pennsylvania Avenue shook their heads in disbelief when they were told that Bob and I didn't regularly exchange information over dinner. After all, they reasoned, he was writing tax law and I was promoting them as the Administration's number one priority."[118] Sometimes she was asked to pass along messages to him, but she said her husband did not want to talk shop at home. Some wondered as well when she became secretary of transportation whether she would work too closely with her husband on the same projects. The Doles, however, did not always agree with each other's positions; in fact, once they debated their different views on *Good Morning America*, after which they received many letters suggesting that they should not argue so much, and one even recommended marriage counseling.[119]

There were questions raised throughout Elizabeth Dole's career about whether she earned her positions or whether they were given to her in exchange for the support of her powerful senator husband. According to biographer Carolyn Mulford, some commentators wondered whether she had earned her position at Public Liaison by herself or whether Reagan gave her the position as a favor to her husband, whose support in the Senate the president wanted to count on.[120] Similar questions were raised when George H. W. Bush appointed her as secretary of labor. At the time, her husband was the Senate majority leader. When George Bush was asked if he had nominated Elizabeth Dole to secure the goodwill of her husband, Bush replied that he had chosen her because he thought she was the best person for the position. He also added: "But a harmonious relationship with the leader of the Senate is very important to me. If there's a dividend in there, I'd accept it."[121] The fact of the matter was that Dole had worked hard for all of the appointments she received during her life. Journalist Stengel made this point in 1996, when he said that her "sugary charm" tends to disguise her ambition, but she has had to lobby very hard for every position she has gotten—beginning with her early positions in Washington, D.C.[122]

An examination of Elizabeth Dole's personal and career choices and her track record in government service has revealed a woman deeply committed to helping other women and minorities succeed. Entering the male-dominated world of government service in the latter half of the 1960s was not easy, and she wrote in personal terms in *Unlimited Partners* about some of the roadblocks she and other women faced at that time. These experiences probably heightened her use of her femininity, as could be expected. Journalist John Carlin of the *London Independent* put the point bluntly:

"In order to make it to the top of a man's world the young Miss Hanford understood that she would have to dissemble, play a twin-track game: pander to meet expectations first, then use feminine wiles to beat the system."[123] Whether this was true or not, at the very least, entering a world largely dominated by men—most of whom had low expectations of women—probably amplified her perfectionist tendencies by putting pressure on her to prove herself. Those who worked with her such as Virginia Knauer described her as "a tremendously dedicated worker."

While her femininity makes it difficult for some critics to place her in a feminist camp, her support of woman certainly qualifies her to have a seat at that table. Her hard work and dedication enabled her to secure positions of power, the kind needed to enforce existing legislation and promote new legislation for the benefit of women and minorities. In one of her speeches to an audience of women, she commented on the necessity of attaining power to cause change. She said: "You have got to be able to have a seat at the table. You are trying to reach . . . goals in a positive way, which means exercising power."[124] During the Reagan administration, she had to mute her support of the ERA in order to bring about the very outcomes that amendment was designed to achieve. Results were key for Elizabeth Dole, not the waving of banners.

Journalist Suzanne Haik Terrell praised Dole—with all her femininity—in an editorial:

> Elizabeth Dole is a woman who throughout her public and private life has taught us that women can be effective, strong and smart without being abrasive, abusive or arrogant. She has shown that class, character and values are admirable qualities. Her hard work and high standards, and her ethics, have earned her respect from people throughout this country who have witnessed her unselfish dedication to the public good. Elizabeth Dole always acts with dignity and professionalism.[125]

And biographer Kozar makes quite a strong statement about her contributions to women: "Elizabeth Dole has probably done more to advance the stature of women in public service than anyone in the last three decades of the twentieth century."[126]

Chapter 5

Advocate for Her Husband, the Republican Party, and Herself

George W. Bush understands there is power—and there is a higher power. He knows there is no strength without integrity; no security apart from strong character.[1]

With these words, Elizabeth Dole did what she has done for more than a quarter of a century—campaigned for the Republican Party. Campaigning for what she wants is nothing new for Dole. Since the time she was a little girl, Elizabeth began to foster the skills she would use later in life, such as leadership and public speaking. Her oratory skills became so finely honed from years of experience that Jeb Bush, governor of Florida, could say about her recently, "She's just a great speaker."[2] As a child, Elizabeth Hanford was an organizer and ringleader among her friends. In high school, she participated in student government, running for, but not winning, the office of school president in her senior year. At Duke University in 1957, she was elected student government president and in 1958, she was awarded the "Leader of the Year" honors by the student body. At the time, her interests were more academic and political than social. In *Unlimited Partners*, she admitted, she preferred writing a paper on "the decision making process leading up to America's use of the first atomic Bomb" than going to a dance.[3] Pragmatic even then, the analytical skills she would learn by writing the paper and the insights she would gain on public policymaking would serve her for the rest of her life.

After graduating from Duke University, Hanford learned a valuable lesson while interviewing for a job at the *Charlotte Observer*: "If you couldn't or wouldn't make the case for why you should get the job, you could hardly expect a prospective boss to make it for you."[4] She was

Elizabeth Dole speaking at the podium to a huge audience at the 2000 Republican National Convention. (Photo by Nichola Gutgold)

beginning to understand that she would have to sell herself, rather than relying on her resume and attractive appearance. This lesson would prove priceless in her future search for positions and as a political campaigner. In New York, she worked as a tour guide for the United Nations and in Washington, D.C., as a secretary in the Peace Corps office. Although these were modest positions for the young North Carolinian with aspirations of a career in government service, they offered her public speaking training and a chance to make important connections that would lay the foundation for her future.

Looking back at all of the positions she has held since those early days, Elizabeth Dole's life could be described as a constant flurry of advocating—for herself to break into the male bastion that dominated government service and politics in the United Sates; for her husband, Robert Dole, who ran for president or vice president in most cycles between 1976 and 1996; and for the Republican Party, for which she has become a highly valued spokeswoman. Her achievements are especially remarkable given the generation into which she, as a female—a Southern female—was born.

Although critics of Elizabeth Dole say that she is rigid, inflexible, and overly scripted as a public speaker, this chapter highlights her versatility and exhibits how adaptive her rhetorical skills have become, especially on the campaign trail. Her biography as an orator must include her impromptu speeches where her remarks have been formulated on the spot from her knowledge and her years of experience. Consider the rhetorical agility necessary for anyone to move as she has done from the sheltered life of a Southern belle to class president, May Queen, consumer advocate, cabinet member, president of the Red Cross, presidential candidate, key Republican spokeswoman, and now a U.S. senator. Without question, Dole is a rhetorical multitasker, and this becomes evident from studying her record as an advocate for causes she championed as a cabinet secretary and for candidates she has promoted during years of political campaigning.

Elizabeth Dole first became known on the national stage when she campaigned for her husband and Gerald Ford during the 1976 presidential election. She emerged at that time as one of the most articulate and accomplished spouses of a major political figure. Before that time, she had been an active spokeswoman for the Republican Party and for herself as she climbed the male-dominated Washington, D.C., career ladder. Throughout the 1980s and 1990s, she spoke to audiences all across America on behalf of her husband and other political candidates. In the late 1990s, she campaigned for herself during her unsuccessful run for the presidency and in 2002, during her victorious run for a U.S. Senate seat from North Carolina. Dole developed her natural talent as a public speaker by speaking extensively, and she become exceedingly effective on the campaign trail.

EARLY CAMPAIGNS

Dole's first foray into political campaigning began in 1976, when her husband was invited to serve as the vice presidential candidate on the Republican ticket with Gerald R. Ford. A new bride, Dole accompanied her husband on the campaign trail and began to get a taste of the associated public speaking demands. Elizabeth reflected on the spontaneity of her early campaign speeches during an interview:

> In 1976, I found myself on the campaign trail. . . . Well, I was in West Palm Beach, Florida, for what I thought was a speech, but when I entered the room, I was walked down the aisle, and instead, with just thirty seconds of notice, I found myself in a debate with Jimmy Carter's son! I had to think fast on my feet, because not only wasn't I prepared for the debate, I wasn't too prepared for campaigning in general, since Bob and I were married in December and then we started campaigning barely eight months after the wedding. I was dropped into the middle of a national campaign.[5]

Although she preferred being prepared, she faced constant surprises that included schedule and event changes, often at the last minute.[6]

At the beginning of the campaign, Bob Dole and his advisors were uncertain about the role Elizabeth should play. On the one hand, she had no experience as a campaigner for elective office, even though she had lobbied successfully to achieve top government positions. On the other hand, while working at the White House Office of Consumer Affairs and as a member of the Federal Trade Commission, she had gained valuable experience navigating through press conferences and speaking before congressional committees. "Public speaking and press conferences are old hat to her,"[7] said Virginia Knauer about Dole's abilities at that time. Figuring out how best to use her skills became the issue, which was further complicated because her husband wanted her to travel with him.

"For the first week or so after the [Republican National] convention," Dole wrote in *Unlimited Partners*, "I pretty much played the traditional political wife, standing at my husband's side and smiling for the cameras."[8] This supportive role did not quite fit a woman of Dole's experience and ability. Speaking to constituents was a better role for her, but "the last thing . . . anyone had thought about was what the candidate's wife should say." In addition, women from the Republican National Committee urged Dole to campaign for the ticket on her own. They advised her to "carve out a separate campaign schedule and cover as much territory as possible." Dole's "instincts" told her "they were right." As a compromise, the Doles traveled together whenever they could, but they addressed different audiences in each city.[9] Often she campaigned by herself in the day, then with her husband in the evening.

Unlike other wives who might enter a campaign with professional skills in education or medicine, Elizabeth Dole spoke to audiences from a background of political experience. Many of the events she attended were ceremonial, but Dole studied her husband's positions on issues and spoke about them whenever she found an opportunity. Biographer Kozar quotes Dole as saying, "As an independent career woman and an FTC commissioner with ten years of government experience, I wasn't going to spend the whole campaign answering reporters' questions with a demure 'I don't do issues.' I did do issues. Six days a week. The genie couldn't be put back in the bottle."[10] During one of her earliest stops in Baton Rouge, Louisiana, Dole spoke about issues and surprised her husband by showing him a local newspaper with four pictures of her on the front page. Included were "news stories discussing the issues. Real issues," she wrote in *Unlimited Partners*.[11]

Not only did Dole present her husband's positions on issues, she also expressed her own opinions, especially when she spoke to women. She stressed the importance of education for women so they could stand on their own two feet. She told her audiences about her personal experience climbing the ladder of achievement: "I just took the best opportunity I saw when I turned a corner. That's why I think it's important for a woman to get a good education. When the options turn up, she's prepared to choose one she wants."[12] Her enthusiasm and skill before an audience on subjects such as education were well received. Her hometown of Salisbury, North Carolina, eagerly welcomed her, naming the day she campaigned for her husband in that city, the "Elizabeth Hanford Dole Day."[13]

The experience of campaigning was a positive one for Dole, even though the Ford/Dole ticket was defeated. In *Unlimited Partners*, she called campaigning a "civics lesson you can't possibly get in the classroom or in Washington."[14] She had done so well that rumors began to circulate in North Carolina newspapers, saying she was thinking of running for a congressional seat.[15] Instead of Elizabeth's running for office, however, Bob Dole announced his interest in running again for the presidency in the 1980 election. In *Unlimited Partners*, she wrote about how much she welcomed the opportunity to campaign for her husband. "A national political campaign," she wrote, "would be an unparalleled learning opportunity,"[16] a comment that was proven true for her. She and her husband campaigned actively for his nomination. They traveled extensively, and when they were in Washington, D.C., they attended two or three political events a night. Since her husband was busy with the Senate, Elizabeth did more campaigning than was typical of a spouse, so much so that some constituents began to think that she was running for office. When it was clear that Ronald Reagan would receive the Republican nomination, Bob Dole pulled out of the race, joking that he was quitting because Elizabeth passed him in the polls.[17]

Elizabeth campaigned for the Reagan/Bush ticket during 1980. About this decision, she told biographer Mulford: "It all just sort of flowed. There was no time to stop and think." Yet she knew that her days of climbing up through the ranks were over. "I was at a point where you were going to serve at the pleasure of the president or you weren't going to serve."[18] Even though Reagan did not support the Equal Rights Amendment and Dole did, the future president promised to root out discrimination in the legal code. To help Reagan and Bush defeat Jimmy Carter and Walter Mondale, Dole helped them appeal to women's groups. She set up voter groups such as "Women for Reagan/Bush" and "Blacks for Reagan/Bush." She also joined their "truth squads," which consisted of campaigners who went into areas where Carter was scheduled to speak to suggest questions to members of the press and who remained after Carter had left to comment on his answers.[19]

Reagan appreciated Dole's loyalty and ardent campaigning. When he won the presidency, she became part of his transition team as chair of the human services group, before becoming head of Public Liaison, a position that required her to garner support for his policies from grassroots and more formal organizations. In 1982, she became head of the White House Coordinating Council on Women, which helped Reagan honor his campaign promise to women. Early in 1983, when Drew Lewis resigned as secretary of transportation, Reagan invited Dole to take his place. All of these positions required a great deal of advocating, this time for policies and appointments and not just candidates for elective office.

When Reagan was nearly fatally wounded, his decision to run for a second term was not a certainty. Rumors abounded about whether Bob Dole or even Elizabeth would run for the presidency in 1984, if Reagan chose not to do so. On several occasions, the Doles joked about one or the other of them running for president. For example, in 1983, at the Gridiron Dinner where politicians and members of the press "toast" each other, Bob Dole said to his audience, "Dole will not be a candidate for president in 1984." Immediately, Elizabeth jumped to her feet and exclaimed to all present, "Speak for yourself, sweetheart!"[20] A year later at the 1984 Gridiron Dinner, it was Elizabeth's turn to speak. Joking with the audience, she told about how her husband had been asked by a reporter how he feels being married to such a powerful woman. Instead of allowing him to answer the reporter, she said to her husband, "Hold it cupcake, I'll take this one." She also expressed her political ambitions humorously by relating a "conversation" she had with Vice President George H. W. Bush: "George asked how I felt about the vice-presidency in '88. I said 'If you're interested in staying on, George, I'll keep you in mind."[21] According to journalist Donnie Radcliffe, Elizabeth won "raves from the Washington Establishment" for her performance.[22] In the end, Ronald Reagan ran for reelection in 1984, and once again Elizabeth Dole campaigned hard for the Reagan/Bush ticket.

Elizabeth was an active campaigner for Reagan and Bush, as well as for other Republicans running for House and Senate seats. She would sometimes campaign in four or five towns in one state on a single day, only to travel to an adjacent state and do the same thing the day after.[23] Dole raised a considerable amount of money for the Republicans, and she spoke at many different kinds of events, including press conferences, lunches and dinners, and rallies. Often she spoke from a manuscript, but at other times she spoke extemporaneously from notes. The most important speech she gave was at the 1984 Republican National Convention.[24] This speech was significant because in 1984, a woman was put on the Democratic ticket; Reagan and Bush ran against Fritz Mondale and

Geraldine Ferraro. During Dole's speech, she stressed how much the administration was trying to make employment opportunities for women.[25] Both of the Doles attracted attention at this convention; media coverage suggested that one or both of them were on "everyone's short list" for the presidency in 1988. Their hotel rooms were 1988 and 1989, and campaign buttons were circulating with "Dole & Dole '88."[26]

THE SOUTHERN STRATEGY

When Bob Dole decided to make a bid for the presidency in 1988, he could not have asked for a better spouse than Elizabeth. Her skills as a campaigner were, by then, expert. During the primaries, she raised $1 million in campaign funds by herself and was hailed in a *Newsweek* article as her husband's "secret weapon."[27] She was also called his "Southern strategy" by the press and by members of the Republican Party. As early as July 1987, Elizabeth gave a speech to about four hundred Republican women in Huntsville, Alabama. Her speech was reported in the *New York Times* as casual and conversational as well as genteel and unthreatening. The audience responded well to her, cheering her enthusiastically and surrounding her when she finished speaking. Her credentials, presence, and Southerness were all seen as assets to the Dole campaign.[28]

When Dole stepped down as secretary of transportation in the fall of 1987, she began a swing through the South. Her husband was the majority leader in the Senate, and it was difficult for him to get away to campaign. Since he only had about a month to hit the campaign trail at the end of 1987, he relied a great deal on her.[29] Journalist Stephen Fehr praised Dole's ability to win over audiences: "Everywhere she went," he wrote, "through Missouri, Texas, Oklahoma, and Iowa, Dole engaged voters. Interviews with voters who came to see her in nine states make it plain that her message is getting through."[30]

Dole was somewhat of a celebrity on the campaign trail, garnering attention from the public and the media. She drew large crowds and was requested as a speaker more than she had time to accept.[31] Articles on her appeared in *Business Week*, *Fortune*, *Harper's Bazaar*, and *Vogue*.[32] In 1988, *Esquire* named her "Woman of the Year."[33] Peter Hart, a public opinion analyst in Washington, D.C., wrote about Elizabeth Dole's influence on her husband's campaign: "She has more [name] recognition than many of the presidential candidates themselves. Americans like her. . . . He's had kind of a tough image over the years. She softens him."[34] Others sang her praises as well. Andy Card, advisor to George H. W. Bush, stated, "she's not just an asset for Bob Dole. She's an asset for the Republican Party."[35]

Given Dole's appeal, it is not surprising that she was asked whether she would be interested in running for elective office herself. Once it became obvious that George H. W. Bush would win the 1988 Republican presidential nomination, journalists began to recommend her as a vice presidential running mate. Ellen Goodman praised Dole: "she is the sort of ladylike women's rights advocate that passes muster in Republican circles while widening those circles."[36] An *Esquire* article advised Bush to make her his running mate because she would add excitement to his campaign. Bob Dole was also said to be on the short list. At the 1988 Republican National Convention, both Doles joked about each other's eagerness to get the call from Bush.[37]

Elizabeth spoke at the Republican National Convention, a move designed to rally support from women voters, who were her target audience. Her chief purpose was to persuade them to vote Republican; at the time, the economy was fragile and many women voters—especially single mothers—faced difficult economic conditions. Dole wanted to convince her audience that George H. W. Bush and the Republican Party would have their best interests at heart.

Gaining the confidence of women voters in 1988 was not an easy task because of a phenomenon known as the "gender gap." During the Reagan presidency, women's support for his administration's policies declined, even though Dole worked diligently in that area. When he was first elected in 1980, Reagan had received almost as many votes from women as he had from men; the difference was only eight percentage points, with fewer votes being cast for him by women. Two years later, however, public opinion polls and other sources revealed that the gap between male and female supporters was widening. Elizabeth Dole was asked to address this problem in 1984, and again during the 1988 convention.[38]

Shortly before Dole took the platform in the large New Orleans Superdome on August 15, 1988, Theresa Esposito, a Republican state representative from North Carolina, introduced her, telling the audience that Dole was an "educated daughter of the South" and describing her career achievements. Esposito's recitation of Dole's resume suggested the importance of the Republican Party in helping Dole build her career. Dole echoed this theme in her speech by detailing the ways in which the Reagan administration provided opportunities for women and how George H. W. Bush would continue to do so. Dole's ultimate goal in speaking was to show women that a Bush presidency would be consistent with their needs.

The claims Dole made in her speech helped her to achieve her goals, as did the techniques she used. She spoke about jobs, child care, and education, subjects that would appeal to women. For example, she summed up achievements under President Reagan that helped women workers:

"President Reagan has created an incredible jobs machine, more jobs for more Americans than ever before. And two thirds of the 17 million American new jobs went to women—good jobs, not bad jobs—real work, not make-work." She promised a continued commitment to "good jobs" if George H. W. Bush would be elected. She also asked her audience to think back to the Carter administration and consider the employment situation at that time: "Remember the Carter years," she asked, "when workers were afraid to open pay envelopes because there just might be a pink slip inside, when families gave up hope of ever owning their own home, when parents feared their children's generation would be worse off than their own? That was real economic violence. We have been there before and we must never go back there again."[39] Dole suggested that a vote for Dukakis would mean "pink slips" for people and loss of the American Dream.

Dole used effective verbal and nonverbal techniques in this speech. She used storytelling to recite the achievements under Reagan and to forecast the potentially disastrous consequences of a Dukakis presidency. Many of the narratives in the speech were not pleasant or entertaining; instead, they were designed to instill a sense of urgency, perhaps even fear in American women voters. She also used inclusive language, especially geared toward women: "We women . . . we're always vulnerable when jobs are cut back and the economy stagnates." Nonverbally, Dole used a rousing tone of voice, and she involved her audience by repeating the same rhetorical question three times about increased employment under Reagan. She shouted to her audience: "Are we going to let them take it away?" And they shouted back to her: "No." Dole's physical appearance also seemed strategic. Her bright blue polka-dot dress was the kind of outfit many women would wear, and dressing that way helped her achieve identification with women in her audience.

When the election was over, George H. W. Bush became the forty-first president of the United States. He hoped to close a gender gap in his administration when he named Elizabeth Dole secretary of labor. American Federation of Labor-Congress of Industrial Organizations President Lane Kirkland quickly made approving comments on Elizabeth's appointment, calling her "a person of proven stature."[40] Dole had no difficulty during the confirmation hearings, and for the next two years she worked in earnest to make good on her promise to make life better for working Americans. Her reason for stepping down as secretary of labor nearly two years later was to become president of the American Red Cross. There can be no doubt that she was an excellent fund-raiser in that position and persuasive as well in meeting their other goals. For example, she admitted how much more effective she was as a speaker when she left the podium to walk around her audiences. Her listeners would understand more personally why they should choose to give blood.[41]

THE MOST SPECTACULAR SPOUSE IN 1996

During the years when she was secretary of labor, Dole continued to campaign for the Republican Party. In October 1989, she campaigned in Chicago for Republican candidates for governor, senator, and other positions. In the fall of 1990, she campaigned for about sixty candidates in races scattered around the country. A typical campaign stop would be like the one she made in Kansas City, where she arrived at night and the next day she spoke to an audience of college students and attended a news conference, an official opening of a job corps center, and a fund-raiser. After Kansas, she was scheduled for trips to Dallas, North Carolina, Denver, and back to Washington, D.C.[42]

Dole turned her attention to her husband's campaign when he decided to run for the presidency against incumbent Bill Clinton in the 1996 election. She took a fourteen-month unpaid leave of absence from the American Red Cross from November 1995 through January 1997. As the spouse of a presidential hopeful, Elizabeth Dole drew attention from the press and public, and gained a reputation for her enthusiastic speaking style and her ability to interact with her audience. "When she talks, people listen," wrote one journalist, "and they believe her."[43] She often used a conversational style of speaking; for example, she spoke to the Chamber of Commerce in Evanston, Illinois, without pause for thirty minutes with no notes and no microphone.[44] A journalist who traveled with Dole for three days described the way she worked a crowd of five hundred, mostly women, at an afternoon picnic in Kentucky. Dressed in a black skirt, high heels, and a silk blouse, she clipped a wireless microphone to her and strolled among the blankets and lawn chairs telling her audience why they should vote for her husband. Speaking without notes in her creamy North Carolina accent, she riveted her audience.[45] Dole became such a formidable campaigner in her own right that when her husband received his matching funds from the government, she was given a $1.5 million traveling budget, a staff of thirty people, and a fourteen-seat Challenger 600 jet. An article in the *New York Times* by Elizabeth Bumiller declared this to be a first for Elizabeth: this was the "first full-time, on-the-road campaign operation for a First Lady candidate."[46] Bumiller also felt Dole would have received more coverage in the press if she had been given a bigger jet to carry more reporters with her.

Elizabeth Dole's chief function during the campaign was to persuade women to vote Republican, a task assigned to her since the 1980s, in particular, to vote for her husband. During a speech she gave in Kentucky, for example, she talked about her husband's record on women's issues and his hiring practices. A banner at this event said: "Elizabeth Dole salutes working women." She also performed other functions, such as her husband's speech coach and editor. For example, she edited a portion of the speech he gave when he accepted the Republican nomination because she found the language too dense, and in another speech, which he gave in Colorado, she asked him to explain the benefits of his crime package to women.[47] In addition, she helped him moderate the tone of his messages. He had the reputation of shooting from the hip, and she wanted him to exercise verbal restraint.[48]

Dole gave her most memorable campaign speech on August 14, 1996, at the Republican National Convention, held in San Diego. When she descended the platform stairs that evening, her purpose was not to address the gender gap issue, but to humanize her husband to the American public.[49] What another wife might say about her husband at a political convention may be very similar to what Elizabeth Dole said about Bob Dole in this speech. But the ingenious way she said it, by strolling through the audience while telling stories and visiting with witnesses of his kindness, showed her ability to create a new kind of speech under a controlled condition.

Immaculately dressed in a mustard yellow, form-fitting silk suit, a slim, sophisticated, and utterly feminine Elizabeth Dole appeared at the podium. She opened her speech by saying that she wanted to get comfortable with the audience, since her speech would be very personal, directed to friends, about "the man I love." She stated the overall purpose of her remarks with the metaphor of "put[ting] the finishing brushstrokes on [the] portrait" of her husband, which the public had seen throughout the campaign. The American people needed to know important information about Bob Dole's character, she explained, so they would make the right decision when they voted in November. She signaled the importance of her remarks by describing the election as she perceived it: "a defining moment in our nation's history. This election is about the vision and the values that will shape America as we move into the next century, and it's about the character of the man who will lead us there."

Dole descended the twelve platform steps in high heels to walk among a surprised audience of delegates. She used a wireless microphone clipped to her lapel, and when that failed, she switched to a handheld one without missing a beat. When a live image of her husband appeared on a giant video screen, she acknowledged him briefly, and then turned to tell stories about his life, starting with his birth in a small Kansas town to humble parents. As she spoke, she hugged and briefly chatted with people in the audience who had been sources of inspiration to her husband. She talked to audience members who attested to her husband's fine character. Her tone was warm, and she smiled genuinely as she spoke to the delegates. Even though she was a politically astute woman, she chose to present herself more as a loving helpmate to Bob Dole than a political insider. Her goal was to portray her husband's sterling character and trustworthiness. Her strategy was to make his personal qualities as public as his record of achievements, not only by telling stories of what Bob Dole had done for others, but also by bringing in witnesses who could verify the truth of her claims.

Concomitant with her goal of promoting her husband, Elizabeth Dole also wanted to present herself as his marriage partner, not his political partner. She wanted to draw a sharp contrast between herself and Hillary Clinton, and she did so by foregrounding her role as her husband's helpmate. At the same time that she lovingly presented stories about her husband's generosity, she came across as a devoted wife who has noticed and appreciated her husband's essential goodness. Her "Oprah-style" speech showed her more as a Southern hostess, circulating around a well-attended party, than a tough political insider campaigning for her husband to win the White House.

Reactions to Dole's speech came from different quarters. For example, Dan Rather announced, "What you have witnessed here tonight is the birth of a new form of campaigning and a new standard for convention speeches by which all others will likely be judged for a long time."[50] Oliver North, a radio talk show host who was at the convention said about the speech, "I think it is absolutely astonishing. What a tour de force. She didn't have a TelePrompTer. It was captivating. It was unprecedented."[51] Other members of the Republican Party loved the speech as well. Delegates who were interviewed after the speech made statements such as: "For Elizabeth, it is very natural. She exudes compassion. She's able to show the . . . caring side of Bob Dole we all know is there." Ann Stone, president of Republicans for Choice told an interviewer: "She connects so well and the best part is, she's never had to compromise her femininity for all her accomplishments." Another delegate said: "She's a great example to young women of how you can accomplish whatever you set out to and still be a caring person."[52] Even Democrats expressed their approval,[53] including Clinton's political advisors, who were awed by her performance and concerned about its possible impact on voters.[54]

Media and communication experts expressed their admiration for her speech, as did ordinary viewers. Kathleen Hall Jamieson called the speech a "model of traditional narrative—tied to self disclosure and conversational style,"[55] and Colleen Kelly compared her performance to Bill Clinton's town hall sessions during the 1992 election.[56] Media expert Terry Pearce praised her decision to remove the podium and teleprompter between her and the audience, commenting on the risks she took and the advantages she gained.[57] Viewers who were interviewed in Houston after the speech regarded it as a "smash hit," claiming, "It was an inspiration to modern women," and "it was wonderful to hear a woman speak her mind, speak from her heart and soul and one who loves her husband. It was just such a pleasure to see her, to look at her face and to know what she was saying was genuine."[58]

Reactions to the speech were overwhelmingly, but not universally positive. Even though some viewers regarded her speech as natural and genuine, Helen Thorpe wrote that Dole's skills incited a backlash with some pundits who said she was too perfect and too scripted. Journalist Martha Brandt alleged that Dole began to memorize her convention speech a year before it was given and that she "choreographed every head toss and heel pivot."[59] Another journalist admitted: "Sure it was scripted, but it was exquisitely scripted,"[60] while Cheryl Lavin of the *Chicago Tribune* admired Dole for sticking to a script.[61]

More serious criticisms of Dole were raised, such as the question that perhaps she was "too good," and her performance upstaged her husband's. Steve Goldstein, writer for Knight-Ridder newspapers, discussed the difficulty Bob Dole's staff had in determining what role to give Elizabeth at the convention. There was a fear that she would draw attention away from him. During July, both Doles had appeared on the *Larry King Live* show and Elizabeth had finished some of Bob Dole's sentences, announced new campaign themes, and helped explain details of some of his programs.[62] Their fears may have been justified, because comments urging her to run for office began to surface after the convention speech. John Carlin of London's *Independent*, for example, wrote that Elizabeth "was so good, so dazzlingly in command of the medium which shapes U.S. electoral outcomes that viewers wondered why she was not running for president."[63] Even though she had extolled the virtues of her husband during her speech, her sheer competence, charisma, and qualifications all pointed back to her as a viable political candidate. Tom Brokaw said, "You can almost hear, if you listen carefully now, across the country in living rooms and bars, and wherever people watch this, folks are running to each other and saying 'Wow, why isn't she on the ticket?'"[64] And, of course, there was the question of whether the Doles came across as did the Clintons in 1992—as a "buy one, get one free" presidency.

In the aftermath of Elizabeth Dole's 1996 Republican National Convention speech and throughout the campaign, she and Hillary Clinton were widely covered in the press, mostly in ways that compared them. Hillary Clinton's speech at the Democratic National Convention on August 27—less than two weeks after Dole's—made the comparison inevitable. Journalists commented on the similarities between the two women, as well as their differences. Both women were described as smart and driven, both received law degrees from ivy league schools (Dole, Harvard; Clinton, Yale), both were elected presidents of their classes, both went to Washington, D.C., to begin their careers, both married ambitious men of modest means, both were raised in privileged circumstances by wealthy parents, both were faithful Methodists with an evangelical desire to improve the world,[65] and both were women's rights advocates. Given all the similarities, First Lady scholar Betty Boyd Caroli admitted there are "more similarities than differences between them."[66]

Journalists identified the most pronounced difference between Dole and Clinton to be one of style. John Carlin drew the contrast this way: "Mrs. Dole is 60 years old; Mrs. Clinton is 47. Mrs. Dole graduated from university in the 50s; Mrs. Clinton in the early 70s. During Mrs. Dole's formative years, women's liberation had not been invented; during Mrs. Clinton's, women were marching in the streets."[67] Getting ahead when Dole was coming-of-age meant being feminine, especially around men and not ruffling any feathers.[68] For Clinton, having grown up in the militant 60s, success meant speaking truth to power without wincing.[69] Republican Ann Stone put the point succinctly when she said: "Elizabeth is an iron fist in a velvet glove. Hillary is an iron fist—period."[70]

Without question, both Dole and Clinton are skillful, politically wise women and both have gone on to achieve independent careers of their own as U.S. senators. During the 1996 campaign, Dole was often questioned about aspirations and whether she would be content serving in the role of First Lady, given her experience in government service. Dole pledged to keep her position as president of the American Red Cross if her husband was elected president. Without trumpeting or fanfare, that would have made her the first First Lady to have a paid position outside of the White House, and it would have helped enormously to change perceptions about the role of women in the United States. When her husband lost the election, speculation about her running for the presidency surfaced. When questioned about the possibility, Dole said she had no plans of running, but wasn't going to rule it out either.[71] During a luncheon speech presented to nearly one thousand people to honor Republican women in elective office, she said, "Just looking around this room today, I'm sure that, in the very near future, the spouse of the nominee for president of the United States will enjoy his time here every bit as much as I have."[72] Comments such as this only spurred speculation about whether she would run for the presidency in 2000; already, a movement was started to "Draft Elizabeth Dole."[73] The speech she gave at the 1996 Republican National Convention may have done more to raise her credibility than her husband's.

THROWING HER HAT IN THE PRESIDENTIAL RING

Rumors of a bid by Elizabeth Dole for an elected political office began in the 1980s and persisted. During Campaign 1984 for the presidency, Bob Dole made a statement about the next election: "There are a lot of people around here talking about 1988," he said, "they're not talking about me, they're talking about Elizabeth." Her performance at the 1996 Republican National Convention and on the campaign trail stumping for her husband served to increase interest in her as a potential candidate. In January 1997, while speaking in Wisconsin to some of the most powerful business and political leaders in that state, Governor Tommy Thompson announced Dole by saying: "In the political arena, we haven't heard the last of the Doles. Only this time, I'm confident that Elizabeth Dole will be a candidate for the highest office in the land."[74] The prospect of an Elizabeth Dole presidential bid was kept alive by her husband, who told a journalist from *Newsday* that there are several capable women coming up through the ranks who could run for the presidency—in particular, his wife: "She is very bright and able . . . We all remember her convention . . . and campaign appearances"; and "the biggest applause I get right now is when I say, 'Well I have one more chance to get into the White House'. . . people go wild at the mention of Elizabeth."[75] Several weeks later, he was on *Meet the Press* and talked about Elizabeth's candidacy again: "I think she is a serious candidate, yes . . . Now whether she runs or not, she hasn't discussed it with me."[76] Elizabeth continued to deny her interest in the presidency, as she almost had to do, given the nonpartisan nature of the position she held as president of the American Red Cross. In a joint interview with the Doles on *CNN*'s "Late Edition," in December, once again she said she had no plans to run, and once again her husband said she was his last chance to get into the White House.[77]

During 1998, the question of whether she would run for the presidency followed her wherever she went. Early in the year, she presented two speeches on women and the economy, one in Alabama, the other in Utah. After both of her speeches, she was asked whether she would run for the presidency, and she answered that she had no plans to run. A seventy-year-old man stood up and requested that she enter the race because he did not like any of the other candidates. *Newsweek* ran a story in March reporting that Dole's "friends say her husband is encouraging her to run for president," and Governor George Voinovich of Ohio said she'd be "a very formidable candidate."[78] In late 1998, the D.C.-based Public Affairs Council polled thirty corporate spin-meisters on their guesses for the major parties' vice presidential nominees. Elizabeth Dole and then New Jersey governor Christine Whitman were named as likely running mates of George W. Bush.[79] This is just a sample of the press coverage she received on her potential candidacy. Yet, until the day she resigned as president of the American Red Cross in January 1999, she was often quoted as saying "I have no plans to run" whenever the inevitable inquiry into her own political aspirations was made.

When Elizabeth Dole stepped down as American Red Cross president on January 4, the press speculated about her motives. Her announcement was broadcast live on *CNN* and *C-SPAN*, and the story was covered widely on *ABC*, *CBS*, and *NBC* evening news programs. Such media attention signaled to viewers that her announcement meant something more than simple a resignation from a humanitarian organization. In *Lessons from the Top*, Thomas J. Neff and James M. Citrin described Dole's savvy media event as a shrewd political maneuver: "She turned a potentially mundane event—the resignation of an organization's CEO—into a veritable pep rally, where she was repeatedly praised for her leadership, vision, and impact on the country. She also picked a slow news day to announce she was leaving, guaranteeing substantial press coverage."[80]

Speaking to about five hundred Red Cross staff members gathered in the historic Red Cross building along the Ellipse in Washington, D.C., as well as to countless television viewers, Elizabeth Dole appeared at the podium in a watermelon red tailored suit to bid farewell and to hint at her possible entry into presidential politics. She greeted her audience warmly: "Good afternoon, everyone! And to those of you who are visitors, welcome to the American Red Cross and Happy New Year to you all!" With this cheerful salutation, Dole indicated that her speech would be upbeat. After patriotic remarks about the greatness of America, she continued her speech by getting her immediate audience involved: "I'd like to start out the New Year by asking you to join me in giving all of you a well-deserved pat on the back and a big round of applause. Shall we? [Clapping begins.] This is for you. [Sustained applause.] What a team! What a great team!" Dole recounted all they had been through together in the years she was president and summarized what they were able to accomplish under her leadership. She said the organization was now "as solid as a rock," and noted how important the position had been to her: "The Red Cross has been a glorious mission field." She told them she might have "other duties left to fulfill," subtly suggesting a future of political leadership, although she also noted that she "had not made definite plans about what I would do next."

Dole's speech was covered extensively in the press. *CNN*'s "Inside Politics" gave her the "Political Play of the Week Award." *Newsweek* reported on January 18, 1999, that "Elizabeth Dole may soon establish a campaign committee." Ralph Reed, former Christian Coalition head said that she "could be a very formidable candidate if she emphasized her North Carolina bible-belt roots."[81] When she officially announced her plans to make an exploratory bid for the presidency in mid-March 1999, she became the first woman in more than twenty years to make a serious bid for the U.S. presidency. Until she withdrew from the race in October 1999, she consistently ran second in the polls to George W. Bush and well ahead of John McCain, Steve Forbes, Gary Bauer, and Alan Keyes.[82] In the August Iowa Straw Poll, she placed third, behind George W. Bush and Steve Forbes.[83] Her campaign seemed to be picking up steam, and in a letter to supporters, Dole wrote: "Without question, my strong showing in Iowa was a big breakthrough for us. It proved we can win."[84] She gave numerous speeches on important issues such as rebuilding the U.S. military, gun control, and education reform.

Dole spoke at the U.S. Naval Academy on April 14, 1999, to an audience of midshipmen and others. This speech was a significant one for her because the presumption against a woman candidate is that she will not know much about foreign policy and the military. Dole demonstrated her firsthand knowledge of hotbed areas around the world from her experience in the Red Cross when she worked with the military to send supplies to victims of violence in Africa, the Middle East, and Eastern Europe. She acknowledged global areas of crises and discussed as well the threat from computer viruses to military operations. She insisted that "missile defense is an absolute requirement" and pledged to "make the investment we need to bring an effective system into reality." The next day, an article in the *New York Times* praised Dole's directness, saying the speech "allowed her to show that a woman can talk tough on military matters."[85]

Dole addressed the issue of education in a campaign speech at Melrose High School on September 22, 1999, where she had taught history to eleventh graders while earning a master's degree in education and government at Harvard University. In this speech, which was extensively covered by the press, Dole told her audience that American schools were once great, and they can be great again. Showing her audience a huge stack of papers to represent bureaucracy, she said she would ease federal regulations and she outlined a three-point plan—her "three R's" for improving American Schools: "Return, Restore and Reinforce." She said: "First, return control to states and local school districts. Second, restore discipline in the classroom and respect for teachers. Third, reinforce parents' control of their child's education."[86] Because Dole recommended locker searches and drug testing with parents' permission, the *Boston Globe* reported that she had selected a "sentimental setting" to offer "an unsentimental prescription" for healing "what ails education."[87]

Elizabeth Dole appealed to many women as she spoke across the United States on the campaign trail. An article in the *Washington Post* commented on her attractiveness as a presidential candidate: "The audiences are overwhelmingly female: younger women, older women, women with babies, women with husbands, women who are Republican Party veterans and women who have never participated in the political process before."[88] Unfortunately for Dole, even though women have enormous voting power, they have not yet realized that power by voting as a block. In a *Newsweek* article, Howard Fineman made a telling statement: "As female clout raises, female candidates aren't automatically raising as well. Older women, pollsters say, distrust other women as executives; young women tend to be turned off by 'I Am Woman' appeals to feminine solidarity."[89] And many women who call themselves feminists will not support any candidate—male or female—who is not pro-choice. The National Organization of Women did not support Dole's presidential candidacy in 1999 because of her pro-life position.[90]

Elizabeth Dole's chances of being the first female president dwindled as did her campaign funds. Press reports began to emerge suggesting that she would make an attractive vice presidential running mate for George W. Bush, who seemed financially and, by the polls, virtually guaranteed the Republican presidential nomination. On October 20, 1999, Dole withdrew from the race, stating her reasons heroically: "All my life, I have been accustomed to challenging the odds," she said, but the depletion of her resources made the odds "overwhelming."[91] With this statement, Elizabeth Dole left the presidential stage. A *New York Times* article reported that her supporters started a petition to make her the Republican Party's vice presidential nominee,[92] but that did not happen for her either. The vice presidential nomination went to longtime Republican politico, Dick Cheney, who served in the first Bush administration. Nonetheless, faithful to the party, Dole accepted the invitation to speak at the 2000 Republican National Convention in support of the Bush/Cheney ticket.

During this speech, Dole acted as a senior spokeswoman for the Republican Party. She spoke after Condoleezza Rice, who would be named Bush's national security advisor after his election. Also speaking that evening was her husband, Bob Dole, who presented a tearful tribute to America's veterans. Elizabeth appeared before the audience in a jubilant mood, and she was well received by the audience. Dressed in a light green fitted suit, smiling broadly, she began: "Thank you very much. You have heard Condoleezza Rice speak eloquently of America's place in the world. I, too, wish to address our nation's security tonight. I speak not of military weapons, but of moral ones, of the defense of values as well as territory."[93] Dole's speech was a moral one, reminding her audience of how much Americans value freedom and how important it is for American leaders to herald peace around the world. "I learned long ago that you don't have to be a missionary to be filled with a sense of mission," she said, "The 20th century was America's century—not because of our power, but because of our purpose. Today, millions of Americans—of both parties and of no party—are seeking a politics of purpose."[94] And with her mention of "purpose," Dole emphasized why George W. Bush represented the moral choice for president. How different this speech was from her speech supporting her husband's bid for the presidency four years earlier.

ELIZABETH DOLE'S SENATE BID—YOU *CAN* GO HOME AGAIN

In 2002, Elizabeth Dole announced her candidacy for a U.S. Senate seat from her home state of North Carolina. Legendary American author Thomas Wolfe may have immortalized the phrase "you can't go home again," but Elizabeth Dole didn't heed the warning. When five-term Republican senator Jesse Helms decided not to seek a sixth term, there was strong Republican support for Elizabeth Dole to run. She decided to enter the race, and set about proving her deep-seated ties to her home state, even though she had lived in Washington, D.C., since the 1960s. She said in an interview, "Washington is where I've gone to work. My home is in North Carolina."[95] Indeed, Dole had been affirming her North Carolina roots in dozens of speeches given throughout those years. Senator Jesse Helms helped to legitimize her candidacy when he praised her highly.

During her campaign, Dole criss-crossed the state of North Carolina, talking to constituents about issues important to them. Wherever she went, she reminded her audiences of her experience in government positions. On July 19, 1999, she presented the "Dole Plan,"[96] which detailed her goals for improving life for the people of her state. Financial concerns were critically important. "North Carolina's economy is going through a transition," she wrote in her campaign literature and posted on her Web site. "A lot of people have lost their jobs, or they're worried about losing their jobs. Textile workers have really suffered during the last recession. We've got to open up foreign markets."[97] Other areas targeted in her campaign speeches and literature included tax relief, fiscal responsibility, global markets, rural renewal, tobacco quota buyouts, and more.

Dole presented her message in many venues. Even though she had been accused of being scripted during her run for the presidency, most of her campaign speeches for the Senate were delivered impromptu, and she altered what she said depending on circumstances, sometimes even last-minute changes of plan.[98] What she stressed in all of her speeches was her family, her faith, and her commitment to her constituents. A rare campaign speech text from this race makes her identification with her fellow North Carolinians clear: "Let's face it, folks, North Carolina's economy is going through a painful transition. There's no getting around it. We find ourselves under assault by a recession, a downturn that spares few, if any, sectors in the state's economy. Many are hurting, and many need help. They live in the small towns, on the farms and even in the shade of those glorious buildings that rise to the sky in Charlotte and Raleigh."[99] She employed a conversational style in her speeches, speaking with warmth and friendliness. Her tone was tougher during her television debate with her opponent, Democrat Erskine Bowles, former chief of staff in the Clinton White House. From the first question asked of her, Dole promised to work on the issues. "I'm results oriented," she said, and interested in "working across the aisle."

President George W. Bush visited North Carolina five times during Dole's run for the Senate, speaking heartily on her behalf. First Lady Laura Bush also traveled to North Carolina right before election day. She told an audience of twelve hundred, the majority of whom were women, that President Bush wanted her to send greetings and tell them that "as soon as you leave this rally, get back to work to elect Elizabeth Dole your next senator." Vice President Dick Cheney visited twice, as did other well-known Republicans such as Senator Kay Bailey Hutchinson of Texas and Rudy Giuliani, former mayor of New York.[100]

On November 5, 2002, Elizabeth Dole became the first woman ever to win a Senate seat from North Carolina. Flanked onstage by her husband, she joyfully addressed an exuberant crowd that had gathered election night in her hometown of Salisbury, North Carolina. "Oh, wow, what a night! I'm so proud to be a North Carolinian! I'm just as thrilled as you are! We'll never forget this night, will we?" Gracious in victory, as she had been two years before when her bid for the presidency was defeated, Dole reached out to voters who had cast their ballots for her opponent: "A few moments ago I got a call from Erskine Bowles, he congratulated me on my victory and he was very gracious. He obviously cares very much about the people of North Carolina and I want to say to those who voted for Erskine Bowles, give me a chance. I intend to be a senator for all of North

Carolina!"[101] The theme song from the movie *Rocky III* played in the background as the crowd stomped and cheered.

With this win, Elizabeth Dole demonstrated the value of the lifelong lesson she had learned years before, when she failed to get a position at the *Charlotte Observer*. In her words: "If you couldn't or wouldn't make the case for why you should get the job, you could hardly expect a prospective boss to make it for you."[102] Throughout the years, Dole learned to make the case for the passage of policies and the election of candidates, including her husband and herself. Her passion for what she believed propelled her to become an eloquent and versatile advocate. From examining her speeches, it is evident that she has learned to use the art of rhetoric in service of the multiple goals she has set for herself.

Chapter 6

Conclusion: A Leader "A Long Way from the Twilight"[1]

Why not dispense with labels altogether? After all, what is a label but a preconception brought to life, a marketing tool that blurs your identity and judges you by the car you drive, the jeans you wear or the CDs that you buy? In such a culture, we don't know people—we categorize them. Replacing subtlety with stereotype, we rob citizens of their most precious possession—their individuality. In any event, America needs leaders, not labels.[2]

This study of Elizabeth Dole's rhetoric might be summed up with a proposal to "dispense with labels," as she suggests in a speech given at her alma mater, Duke University, in May 2000. When Dole uttered this passage, she was fresh from withdrawing her bid for the U.S. presidency, and she was ready for new challenges. During the campaign, commentators and pundits had labeled her pejoratively as a "perfectionist" and caricatured her as "rigidly scripted," when they just as easily could have called her a "true professional" for her carefully prepared and rehearsed speeches. Perhaps Dole had learned a lesson, too, from being married to a man whose verbal style had sometimes been labeled as "shooting from the hip." Her call to remove the labels during her speech at Duke must have been issued from nothing other than wisdom born from experience. For if there is one call to action that is needed for any woman to have her voice heard, it is the removal of labels that can function to silence her.

Four years earlier, on August 14, 1996, Elizabeth Dole was invited to be the guest speaker at the San Diego Sports Center at a ceremony honoring a number of women who had triumphed over adversity. As they were introduced onstage, she handed them red Bibles and congratulated

Portait of Elizabeth Dole as United States Senator. (Photo
courtesy of Elizabeth Dole)

them for their ability to define themselves by taking control of their own
lives.[3] Rather than a general call to remove stereotypes or labels as she
had given the graduating seniors at Duke University, Dole presented these
honored women with specific suggestions to help them continue developing practical skills to become successful individuals. She told them the
secret of success was "preparation"; it was being ready to seize opportunities when they arise. "It is very important to be prepared and to know
what your strategy is going to be," she said. She also stressed the kind of
individuality that allows a person to make choices that are right for her:
"If we don't march to our own tune," she told them, "we'll be marching
to someone else's."[4] Later that same day, Dole presented her "spouse
speech," widely praised with superlatives, at the Republican National
Convention in support of her husband's nomination for the presidency.

These two speeches given the same day bring forward themes important in our study of Elizabeth Dole as a rhetorician.

Elizabeth Dole's career in public life has been one of providing leadership to others through her wise and inspirational words. Through her eloquent oratory, she has forged an impressive, history-making career at a time when women in America are still lobbying to expand their sphere of influence. As a role model, the message she gives women is to be prepared to say "yes" to opportunities by getting a good education, gaining as much experience as possible in positions of increasing responsibility, learning to use your voice in the service of others and yourself, and above all else, exercising your individual right to make your own choices and decisions.

THE IMPACT OF STUDYING ELIZABETH DOLE'S CAREER AS A SPOKESWOMAN

The study of Elizabeth Dole's career as a highly visible spokeswoman is vital to an understanding of the position of contemporary American women who choose to engage in public service through politics. Probably more so than any other woman on the national stage today, Dole's career accentuates the choices female politicians must often make and the shifts of role they experience. As speechwriter Kerry Tymchuk notes in the foreword of this book, Elizabeth Dole has had many firsts for women in America. She has been the first woman to hold cabinet posts in two different presidential administrations, the first Republican woman in more than thirty years[5] to run for the presidential nomination, and the first woman elected as a U.S. senator from her home state of North Carolina. Her service in these positions has helped American women hit the critical mass necessary to desensitize the public to the new roles women do and will continue to play in the political arena.

At the same time that Elizabeth Dole has paved the way for other women, she has experienced many transitions in her own career. Very eloquently and with rhetorical distinction, she has changed roles from being a political appointee to the spouse of a presidential candidate. She has shifted from the role of a campaigning spouse to that of a presidential candidate in her own right. With her successful run for a U.S. Senate seat from North Carolina, she has shifted her role once again to that of an elected official. All of these shifts demonstrate her rhetorical agility. She has proved that a woman can serve as an effective surrogate for her husband as well as a leader in her own right. During the 1996 campaign, journalist Elizabeth Bumiller highlighted the many sides of Elizabeth Dole when she said: "Mrs. Dole represents the last gasp of the traditional First

Lady, ratcheted up to running mate, and a bridge . . . to a day when America will have a woman in the White House."[6] Moderator Kathleen Hall Jamieson, dean of the Annenberg School of Communication at the University of Pennsylvania, echoed these sentiments at a forum when she lamented Dole's departure from the presidential race before she had an opportunity to participate in the debates. According to Jamieson, the case for a woman president would have been strengthened if Dole had participated because she "would have looked like she belonged there."[7]

What strikes many people when they hear Elizabeth Dole speak or meet her in person is her gracious Southern persona. While a thoroughly modern woman, in some ways she seems like a person from another, more refined era, with her highly cultivated social skills and her projected moral character. Her youthful exuberance belies her age, making it difficult for those who meet her to comprehend the scope of her career. She further confuses those who wish to compartmentalize her because she is utterly feminine, yet powerful; beautiful, yet intelligent; well rehearsed, yet spontaneous; serious, yet good-humored. She has publicly played out the tensions that many career women face—whether to pursue her own aspirations or promote her husband's. She is unique in that she has left vital government appointments to help her husband campaign for the presidency. While feminists saw her leaves of absence and resignations as career interruptions and sacrifices, Dole saw them as matters of personal choice. She chose to help her husband, because she knew she would be an asset to his campaigns and because she believed he would make an excellent president. And by campaigning so ardently for him, she knew she would gain valuable speaking experience and public visibility that would help her launch independent campaigns for elective office of her own. Distinguishing *herself* while campaigning for her husband has led to her run for the U.S. presidency in 2000, and her election as a U.S. senator in 2002. She has demonstrated well an ability to serve more than one purpose in her speeches, a phenomenon we have coined "rhetorical multitasking." This is one of the most important features of her speech and one of the most useful lessons others can learn from her.

When Dole withdrew from the presidential race, the statement she made noted how much her campaign had contributed to the day when there will be a woman elected president of the United States: "In terms of women and their views of my withdrawing from the race right now, I think that what we have done is paved the way for the person who will be the first woman president, and I'm just delighted at what just happened because I feel like we have really made a giant contribution."[8] Authors

Eleanor Clift and Tom Brazaitis corroborate Dole's assessment in their book *Madame President,* where they report how much Dole's bid for the presidency did to spur on other women, especially Hillary Rodham Clinton. Clinton's interest in running for a Senate seat from New York surged after Dole stepped down from the presidency of the Red Cross in January 1999 to launch her exploratory committee for the presidency. Apparently, according to the authors, that accelerated Clinton's interest in getting herself in the public eye. "'She'd love to be the first [woman president],' one of her aides said."[9]

Indeed, Dole's "failed" presidential run was a great victory for the women's movement. As this book is going to press, there is much banter in the media about the 2008 election and the possibility that Hillary Clinton will run for the Democratic presidential nomination if John Kerry loses the 2004 election. If Elizabeth Dole owed a gratitude to Hillary Clinton for being the first "spouse turned senator" then, should Hillary Clinton make a White House bid, she would in turn owe Elizabeth Dole deep gratitude for bearing the burden of being the first woman presidential candidate in twenty years to poll well and to be taken seriously by the press and the public. And both are paving the way for other women who will run for offices in the future. Dole put the point well when she commented on the criticism she received: "If you are going to be in the forefront of a revolution, you have to keep taking the flak until it's won."[10]

Women's groups and other organizations have recognized Dole's contributions and given her numerous awards, ranging from honors for civil service and leadership in government to accolades for her charitable commitments and dedication to women in the workplace.[11] She has been recognized by the media, being named in 1996, the top news maker by *Newsweek,* one of the ten most fascinating people by Barbara Walters, and the most inspiring political figure by *MSNBC.* In 1997, *Glamour* named her "Woman of the Year," while in 1998, *Good Housekeeping* designated her one of the ten most admired women and the *Gallup Poll* designated her one of the world's top three most admired women. Throughout her career, she has also received honorary doctorate degrees from forty colleges and universities. All of these awards and recognitions are a testament to the effectiveness of her oratory in her political and humanitarian service to others. Dole has advanced the cause of American women at the same time that she has contributed to the quality of life for the American public. She has advocated for the public good, spoken out for morality and patriotism, promoted the rights of women and minorities, and engaged actively in the political process.

AN ADVOCATE FOR AN "AMERICA WE CAN BE"[12]

Throughout this book, we have seen how Elizabeth Dole advocated for the public good, beginning with her early work in Washington, D.C., when she was a consumer advocate. As secretary of transportation, she focused on the safety of the traveling public in the air, on the highways, on the rails, and on the seas through the Coast Guard. Her work with the Federal Aviation Administration (FAA) culminated in "white glove inspections," affecting more than 370 separate airlines. As a result of her leadership, the entire FAA received a major overhaul. On the highways, Dole achieved the addition of a rear brake light to automobiles, adding to a driver's ability to see the brake on the car in front of her. Airbags and mandatory seat belt laws were also targeted during Dole's tenure. When she served as secretary of labor, Dole made sure that the least privileged in our society, such as the homeless and at-risk youth, would have an opportunity to obtain skills that could help them become contributors. She mediated to end a bitter coal strike in Pittston, West Virginia. She initiated an important study of the "glass ceiling," which continued after she left office under the direction of Lynn Martin and Bob Dole, who introduced legislation into the Senate. The mantra "everybody counts" became her special focus. As American Red Cross president, Dole raised funds with a missionary's zeal for critically important projects. She began her term as president at a difficult time, when the AIDS epidemic was in full swing, when there were a record number of natural disasters, and when resources were needed to support soldiers and victims in the Persian Gulf. She raised $46 million for the American Red Cross,[13] and used the money to modernize the U.S. blood collection and distribution procedures, to replenish the disaster relief reserves, and for other purposes such as instituting a national disaster control center and for international humanitarian aid. Dole held the position of Red Cross president longer than any of her other positions. The Red Cross was a mission field for her, and the work she did there rang most true to her nature—to make a difference in the world. In this position, she was also her "mother's daughter"; Mary Hanford had said about her own work for the American Red Cross, "nothing I ever did made me feel as important."[14]

ADVOCATING FOR HER RELIGIOUS CONVICTIONS

"Like azaleas in the spring"[15] is how natural Elizabeth Dole's faith came to her in her life. She attributes her foundation of faith to her North Carolina upbringing, when her grandmother, "Mom Cathey," read the Bible to Elizabeth and her friends. She learned how to put her faith into action by following her father's practices as a landlord and from her mother's volunteerism. Mary Hanford died recently at the age of 102, just as this book was being completed. She was eulogized by Elizabeth and her brother, John Hanford of Charlotte, in a family statement: "Throughout her life, Mother provided us with an example of what it means to live every day of your life with grace, dignity, generosity, and spiritual strength, and what it means to love a community and to work tirelessly to make it a better place."[16]

Elizabeth Dole's faithful service to others is evident by the career choices she made, beginning with what was a unique decision for a young woman to make at the time—to enter government service. Choosing to serve others instead of simply making a living indicates the level of purpose Dole wanted in her life. She wanted her work to be a mission field so that she could help make life better for others. She felt blessed, and wanted to be a blessing. The theme that connects her faith to her work is her dedication to the well-being of others as she moved from ever-widening positions serving her country and beyond its borders.

Even her early career moves—organizing a conference for the deaf, working as a public defender and a consumer advocate—demonstrate her desire to put her faith into action by giving back some of the blessings she had been given. Her work at the Federal Trade Commission focused on educating consumers about food contents so they could make healthier choices. Once again, she was devoted to making a positive difference through her work.

As secretary of transportation, Dole recognized that lives could be saved by policy initiatives. She was guided by her insight of how difficult it would be to look a family member in the eye if she knew the agencies under her leadership had not done everything possible to prevent accidents. She also worked tirelessly on preventing drunk driving by advocating a zero-tolerance policy. She knew how devastating accidents can be because of the loss of her uncle to a drunk driver, as well as the injuries she suffered, severe enough to hospitalize her for a month.

Her career choices were also motivated by the constant renewal of her faith. When she was transportation secretary, Dole presented her Queen Esther speech at a National Prayer Breakfast and shared her identification with the biblical heroine with her audience. She described how she had reordered her priorities to make faith the center of her life. For a public person to make such an intimate declaration of faith in front of so many political leaders was a bold rhetorical move. Imagine the intimate atmosphere Dole created when she disclosed: "I consider it one of the greatest possible privileges to be invited to share this morning with fellow travelers a little of my own spiritual journey. . . . I am grateful that members of the congressional prayer groups have asked me to speak from the heart about the difference Jesus Christ has made in my life."[17] She presented the Queen Esther speech many times during her career, promoting her well-deserved reputation as a person of deep religious commitment. Without fail, Dole daily renews her faith by spending at least thirty minutes in devotional time, often by reading her most cherished Bible from "Mom Cathey."

Everything Elizabeth Dole did as president of the American Red Cross stemmed from her core faith. She traveled extensively across the United States and abroad, often to places desperate for humanitarian aid from natural and man-made disasters. Her work as leader of the American Red Cross could be seen as her effort to mother those in need, to wrap protective arms around the most vulnerable by delivering nourishing food, warm blankets, and lifesaving medications. As American Red Cross president, she expressed such sentiments, facing squarely Mother Nature's power: "no matter how fast the winds may blow, or how high the water may rise, the Red Cross has always weathered out the storm providing food, clothing, money, shelter, and hope."[18] The Red Cross staff and army of volunteers stood ready under Dole's leadership to help those who needed it.

THIRTY PLUS YEARS WORKING FOR WOMEN'S RIGHTS

Even though Elizabeth Dole does not label herself a feminist, she has said: "The key to happiness for a woman is to be able to stand on her own two feet and become a person in her own right."[19] Avoiding the label while simultaneously rolling up her sleeves to help women by promoting legislative actions renders meaningful the title Bob Dole once gave her, a "sensible feminist." At a time when the label "Old Maid" was applied to any woman not married by the age of thirty, she waited until she was thirty-nine to marry, retaining her own name until "Dole" gradually replaced "Hanford" during her tenure as secretary of labor. More than any single initiative pursued during her career, Elizabeth Dole's life serves as the best testament to her commitment to equal rights. She took the challenging road to Harvard Law School and a thoroughly untraditional career path, even though her life at home was comfortable, even privileged. She could have done nothing and lived very well. But that simply wasn't and isn't Elizabeth Dole.

Dole worked to protect consumers when she served on the President's Committee on Consumer Interests, championing the Equal Opportunity Credit Act that guaranteed women access to credit, even when their spouses die or when they divorce. She was the first woman appointed to serve in the Reagan administration, heading the White House Office of Public Liaison. Because of her commitment to make life better for women, she was named head of the White House Coordinating Council on Women, helping Reagan honor his campaign promises to women. As the first woman ever to serve as secretary of transportation, she helped boost the DOT's female and minority workforce.

One of the reasons Dole accepted the secretary of labor position was to advocate for the rights of women and minorities in the workforce. Issues such as child care, minimum wage, and family leave time became central focuses under her leadership. As labor secretary, Dole investigated the "glass ceiling" phenomenon and called national attention to the low numbers of women and minorities in top management positions. She appointed women and minorities to serve in half of the senior staff positions at the Labor Department, and continued to hire them when she became president of the American Red Cross, the first woman since Clara Barton appointed to the post.

BLAZING THE CAMPAIGN TRAIL

Elizabeth Dole traversed the campaign trail in the United States for nearly thirty years, speaking passionately for the election of her husband, other Republican candidates, and herself. She did "do issues," learning to speak forcefully in support of them by using stories and statistics to rally her audiences. Her training as an advocate began early, when she campaigned against the provincial choices other young women were making in Salisbury, North Carolina. Not wanting to marry early, she surprised her family by choosing to earn a law degree from Harvard and afterward to work in government service on the national level. Dole was well qualified for her first position at Health, Education, and Welfare; nonetheless, she still had to make a case for why she should be hired. Her desire to make it happen and her perseverance helped launch her career when no one in the nation's capital knew her. Her determination, hard work, and sense of mission for the work she was doing helped Dole become enormously successful. Her early supervisors recognized her dedication and talent, giving her more responsibility. Even without a blueprint for her future, she was poised to make important contributions as opportunities for increasingly powerful positions presented themselves. Her desire to live a meaningful life, consistent with her core values, guided her choices among the alternatives.

Dole had little experience as a political campaigner during the 1970s, just her volunteer work one summer to help Lyndon B. Johnson win the vice presidency. Her marriage in 1975, however, changed all of that. Eight months later, she was on the campaign trail, persuading constituents first to vote for her husband and then to vote for the Ford/Dole ticket. As the wife of Bob Dole, she would campaign for his election to the presidency over the next twenty years. She was congenial and effortlessly inoffensive, while her husband gained a reputation for sarcasm and never felt fully at ease in front of cameras. She became his speech advisor, toning down his biting humor, encouraging him to smile and to practice his speeches. Elizabeth was only telling him what she knew to be effective for her. He admitted that his experience in the Senate may have fostered bad habits: "the old story in the Congress is that you only give a speech once, and that is when you read it for the first time. That's why we're not any good." He said during a recent interview, "You don't hear any good speeches in the Senate anymore, and that is because we're reading them."[20]

Elizabeth Dole's careful preparation through months of campaigning for her husband's bid for the presidency in 1996, culminated in her Republican National Convention speech that won superlatives from the media such as "fabulous" from Cokie Roberts, "flawless" from Maria Shriver,[21] and "by anyone's standards a tremendous performance"[22] from Dan Rather. Turning her attention to her own presidential bid in 1999, she used her skills as a campaigner to raise money and speak on issues. What she achieved as a role model for women, especially women speakers on a national stage, cannot be denied. In her own voice, she demonstrated the possibilities of leadership to woman and young girls alike.

Dole was successful in winning a U.S. Senate seat from North Carolina, during her campaign in 2002. When she announced her candidacy, she highlighted her experience as secretary of transportation and labor, and as president of the American Red Cross. She spoke eloquently about Ground Zero, emphasizing her faith: "Since September 11," she said, "we have experienced a sense of universal fraternity—love of country, love of community, love of neighbor."[23] Dole encouraged her fellow senators to apply that love to help others during her Maiden Senate speech on June 5, 2003. Given on "National Hunger Awareness Day," Dole campaigned for government action to help feed the poor: "Mr. President, in my lifetime, I have seen Americans split the atom, abolish Jim Crow, eliminate the scourge of polio, win the Cold War, plant our flag on the surface of the moon, map the human genetic code and belatedly recognize the talents of women, minorities, the disabled and others once relegated to the shadows."[24] Now is the time, she told them, to wipe out hunger.

RHETORICAL TRAITS OF ELIZABETH HANFORD DOLE

This treatment of Elizabeth Dole as a public spokeswoman would not be complete without a final analysis of the rhetorical features that make her so successful with contemporary audiences. Every generation has to define the characteristics of effective oral presentation for itself. The traits that make Elizabeth Dole popular with audiences and valuable as a spokeswoman include her use of novel nonverbal and verbal actions, her shrewd use of the media, her combination of traditional femininity and power, her commitment to hard work and preparation, and her ability to accomplish more than one task when she speaks—what we have termed "rhetorical multitasking."

Elizabeth Dole's speeches demonstrate the use of novelty to gain the attention and to hold the interest of her audience. For example, she knew she would gain attention nonverbally when she descended the steps in high heels at the 1996 Republican National Convention. She also knew she would hold the audience's attention as she circulated around the room. She admitted as much during an interview:

> The first thing that I considered about the convention was that everyone is talking on the floor. How do you keep the audience quiet? But when the audience saw me descend the podium by walking down twelve steps in heels, it caught everyone by surprise. . . . they all got quiet. They hadn't seen this before. They all wondered 'what is she doing'? And because of that, they were more attentive and cooperative as I walked around the room.[25]

The stories Dole told and the witnesses she visited in the audience all helped to make her speech what Tom Brokaw called a "gold-medal performance."[26] About the speech, Bob Dole said during a recent interview: she "hit a homerun."[27] Dole also used props effectively such as the stack of papers she held up during her speech at Melrose High School in 1999, demonstrating how much bureaucracy interferes with a community's task of educating its students. Her use of stories contributes to the novelty of virtually every one of her speeches.

Elizabeth Dole has also demonstrated a great deal of media savvy, especially in an age of television, which puts a premium on the visual impact of the speaker. With her attractive appearance, her animated delivery, and her brightly colored suits of watermelon red, daffodil yellow, and bright green, Dole makes as much of a visual impact as a verbal impact. In addition, her timing of media events has helped her gain wide exposure for her messages. She has displayed an uncanny sense of public relations, probably developed from many of the positions she has held over the years. When she was president of the American Red Cross, for example, she traveled to disaster zones, inviting the media to interview her on location. Surrounded by devastation visible to her listeners, she would appeal for donations and other help for the victims. This was an effective fund-raising technique, and when Dole resigned from the Red Cross, she left their disaster relief fund in the black. The resignation, too, proved a tremendously successful media event. Thanks to a well-planned "leak" about Dole's future political plans, the media sent camera crews to record her farewell; they hoped to hear her announce her decision to run for the U.S. presidency. Instead, they learned how rock solid the American Red Cross had become, including a list of all that the organization had accomplished during her eight years as their president. Without question, this event alone proved her to be a savvy politician.

Dole's femininity has also been an important component of her appeal as a public speaker and it reverberates on different levels. Her self-presentation exudes a Southern graciousness of voice and manner, making her an attractive model as a public speaker, especially for women who want to retain their femininity as they vie for political office. Doing so is not easy, say scholars Eleanor Clift and Tom Brazaitis; often, femininity is "the price tag" women pay as they enter public life.[28] Dole has not forsaken her traditional feminine style; instead, she uses it, for example, in the way she dresses and how she moves around audiences like a hostess at a party. Her femininity has also come into play in carrying out official duties, such as when she helped mediate a settlement between the United Mine Workers Union and the Pittston Coal Company. Her ability to favor "consensus over confrontation," is clear as well from the slogan Dole used in her campaign literature during her run for the presidency. In speeches, she has praised the conciliatory skills of women, saying that women can choose to be more like women once we have equal rights. Thus, not only does Dole engage in feminine speech and manner, she admires women's traits, regards them as effective, and chooses to perform them.

Dole's penchant for preparation has been a much-discussed feature of her public speech. She prefers not to leave her words to chance, and when she is hired to present a speech, the organization can be assured of a well-prepared presentation tailored to the specific occasion. She has formed close working relationships with her speechwriters, who have learned to write in her voice, though she discusses with them what she wants to say in her speeches and is a careful editor when she gets the drafts. Dole rehearses her speeches as well, and she likes to stick to a script. But the criticism she received during her run for the presidency for being overly scripted is surely an exaggeration and shows how uninformed some pundits can be about the reality of campaigning. A good example is Dole's 1996 Republican National Convention speech, which some commentators faulted because they said she had it memorized. Before she spoke, Dole did say, "I have my speech in my head,"[29] but how could it be otherwise? Imagine campaigning all those prior months and not having your speech in your head. In the weeks after the convention, Dole covered as much ground as she could, presenting her fifty-minute speech about her husband's achievements and character at twenty to thirty events a week.[30] Her activity before the convention must have been nearly as hectic. The surprising part may not be how scripted Dole sounded, but how she managed to sound spontaneous about material she could probably recite in her sleep.

Elizabeth Dole's beliefs, her work, and her words are closely interwoven, and what emerges from our study of her speeches and rhetorical actions is her determination to make her life's work meaningful. She has paid attention to how she presented herself, and developed her skills in front of audiences. Although she has asked her Duke University audience to "dispense with labels,"[31] we think her penchant for multitasking helps her to defy them. She has gained a reputation for speeches that are exceptionally well crafted and delivered, while at the same time presenting her positions on policy, which emanate from her deeply rooted commitment to religious fundamentals. She is a deeply patriotic woman who believes in God and country, often quoting from the Bible: "We have been blessed to be a blessing . . . we have received that we might give." This line describes the course of her life, and shows what a person can do when she uses all her skills and her voice in the service of her heart. In the process of being a blessing, Elizabeth Hanford Dole has built a reputation for herself as a public speaker worth studying—and a national leader worth our deepest respect.

Appendix: Dole's Speeches

Elizabeth Dole gave the following speeches when she served the public in Washington, D.C., both in appointed positions in national government and as president of the American Red Cross. Also included are speeches from her run for the U.S. presidency and for a U.S. Senate seat from her home state of North Carolina. Taken together, they demonstrate how Dole adapted her messages to different situations, audiences, and purposes. Her characteristics discussed in the introduction and demonstrated throughout this book are evident in these speeches. We have provided brief notes before each speech to indicate where and when it was given. In many of her speeches, she speaks with more than one purpose, a phenomenon we have called "rhetorical multitasking." We recommend this efficient use of time and words as an effective model for women leaders who can appeal simultaneously to more than one audience and advance more than one purpose when they speak. Several of the following speech texts are difficult to locate and we have included them for use by the scholarly community. They are included with Elizabeth Dole's permission, and we would like to acknowledge her great generosity in making them available.

NATIONAL PRAYER BREAKFAST SPEECH
Washington, D.C., February 5, 1987

The National Prayer Breakfast Organization annually selects a well-known Christian to serve as a keynote speaker for its renowned prayer breakfast. Elizabeth Dole happily accepted the invitation to acknowledge the place of faith in her life. She was secretary of transportation when this speech was given, and a

well-known Republican, the only woman serving in the cabinet of President
Ronald Reagan at the time. In the speech, Dole talks about the central place of
faith in her life. The authors received this text from Elizabeth Dole.

I consider it one of the greatest possible privileges to be invited to share
this morning with fellow travelers a little of my own spiritual journey. Like
most of us, I'm just one person struggling to relate faith to life. . . . but I
am grateful that members of the congressional prayer groups have asked
me to speak from the heart, about the difference Jesus Christ has made
in my life.

But first, I must mention a political crisis. . . . a crisis from which I have
learned some very important lessons.

Now, this is a political crisis involving high stakes, intrigue, behind-
the-scenes negotiations, influence in high places, and even an element of
romance.

Where have I learned of this crisis? On the front page of the newspapers?

No. The newspapers haven't carried this story.

No, the political crisis I'm talking about occurred around 2,450 years
ago.

And we learn about it . . . in the bible . . . in the book of Esther.

Esther is the saga of a woman forced to make a decision concerning the
total commitment of her life—a decision she was reluctant to make. She
had to be vigorously challenged, and it's this part of her story to which I
can so easily relate in my own spiritual journey. For while the particulars
of her challenge may differ greatly from the challenges you and I face, the
forces at work are as real as the moral is relevant. The basic lessons Esther
had to learn are lessons I needed to learn. Thus, the story of Esther, over
the years, has taken on great significance for me. Indeed, it reflects an
individual's discovery of the true meaning of life.

The story takes place in the ancient kingdom of Persia where there lived
a particularly faithful man of God named Mordecai. Now, Mordecai, a Jew,
had a young cousin named Esther, whom he had adopted after the death
of her parents and raised as if she were his own daughter. In fact, Mordecai
had raised a young woman literally fit for a king . . . for Esther grew into
a woman of extraordinary grace and beauty.

Then, one day Xerxes, the King of Persia, commanded that a search be
made throughout all the provinces for the most beautiful woman so that
he could choose a new queen—a sort of Miss Persia Pageant. Esther, above
all others, found favor in the eyes of the king. And this young orphan girl
was named Queen of Persia.

The king was so delighted with his new queen that he threw a magnificent banquet and even went so far as to lower all the taxes. Mr. President, I thought you would especially like that part of the story.

Meanwhile, Mordecai, out amongst the people, learned to his horror, that one of his top men in government had developed a very careful plan to put to death all of God's people, the Jews, throughout the entire kingdom.

Of course, Mordecai immediately thought of Esther and he sent an urgent message saying "Esther, you must do something—you may be the only person who can persuade the king to call off this terrible plan."

But Esther wants no part of this. Her response to Mordecai: "All the King's officials and the people of the royal provinces know that for any man or woman who approaches the king in the inner court without being summoned, the king has set but one law: that he be put to death. The only exception to this is for the king to extend the golden scepter to him and spare his life. But thirty days have passed since I was called to go to the king."

In other words, Esther is saying, "Mordecai, you don't understand protocol. I have to follow standard operating procedures. Chances are that if I go to the king, I just might lose my head!" Mordecai has no sympathy with Esther's refusal to help. Tens of thousands of her own people stand to lose their heads. Mordecai feels compelled to send a second message to Esther.

I once heard a very insightful pastor, Gordon Macdonald, highlight three distinct parts to this second appeal—three profound challenges which strike at the heart of Esther's reluctance.

First: Esther, think not that you'll escape this predicament any more than other Jews—you'll lose everything you have if this plan is carried out—all the comforts, all the fringe benefits. It seems that Mordecai is saying: if the thing that stops you from being a servant to thousands of people is your comfort and security, forget it, lady—for you're no more secure in there than we are out here. Esther shares the predicament.

The second theme is privilege: If you keep silent, Esther, at a time like this, deliverance and relief will arise from some other place.

God has given you, Esther, the privilege to perform. If you don't use that privilege, he may permit you to be pushed aside and give your role to someone else.

The third theme is providence. Mordecai says: Esther, who knows—but that God has placed you where you are for such a time as this.

Finally Mordecai's appeal struck home—Esther's response: "Go, gather together all the Jews and fast for me. Do not eat or drink for three days, night or day. I and my maids will fast as you do. When this is done, I will go to the King, even though it is against the law. And if I perish, I perish."

That's total commitment. Indeed, the story of Esther is for me a very challenging and humbling one. For there came a time in my life when I had to confront what commitment to God is all about.

My witness contains no road to Damascus experience.

My spiritual journey began many years ago in a Carolina home where Sunday was the Lord's Day, reserved for acts of mercy and necessity, and the Gospel was as much a part of our lives as fried chicken and azaleas in the spring.

My grandmother, Mom Cathey, who lived within two weeks of her 100th birthday, was my role model.

I remember many Sunday afternoons with other neighborhood children in her home—the lemonade and cookies—I think that's what enticed us— the Bible games, listening to Mom Cathey as she read from this Bible— now one of my most cherished possessions.

She practiced what she preached, and lived her life for others. In a tragic accident, Mom Cathey lost a son at the hands of a drunk driver. The insurance policy on his life built a wing in a far-off church mission in Pakistan. Although Mom was not at all a wealthy woman, almost anything she could spare went to the ministers at home and missions abroad. When it became necessary in her 90s, to go into a nursing home, she welcomed the opportunity. I can still hear her saying, "Elizabeth, there might be some people there who don't know the Lord, and I can read the Bible to them."

I love to find her notes in the margins of her Bible, notes written in the middle of the night when she couldn't sleep. For example, I find by Psalm 139, this notation, "May 22, 1952, 1:00 A.M.—My prayer: Search me, O God and know my heart. Try me, and know my thoughts. And see if there be any wicked way in me, and lead me in the way, everlasting."

I can't remember an unkind word escaping Mom's lips in all the years I knew her or an ungracious deed marring her path. My grandmother was an almost perfect role model.

And I wanted to be like her. From an early age, I had an active church life. But as we move along, how often in our busy lives something becomes a barrier to total commitment of one's life to the lord! In some cases, it may be money, power or prestige.

In my case, my career became of paramount importance. I worked very hard, to excel, to achieve. My goal was to do my best, which was all fine and well. But I'm inclined to be a perfectionist. And it's very hard, you know, to try to control everything, surmount every difficulty, foresee every problem, realize every opportunity. That can be pretty tough on your family, your friends, your fellow workers and on yourself. In my case, it began crowding out what Mom Cathey had taught me were life's most important priorities.

I was blessed with a beautiful marriage, a challenging career. . . and yet . . . only gradually, over many years, did I realize what was missing. My life was threatened by spiritual starvation.

I prayed about this, and I believe, no faster than I was ready, God led me to people and circumstances that made a real difference in my life.

I found Ed Bauman of Foundry Methodist Church, a tremendously sensitive, caring pastor, who helped me to see what joy there can be when God is the center of life, and all else flows from that center.

A spiritual growth group gave me renewed strength as I began to meet each Monday night with others who shared my need to stretch and grow spiritually, and I was strengthened through Bible study with other senate wives. I learned that Sundays can be set aside for spiritual and personal rejuvenation without disastrous effects on one's work week. And suddenly, the Esther story took on new meaning.

I finally realized I needed to hear and to heed those challenges Mordecai so clearly stated. Mordecai's first challenge: Predicament: "Don't think your life will be spared from the slaughter, Esther. If you try to save your life, you'll lose it all!" It's a call to total commitment, to literally lay her life on the line.

But I can sympathize with Esther's dilemma. She had all the comforts, a cushy life, and when you get all those things around you, it can build up a resistance to anything which might threaten the comfort and security they seem to provide.

I know all too well how she felt. Maybe you do, too. I enjoy the comfortable life. I had built-up my own self-sufficient world. I had God neatly compartmentalized, crammed into a crowded file drawer of my life somewhere between "gardening" and "government." That is, until it dawned on me that I share the predicament that the call to commitment Mordecai gave to Esther is like the call which Jesus Christ presents to me.

"If anyone would come after me," Jesus tells us, "He must deny himself and take up his cross and follow me. For whoever wants to save his life will lose it, but whoever loses his life for me and for the Gospel, will save it. What good is it for a man to gain the whole world, yet forfeit his soul?"

Hard words to swallow, when you're busy doing your own thing—but the most compelling logic I've ever heard. For if Christ is who he says he is, our savior, the central figure in all of history who gives meaning to a world of confusing, conflicting priorities, then I had to realize Christ would not be compartmentalized.

It would be different if I had believed that Jesus was just a man, as some do. Then I could easily have compartmentalized Him. Or, if I had believed he was just a good teacher of morals, then perhaps, I could have just put his book away on my shelf. Or if I had thought he was just a prophet, even then, I might have been tempted to file him away.

But I knew that Jesus Christ was my Lord and my Savior, the Risen Lord who lives today, Sovereign over all. And I knew it was time to cease living life backwards, time to strive to put Christ first, preeminent with no competition, at the very center of my life. It was time to submit my resignation as master of my own little universe, and God accepted my resignation!

Mordecai's second challenge was privilege. "If you don't take this privilege seriously, Esther, God will give it to another."

This, too, was a challenge I needed to hear.

What God had to teach me was this: It is not what I do that matters, but what a sovereign God chooses to do through me. God doesn't want worldly successes. He wants me. He wants my heart, in submission to him. Life is not just a few years to spend on self-indulgence and career advancement. It's a privilege, a responsibility, a stewardship to be lived according to a much higher calling, God's calling. This alone gives true meaning to life.

Mordecai's warning to Esther is sobering. God forbid that someday I look back and realize I was too distracted by things of this world, too busy, too driven, and my work was given to another.

The third challenge, Providence: "Esther, who knows, but that God in His providence has brought you to such a time as this."

What Mordecai's words say to me is that each one of us has a unique assignment in this world given to us by a Sovereign God: to love and to serve those within our own sphere of influence.

We've been blessed to be a blessing; we've received that we might give.

The challenges Esther needed to hear were challenges I needed to hear, and continually need to hear: the call is total commitment.

But there is one last lesson I had to learn from Esther: the way in which her heart responded.

Esther called on her fellow believers to pray and to fast. And then she cast herself, indeed, her very life, upon God in dependence on Him: "If I perish, I perish!"

And how did God work in this situation? What was the outcome of Esther's commitment and dependence on God? Scripture tells us that the King extended the golden scepter, sparing Esther's life. That his heart went out to her cause, and that God's people were gloriously rescued!

Esther could have played it on her own wits and charm and just left God out of the picture. But she knew her cause would only succeed if God were with her. And she rallied others to join her in spirit of humble dependence through prayer.

It has struck me that this is really our purpose in gathering together this morning at this, the Annual National Prayer Breakfast. We have come to humbly acknowledge our dependence on God. We have come, as our invitations to this event state: To seek the Lord's guidance and strength in our individual lives and in the governing of our nation, with the hope that the power of Christ may deepen our fellowship with one another.

But in this city accustomed to giving directions, it's not easy to seek them instead. Dependence on God is not an easy thing for Washington-type achievers, and it has not been easy for me. Often, I find myself faced with tasks demanding wisdom and courage beyond my own. And not just on the big decisions. I am constantly in need of God's grace to perform life's routine duties with the love for others, the peace, the joy, inherent in God's call.

I've had to learn that dependence is a good thing, that when I've used up my own resources, when I can't control things and make them come out my way, when I'm willing to trust God with the outcome, when I'm weak, then I am strong. Then I'm in the best position to be able to feel the power of Christ rest upon me, encourage me, replenish my energy, and deepen my faith. Power from God, not from me.

Yes, the story of Esther is actually a story of dependence. It's a story not about the triumph of a man or a woman, but the triumph of God. He is the real hero of this story.

And in the same way, I've come to realize there can be only one hero in my story, too: God in Jesus Christ.

Total commitment to Christ is a high and difficult calling. And one I will struggle with the rest of my days. But I know that for me, it's the only life worth living, the only life worthy of our Lord. The world is ripe and ready, I believe, for men and women who will accept this calling, men and women who recognize they are not immune from the predicaments of the day, men and women who are willing to accept the privilege of serving, and who are ready to see that the providence of God may have brought them to such a time as this.

Thank you and God bless you.

UNIVERSITY OF VIRGINIA COMMENCEMENT SPEECH
Charlottesville, Virginia, May 17, 1987

Elizabeth Dole's popularity has made her a highly sought after graduation speaker. She presented the following speech when she was serving as secretary of transportation. In it, she shows her patriotism and shares with her audience the historic relevance of Thomas Jefferson and the University of Virginia. She comments especially on the Constitution, reminding her audience of its 200th anniversary and the obligations democracy entails. She invites the graduating seniors to consider a life devoted to public service. Multitasking, Dole takes time in her speech to praise the Reagan administration's policies, especially on the economy. This text was provided by Elizabeth Dole.

This morning I stand before you on this historic lawn in the very center of the University Thomas Jefferson built. I know it's been said that Mr. Jefferson is everywhere on these grounds, and from looking at the Rotunda . . . and thinking about the history of this great seat of higher education, it is no wonder it's considered to be one of the nation's outstanding universities . . . as well as one of the finest architectural wonders of North America.

It has always impressed me that Mr. Jefferson, a man who served as both President and Vice President of the United States, requested only three things listed on his tombstone: Author of the Declaration of Independence, author of the Virginia Statute on Religious Freedom, and founder of the University of Virginia. Jefferson chose these three among many, I believe, because he understood the importance of ideas. He knew that ideas have their consequences—indeed, he experienced the power of ideas and their consequences first-hand.

But he also knew that the ability to appreciate the role of ideas in human affairs, and more crucially, to distinguish good from bad ideas, must ultimately be rooted in an educated citizenry.

Thomas Jefferson, in founding the University, made his position on the importance of education very clear. He summed it up in one simple sentence: "I cannot live without books." He knew the power of an educated mind and the dangers of an ignorant society. Enlightenment was the key to freedom, for only enlightened people could rise up and throw off the shackles of tyranny and oppression which had characterized so much of world history. No doubt all of you have benefited from Mr. Jefferson's wisdom in your years at U.Va. The time you have spent here has prepared you well for the creative tensions of modern life. Here, you have learned that so long as books remain open, minds will never be closed.

Education was foremost in Mr. Jefferson's mind, as was the question of governing a free people. The father of our Declaration of Independence was ever vigilant in warning his contemporaries of the dangers of an all-consuming government.

In his First Inaugural Address, he stated, "Sometimes, it is said that man cannot be trusted with government of himself. Can he, then, be trusted with the government of others? Or have we found angels in the forms of kings to govern him? Let history answer this question."

I believe America has answered the question, and I'm sure Mr. Jefferson would agree, if he could speak to us today. For the system of government Jefferson envisioned in the Declaration of Independence has stood the test of time and has made the United States the strongest bastion of freedom on the face of the earth.

Two hundred years ago this week, 55 men gathered in what was then known as the Pennsylvania State House to consider alternatives to the existing Articles of Confederation. History tells us that what we know was the Constitutional Convention didn't get underway on time. In fact, it started two weeks late—because the roads to Philadelphia were so bad! It took George Washington four days to travel by carriage from Mt. Vernon to Philadelphia. Today, that same trip on the Metroliner takes one hour and thirty-seven minutes. Of course, if the convention were held today, there'd not only be men representing the colonies, but women as well.

Two hundred years later, we pause to remember the men of Philadelphia. Yet it isn't their daily debates that we recall, nor even the individual signers, most of whom are lost in the pages of time. No: it's the idea behind the document—the idea that America was different because here, we the people would rule ourselves.

The document whose bicentennial we observe this year was tailored to fit the changing needs of a dynamic and fluid society. It was a coat woven to fit an infant republic of three million souls, and which now clothes the 240 million Americans in opportunity and freedom. The framers wrote for the ages. They embraced timeless beliefs in self-government and shared responsibility. For they believed in the ability of seemingly ordinary people—people like you and me—to accomplish extraordinary things, to make their own decisions, to realize their own destinies.

The drafters of the Constitution drew up a challenge as well as a charter. They fashioned a popular government, knowing that the only way it could survive was to enlist the energies and devotion of the people themselves.

They crafted a government strong enough to protect our liberties—but limited enough to keep from crushing them in its embrace. Thomas Jefferson said it well: "That government is best which governs least, because its people discipline themselves."

Recently, I happened to come across a speech on citizenship and democracy which I gave in 1978, when I was a member of the Federal Trade Commission. In that speech, I indicated my concern that many citizens seemed to have lost the sense of pride and commitment to the ideal of America that once prevailed among our people. I spoke of a decline in national confidence, and the rise of public apathy in its place. Sadly, many Americans no longer felt that as individuals they could make a difference. And if they stopped believing in themselves, I wondered, then how could they believe in the American dream of individual effort and national service? As our citizens turned inward, we were in danger of turning out the lights in America. Little wonder that the 1970s were dubbed the "Me Decade."

Happily, I stand before you nine years later to report what you already know—all that has changed. The "Me Decade" has been replaced by the "We Decade," as citizens all across America have regained confidence in themselves and in the mission of their country to serve as a beacon of hope to an oppressed planet.

Today, we are witnessing nothing less than an American renaissance, a grassroots revival of those fundamental principles that give character to our land and reality to our dreams. We are renewing the ancient ideals of hard work, pride of family, love of freedom and trust in God. We have rediscovered our roots—and we are reaching for the stars.

President Ronald Reagan came to office sensing this thirst in Americans for a return to basic principles. He has helped restore faith and confidence in our institutions and in ourselves. He has reminded us that we can strengthen the land we love by meeting several important challenges. These challenges go to the heart of who we are and who we want to be.

First, there is the economy. Few doubt the strength of the American economy today. For 53 consecutive months we have enjoyed the benefits of economic growth. During that time, productivity has risen. Inflation has declined to its lowest levels since the 1960s. Unemployment is at a seven year low, and over 13 million new jobs have been created.

Simultaneously, we are called on to meet the challenge of defending freedom in a dangerous, sometimes desperate era. Since taking office, the President has made significant headway in rebuilding our defenses and making America more secure. But now is not time to rest on our laurels, or let down our guard. Skimping on defense now could undo all we have achieved. It could undermine not only our own security, but that of our closest friends.

There is nothing new to the cries for less defense and more domestic spending. During one debate in the Constitutional Convention, a delegate rose to his feet and moved that "the standing army be restricted to 5,000 at any time." This prompted George Washington, as presiding officer, to suggest an amendment of his own—to prohibit any foreign enemy from invading the American soil with more than 3,000 troops!

But what are we defending? We defend more than factories—more than shopping malls—more than territory. We defend the values that have blessed this land and set it apart in the family of nations. The record of the Constitutional Convention leaves no doubt that our nation's founders were sustained by their faith in God. As George Washington once said, "Of all the dispositions and habits which lead to political prosperity, religion and morality are indispensable supports."

This morning, I am looking at America's first and ultimate line of defense. For surely we share the belief that the source of all our national strength lies in the inner strength that forms our attitudes, shapes our ambitions, and turns our aspirations into achievements.

To meet these several challenges is to be reminded every day of what it is that distinguishes this constitutional republic from the rest of mankind. Today, I would like to add another challenge. For each of us, in our own way, is called to service. The Constitution does not merely grant rights to America. Benjamin Franklin, who could have written America's first manual on public service, once said, "The most important task we are undertaking as a nation is to solve the magnificent challenge of being a free people." Two centuries later, his words have not lost their resonance. They still shine forth, from the red brick state house of colonial Philadelphia to guide our steps along the narrow path of duty.

There is a famous story about Justice Oliver Wendell Holmes, who once found himself on a train, but couldn't locate his ticket.

While the conductor watched, smiling, the 88-year old Justice Holmes searched through all of his pockets without success. Of course, the conductor recognized the distinguished Justice, so he said, "Mr. Holmes, don't worry. You don't need your ticket. You will probably find it when you get off the train and I'm sure the Pennsylvania Railroad will trust you to mail it back later."

The Justice looked up at the conductor with some irritation and said, "My dear man, that is not the problem at all. The problem is not, where is my ticket. The problem is, where am I going?"

Where, indeed. That's a good question for you who are graduating to ask yourselves as you prepare for the next chapter in your lives. It's a question every American should constantly ask himself. This bicentennial year of the Constitution offers a special opportunity to ponder the meaning of that sacred document, and the challenge it poses to your generation and to mine. For the decisions we make today can affect the lives of other people as dramatically as the Founding Fathers have affected us.

Daniel Webster was not in Philadelphia in 1787. But no one studied the handiwork of Madison, Washington and Franklin with greater care. And the result of Webster's lifelong study was a warning to those who would come after him. "We may be tossed upon an ocean where we can see no land—nor perhaps, the sun or stars," he said. "But there is a chart and a compass for us to study, to consult, and to obey. The chart is the Constitution."

As a people who have lived with the freedom under the guidance of the Constitution for two centuries, we can forget how precious and rare that freedom is. All of us have an obligation to participate actively in the system of self-government the Constitution establishes. It is an obligation we owe not only to ourselves, but to the framers of our government—men and women who risked everything for freedom, brave men and women who have bonded this nation with their blood and their toil and their sacrifice. And graduates, you are now being given the opportunity to help shape the character of your country and your times. The inheritance into which you are entering includes a land in the throes of national renewal—an America born again, yet, as never before, in need of leaders whose character is matched by their commitment. In the words of another great Virginian, Woodrow Wilson, "We should not only use all the brains we have, but all that we can borrow."

Today, America herself applies for a very special loan—borrowing not only the brains here today, but the character, the sensitivity and the courage that guides them. To be secure, as a nation we require all the breakthroughs of which modern thought is capable. We need inventive thinkers to guide our economy, protect our environment, secure our rights and establish our place in the world. But most of all, we need individuals—committed men and women, for whom conscience is the North Star by which they guide their steps—and those of the nation they love.

When Ronald Reagan was governor of California, he recalls how he first learned to deal with enormous challenge and stress as a newly-elected governor of California. "Each morning began," he says, "with someone standing before my desk describing yet another disaster. The feeling of stress became unbearable. I had the urge to look over my shoulder for someone I could pass the problem to. One day, it came to me that I was looking in the wrong direction. I looked up instead of back. I'm still looking up. I couldn't face one day in this office, if I didn't know I could ask God's help!" Let us never forget the source of our strength and courage.

I invite each of you to make your own contribution, in your own special way, to the land and its people. I especially hope you will consider the life of public service. For while you may not get rich, you will enrich the lives of millions of your countrymen. Your rewards may not be material, but rather the satisfaction of service—making a difference—a positive difference—in people's lives.

In closing, let me share with you an experience that Bob and I had when we visited the Soviet Union a few years ago for the US-USSR Trade Conference—an experience I will never forget.

At our embassy in Moscow, I talked to members of two families from Siberia, who had sought asylum from the religious persecution they had encountered in their own mother country.

In attempting to reach our embassy's gates, one of the young sons was caught by Russian guards, beaten in full sight of the two families, and then dragged away. Not until three weeks later, did they learn that he had been thrown on a train back to Siberia. It was nearly five years—separated from their friends and family and living in the basement of that embassy— before the Soviet government allowed those families to emigrate to Israel.

As we drove up to the airport to begin our long trip home and I looked at the airplane sitting on the runway with "United States of America" emblazoned on its side, I just thanked God I could come home to a country where freedom and democracy are more than just hollow spaces.

Every citizen has a stake in government that lives up to its noblest promises. Each one of us is obliged to pass on to our children the freedoms that Thomas Jefferson and the rest of the men of Philadelphia entrusted to us. They created something unique in the annals of history. Let us not only preserve their past—let us make certain that the present is worthy of preservation, so that, in another 200 years, our descendants can say as proudly as we do today, "I am an American."

Congratulations, and God bless each and every one of you.

DEPARTMENT OF TRANSPORTATION AWARDS CEREMONY SPEECH
Washington, D.C., September 16, 1987

This speech was Elizabeth Dole's swan song as secretary of transportation. It shows the emotion and personal fulfillment Dole felt about what she and the Department of Transportation staff were able to accomplish together during her four and a half years of service. She reminds her audience of the 200th anniversary of the Constitution, and how that document calls "we the people" to fulfill the obligations of self-government. Looking ahead to the presidential campaign of 1988, Dole forecasts her husband's bid by hinting that she "will be working for another cause" in which she strongly believes. This text was provided by Elizabeth Dole.

Ladies and gentlemen, let me begin with a personal note. I can't tell you how it touches my heart to look out at this audience and know it's the last time I'll address you at this event as Secretary of Transportation. I must tell you that reaching my decision to leave was a bit of a wrenching experience because I care so much for our DOT family and the work we have done together. And there is much more ahead of us. I will be working on another cause, soon, in which I also strongly believe, but a part of my heart will be with you, the strong, able men and women of DOT, as you continue to carry out the high goals and many opportunities to help other people, which we have shared.

So, while Monday was a great moment in my own life, today is a very special day for the Department—and the nation. While this morning we honor our award recipients, this afternoon we will celebrate the 200th anniversary of our U.S. Constitution. It's worth noting that while other countries may have more ancient cities and cultures—no constitution is older, more revered or better equipped for serving the needs of democracy than ours. Two hundred years isn't bad, is it? I mean, who says American products aren't built to last!

This week, the nation pauses to remember the men who drafted the Constitution. Yet it isn't their daily debates that we recall, nor even the individual signers, most of whom are lost in the pages of time. No: it's the idea behind the document we honor—the idea that America was different because here, we the people would rule ourselves.

The framers wrote for the ages. They embraced timeless beliefs in self-government and shared responsibility. For they believed implicitly in the ability of seemingly ordinary people—people like you and me—to accomplish extraordinary things, to make their own decisions, to realize their own destinies.

The drafters of the Constitution drew up a challenge as well as a charter. They fashioned a popular government, knowing that the only way it could survive was to enlist the energies and the devotion of the people themselves.

This bicentennial year of the Constitution offers a special opportunity to ponder the meaning of that sacred document, and the challenge it poses to our generation. For the decisions we make today can affect the lives of other people as dramatically as the Founding Fathers have affected us.

To meet this challenge is to be reminded every day of what it is that distinguishes this constitutional republic from the rest of mankind. For the Constitution calls each of us, in our own way, to service. The Constitution does not merely grant rights to the people. It reminds us of our responsibilities to each other and to America.

This morning, we recognize our colleagues who have demonstrated their own commitment to serve others with the dedication and selflessness which are the hallmarks of government service. Our government's strength lies in the quality of those who do their jobs outside the headlines and without great fanfare. As John Gardner has said, "Democracy is measured not by its leaders doing extraordinary things, but by its citizens doing ordinary things extraordinarily well."

The Department of Transportation is blessed with a strong team of outstanding people, men and women dedicated to doing their job extraordinarily well. Though we specifically honor our award recipients today, they represent thousands of others who also merit recognition—for outstanding performance every day of the week.

When I came to the Department back on a cold day in February, 1983, I had already been told that DOT employees had a reputation in government circles as the very best. Four and a half years later, I can gratefully and proudly state that your professionalism and commitment exceeded my already high expectations. From that first day, we embarked on a campaign to make life better, economic prospects brighter and transportation safer for all Americans.

Back in early 1983, deregulation of America's transportation industries had not yet fully impacted our country, due to the final stages of the recession and high fuel prices. All this changed when the President's economic policies took hold, and our transportation industries grew beyond even their own expectations. For example, in aviation millions of people who never thought they would have the money to fly are in the air, and the number of people flying has increased dramatically. Thanks to deregulation, consumers are saving an estimated $6 billion a year in air travel alone. Our challenge in the era of this post-deregulation boom is to make sure that the world's safest transportation system continues to become even safer, by staying ahead of the growth curve and making the changes necessary to keep pace with a dynamic transportation system.

Together, we've come a long way in the past four and a half years to fulfill that mandate. Our Safety Review Task Force examined, carefully, each mode, and led the way to significant improvements in transportation safety: a total overhaul of FAA's inspection system, the unprecedented NATI program of 14,000 inspections of over 300 airlines.

The number of FAA inspectors increased 60 percent since 1983, the number of fully qualified controllers increased 67 percent; and if we get our way for FY 1988, the controller workforce will increase by 24 percent. And while every agency has been hit with budget reductions, we've been able to increase the budget of FAA by 50 percent in response to the growth of the system. Recent initiatives are designed to make sure small aircraft do not cross the path of commercial carriers, and the large carriers will carry collision avoidance warning systems.

We can be proud of the fact that the last three years have been the safest in U.S. history. We had the lowest automobile fatality rate in history both in 1985 and 1986, and last year was the safest ever on the railroads.

Our campaign against drunk driving, the "Age 21" legislation, coupled with the passage of seat belt laws in 29 states, spawned by our regulation 208, have saved countless lives and prevented thousands of crippling injuries. Seat belt usage has risen from 12 percent before seat belt laws to 42 percent today. With 208, we ended a twenty year long battle over passive restraints, and today they're available in 25 percent of all new cars. And because of an incentive we placed in rule 208, airbag technology was preserved, and soon 10 manufacturers will offer an airbag option.

We've also taken action to assure the American public we're doing all we can to eliminate drugs and alcohol in our transportation system. We broke a twelve-year logjam by issuing the first requirement for alcohol and drug testing after serious railroad accidents. And with your understanding and cooperation, DOT is the first civilian agency to undertake random drug testing to assure a drug-free workplace.

And a word of praise and gratitude for the men and women of the Coast Guard, engaged as never before in patrolling the waters which surround America for illicit drugs. I felt a great pride as I visited the Coast Guard Academy last week for the launching of the Eagle's voyage to Australia. I thought about the daily missions of mercy, and our Coast Guard's tremendous humanitarian role.

Thanks to the work of our Research and Special Programs Administration, emergency response programs for hazardous material spills are being tightened up. And the Federal Highway Administration is deeply committed to improving truck safety—eliminating multiple licenses, and reviewing all our regulations.

And while ensuring the safety of the traveling public, we are reshaping the federal role in transportation. Despite long odds and tremendous obstacles, we sold our freight railroad to the public for almost $2 billion in the largest initial industrial stock offering in U.S. history—and we sold the Alaska railroad to the state. And in perhaps the sweetest victory of all, we did what nobody could do since they started trying in 1949—transferred Washington National and Dulles Airports to a regional authority so that $700 million in improvements to these gateways to the nation's capital can go forward, but not at the taxpayers' expense.

In UMTA, we are aggressively seeking to cut costs and provide better service by involving the private sector. UMTA has been a leader in privatization, and an example the rest of the government looks to for creative programs. And thanks to Jim Emery, the Saint Lawrence Seaway has been aggressively and successfully marketed among our trading partners. The Maritime Administration can take credit for leading the effort which streamlined regulation of U.S. international maritime carriers, a goal pursued unsuccessfully for 7 long years. And now we've set our sights on the stars, as DOT argued and won the battle to privatize space. This new space industry already has 20 reservations to launch routine commercial satellites as we compete with the French, the Russians and the Chinese.

On October 1, as I move on to the next great challenge of my personal life, I will always remember your outstanding performance and the joy you have given me. Historians tell us that the men of Philadelphia were miracle workers. As I look out over this audience, I can see that the age of miracles has not passed. For four and a half years, when the odds were sometimes long, the challenges great, the conventional wisdom most daunting, you and I and literally thousands of our colleagues were willing to stand up for what we knew to be right. In the process, we made a lot of headlines. We made a lot of history. Best of all, we made a positive difference in the lives of millions of our countrymen. But as this week reminds us, nothing lasts forever—not Constitutional Conventions, not cabinet secretaries. Of all the words in the language, I think perhaps the hardest to pronounce is the word "good-bye." So let's not even attempt it this morning. Let me instead tell you something straight from the heart.

Awards are wonderful. But there's no plaque and no certificate that can fully convey what I feel for each of you, nor my own personal pride and admiration that I take away on the road to tomorrow. However crowded the years ahead may become, they can never crowd the memories of your selflessness and friendship—memories that I will cherish always. There are many ways to define the greatness of America. Some look to documents. Some find it in institutions. I have a simple formula: I think any country must be great that can inspire people like you to devote your lives to service.

And now let me exercise my constitutional right to wish you all God-speed, good luck, and the fulfillment of every hope for future happiness. God bless each and every one of you.

REPUBLICAN NATIONAL CONVENTION SPEECH
New Orleans, August 16, 1988

In 1988, after a glowing introduction by Theresa Esposito, a Republican state representative from North Carolina, Elizabeth Dole spoke to the women of America during the Republican National Convention about the fragile economic conditions facing the country. She understood that some women were not comfortable supporting a Republican candidate, and she wanted to assure them that George Herbert Walker Bush would work hard to protect their interests: "Let me say to the women of America: I respect the fact that some of you have questions. I also ask you to have an open mind." The implicit message here is how well a woman can do as a Republican, even one like Dole, who at one time was a registered Democrat. This text was provided by Elizabeth Dole.

Thank you. Thank you very much.

Theresa, you're an outstanding member of the North Carolina Legislature, and I know that you're going to have a resounding re-election victory in November. Thank you so much.

Peace, progress, opportunity. That's what we're here to celebrate. That's the legacy of a great president, Ronald Reagan. And that will be the living legacy of the next president of the United States, George Bush.

First, let me thank the Democratic Party leaders for televising their Convention. What I saw and heard reminded me and millions of other former Democrats why we're proud to be Republicans.

The Dukakis convention speech was just like the Democratic platform, hedging on defense, hedging on taxes, hedging on spending. We're not running against Bentsen and Dukakis, we're running against Bentsen and Hedges.

"Governor Hedges," "Governor Hedges," "Governor Hedges" tried mightily to paint over his liberal policies with pretty rhetoric. But the make-up job failed. As an old Federal Trade Commissioner, I want to know—whatever happened to truth in advertising?

But we've come to New Orleans not to pin the tail on the donkey. We're here to pin our hopes on the American future. And we're not buying the Dukakis deception. Despite what he says, this election is about ideas and ideology. They do matter. They will matter to Americans who face a choice this year as stark and dramatic as any in memory.

We Americans faced a similar choice in 1980. And what did we get for our choice? We got a president who doesn't apologize for American interests—he asserts them.

We got a breakthrough in Soviet relations and the INF treaty. We got the longest economic boom in peacetime history.

It was my privilege for seven years to serve the man who made this happen—one of America's greatest presidents, Ronald Reagan. Thank you, Mr. President. Thank you, Mr. President, for that opportunity.

Today's strong economy means stronger families. And we affirm the woman who chooses to work in the home. But our strong economy has also provided needed jobs for millions of women, and let me say to the women of America: I respect the fact that some of you have questions. I also ask you to have an open mind.

You know better than anyone that a job—a good job—is absolutely basic to a family's happiness and stability. That's our freedom. Are we going to let them take it away? [Crowd yells, "No."]

In the past eight years, President Reagan has created an incredible jobs machine—more jobs for more Americans than ever before. And two-thirds of the 17 million new jobs created since 1982 went to women. Good jobs, not bad jobs.

Real work, not make-work. That's our freedom. Are we going to let them take it away? [Crowd yells, "No."]

You did it. You were the expansion. You, the women of America—who are holding jobs as never before, who've started businesses as never before, who have invested as never before. This expansion—it's your triumph. But it was Ronald Reagan and George Bush who set in motion the forces, which allowed that growth to occur and the economy to bloom. That's our freedom. Are we going to let them take it away? [Crowd yells, "No."]

America is on a roll. If this great economic upsurge is stopped, if we have a President who raises taxes again and increases regulation again and stifles growth again—and believe me, that's what Michael Dukakis will do—if we let the liberals back in, we lose all that progress, your progress.

We women would be especially vulnerable. We're always vulnerable when jobs are cut back and the economy stagnates.

Remember the Carter years, when workers were afraid to open pay envelopes because there just might be a pink slip inside, when families gave up hope of ever owning their own home, when parents feared their children's generation would be worse off than their own. That was real economic violence. We have been there before, and we must never go back again.

So I ask you, women of America, not just to support us. Work with us, to ensure that this growth continues. Work with us, so that each American has a chance and a choice. Work with us, to change what needs to be changed.

The future belongs to our children, and childcare is one of those changes. Michael Dukakis wants to march our kids lockstep to a government institution where Washington will set all the rules.

Only one kind of childcare deserves federal aid, he says. But governor, people work part-time, full-time, night shifts, day shifts, and swing shifts. One size does not fit all.

George Bush, a father of five, a grandfather of 10, will give American parents what they want—child care supervised by people who share their values: in a community-based setting, a relative's or neighbor's home, a church-sponsored center, or by the mother or father who works full-time at home. George Bush believes the parents should choose.

But taking care of children also means making bad schools good and good schools better. George Bush and Barbara Bush, too, who have worked tirelessly to end illiteracy, understand what we have to do.

We must rescue a generation of children from the social experiments and educational fads that gave us erratic school policies, declining skills and low SAT scores. Ronald Reagan and George Bush have reordered our educational priorities. Commitment to excellence will continue to be our watchword.

But education is more than molding the intellect—it means shaping the character as well. It is character that will enable our children to say "yes" to the intellectual challenges of a new century and "no" to the physical and moral dangers of drugs.

The war on drugs must be fought by the Coast Guard patrolling our waters, and police officers in the alleys of our cities. These brave men and women can win battles, but George Bush knows that ultimately the war can only be won when the fathers, the mothers, the sons and the daughters of America unite to speak with one voice to just say no.

Nancy Reagan saw this solution when most politicians didn't even see the problem. What a great first lady she has been.

Next spring marks the 200th anniversary of the first inauguration of a United States President. There have been many changes in our nation since that day when George Washington took the oath of office. Yet the values on which this great nation was founded are just as vital today as they were 200 years ago.

We would do well to remember the parting words of that first president who said: "Of all the dispositions . . . which lead to political prosperity, religion and morality are indispensable. The mere politician, equally with the pious man, ought to respect and cherish them."

What wise words from our first president.

It is reassuring in this day, when we find faith and morality under attack, to know that George Bush is a man who truly respects and cherishes these guiding principles.

As we go forward to elect a new President, let us then select a man who will keep faith with the timeless values on which this great nation was founded, even as he leads our nation into a greater future.

Tonight, I am proud to be an American. Tonight, I am proud to be a Republican.

And tonight, I am proud that a great man, George Bush, will be our candidate for the next President of the United States.

Thank you. God bless you all.

AFL-CIO CONSTITUTIONAL CONVENTION SPEECH
Washington, D.C., November 13, 1989

As secretary of labor, Elizabeth Dole had the opportunity to speak to members of the American Federal of Labor–Congress of Industrial Organizations (AFL-CIO). In this speech, she discusses the recent increase in minimum wage and especially the compromises required before President Bush could sign it into law. She describes how work done today is growing increasingly complex, demanding a more educated workforce. She pledges to work with labor to find creative ways to meet the needs of workers at home in America and abroad. She also uses the opportunity to review other initiatives she plans to undertake at the Department of Labor (DOL). This speech, which reinforces her credibility with labor, was provided by Kerry Tymchuk.

Thank you, Lane, for that gracious introduction. It is a privilege, indeed, to be here this morning with the members of the AFL-CIO.

As Labor Secretary, I have often spoken from the heart about the contributions of our unions to the fabric of American life. My words, however, are certainly not as eloquent as those of Lech Walesa.

Eight years ago, Walesa appeared, for the first time, before the International Labor Organization. And though he spoke of Solidarity, his words define you—the working men and women who are the AFL-CIO. He said: "Members have different occupations and vocations, different philosophical and religious opinions. But they are joined by one common aspiration—that of ensuring for workers, blue-collar and white-collar alike, a life in civic freedom, freedom of thoughts and speech, and human dignity." I know those aspirations are shared by Lane Kirkland, Tom Donahue, and the entire membership of the AFL-CIO.

And, Lane, thank you for the candor and cooperation you have provided during my first nine months as Secretary of Labor. Whether it was before the AFL-CIO Executive Council in Florida, or the International Labor Organization in Geneva, I have appreciated your wisdom, and found inspiration in your words.

Over the past months, my door has been open and our discussions frank. This does not mean that we haven't had disagreements. Of course, we have. Will we continue to have disagreements in the times ahead? Of course, we will.

But President Bush and I have also worked with you to find much common ground. And where there are disagreements, I believe they are on the mechanics to reach goals, and not on the goals themselves. I am very pleased that the long process to reach one of these goals was completed last week with final passage of legislation to increase the minimum wage.

It was my pleasure to work with organized labor in negotiating and drafting the compromise, the first increase since 1981, which will help working men and women.

And let me assure you, whether the discussion at the Cabinet table concerns clean air, or a trade issue, such as steel VRA's, or "Super 301," I vigorously present the impact on jobs and America's working men and women.

I am reminded this morning of a story about George Meany. Meany called a particular cabinet officer to ask about a problem that had crossed his mind. The cabinet secretary made the mistake of failing to see why this issue would concern Meany and he said, "George, what the blazes has that got to do with labor?"

"Sonny Boy," Meany replied, "Everything that happens today has to do with labor."

Those words are truer now than ever before. Labor, indeed, has to do with everything that happens today. For as we enter a new decade, we find ourselves in a new age. An age of increasingly competitive global markets, and increasingly complex jobs. An age which presents historic opportunities and challenges to our unions, because working men and women are the cutting edge that determines the success of any enterprise, and of America herself.

What seized my attention when I came to the Department of Labor was the fact that we are on the brink of some revolutionary changes in American business and in the American workplace. These pose some complex challenges, and require some very fundamental, long-term changes in our workforce environment. They are challenges that are ill-served by short-term, quick-fixes that can tend to grab headlines.

Over the past months, I've spent a great deal of time consulting with workers and labor unions, with business leaders and educators, to receive their expertise and assessment on how we could effectively confront these problems.

If we are to take advantage of this new age, we must first work together to bridge a disturbing and increasing skills gap. Across the board, jobs are demanding better reading, writing, and reasoning skills. More math and science. Jobs that once required only manual ability, now require mental agility.

And this trend will continue. While manufacturing jobs have increased in real terms, the jobs experiencing the most growth now, and in the coming years, will be in the service, managerial, and skilled technical fields. Most notably, over half the jobs in our economy will soon require education beyond high school.

And the fact is, that as we enter the last decade of this century, America also enters a workforce crisis.

A crisis resulting from the fact that 25% of our young people—perhaps as many as one million students a year—are dropping out of high school. And of those who do graduate, a surprising number can't even read their diplomas. And our problems extend beyond our future workers to include our current labor force. At least 20 million and possibly as many as 40 million adults experience substantial literacy problems.

Two weeks ago, I proposed a series of initiatives to help address this skills gap. They involve some innovative, what some might call revolutionary changes in the way we think about business, labor, and education. And I need your help to implement these needed reforms.

I believe public education is a public responsibility. And all sectors of American society must work to make the changes necessary for our economic survival. Employers tell me constantly that the curriculum in our schools is not providing students with the skills required in today's jobs.

To address this mismatch, I will soon appoint a blue-ribbon panel, which will include top leaders from business, labor, and education, and I will charge them with the mission of hammering out national competency guidelines that reflect work readiness.

These guidelines, or norms, will serve as working definitions of what skills employers require and workers need on the job. Local schools and educators, as well as training programs, can use these guidelines to help develop relevant curriculum for promotion and graduation.

I want to redesign the Employment Service to equip it for the dynamics of the 1990s—not the 1960s. And, I will focus on the 40% of our high school graduates who don't go on to further education. These "forgotten youth" often kick around for a year or two trying to "find themselves." With our workforce growing at a rate of only 1% annually—the slowest rate in forty years—we can't afford this random, "catch-as-catch-can" approach to work any longer. The United States is one of the few modernized nations without a formal school-to-work transition. With your help, I will address this issue through partnerships to conduct model school to work transition programs.

The slow workforce growth means that issues once defined as social problems will be dealt with more out of economic necessity. In tighter labor markets, employers can't afford to discriminate; they cannot afford to put workers at health and safety risks; and they cannot afford to ignore workers' obligations to family. Employers who do will simply lose out to employers who don't. Such employers will falter or fail—and they deserve to.

I found the results of a recent survey of workers quite interesting—a survey which reported that nothing was more important to working men and women than a safe workplace. Public safety has been a mission of mine throughout my government career. It's a mission that continues at the Department of Labor.

I am sending a clear and unequivocal message to those who are responsible for the health and safety of workers: They must be aware of our standards, and they must comply with them fully.

If they fail to do so, we will proceed against them using our full authority under the Occupational Safety and Health Act. I can assure you that this is not mere rhetoric.

Already this year, I have sought to increase OSHA inspectors by 10%—the first enforcement budget increase for OSHA since 1981, and we have assessed the largest-ever OSHA penalty—$7.2 million in a case involving USX. We have also used, for one of the few times in the history of the Act, the Department of Labor's authority to force a company to immediately abate an imminent hazard—and we have gone to the courts to make that stick.

Those are only a few examples. Where we have a law or standard to enforce, we will do so fairly, vigorously and without hesitation.

We will also not hesitate to increase safety standards, where necessary. For instance, fires and explosions due to inadequate ventilation of mines are the leading cause of mine fatalities. The Mine Safety and Health Administration is aggressively moving forward on revised standards which will incorporate new technologies to make mines safer.

Woodrow Wilson once said that "Labor is not a commodity. It is . . . cooperation." Promoting that cooperation is also a guiding principle of mine as Secretary of Labor.

The tireless efforts of America's unions have resulted in protection for all workers, regardless of whether they are union members. Protections such as child labor laws, wage and hour benefits, worker safety, and pension benefits are the legacies of organized labor.

And recent agreements, such as the one between the Communications Workers of America and AT&T, prove that you continue to be on the cutting edge of America's social agenda, as bargaining moves to benefits such as child care, elder care, and parental leave.

This spring, I also had the pleasure of seeing, first-hand, a fine example of union-management cooperation when I visited the new United Motors Manufacturing plant in Fremont, California. By listening to employees, whose creative ideas have increased productivity, NUMMI [New United Motor Manufacturing, Inc.] has positioned itself as a model organization ideally suited to the rapidly changing workplace.

My visit to the NUMMI plant underlines my commitment to productive labor-management relations, which I view as essential in an ever more competitive global market. This is a commitment—and a responsibility—I take very seriously.

In July of this year, I met with Paul Douglas, Chief Executive Officer of the Pittston Coal Company. I met with Rich Trumka, President of the United Mine Workers. And I met with Bob Baker, the Acting Director of the Federal Mediation and Conciliation Service. Mediation, Baker told me, would be underway the next day. I have great respect for the FMCS, but several months later, the parties were still meeting in separate rooms, and it was clear that no solution was in sight.

I traveled to Southwest Virginia to talk with the miners, and the following day, Paul Douglas, Rich Trumka, and I met at the Department of Labor. It was my view that the good offices of the Secretary of Labor should be used to facilitate the collective bargaining process. We talked for almost two hours. Each assured me he was committed to resolving this dispute. Each agreed with my decision to appoint a Super Mediator. And late last month, I named Bill Usery, former Secretary of Labor, and former Director of the FMCS, to serve in that role.

It is my hope and my prayer, that the process I have started in this very difficult and protracted strike, will help the parties to reconcile their differences.

Let me add how proud I was to sit with Lane Kirkland and Rich Trumka at the Labor Hall of Fame Ceremonies just days before the announcement of the historic re-affiliation of the UMW and the AFL-CIO.

Yes, these are historic times for America's working men and women. And there can be no doubt that they are also historic times for workers throughout the world. From Europe to the Far East, from Africa to the Americas, the world is being swept by powerful tides of democratic change. Change fueled by mass movements of working men and women demanding a voice in their own economic and political future. Changes happening even as we meet, as the Berlin Wall crumbles under the force of freedom-loving people.

And when the story of our time is written, it will reflect the fact that one of the motivating forces influencing this tide of democracy was the AFL-CIO. As proof of this conclusion, future historians will point to Poland.

The birth of Solidarity in 1980 and 1981 captured the hearts of AFL-CIO members across America. Yours was a relationship based on common goals. The trademark of the American Labor movement has always been an unyielding commitment for human rights, individual dignity, and economic justice. And these were the simple yet stunning aspirations of solidarity.

In December of 1981, however, the first rays of freedom's sunlight were snuffed out by martial law. And Lane Kirkland and Irving Brown, who shortly before his death in 1988, received the highest civilian honor this nation has to offer—the Presidential Medal of Freedom, committed themselves to assist Solidarity in every possible way. Your work was quiet, because you believed the permanent glory of freedom was more important than the temporary spotlight of fame.

And what a difference you made. Money channeled through the AFL-CIO's Free Trade Union Institute bought printing presses, ink, computers, cameras, broadcasting equipment, and food and clothes for the families of imprisoned Solidarity members.

Your support was so influential that the Communist government singled out Lane Kirkland for a distinct honor—they refused to let him enter Poland. I'm pleased that Lane will make that trip to Poland as part of our Presidential Mission, departing on November 29. Lane will join Bob Georgine, Agriculture Secretary Yeutter, Commerce Secretary Mosbacher, Chairman of the Council of Economic Advisors Boskin, myself, and agriculture and business representatives, on this most important journey.

Our optimism for Poland, of course, must be tempered with realism. The road to economic and political freedom for Poland and her people remains very long. The transition from a state-supported economy to a free market economy will not be accomplished without some initial pain. Our support is needed now more than ever.

American experience and American know-how can help Poland in this transition. In August, I met with Prime Minister Mazowiecki and Lech Walesa in Poland and offered our assistance. We are now nearing implementation of a comprehensive program which calls upon the expertise of government, business, and labor.

Specifically, our discussions in Poland to finalize their priorities will focus on: establishment of an effective unemployment insurance system to provide a safety net for workers during their transition; employment services to match workers with jobs; worker training and retraining; and reliable labor statistics, which are key to investment and policy decisions.

If Poland succeeds—and she must—the ramifications for democracy are limitless.

Our concern for the workers of Poland stems from a deep, moral belief in the basic rights of all workers. And, let's not kid ourselves, the abuse of fundamental worker rights abroad provides those who engage in such practices with an unfair trade advantage in competition with American products. More importantly, the abuse of basic worker rights anywhere in the world is immoral and wrong. I know that Lane and I share a commitment to work through the International Labor Organization to ensure human rights and worker rights throughout the world.

As we have in times past, America is asking much of working men and women. You are needed to shoulder the responsibility of producing not only for our people, but for freedom-loving people around the world.

And as we prepare for the upcoming century . . . as we prepare to meet our challenges, let us take heart from the words of a great President. Almost 100 years ago, Teddy Roosevelt confronted the 20th century and said: "We are face to face with our destiny, and we must meet it with a high and resolute courage. For ours is the life of action, of strenuous performance of duty. Let us live in the harness, striving mightily. Let us run the risk of wearing out, rather than rusting out."

By continuing to work together toward shared goals and aspirations, we will run that risk and we will meet our challenge. America deserves it, history demands it, and our children will reward it.

300 GROUP SPEECH
London, England, November 15, 1989

Elizabeth Dole spoke to the 300 Group in London, an organization committed to women's economic equality. She established common ground by describing her stay in England as a university student, and the emigration of the Hanford family from England to the United States. She was secretary of labor when she gave this speech. In it, she highlights the need for women to use the knowledge and power they have gained through grassroots initiatives to improve the conditions for women. Dole presents startling statistics from research to reveal the factual basis of the phenomenon called the "glass ceiling." She closes the speech by pledging to work with others to end economic discrimination against women and minorities. This text was provided by Kerry Tymchuk.

Thank you, Andrea, for that gracious introduction.

What a joy it is to return again to England. Thirty years ago this past summer, I spent a delightful couple of months at Oxford University. While there I studied English history and government, but my education certainly wasn't limited to the classroom.

I will never forget the majesty of Evensong under the vaulted roof of Christ Church, or the beauty of a bicycle ride to the Trout, or the elegance of tea and crumpets at the old Mitre Hotel. And on weekends, I would ramble through Welsh coal mining valleys and come in to London on the train to take in the theatre. And in the fall, there was the Edinburgh Arts Festival.

And for someone eager to experience everything possible in the city of dreaming spires, I remember well the night I deliberately stayed out late, until the gates of Exeter College were closed. Then I climbed a ladder to the top of the wall, jumped over and landed in the Don's garden. I had barely enough time to scamper to my room without the Don identifying the intruder in his yard.

I have returned to Great Britain many times since my days at Oxford, both for business and for tracing family history. But I never imagined I would eventually be asked to address such a prestigious group of enlightened citizens who are themselves dedicated to leaping over walls and knocking down barriers.

Throughout this decade, the 300 Group has devoted itself to the goal of a society which regards as natural the participation of women in public life and private enterprise. Project 2000, training programs, and a network of women to whom others can turn for advice, are just three examples of your innovations designed to help in reaching that goal.

The people of Great Britain should indeed be grateful to you, the members of the 300 Group, for your generosity of time, your creative programs and energy, and your firm resolve. For without them, the goal of equal representation for women would surely be a more distant reality.

Such a goal is most certainly shared by women in the United States; it's a goal for which I've fought throughout my years in public service.

In fact, when I read of the outstanding work of the 300 Group, and sensed the common bond and shared mission that unites us, I thought of the words of Winston Churchill.

In addressing the United States Congress, Churchill said that had he, like his mother, been raised in America, he might have made it to Congress on his own.

Well, to paraphrase Churchill, let me just say that had the Hanford family never left England for North Carolina, I'm confident that I would have joined the 300 Group on my own.

I know that Churchill and Lady Astor often enjoyed matching wits when they disagreed—with most of their matches being draws.

As a woman in a two-career marriage, I've often been asked if my husband and I ever disagree on issues.

Well, several years ago, Congress was debating whether or not there should be a Consumer Protection Agency in the federal government. I thought it would be a good way to unite the twenty-six separate agencies that were dealing with consumer matters into one more effective voice of the consumer. Bob disagreed, believing that we didn't need another bureaucracy.

Somehow, the television program "Good Morning America"—similar to your "Breakfast News"—heard about our disagreement, and asked if we would appear on their show to debate the issue just before the Senate was to take its vote. We agreed to do it. Now, when Bob and I make joint appearances, he always says it should be spontaneous—meaning we don't discuss it beforehand.

Well, ladies and gentlemen, this was one of the most spontaneous events ever seen on television. The host of the program began by throwing out the first—and only—question for twelve minutes. "Should there be a Consumer Protection Agency in the federal government?"

I, for one, forgot there were millions of people watching that morning, it was like sitting at the breakfast table discussing—or you might call it arguing—about an issue. I remember at one point, Bob saying, "Elizabeth, if I could get a word in, I'd really like to say something!" "Bob," I said, "I haven't made my point yet," and I just kept right on going!

When this was over, we received quite a bit of mail, as you might imagine. One lady wrote to Bob and said "Dear Senator Dole: If you ever expect to get anywhere in politics, if you want to get re-elected, you better get your wife to shut her mouth." Then there were those who wrote to me and said "You're right! He's absolutely wrong."

But the one letter I remember most, and that I have saved for posterity, came from a gentleman who said "I do hope you will soon be able to resolve your marital difficulties."

While the Doles may disagree on an issue here or there, one thing on which we most definitely agree is our strong support for critical issues such as economic equity for women, pension reform and tough enforcement of child support laws. And we both understand the value of shared leadership between men and women at all levels. Bob's chief-of-staff is a woman, and he has consistently appointed women to top leadership positions, as have I.

Another thing that Bob and I agree on is our admiration for the abilities of Nancy Astor. And David, it's such a pleasure to be with you tonight. A woman of wit, charm, and principle, Nancy Astor was an American and an English original. I can't say it any better than did a leader for whom I have the greatest respect, your Prime Minister, Margaret Thatcher, with whom I met this afternoon. The Prime Minister said "If you think what kind of person you would need to go into that male-dominated House of Commons, you would have chosen Nancy Astor. You needed tremendous courage and a proper sense of your own views. You needed determination and a certain sense of style, and Nancy had them all."

I am very proud of the fact that Lady Astor was American born, and more specifically, that she was born in the American South. It's heartening to know that had we ever met, we wouldn't have needed an interpreter!

There are a seemingly endless number of stories involving Nancy's meetings with the famous and the infamous. One of my favorites involves an exchange she had with Joseph Stalin. Stalin commented, "How is it possible that a small island like Great Britain can have so much influence and respect in the world?" And Nancy said "Look at the map. It can't be might. It must be right. It's something in their thinking."

In the past decades, many women in public life in England—some of you right here in this room—have succeeded in changing the thinking of many people.

And much credit for the change of thinking goes to the media, who, through reports and articles, have brought public attention to the achievements of women. My congratulations to all the Winners of the "Nancy Astor Awards" for the difference you are making and will continue to make.

We Americans share some anniversaries with the 300 Group. For we meet not only during the 70th anniversary of the election of Nancy Astor, but also the 70th anniversary of women's suffrage in the United States; and in the Department of Labor, we are proud to celebrate the 70th anniversary of the founding of our Women's Bureau, which is dedicated to expanding opportunities for women in the workplace.

While it's true that anniversaries are times for celebration and remembrances of events in the past, they are also times to take stock of what's been accomplished, and what the future will hold. And this evening, I would like to discuss the changing role of women both in public life and in private enterprise.

Though my career in government has been through appointive, rather than elective positions, I believe I've experienced some of the same frustrations as those who stand for office, and certainly as I've campaigned for a large number of women candidates I've witnessed some of the lessons they have learned, and I have benefited, too.

And as my department pursues the opening of doors for women in non-traditional roles such as construction and aerospace, I can't help but think back over my own career—beginning with my days as a student at Harvard Law School.

There were 550 members of the class of 1965, and only 24 were women. On the first day of class, a male student came up to me and asked what I was doing there. In what can only be described as tones of moral outrage, he said, "Don't you realize that there are men who would give their right arm to be in this law school—men who would put their legal education to use?"

That man is now a senior partner in a Washington law firm. And every so often, I share this little story around town. You'd be amazed at the number of my male classmates who've called me to say, "Please tell me I'm not the one! Tell me I didn't say that, Elizabeth."

And I'm sure there were some men who shook their heads when I became the first female Secretary of Transportation, where my responsibilities called for selling three railroads, overseeing ship building and highway construction, and running the air traffic control system of the United States. I also gained a footnote in history as the first woman to head a branch of the American armed forces—the U.S. Coast Guard.

And now, I'm privileged to serve in a Cabinet position that deals with the traditionally male-dominated field of organized labor. Most recently, I've been attempting to settle a protracted coal strike.

These were also issues dealt with by Frances Perkins, who, as Franklin Roosevelt's Secretary of Labor, was the first woman to serve in a President's Cabinet. And the second was the distinguished Oveta Culp Hobby, Secretary of Health, Education, and Welfare, and Ambassador Catto's mother-in-law. Miss Perkins was once asked whether being a woman was a disadvantage in public life. "Only," she answered, "when I am climbing trees."

Perhaps some of you feel, as do many women in the United States, that the progress of women in public life is like climbing trees—and that too many of the branches seem just out of reach.

But the last few years have been especially good for women in American government. More and more we're gaining the confidence to reach out, grab the branches—and pull ourselves up.

And I've always believed that a nation is like a tree—strongest at its grassroots. In America, and here in Britain, the seeds of lasting success for women in public life are being planted at the grass roots.

Six and a half percent of the membership of Parliament are women, slightly higher than in America, where 5% of Congress is female. The numbers increase at local levels, where 19% of the 25,000 members of your local councils are women, as are 11% of our mayors and 15% of our state legislators.

You might be interested to know that Texas—the home of J. R. Ewing and bucking broncos is leading the way for American women in positions of power.

The four largest cities in Texas—Dallas, Houston, San Antonio, and El Paso—all have women mayors. And it's quite likely that the Democrat candidate for governor of Texas in next year's election will be a woman.

All these women have succeeded in politics only after long histories of grassroots service in their communities.

Women have always been active in the organizations important to the fabric of community life—churches, the Parent-Teacher Association, charities, hospital and library boards. It is in these activities where many women learn valuable skills of leadership—consensus-building, mediating, moderating, and a commitment to good government.

A woman who personifies this particular American path to success is Anne Armstrong—who, by the way, is also a Texan. Anne began her career as a volunteer for civic and charitable causes and then toiled in the vineyards as a volunteer in Republican campaigns. Anne would use all these skills and more when my husband recognized her leadership and asked her to serve as his co-chairman of the Republican National Committee, and when President Ford appointed her as Ambassador to the Court of St. James.

By and large, the women who have been prominent in political life have succeeded because, like Anne Armstrong and your Prime Minister, they worked their way up. They started at the grass roots level and developed a sense of mission, dedication, and commitment to causes based on the important values of communities.

And it's interesting that some of the women who rose through the ranks with this dedication to good government, have viewed the achievement of power with mixed emotions or even with distaste. They believed that concepts such as power and ambition were inconsistent with the sense of mission which guided their steps and their conscience.

Over the years, however, women have more and more come to realize that power is a positive force if it is used for positive purposes. They've come to realize that they can not have an impact on the issues they care about, unless they obtain a place at the policy table, direct public attention to their cause by aggressive and creative promotion through the media and other outlets, and, in some instances, get out and raise the necessary money.

Perhaps no issue in American politics better illustrates the use of these principles than the debate on drunk driving—a debate elevated and transformed by women.

For too many years in too many American courtrooms, drunk driving was treated as no worse than a traffic violation. Judges and jurors tended to look past the dangers of drunk driving, by theorizing that they too, might have once had a drink or two before driving, and what's wrong with that?

What's wrong with that? Plenty. In 1988, over 23,000 Americans were killed in alcohol-related automobile accidents. Thankfully, this tragic loss of lives has decreased since we tightened up our laws and raised the consciousness level of the American people to this tragedy. Drunk driving was an issue of special importance to me, as one of my uncles was killed by a drunk driver. As Secretary, I worked to stiffen drunk driving laws throughout America. And my most important and effective ally was a volunteer organization that became a real political force.

That organization is MADD—Mothers Against Drunk Driving. Using their moral force and their passion as mothers whose children had been killed or injured by drunk drivers, they orchestrated a dynamic campaign for stiffer penalties, mandatory sentences and a change in attitude. And they succeeded.

Women have also succeeded in changing the public debate on human resource and education issues. Once regarded as "women's concerns," these are now considered as economic issues that define our future. For instance, child care was one of the most prominent issues during last year's presidential campaign, and it's a top priority in this session of the United States Congress.

At the Department of Labor, we are the lead agency responsible for ensuring that work and family are complimentary—and not conflicting goals. Child care, parental leave, flexible work schedules, and flexible benefit packages, are the major areas of our focus.

Likewise, President Bush often states his desire to be the "Education President." And education has risen to the top of my priority list, as it has become increasingly apparent that improving our education system is absolutely vital to providing America with the skilled workforce needed in today's competitive and complex world marketplace. We share with you a concern for job training and providing our workers with the higher skills needed to compete.

These are issues that face government. They are issues that have been advanced by women, and that need the continuing contributions of women as policies are formed. As a woman in government, I take very seriously my role to encourage and mentor others who seek to enter public service.

Back in the early 60s, I spent a summer in Washington working for a home state Senator. While there, I sought out several prominent women in government for professional guidance. Topping my list was Margaret Chase Smith, who was regarded by many as the conscience of the United States Senate. I don't know how many U.S. Senators would share an hour with a 22-year old total stranger seeking advice. But Margaret Chase Smith did, and she recommended that I bolster my education with a law degree.

Having had this experience, I feel a keen responsibility to do the same for young people who seek similar advice and counsel. My door is always open to them. And almost one-half of my senior level appointments at the Department of Labor are women. I tell young people that by public service, you may not get rich but you'll enrich the lives of millions. And speaking of committed women, I'd like to introduce an outstanding public servant who worked with me at Transportation, and who now serves as Assistant Secretary of Labor for Policy—Jenna Dorn. Believe me there are some men who work at the Labor Department!

Incidentally, I am very proud to report that in his first nine months in office, President Bush has appointed more women to senior positions than any previous administration has appointed in a whole year.

About twenty years ago, a group of women appointees and I organized a club called "Executive Women in Government," which still flourishes today. Its purpose was twofold: To help younger women who wanted to follow us into government service with information and perhaps advice on how to avoid some pitfalls and to provide women in policy-making positions with an opportunity to relate to one another across government.

Such networking is also key to the success of women in private enterprise. Decades of male domination of top corporate positions have ensured that the existing informal network system is often for men only. Days at the golf course, weekends at the hunting lodge, and afternoons at the club still close out women.

True, changes in the law have forced many traditionally male-only clubs to open their doors to women. But just making a club co-ed does not automatically change attitudes or generations of thinking. The 300 Group has correctly realized the absolute necessity of changing attitudes and preconceived notions of what women can and cannot do. And I do believe that attitudes are gradually changing as women make gains in the public and private sectors.

As you in the 300 Group so aptly stated, "The characteristics perceived as being necessary—opinionated, articulate, self-confident, assertive—are deemed suspect in women, who are more likely to be described as strident, brash and bossy, if they display them."

And our own attitudes are important, too. Part of the change must continue to come from within us—in the way that we prepare ourselves to accept greater responsibilities and the risks that accompany them. And part of the change must also come in the way that we rear our children, ensuring that our daughters, as well as our sons, recognize they have a full range of choices, and that they are fully trained to make the right choice for them.

America is now in a record 84th consecutive month of economic expansion. Since 1982, we have created over 20 million new jobs—and over half of those jobs have been filled by women.

Among small businesses [that are] responsible for three out of five new jobs created in America, women-owned businesses are growing at a rate five times that of male-owned—representing the largest increase in the most significant area of our economic expansion.

Today, women comprise the majority of workers in finance, insurance, real estate, banking, and health and legal services.

The number of women professionals—lawyers and doctors, for instance—has almost doubled since 1972. And the number of women in managerial jobs has almost tripled. But who among us can say that discrimination has disappeared? Who among us can say that the prejudice I call the tyranny of perfection has been banished?

Social critic Marya Mannes put it best, I think, when she wrote "Nobody objects to a woman being a good writer or sculptor or geneticist if, at the same time, she manages to be a good wife, a good mother, good-looking, good-tempered, well-dressed, well-groomed, and unaggressive."

In other words, a woman, too, can be treated the same as a man—so long as she outperforms him.

And who among us can deny the very real presence of a wage gap? The median-weekly earnings of women working full time last year were 70% of men's wages, similar to your experience here.

There can be little doubt that a woman, no matter how well schooled, what her age, or how thick her portfolio or credentials, enters many business organizations with limited or no hope of reaching the top. The positions of power and decision-making in business are still held primarily by men. For example, of the 500 largest companies in America, just two— two out of 500—have a woman Chief Executive Officer.

A woman manager may indeed have all the tools of the trade in her toolbox, and still not reach the top. There is a "glass ceiling," if you will, where women can see that top, but are blocked from reaching it by often invisible, impenetrable barriers.

The end result of these barriers for the businesses that maintain them may be the loss of talented human resources—as women take their skills and talents to other employers, or they start their own businesses.

Fortunately, demographics may help to remove this glass ceiling. America's workforce is growing at a rate of only 1% annually—the slowest rate in 40 years. And we expect that slow growth to continue into the next century. And two-thirds of the new entrants into the workforce between now and the end of the century will be women.

The slow workforce growth means that employers are competing for employees. Issues once defined as social problems will be dealt with more out of economic necessity. In tighter labor markets, employers can't afford

Assistant to the President, I worked hard at the White House for legislation that now makes it easier for mothers to collect child-support payments, and we fought for pension reform, such as equalizing Social Security pension benefits, for widows and widowers. And at the Department of Transportation, we implemented a ten-point program that boosted the number of women in a 100,000-member workforce by several percentage points. I knew we were making progress when a pilot told me that in his approach to a major U.S. airport, he was assisted by three distinct voices over the air traffic control system—and all three were women's voices.

And it didn't take me long in Washington to realize that one of the most important voices for women was, indeed, the Labor Department's Women's Bureau. I have long been an admirer of the Bureau, and of the outstanding women who have served as its Directors. And we are blessed, indeed, to have four of those women with us this evening. Special greetings to former Directors Mary Keiserling, Carmen Rosa Maymi, Shirley Dennis, and one of my most cherished friends, Esther Peterson.

I have long relied on Esther's counsel and wisdom, and am fortunate, indeed, to be one of many who regard her as a mentor and a role model.

And Elizabeth Duncan Koontz, who served under President Nixon, was a woman I greatly admired since the days when both of us lived in Salisbury, North Carolina.

Libby passed away last year, but her spirit as well as her words remains with us. Twenty years ago, at the 50th Anniversary celebration of this Women's Bureau, Libby said, "We have not come far enough, nor fast enough. And time is running out. The pace of our entire civilization is accelerating, and so must the pace with which our society brings equality to all its people."

Bringing equality to people by promoting the welfare of the working woman—that has been the work of the Women's Bureau for seven decades. And this work . . . our work . . . has never been more important than today.

America's workforce is growing at a rate of only 1% annually—the slowest rate in forty years. And we expect this slow growth to continue throughout this decade—a decade where fully two-thirds of new entrants into the workforce will be women.

The bottom line is simple. If employers want to compete in today's complex global market, then they can't afford to discriminate. They can't afford to ignore the needs of working women. Employers who do will simply lose out to those who don't. And, in the final analysis, America will lose out.

For the past twenty months, the Women's Bureau, through the national office here in Washington and our excellent regional offices across the nation have focused on four missions.

The first: ensuring that both men and women have the skills necessary to succeed in today's more complex jobs.

And much of my agenda this past year has been devoted to providing the skills, counseling, training, and literacy, needed by the least skilled and most disadvantaged Americans.

The Women's Bureau has sought to maximize opportunities by encouraging women to raise their math and science levels, and to assist women in obtaining careers in non-traditional fields like aerospace and construction.

Our second mission is to ensure that the relationship between work and family is complimentary, and not conflicting.

Women have entered the workforce at an astonishing rate in the past several decades. Approximately two-thirds of mothers with children under high school age are now in the workforce either full-time or part-time, and we have sought to mobilize America's employers to initiate childcare programs.

Throughout this Congress, President Bush and I have fought for childcare legislation which held fast to four principles. Parents are the ones best able to make childcare choices for their families; childcare options should be increased and not limited through a one-size fits all government mandate; aid should be focused on low-income families who need help the most; and parents who sacrifice a second income to remain at home with a child should not be discriminated against.

As this Congress approaches its final hours, I am very proud that the legislation on the table is true to these four principles.

I am also proud that our Work and Family Clearinghouse in the Women's Bureau was designed to assist employers in identifying the most appropriate policies for responding to the childcare needs of employees.

Employers who want to learn what is available . . . what works and what doesn't, can phone 1-800-827-5335 or write to the Clearinghouse seeking information about existing childcare and elder care programs across America. And through the Clearinghouse and a countless number of conferences and workshops at the local level, the Women's Bureau continues to stand up for America's most important institutions—her families.

Our third mission is one of workplace safety and health—a priority of mine throughout my years of public service. Since taking the oath as Secretary of Labor, I have sent an unequivocal message to those who are responsible for the health and safety of workers. The only acceptable compliance with safety requirements is full compliance.

The Women's Bureau has provided invaluable assistance in seeing that this message is being heard loud and clear in businesses and industries with a large number of women.

Our efforts are focused on safety in high hazard areas, such as construction. And on tackling the most pressing issues, such as repetitive motion illnesses, which account for about 48% of workplace illnesses, and safety belt regulation, since motor vehicle crashes accounted for 37% of deaths on the job last year.

By providing skills, building cooperative work-family relationships, and ensuring safety and health, we have greatly assisted in bringing women into the workforce and enabling them to remain there. Our fourth mission is a natural progression—to see that once a woman enters the workforce, there are no limits to the heights she can reach.

Since 1982, we have created over twenty-two million new jobs in this country—over half of which have been filled by women. Among small businesses—responsible for three out of five new jobs created in America—women-owned businesses are growing at a rate five times those owned by males.

Today, women comprise the majority of workers in finance, insurance, real estate, banking, and health and legal services. The number of women professionals—lawyers and doctors, for instance—has almost doubled since 1972. And the number of women in managerial jobs has almost tripled.

But despite this growth, who among us can say that discrimination against women has disappeared? Who among us can doubt that a woman, no matter how well schooled, or how golden her resume, enters many business organizations with limited or no hope of reaching the top?

Any overview or examination of the make-up of the American workforce finds women—and minorities—reaching plateaus from which they feel they cannot climb. For example, *Fortune Magazine* recently studied 800 of the largest U.S. companies. Of the 4,012 people listed as the highest-paid officers and directors of these companies, only 19 were women—that's less than one-half of one percent.

Additional evidence of the presence of what has been called the "glass ceiling" can be found in a recent survey of the nation's 1,000 largest corporations by Korn-Ferry and the UCLA Anderson Graduate School of Management. Their study revealed that minorities and women, who today account for more than half of the workforce, hold less than 5% of top managerial positions.

I can't help but think back over my own career—beginning with my days as a student at Harvard Law School. There were 550 members of the Class of 1965, and only 24 were women. On the first day of class, a male student came up to me and asked what I was doing there. In what can only be described as tones of moral outrage, he said, "Don't you realize that there are men who would give their right arm to be in this law school—men who would use their legal education?"

That man is now a senior partner in a Washington law firm. And every so often, I share this little story around town. You'd be amazed at the number of male classmates who've called me to say, "Please tell me I'm not the one! Tell me I didn't say that, Elizabeth!"

The objectives of our "glass ceiling" effort is to serve as a catalyst for change in both attitudes and policies, thereby ensuring women and minorities equal access to senior management opportunities.

Our initiative has everything to do with promoting opportunity, and nothing whatsoever to do with quotas. Under the leadership of the Office of Federal Contract Compliance, we aim to give a "wake-up" call to businesses, to alert them to the fact that it's in their vested interest to help ensure that the "glass ceiling" meets the same fate as the Berlin Wall.

The first step in this wake-up call is currently underway—a series of nine compliance reviews of government contractors. We are investigating how senior management positions are filled, and whether minorities and women are being developed for such opportunities. Specifically, we are examining training, rotational assignments, developmental programs, and reward structures—all the indicators of upward mobility in corporate America.

The pilot initiative has been ongoing for several months, and I believe it is having a positive effect. I have heard from many companies who were already taking positive steps to dismantle their glass ceiling. Several companies have developed tracking systems for identifying and developing high potential minorities and women for their workforce. Others have now asked executive search and recruitment firms to make an extra effort to include minorities and women in their candidate pools.

And, in just a few minutes, I will present this year's "Opportunity 2000 Award" to Digital Equipment Corporation. This award is presented annually to federal contractors, who, through a strategy of comprehensive programs, anticipate and take control of the changing demographics of the workforce.

Digital Equipment was selected because of their commitment to shattering the glass ceiling. Through an aggressive and ambitious agenda of early intervention programs, scholarships, work study, and pre-employment training programs, Digital Equipment is assisting women and minorities to become a significant part of its work force at all levels.

Their commitment to equal employment opportunities for all Americans is shared by the others we honor tonight—the nine recipients of the prestigious Exemplary Voluntary Efforts Award. These businesses are meeting the realities of today and tomorrow head-on. By opening their doors wide to minorities, to women, to individuals with disabilities, and to veterans, they not only help to ensure their own success, but America's as well. I might add that I am proud to work for a President who has appointed more women to senior positions than any other President in history, and I am delighted that 62% of my senior staff are women and minorities.

And to our honorees, let me just say that I am confident that you consider your awards as not just recognition of past achievements; rather, you consider them as recognition of a never-ending commitment to building a quality workforce.

Because for all that you've accomplished—for all that the Women's Bureau has accomplished these past seventy years—our missions are far from complete.

And as we look to the challenges ahead, let us take heart from the words of a woman who conquered incredible challenges. Unable to see or hear, she never ran for office, never raised a family, and never entered the job market. Yet she inspired millions.

"One can never consent to creep," said Helen Keller, "when one feels an impulse to soar."

All Americans, regardless of their race or gender, share that impulse to soar. To go as far and rise as high as their skills and talents will take them. And, more important, we also share an understanding that at the end of our days, our success will be judged not by the achievement of power for power's sake. Rather, we will be judged by how we used that power, what we stood for, and the difference—the positive difference—we made in the lives of others.

And that, ladies and gentlemen, is what the Women's Bureau is all about, and, indeed, what America is all about. Thank you and God bless you.

EVERYBODY COUNTS: THE FOURTH ANNUAL STATE OF THE WORKFORCE ADDRESS
Washington, D.C., October 24, 1990

This speech was Elizabeth Dole's "good-bye" to the staff at the Labor Department, who knew she had accepted the position of American Red Cross president.

Dole presents a summary of what she and her staff were able to accomplish in the areas of skills, safety, and security for the American worker. Eloquently, she argues that the social contract in America is based on the idea the "everybody counts," everyone should have a job worth doing that pays them a good wage. This speech was provided by Kerry Tymchuk.

Good afternoon. As you undoubtedly already know, this morning I visited with President Bush to announce that I would be resigning as Secretary of Labor in order to become the President of the American Red Cross.

Protocol required that I talk with him first. But I wanted you, the men and women of this remarkable department, to know just how much this experience has meant to me, and why.

Almost two years ago, I stood before you in this very hall to take the oath of office and begin my tenure as your Secretary. It was one of the proudest moments in my twenty-five year career in public service. I truly believed that this—the people's department—would be my mission field, a place where I would have the opportunity to work with people such as each of you, who are dedicated to making a difference—a positive difference—in people's lives. And, indeed, as we got to know each other, as we fought the good fight, we have succeeded in making that positive difference.

For the past four years, it has been traditional for the Secretary of Labor to deliver a "State of the Workforce Address." And last year, like Secretaries Brock and McLaughlin before me, I ventured outside the Francis Perkins Building to deliver the address. But over the past few days, as I thought about what I wanted to say in this year's address, and what you mean to me and to America, I realized that there was no one more important to the state of our workforce than you—the men and women of the Department of Labor.

After all, it's you who have worked so hard and done so much this past year to improve the skills, safety, and security of America's workforce, and it's you who must continue to make that difference—that positive difference—in the challenging times which lie ahead. The contributions of each of you matter. Everybody counts.

"Everybody counts." This simple belief was stated more eloquently by Thomas Jefferson who wrote that we're each endowed with certain inalienable rights, including life, liberty and the pursuit of happiness.

And, over the years, we have come to understand this to mean that the government would work to ensure that everyone has a chance at a good education, a decent job, and a secure retirement. And, in return, all citizens would accept a responsibility to work hard, provide for their family, and obey the law.

For more than 200 years, this "social contract" has served as the glue that holds our society together. It provides the momentum which keeps America moving forward, ever forward. But I have seen troubling evidence that this contract is being breached. And I believe that the mission of the Department of Labor must be to improve the state of our workforce, and the state of our nation, by doing what we can to ensure that, indeed, everybody counts.

Soon after my swearing in, I traveled across America—to inner cities, and small-town farms and everything in between. I met with the shop owners and merchants on Main Street, the factory workers and coal miners, and with those who live on the outskirts of hope—the drop-outs, mothers on welfare with no skills and little education, children working illegally, and migrants.

And through these meetings, it became clear to me that while our remarkable economic growth brought unparalleled opportunity for most Americans, there are those who have been left behind.

In 1981, the American economy and the American spirit were at their lowest levels. Families buying a home faced the highest interest rates since the Civil War. Senior citizens buying groceries were forced to make do with a 12% inflation rate. And young men and women seeking a job were staring at a double digit unemployment rate.

It was clear that economic policies had to be altered. And they were. As a result, twenty-two million new jobs were created, and the income of citizens in all five economic quintiles was increased. Yet, as our economy moved to a new and higher level, it bypassed some with minimal education or skills.

Now, I've been around public service for twenty-five years—long enough to know that the Labor Department doesn't have all the answers, and can't solve all our problems. But I believed that through the policies and programs of the Labor Department—the "people's department"—you and I could help in seeing that everybody counts.

I set three goals—I call them skills, safety and security—to guide our policies. Goals that would help achieve not just full employment, but fulfilling employment; not make-work, but real work—for all Americans who are willing to work. Goals that involve every agency of the Department of Labor—from ETA [Employment and Training Administration] to OSHA [Occupational Safety and Health Administration], for PWBA [Pension and Welfare Benefits Administration] to ESA [Employment Standards Administration], from the Women's Bureau to the Office of Policy.

First, fulfilling employment requires the education and the skills demanded by today's marketplace—a marketplace that becomes increasingly more global and more complex day by day. I will never forget the faces of the young men and women I have met in job training programs across America. People like Tim Douglas, a young man I met in Brooklyn, who told me—and later a hearing room full of Senators—that he was "evil" until one of our programs turned his life around, and gave it meaning.

There are too many children who face the future not with hope, but with pessimism, as Tim once did, who believe they don't count, that their lives don't matter. And this attitude has bred, in return, an unwillingness to fulfill the basic duties of citizenship. As columnist William Raspberry has written, "They drop out of school, or get through school with minimal academic effort, because they don't believe that academic exertion will make much difference in their lives. They become adolescent parents because they see no reason for postponing, or even being particularly careful with sexual activity. They sell drugs because the money is attractive and the risk of a police record seems small when measured against their chances of success in the legitimate world."

Ladies and gentlemen, where these young Americans are concerned, the social contract is in tatters. And we can take great pride in the fact that much of our work here at the Department has been aimed at helping turn these young lives around, putting the social contract back together for America's at-risk youth.

Our mission includes helping kids understand that doing well in school means they will do well at work—and helping schools understand that they must prepare students for the realities of today's workplace. And our innovations make this happen.

And while government can not heal the pain of broken families, or instill values when parents fail to, we can work to create an atmosphere which lets our youth know they do count. Through our Youth Opportunities Unlimited, or YOU grants, we are reaching into high poverty areas, and strengthening communities. We want to make youth feel they are the center of their communities; that there is much to hope for in their future, indeed, that they are the hope of our future.

In this mission, I've asked for the help of America's businessmen and women. After all, our workforce is growing at its slowest rate in forty years. Businesses will no longer have the luxury of skimming the cream off the labor market. America will need every one of us. Business must do more to help provide the skills, education, and motivation to give all our young people a chance.

I have asked America's businesses to allow 10% of their workforce the leeway to become involved in mentoring—in helping to point out the potholes on the road of life—to listen, to offer support—to let kids know that they count. And heartfelt thanks to the inspiring number to DOL employees who are helping us set a shining example by serving as mentors in their schools and communities.

And then there are the forgotten youth—the 50% who graduate from high school and don't go to college. Many of these move from low-paying job to low-paying job, with little chance of moving up the wage ladder. Businessmen and women tell me constantly that they have jobs to offer, but the youth coming out of high school don't have the skills—the credentials—to fill them.

Teddy Roosevelt once said that, "Far and away, the best prize life has to offer is the chance to work hard at work worth doing." Well, from developing working definitions of what skills employers require on the job, to building new school-to-work transition programs, to expanding the principle of apprenticeship so that workers will have "portable credentials," we are ensuring that all Americans can claim that prize . . . that they all have the opportunity to work hard at work worth doing.

Our second goal is safety—protecting our workers on the job. And, as with skills, this also begins with our young people. The laws prohibiting kids working too many hours in dangerous jobs have been on the books for more than fifty years. There was no need to create a new child labor program to deal with a growing number of violations. I just told my compliance officers to enforce the law. So four strike forces went into the field, and we got the message out that the "cop is on the beat," and we're going to stay there.

Physical safety is a concern, indeed, a basic right, of all our workers. And from the moment I took office, I have sent an unequivocal message to those who are responsible for the health and safety of workers: Everybody counts. The only acceptable compliance with safety requirements is full compliance. And our actions provide the evidence that this is more than just mere rhetoric.

In my first days at the Department of Labor, I requested and received a 10% increase in OSHA inspectors—the first such request in a decade. And we've set our sights on tackling the highest hazard problems—such as repetitive motion illnesses, which account for 48% of all work-related illnesses, and the occupations with the highest number of injuries—such as mining and construction.

Perhaps the one safety initiative that will save the most lives and prevent the most injuries involves automotive safety, as 37% of the workplace fatalities in America occur in motor vehicle crashes.

The value of safety belts has been proven in the most difficult testing laboratory of all—our highways. Six years ago, during my service at the Transportation Department, I put into place "Rule 208," requiring that every new car have an air bag or automatic safety belt. This rule also spawned thirty-six state safety belt laws, and has saved almost 20,000 lives to date. It totally changed the climate for automotive safety in America, and without this foundation, our actions at the DOL would have not been possible.

By providing skills, we ensure that those who want to work, count. By providing safety, we ensure that those who are working, count. And by providing security, we ensure that those who have retired from work, count.

When I traveled to the coal fields of southwest Virginia last fall to witness first-hand the dispute between the Pittston Coal Company and the United Mine Workers, I saw a community in turmoil. I walked the picket lines, and spoke with miners, their wives, and their families. There were many tears as they told me of their worry that commitments had been broken, that the system was failing them. Funds for retiree health benefits were in the red. Health care costs were skyrocketing. And the percentage of coal companies contributing to the retirement fund had dropped from 80% to 30%.

I will always be proud that the Department of Labor stepped in—calling in the parties and appointing a Super-mediator. We reached a settlement when most said none was possible. And to address the problem of retiree health benefits—a pivotal issue of the '90s—I appointed a Blue-Ribbon Commission charged with reviewing the pension and health care issue. The Commission reported last week with forward-looking cost containment recommendations.

As I expected on such a complex issue, the Commission debate was lively and contentious—on all sides. In my opinion, that's because it's controversial. It's precisely because the problem is big, because it's contentious, because it's fundamental to both our workers and our businesses, that we must address it now. The sooner we tackle it, the sooner it will be behind us—and that's good for everyone.

Ladies and gentlemen, as I said, the Labor Department does not have all the answers, nor can it address but a small portion of America's challenges. But each of us must start with our own corner of the world. Each of us in this room and all across the nation must do what we can to ensure, that here in America, everybody still does count. It's part of the deal—it's fundamental to the social contract. If the state of our nation and the state of our workforce is to remain strong, then that contract must be strong.

And so, my colleagues, what is the state of America's workforce this October afternoon? I believe it's more skilled, safer, and more secure, thanks to our efforts—your efforts—of the last two years.

There are so many memories I would like to share today . . . so many thanks to offer, but there will be other times for that in the coming months, and if I said all I want to say I'd end up being here for as long as Francis Perkins!

Let me just leave you this afternoon by sharing one of the most memorable experiences of my life—walking through the shipyards of Gdansk, Poland, with Lech Walesa. We talked about the history being written by the courageous citizens of this country, across Europe, and around the world. And, with a smile, Walesa told me the definition of a Communist economic enterprise: "100 workers standing around a single shovel." Then he said, "What Poland needs is 100 shovels."

Since then, I have thought a lot about that conversation. He was talking about men and women who had no role to play in their economy or their nation, their destinies decided not by individual effort, but by government. In short, they just didn't count. That feeling of futility, as much as anything, helped bring about the remarkable springtime of democracy that soon swept Eastern Europe. Millions of working men and women were finally fed up with a system in which they made not a dime's worth of difference.

It wasn't all that long ago in the sweep of history when we, too, were governed by absentee landlords who refused to allow us a voice in our own destiny. Our voice was gained, and our destiny changed, by a group of patriots who met in Philadelphia in 1776.

The world has turned over many times since, in the past two centuries, and the torch has been passed from generation to generation. But our mission remains the same . . . our cause endures. My service at the Department of Labor will soon be complete, as I leave the organization dedicated to serving people for another dedicated to the same purpose. And if I could write my own legacy for our time here, it would simply be, "They did their best to keep the contract intact. They did their best to ensure that everybody counts."

Thank you and God bless you.

A TRADITION OF TRUST SPEECH
Washington, D.C., February 4, 1991

In this speech, Elizabeth Dole introduces herself to the staff at the American Red Cross, describing what the organization means to her and to people all across the United States. To earn the trust of the Red Cross volunteers, she announces that she will work for a year with no pay. She describes the challenges facing the organization and pledges to meet them, asking the staff and volunteers to help her. This speech was provided by Kerry Tymchuk.

Thank you for that very warm welcome, and thank you, for those very kind words of introduction. This is the first time I've been introduced as the President of the American Red Cross, and I sure do like the sound of it.

I'm not going to take you away from your work for long today. In the next few weeks, as I find my way through the tunnel, I hope to drop by as many offices as I can, so we can become better acquainted. I am confident, however, that you and I are a good match. After all, we are united in a common mission—a mission of making a difference for people.

For me, the most rewarding times in my public service career were not spent in smoke-filled rooms exchanging political gossip. Rather, they were in classrooms, listening to at-risk youth and teen mothers who were turning their lives around; in fields, meeting with migrant workers who needed a voice; deep in coal mines, meeting with miners concerned about their safety; in businesses, ensuring full compliance with our child labor laws; and in far flung corners of the world where people needed help.

The opportunity to devote myself to these causes on a full time basis is what led me to the Red Cross. And, over the past four months, I've done a great deal of thinking about what it would take to earn my place among you, here at the world's largest humanitarian organization.

I found myself remembering the many ways in which the Red Cross has touched my life. When my brother was stationed in the Pacific in World War II, his load was made lighter by the presence of Red Cross Volunteers. Back in Salisbury, North Carolina, my mother was a Red Cross volunteer, telling me that she couldn't remember when she felt so important.

I married a man, who, like my brother, also fought for freedom in World War II. And when Bob Dole was wounded, the Red Cross was there with kind words and support, every step of the way. Bob returned the favor by serving as Chairman of the Russell County Chapter of the Red Cross in Kansas. And how proud I've been during my fifteen years of marriage to Bob, to be a member of the Senate Wives Red Cross Unit.

My story is not unique. In the past few months, countless men and women have come up to tell me how Red Crossers touched their life . . . How, during their years in the armed services, time spent in a Red Cross facility or a kind word from a volunteer made home seem that much closer. How Red Cross services after a flood or a tornado helped them survive financially and psychologically . . . how blood collected by the Red Cross had saved their life or the life of a relative. . . . how they learned to save lives through our safety programs. *Our* safety programs. I do like the sound of that!

What struck me the most during these conversations was the absolute trust that these men and women placed in the Red Cross. They trusted the Red Cross to be there when needed. They trusted the Red Cross to do what was right. This tradition of trust is our most valuable and irreplaceable asset . . . an asset which must be protected at all costs.

When the search committee first approached me about coming here, they told me of the great challenges facing this organization—about an organization struggling mightily to preserve that tradition of trust. The Red Cross is challenged because this country is challenged. You are meeting those challenges head-on and I salute you.

Specifically I salute the work that went into SD 21 [Service Delivery for the 21st Century], and predict that SD 21 will go a long way toward strengthening trust and respect for the Red Cross and her people across America and around the world.

As you know, in January, the Executive Committee delayed for a few months Board action on the SD 21 recommendations. The SAF [Service to Armed Forces] portion needs a second look, given the war in the Gulf, and the Board and I are eager to review all final recommendations before we go forward. I assure you, however, we *will* go forward.

I have also announced other changes in the management structure, including the selection of a chapter manager to Senior Vice President for Operations Management. The board and I look forward to completing this search and selection process expeditiously. Additionally, I have established the position of comptroller, to examine issues of quality control to ensure fiscal accountability. I am determined to do everything we can to see that the Red Cross services are delivered even more efficiently.

These changes are evolutionary, rather than revolutionary, and they are designed to strengthen coordination, improve communication, and increase effectiveness. I hope these strategic shifts will make it easier for chapter voices to be heard in headquarters, and for headquarters to respond even more quickly, efficiently and cost effectively.

As we build for the future, and reinforce our tradition of trust, we must remember that while times and management styles may change, basic human needs do not. I promise as your president to always remember from where we came. For by always remembering that service to people is our reason for being, our mission will evolve, still true to our heritage, still worthy of trust.

And, as we set about our work, we will follow the principle of Noah, that first great proponent of disaster preparedness: "No more prizes for predicting rain. Prizes only for building arks."

Like Noah's ark, the Red Cross was built by volunteers. And our tradition of trust was built from the grass roots, in communities across the country. Our assistance is not delivered by strangers or faceless bureaucrats, rather it's given by friends and neighbors. The Red Cross patch can be found on the arm of the merchant on Main Street or the retired teacher, two houses down.

I've thought a lot about that patch, and the over one million volunteers who wear it today. I've thought about how I wanted to get the message out that it is the volunteers who are the heart and the soul of the Red Cross. And I decided that the best way I can let volunteers know of their importance is to be one of them—to earn the patch on my sleeve.

Therefore, during my first year as President, I will accept no salary. I, too, will be a volunteer.

The first volunteer of the Red Cross was, of course, Clara Barton, who earned her patch on the battlefields of the Civil War.

War has been an unfortunate reality of modern history. A history that has reflected the fact that wherever you find American soldiers defending freedom, you will also find the American Red Cross. And serving our soldiers and their families, in times of peace, as well as war, contributes immeasurably to the Red Cross tradition of trust. The tradition continues today as we will soon have 154 staff members stationed in Saudi Arabia, and we stand poised to ship as many as 7,000 units of blood per week to the forces of Operation Desert Storm, should they be needed.

However, modern realities have changed the services the military requires, and put pressure on the ability of our chapters to pay for them. Those services must evolve, and that pressure will be relieved. But let there be no doubt that we *will* find ways to live up to this trust.

We will, because we must. After all, the building was dedicated as a memorial to the "women of the north and the women of the south . . . that their labors to mitigate the suffering of the sick and wounded in war may be perpetuated. Until the day comes when wars are no more, then the Red Cross must remain true to those words."

Re-emphasizing both the volunteer nature of the Red Cross, and our enduring commitment to serving America's armed forces, are just two steps on the road of strengthening our tradition of trust.

There can be no higher trust than the blood of life we distribute to hospitals, and now to our men and women in the Gulf.

As Secretary of Labor, I was responsible for the safety of America's workforce. And when presented with evidence that a workplace was endangering that safety, I told them clearly and unequivocally to clean up their act or we would shut them down. I know you are already taking dramatic steps to ensure universal standards of excellence among our Blood Regions. I will not let you down in this regard. My goal and my commitment is that all of our Blood Regions must meet or exceed exacting standards of quality, or they will not collect blood.

This month marks the 50th anniversary of the blood services program of the American Red Cross. What better way to celebrate this milestone than by taking every step possible to ensure that the blood supply is as safe as we can make it.

One of the most moving experiences of my life came in the fall of 1989, when I visited Armenia soon after the devastating earthquake. There, amidst the rubble and ruin, I found representatives of the American Red Cross, continuing a tradition that dated back before Clara Barton made her own trip to Armenia in 1896.

Just as blood is necessary to sustain life, so, too, is hope. And hope is what we offer through our disaster relief services. Hurricanes, floods, fires. . . . there is no doubt that forces of nature are strong forces, indeed. However, as the volunteers and staff of the American Red Cross have proven time and again, the force of people helping people can be much stronger. For no matter how fast the winds may blow, or how high the water may rise, the Red Cross has always weathered out the storm, providing food, clothing, money, shelter, and hope.

Here, our priorities are clear. When disaster strikes, the Red Cross will respond quickly, efficiently, and with volunteers who know the needs of the community. We are currently engaging in a comprehensive review of disaster services, with a goal of improving the efficiency and effectiveness of our assistance to disaster victims.

Assisting military personnel and their families . . . blood services. . . . disaster relief . . . international assistance to refugees and victims of war . . . health and safety education. . . . these are just a few of the many ways in which the American Red Cross has earned the trust of our nation. And given these good causes, it is no wonder that Americans have been more than generous when asked to support our mission. In return for their generosity, we will live up to our tradition of trust through complete fiscal accountability, integrity, and just plain good sense when it comes to spending each and every dime.

If I learned one thing during my twenty-five years in government, it is that Washington, D.C. does not have a monopoly on wisdom or ingenuity. I learned that while the national office usually had the best overview, the best answers to problems often came from those in local and regional offices—those translating policy into action, "is where the rubber meets the road." Success comes from finding the right balance between the two.

I believe that the same must be true for the Red Cross. I looked forward to my first day here at headquarters, to taking my place alongside each of you. In the coming months, I look forward to visiting with Red Crossers in every region of the country, to learn from them, as I will learn from you, how to map our future together.

I am reminded of a story told about the night in 1945, when General Dwight D. Eisenhower was walking along the Rhine, thinking of the crossing in which he would lead the allied armies. He met a soldier, and asked him why he wasn't sleeping. The young GI, who didn't recognize the supreme commander said, "I guess I'm a little nervous."

"So am I," said Eisenhower. "Let's walk together, and perhaps we'll draw strength from one another."

Ladies and gentlemen, you have every right to be confident and proud of the Red Cross patch on your sleeve, or pin on your lapel. Yes, there are challenging times ahead, but of one thing I am certain. By walking together, by working together, and by drawing strength from one another, we will ensure that our tradition of trust will endure, and that the best days of the American Red Cross are truly yet to come.

Thank you and God bless you.

REPUBLICAN NATIONAL CONVENTION SPEECH
San Diego, California, August 14, 1996

This campaign speech, presented in support of Bob Dole's nomination for the presidency, received considerable attention from the press and the public. Elizabeth Dole did something unprecedented in political convention history when she descended the platform stairs to present her speech while strolling around the audience. At first she used a lavaliere microphone, and when the sound failed, she switched to one that was handheld. She gained great national exposure, and many who saw and heard her expert performance began to regard her as a woman who could herself run for the vice presidency, even the presidency. The speech was obtained from: http://www.allpolitics.com/conventions/san.diego/transcripts, accessed September 3, 1996.

Thank you so much. Thank you, ladies and gentlemen. Thank you very much. Thank you. Thank you so much. Oh, my. Thank you, ladies and gentlemen. Thank you so much, ladies and gentlemen for that wonderful, warm welcome. And thank you, Governor Wilson, for your very kind words of introduction.

Now, you know, tradition is that speakers at the Republican National Convention remain at this very imposing podium. But tonight I'd like to break with tradition for two reasons—one, I'm going to be speaking to friends, and secondly, I'm going to be speaking about the man I love. And it's just a lot more comfortable for me to do that down here with you. Thank you. Governor, how are you doing tonight? Great. Congratulations.

Now, for the last several days, a number of men and women have been painting a remarkable portrait of a remarkable man, a man who is the strongest and most compassionate, most tender person that I've ever known—the man who, quite simply, is my own personal rock of Gibraltar. And tonight, I want to put the finishing brush strokes on that portrait, if you will. And Bob Dole, if you're watching, let me just warn you . . . I may be saying some things that you in your modesty would never be willing to talk about. But I think that the people you've been serving all these years in America deserve to know—they have a right to know. This is not a time to be silent.

This is a defining moment, ladies and gentlemen, in our nation's history. This election is about the vision and the values that will shape America as we move into the next century, and it's about the character of the man who will lead us there.

Now [Applause] thanks. Bob Dole, as you know, was born in Kansas in a small town. And his family . . . [Applause] Hey, Bob. [Bob Dole appeared on a large video screen.] What are we doing? [Applause] Is he going to speak or am I going to speak? I'm not sure. [Laughter] That was a nice surprise.

But let me say that, yes, he was born in a small town in Kansas. His parents were poor, in fact, at one point, when Bob was a boy, they had to move their family—parents and four children—into the basement and rent out their small home, the upstairs, just to make ends meet. But while they were perhaps poor in material things, they were rich in values—values like honesty, decency, respect, personal responsibility, hard work, love of God, love of family, patriotism.

Those were values that led Bob to risk his life on the battlefields of Italy and these were the values that enabled him to sustain over three years in the hospital. Now, I didn't know Bob back then. But Pat Lynch did. Pat, stand a moment if you would.

Come right up here with me. Pat Lynch is from Boone, Iowa. And she was. . . . Pat was one of Bob's nurses at Percy Jones Hospital in Battle Creek, Michigan.

Pat has told me about Bob's good humor and how they used to wheel him from ward to ward to cheer up the other wounded soldiers. I think we're having a little technical difficulty. She also told me that Bob was very patient and that he tapped his inner resources so that he endured, not just day after day, but month after month—I think we're having a little technical difficulty, yes—also—there we are. [A new microphone was handed to Elizabeth Dole to rectify the audio problem.]

Pat's told me that when Bob was totally paralyzed and people thought he wouldn't walk again, he literally willed himself to walk. He was a person of great perseverance and determination and drive. And he recovered fully except for the use of his right arm in the three years over at the hospital.

But during that period of time, I think that Bob's sensitivity to the problems of others certainly was deepened as well—because he's been there. He's been through adversity. He's known pain and suffering. It was at this time in his life that he got to know Dr. Hamper Kelikian. Now, Hamper Kelikian was a great surgeon . . . [from] Chicago, Illinois.

And Dr. Kelikian had fled Armenia, war-torn Armenia, as a young man. Three of his sisters were not so fortunate. But he came to the United States with only two dollars and a rug from his homeland under his arm. And Dr. Kelikian, at that point a young boy, worked on a farm. And the owner of the farm was so impressed with him that he paid his way through college. And then he went on to medical school, and he became a great surgeon, a master in bone and joint surgery. And so Bob Dole went to Dr. Kelikian looking for a miracle because he wanted to be the person he had been before the war, a great athlete, a person who was on his way to study medicine. Dr. Kelikian performed a number of operations. And then he had to administer some tough love. He had to say to Bob, "You're not going to find the miracle. Now, the choice is up to you, Bob. You can continue to feel sorry for yourself, or you can get on with your life and work to make the most of what you do have."

Dr. Kelikian would not take a penny of money for those operations. And he did the same for many other young veterans coming back from the war who were not able to afford the medical care that they needed. So you can imagine how much we cherished the friendships of Dr. Kelikian's widow, Ovsanna Kelikian, and her daughter, Alice.

And certainly Bob has known the struggle to make ends meet. In fact, he couldn't have had a college education if it were not for the GI Bill. And so, he's going to protect and preserve and strengthen that safety net for those who need it.

And, he's dedicated his life to making a difference—a positive difference—for others because of his own experiences. Whether it's on the battlefield, on the Senate floor, or whether it's in his personal life, he's going to be making that difference for others.

And you know, it was only . . . about 12 years ago that I recall so well Bob coming home from a trip to Kansas. We were sitting in the bedroom talking, and he said, "Elizabeth, my plane was late, and they were trying to rush me into a meeting out there. And there were these two young people who were waiting outside the door to talk with me, and they were severely disabled. And they were there with their parents. Tim and Carla were their names." And he said, "Tim said to me, Senator Dole, we found a source of help for people who have a disability such as ours in another state. Can you help us get there?" And as Bob was telling me about it, he said, "I can't stop thinking about Tim and Carla. Elizabeth, I've been meaning to start a foundation for people with disabilities for years, and I haven't done it yet." Well, very soon thereafter, the Dole Foundation was up and running, and Bob's raised millions of dollars to help people with disabilities. Tim—Tim, I want to thank you for your courage and your spirit. Thank you, Tim, for inspiring Bob Dole to start the Dole Foundation for people with disabilities. We love you, thank you.

And I remember a Thanksgiving, oh, probably three or four years ago when Bob called up and he said, "You know Elizabeth," he said, "I'd like to do something a little different this Thanksgiving." And he sounded kind of sheepish because you see he'd already put the plans in motion. And I said, "Bob, what would you like to do?" And he said, "Well, I've invited 35 young people from some pretty tough parts of Washington and their church sponsors to have Thanksgiving dinner with us." Well, he had already reserved some places for us at a restaurant. He'd had them put in some televisions so the kids could watch the Redskins game. What touched us so deeply was that after they finished the Thanksgiving meal, and they finished watching the game, they began to talk about their life stories. And the common thread that ran through so many of those stories was that these kids, until very recently, had never heard anyone say, "I care about you, I care about you." Ladies and gentlemen, you didn't read about that Thanksgiving dinner in the newspaper or hear about it in the media because Bob Dole never told anybody about it. He did it from his heart.

He wants to make a difference—a positive difference—for others because he cares, because that's who he is. And I certainly will never forget his last day as majority leader of the United States Senate. I was seated up in the balcony, you know, and I was watching as senator after senator, Democrats and Republicans, stood and paid tribute to my husband on the Senate floor. They talked about his countless, legislative achievements, how he had led the United States Senate to successfully pass the largest tax cut in the history of the United States of America.

They talked about how he had saved Social Security and I just want to quote from a letter—this is Claude Pepper. As you know he was the champion of seniors. And he wrote to Bob [on] May 11, 1983. He thanked Bob for his extraordinary contributions saying, and I quote, "You never lost hope and faith in our accomplishing the immeasurable task of saving

Social Security. We could never have produced this result without your skill and sincerest desire to make a meaningful contribution."

That's leadership, ladies and gentlemen. They also talked about how Bob had led the senate just last year to save Medicare, increasing spending 62 percent, only to have the White House veto the legislation, provide no other alternative for saving the system except a multi-million dollar ad campaign to scare our senior citizens.

They talked about Bob's incredible ability to bring people together and his tremendous sense of humor. And you know that reminds me of the time that I was up for confirmation hearings before . . . one of the committees of the senate for Secretary of Transportation. And my husband introduced me. And you know what he did to me? He sort of did a take off on Nathan Hale, he said, "I regret that I have but one wife to give for my country's infrastructure."

That's Bob Dole.

But above all, these senators, Democrats and Republicans, talked about Bob's character, his honesty, his integrity. And I remember Senator Pete Domenici, beautiful speech that you gave, and when you concluded your speech, you said, "The next majority leader of the United States Senate better know that he better be honest. He better tell the Senate the truth because Bob Dole knew no other way." Remember, Pete?

And Dianne Feinstein, Democrat of California said, "Bob Dole's word"—listen to this now—"Bob Dole's word is his commitment. And his commitment is a matter of honor. We often disagree on issues," she said, "but even when we disagree, I know where I stand with Bob Dole, and I know I can trust his word." I can trust his word . . . And that's why, ladies and gentlemen, that's why Bob Dole's fellow senators elected him six times to be their leader—because they know he's honest, trustworthy, a man of his word, his word is his bond, and they know he has exceptional leadership skills. And isn't that exactly what we want in the President of the United States?

These are the people, think about this. These are the people who know him so well, have worked with him, day after day, year after year. They know what his judgment is like under pressure. And that's why they continue to put their faith and trust in him, making him the longest serving Republican leader in senate history—11 years.

Now, I'm also proud of the fact that the employees of the United States Senate, the waiters, waitresses, others who work there voted Bob twice, four years apart in two surveys, as the nicest, friendliest of all 100 senators. I'm sorry about that, Pete.

These are employees like Trude Parker, who is a member of the United States Capital Police, and Trude, bless your heart. Trude was the first person that Bob saw on the way to work every morning while he was in the Senate, and also that final day, I can still see you. I'll remember it forever. You threw your arms around my husband and tears were streaming down your face, and you said, "Elizabeth, everywhere you go, people tell you they love Bob Dole because he always has a kind word for everyone." Bless you, Trude.

Now, let me just say I could go on and on sharing stories about this loving husband and father, this caring friend, but please indulge a very proud wife just one final story which neither I nor my 95-year old mother will ever forget.

When Bob was dating me, he used to go to North Carolina to visit my parents. And, one morning—one morning unbeknownst to me, he left his bedroom and went down where mother was fixing breakfast in the kitchen. And he had a towel over his arm and shoulder that had been disabled in the war. And he said, "Mrs. Hanford, I think you ought to see my problem." Mother said, "That's not a problem. It's a badge of honor."

My fellow Americans—my fellow Americans, I believe that in the years to come, future generations will look back to this November and say, "Here is where Americans earned a badge of honor."

Here is where we elected the president who gave us more opportunities and smaller and more efficient government, and stronger and safer families. Here is where we elected the better man who led us to a better America because here is where we elected Bob Dole.

God bless you all. Thank you.

REDBOOK/MOTHERS AGAINST DRUNK DRIVING SPEECH
Washington, D.C., May 9, 1997

Elizabeth Dole gave this speech at the National Press Club in Washington, D.C., when she was president of the American Red Cross. Her experience with transportation issues and her commitment to safety made her an obvious choice as a speaker for this conference, which was sponsored by *Redbook* magazine to raise awareness about drunk driving among America's young people. She related personally to the speech, disclosing that her grandmother had lost a son in a drunk-driving accident. Present in the audience were members of the support group Mothers Against Drunk Driving. Dole recognized the courage of families who had lost children to drunk drivers, and she pledged to help them promote a zero tolerance to drunk driving in society. This speech was provided by Kerry Tymchuk.

Thank you for that welcome, and thank you, Kate [White, editor in chief of *Redbook*] for those very kind words of introduction. When Kate invited

me to join with you in paying tribute to the five remarkable and courageous women you honor today, I quickly accepted for a number of reasons.

First, because of the tremendous respect I have for the Mothers Against
Drunk Driving Organization—respect that began during my years as Secretary of Transportation, and respect that has only grown stronger over
the years. Second, because I shared *Redbook*'s alarm with the recent increase in drunk driving fatalities in the United States. After all, as President of the organization that collects, processes and distributes half of
America's blood supply, I am keenly interested in doing all we can to stop
needless bloodshed. And, finally, I accepted because doing all I can in the
battle against drunk driving allows me, in some small way, to pay a debt
of gratitude to a woman who taught me lessons that have inspired my
entire life—my grandmother, Cora Alexander Cathey.

I can still vividly recall the Sunday afternoons I spent in "Mom"
Cathey's living room, munching on cookies, and drinking lemonade as
she told us stories from Scripture. It was Mom Cathey's deep faith that
helped her persevere through a tragedy shared by three of today's honorees, and by thousands more across the country—the loss of a child to a
drunk driver.

When Vernon Cathey was killed just out of college, my grandparents
lost a son, my mother lost a brother, and I lost an uncle I was never to
know. My grandmother was not a wealthy woman, but because she was
concerned that Vernon never had a chance to make his contribution in life,
she took the money from his life insurance and built a new wing for a
mission hospital in far-off Pakistan. There was no Mothers Against Drunk
Driving organization when my grandmother suffered her loss, but I know
that had there been, she would have been a dedicated member.

I thought of my grandmother when I read the words of honoree Linda
Hull, who suffered the unimaginable horror of losing two daughters and
a stepdaughter to three drunk drivers in the course of four years. In this
month's *Redbook*, Linda writes that after a period of depression and in-
trospection, "I realized that I can't make these girls come back. The only
thing I can do is make a change." Making a change in both the laws and
attitudes involving drunk driving was on top of my agenda when I became Secretary of Transportation in 1983. And President Reagan and I had
no better ally in advancing this agenda than Mothers Against Drunk
Driving.

MADD was with us every step of the way as we championed legislation encouraging states to raise their drinking age to twenty-one, thereby
bringing an end to the "blood borders" that tempted some teenagers to
drive across state lines to take advantage of more liberal laws next door.

MADD was also with us as we used the bully pulpit to spread a message of zero tolerance for drunk driving. Prior to that time, far too many Americans tended to react to drunk driving with a wink and a shrug, instead of with the outrage it deserved.

It is well worth noting here at the National Press Club that the crusade that dramatically lowered the number of drunk-driving accidents and deaths in the 1980s and 1990s would not have succeeded without the assistance of the print and broadcast media. Through news stories, public service announcements, and the support of entertainment industry celebrities, the public's attention was focused on the costs of drunk driving, and the term "designated driver" became part of our national vocabulary.

Over time, however, the media's and the public's attention have shifted to other issues, and, not coincidentally, in 1995, for the first time in a decade, there was an increase in the number of drunk driving fatalities compared to the preceding year.

It was this increase that led this month's *Redbook* to print one of the most heartbreaking and disturbing headlines I have ever seen. The headline states simply: "Drunk Driving Makes a Comeback."

Ladies and Gentlemen, I know it pained *Redbook* to print that headline. But that pain pales in comparison to the pain of those who know all too well the truth of that headline—the families and friends of more than 17,000 Americans who died in alcohol related traffic crashes in 1995.

Today, I'm proud to join with MADD in issuing a call to arms, and in pledging to do everything we can to write a much different headline—a headline announcing that drunk driving fatalities have reached a record low.

How do we make that headline a reality? We do it by remembering the words of Linda Hull—by making changes.

We do it by changing the attitudes of America's youth. The fact is that the overall death rate for 15 to 24 year olds is higher today than it was 20 years ago, and the leading cause of death in that age group is drunk and drugged driving. MADD correctly realizes that despite the fact that alcohol-related youth fatalities have declined in recent years, there is still much more that needs to be done. I congratulate MADD for sponsoring a National Youth Summit on Underage Drinking, which begins tomorrow here in Washington, and I challenge the media to cover this summit, and to report on the recommendations it makes.

We can also make changes by setting national goals, and sticking with them until they are met. I look forward to this June, when the National Highway Traffic Safety Administration launches "Partners in Progress," which will unite numerous groups behind a goal of reducing yearly alcohol-related fatalities to no more than 11,000 by the year 2005.

Those in the halls of Congress and our nation's state legislatures can also continue to make necessary life-saving changes in the laws dealing with alcohol and drug-impaired driving. I congratulate Senator Lautenberg and Congresswoman Lowey on their leadership on this issue, and wish them well as they work with their colleagues and with America's governors and state legislatures in fashioning legislation that will help keep alcohol and drug-impaired drivers off our streets.

Ladies and gentlemen, it has been a true privilege to be with you, and to join *Redbook* in honoring five very courageous women, and in returning the fight against alcohol and drug impaired driving to the top of America's agenda. In closing today, I want to share with you the words of honoree Kathleen Valone, who along with her husband and two children, are still dealing with injuries caused by a drunk driver seven years ago.

Kathleen explained her involvement with MADD in these words, "there's one reason that drives me to do everything I'm doing. In order for me to live with what's happened to us and to get through each day, I have to make something good out of something bad."

In the days and months to come, let us all remember the words of Kathleen Valone. And let us all resolve to ensure that out of something bad—the "comeback of drunk driving"—can come something very good—a new national resolve to make our streets safer and more sober. Thank you very much.

ECONOMIC SUMMIT FOR WOMEN SPEECH
Albany, New York, May 20, 1997

This speech was a keynote address at a large conference for women sponsored by Governor George Pataki of New York. Elizabeth Dole presents many of her views on equality in the workplace, stressing her belief that women possess excellent leadership qualities. She told her audience, instead of asking, "why can't women be more like men?" which would have been an appropriate question for the 1960s, a better question for the 1990s is, "why can't women be more like women?" In this speech, Dole describes several of the gender-based difficulties she has faced and offers advice for women leaders. This text was provided by Elizabeth Dole.

Thank you for that very warm welcome, and thank you, Libby, for those very kind words of introduction. When Governor Pataki and Charlie Gargano asked me to join you today, I quickly accepted for a number of reasons and let me tell you why.

First, because of the high regard I have for a number of people whose leadership and vision made this Summit possible. Chief among them, of course, are George and Libby Pataki. My husband prides himself on having a keen eye for talented public servants. And I remember several years ago when Bob returned home from a trip to New York and said, "Elizabeth, there's a State Senator running for Governor in New York that the so-called experts say doesn't have a chance. I met him, and I think the experts are wrong."

Bob was right. The experts were wrong. And in the last two and a half years, Governor George Pataki has earned a reputation as one of America's most innovative, effective, and successful governors. The state motto of New York is just one word—the word "Excelsior" which means, "Ever Upward." And those words certainly describe New York's economy ever since Governor Pataki was elected. You know better than I how his tax cuts and regulatory reform have revitalized the Empire State, leading to 150,000 new private sector jobs in the last two and a half years. And I know the economic action items adopted at this Summit, will help to ensure that the women of New York continue to benefit from the economic resurgence.

And in Libby, New York has one of America's most talented and gracious First Ladies. I thought my schedule was busy until I got a look at Libby's—not only does she focus attention on women's health awareness, children's issues, and economic development through small businesses, tourism, and the arts; but she also has become this state's "First Volunteer," donating time to a countless number of organizations, like excellence in education. And drawing great support and guidance from her faith, she hosted the first official Prayer Breakfast in New York State, and is an active member of the prayer Group Movement throughout America. All this, of course, while also managing the Pataki Farm and taking care of four children.

I think I first met Charlie Gargano back in 1983, when I was serving as Secretary of Transportation, and Charlie was Deputy Administrator of the Federal Urban Mass Transit Administration. Charlie later served with great distinction, as you've heard, as our Ambassador to Trinidad and Tobago, and now, of course, he presides as Chair of the Empire State Development Corporation. Charlie also makes a very positive difference in the lives of others as President of the Italian Earthquake Relief Fund, President of the Board of the Children's Development Center, and Chairman of the Suffolk Country Race Against Drug Abuse. Bob and I are honored to call Charlie our friend.

I'm also delighted to be with Elaine Wingate Conway, Director of the New York State Division for Women, and John Sweeney, Commissioner of the Department of Labor. Charlie, Elaine, John and all the corporate sponsors deserve so much credit for the outstanding Summit and many others!

The topic of this conference—removing the barriers that prevent women from participating fully in our workforce—is one that has been a special mission of mine for many years. And I've found that, while a virtual tidal wave of qualified women have entered the marketplace in the recent past, many of us are still seeking answers to some important questions.

Indeed, one question that women have heard all too often in our fight for equality—even well before Henry Higgins asked it in "My Fair Lady," is "why can't a woman be more like a man."

It's the question Abigail Adams wrote to her husband, John, in 1776. She wanted women to have the right to own property. It was not that long ago when a man and woman married, the two became one—and the husband was the one. "Do not put such unlimited power in the hands of husbands," warned Abigail Adams.

I don't know how much affect Abigail's words had on her husband. In a letter John once said to her, "I must not write a word to you about politics, because you are a woman." Perhaps that attitude explains why Adams was just a one-term president!

Why can't a woman be more like a man? I asked myself that question on my first day of class at Harvard Law School, when a male student came up to me and asked what I was doing there. In what can only be described as tones of moral outrage, he said, "Don't you realize that there are men who would give their right arm to be in this law school—men who would use their legal education?"

That man is now a senior partner in a prestigious Washington law firm. And every so often, I share this little story around town. You'd be amazed at the number of my male classmates who've called me to say, "Tell me I'm not the one! Tell me I didn't say that, Elizabeth!"

Indeed, during my tenure as Secretary of Labor, some very interesting facts crossed my desk: like the fact that 60% of new jobs created between 1980 and 1990 were filled by women; and the fact that women-owned businesses are the fastest growing segment of the small business economy in the U.S. . . . and now employ more workers than all of the Fortune 500 companies combined!

But we women certainly have not reached the millennium.

The latest studies show that women who work full-time earn an average of just seventy-six cents for the dollar earned by males.

And while the number of women in top management positions has increased over the past decade, the totals are disturbingly low. The Glass

Ceiling investigation, which I initiated at the Labor Department, revealed that only 6.6% of the nearly 4,500 executive-level managerial positions in the nine corporations we interviewed were held by women.

So, yes, while progress has been made, there is still much work to do before all the barriers are down, before the Glass Ceiling meets the same fate as the Berlin Wall.

I wholeheartedly agree with author Jane White, who writes in her book, *A Few Good Women: Breaking the Barriers of Management*, "If you're going to be in the forefront of a revolution, you have to keep taking the flak until it's won."

But I think the day has come where that "flak" will not involve someone asking, "Why can't a woman be more like a man?"

Indeed, I would submit to you that the much more relevant question for the '90s is: "Why can't a woman be more like a woman?"

In *Reinventing the Corporation*, John Naisbett and Patricia Aburdene argue that the successful companies will be those that aggressively hire, train and promote women.

Why? Well, one reason is simple demographics. The low birth rates of the '60s and '70s mean that there are simply not enough men to fill new managerial jobs. Any business that wants to stay competitive will have to recruit, retrain, and retain women.

Another reason, however, has nothing to do with our numbers, and everything to do with our skills—skills which are being recognized as absolutely necessary to successful management, whether in volunteer or business organizations. Tom Peters, after a decade in search of excellence, has concluded that "soft is hard." Some male CEOs and executives now proudly boast about their "female style of management."

What that means is probably best explained by Rebecca McDonald, former President of Tenneco's natural gas marketing subsidiary—an industry traditionally dominated by "good old boys." She said, "You hear a lot of talk about changing the way we teach little girls because they're taught to listen and accommodate while little boys are taught to win at all costs. I wonder if, really, we shouldn't rethink the way we're teaching boys. The rigidity that comes from expecting to win at all costs doesn't necessarily play to the new skill sets for corporate America."

The management skills which she was referring to include mediation, negotiation, and dealing with needs, issues, and market forces that are often not clearly defined.

And, as McDonald points out, "Women have a higher tolerance for ambiguity because we're always responsible for tending to the emotional needs of others—which are very fluid. We learn to read between the lines and come up with creative solutions for accommodating people. What I'm suggesting isn't touchy-feely at all," she says. "Results, results, results are still the bottom line. I'm just saying that women are especially suited for today's demands: listening, communicating, getting to the root of the problem. It's what we trained for."

In other words, McDonald is saying that progress for women in the workplace of the '90s will continue, as we continue to develop our skills and values as women, because it is precisely those skills and values our country needs most at this moment. By being more like women, we can soar in any work place arena, paid or volunteer. And summits for women like this one help us meet the challenges of our next century.

I have been privileged during my years in the public and not-for-profit sectors to work with a number of women who have achieved and soared. And I would now like to pass along a few common traits I have identified in those women, as well as sharing some lessons I have learned over the years.

In today's fast-paced world the only constant is change itself. Whether or not we expect change . . . whether or not we expect the unexpected, it will find us. So we need a plan for it. And that's the first lesson I want to share today: Always plan for the unexpected.

When I talk about the unexpected, I can't help but think back to the time early in my career when I took a month between jobs to learn my way around the courtroom by observing proceedings in the D.C. Night Court. On my third night there the judge asked me who I was, what I was doing there, and whether or not I was a member of the D.C. Bar. I told him I was Elizabeth Hanford, I was observing the proceedings, and yes, I was a member of the bar.

No sooner had I said that than the judge handed me a file and told me that I was to defend an indigent defendant. Minutes later, I was in a cell block trying to talk to my first client—a Greek national who spoke only limited English, and who was charged with petting, and thereby annoying, a lion at the national Zoo—a violation of a Federal Statute.

When the proceedings got under way that evening—the opposing counsel, by the way, was a Harvard classmate of mine who was editor of the *Law Review*, I argued that without the lion as a witness, there was no way of knowing whether or not he had been "annoyed or teased." By the grace of God, I won the case.

Sometime in the near future, the business where you work—the institution where you volunteer—is likely to find itself looking into an unexpected lion's mouth. And, as a woman, the flexibility that you bring, the ability to think on your feet, and to juggle four or five things at a time is likely to serve you well.

As Madeleine Kunin, former Deputy Secretary at the Department of Education and former Governor of Vermont, has said, "Women need to value their own experiences more, and recognize the skills they have taken from them. Anyone who's been in a volunteer organization or done things in the community is superbly equipped for political life: You have your finger on the pulse of the community that way, and learn to be an organizer . . . most women have learned to organize their lives because they had to juggle so much."

And, I can't help but add that planning for the unexpected is the day-to-day work of the American Red Cross, that grand old organization which I am privileged to lead. We don't know when or where the next hurricane, or flood, or earthquake will hit . . . we don't know when or where someone will need blood, but we do know that we will be called to help, and we will respond. We have learned to plan for what we cannot predict. And that's a lesson we all should follow.

The second lesson I have learned is to trust your instincts. Our judgment of people, situations, and the heart of an issue is often right on target—yet sometimes we women allow ourselves to go against what our instincts are telling us. I bet we've all had the experience of sitting across the table from someone—a man, let's say—with whom we disagree. How many times, in this situation, has your reaction been to question your own perception and judgment, rather than his . . . only to find out later that you were right on the money?

Over the ages we women have perfected this trait of second-guessing ourselves to a high art form. Perhaps it stems from our early and constant exposure to society's message to women—we can never quite measure up to the model on the pages of *Vogue*.

Many business women have been inspired by the story of the young Utah housewife who just knew there was a market for her homemade cookies. There was one problem. Everyone she talked to disagreed. "The bankers and the financial people did not take me seriously," says Debbi Fields. "Everyone thought I would fail."

Needless to say, Debbi Fields went with her instincts, insisting that "No is an unacceptable answer," and I imagine there are quite a few so-called financial "experts" who can't look at a Mrs. Fields chocolate chip cookie without a little bit of indigestion.

In short, we must take our own measurements, and use our own instincts to make choices and decisions, whether it is on the job or in our personal lives. Certainly, we need to seek input and gain support. Yes, we need to look at all the facts and figures we can muster. But when it's time to make the decision, we must, quite simply, rely on our own judgment and do what we think is right.

Sometimes that instinct may lead us to take risks. And that's for the good.

Caroline Nahas—the first woman partner at Korn-Ferry, says, "Risk taking doesn't mean going after the CEO's job. Just reach out a little every day. If public speaking is painful, join a group that makes you get up and give presentations . . . take a leadership position on the local Chamber of Commerce . . . or a community service board . . . do something that pushes you to grow."

I believe your instincts are your guide to the future. Follow them to reach your dream.

The most valuable asset of the American Red Cross is what I call our "Tradition of Trust." Simply put, people trust the Red Cross to be there when needed and to do what is right. Throughout my career, I have also learned that your own personal "Tradition of Trust," your own integrity— is absolutely essential to success. And the third point I offer today is always maintain your integrity. For in the final analysis, it is your integrity—what I call your "moral compass," that counts far more than any line on your resume.

Nancy Kassebaum Baker, Margaret Thatcher and the late Barbara Jordan are women who've succeeded in the world of politics. And agree with their positions or not, total and complete commitment to integrity is a common hallmark of their service.

It is interesting to note that the American Management Association surveyed 1,500 managers around the country and asked the open-ended question, "What values, personal traits, or characteristics do you look for and admire in your superiors?" More than 225 different responses emerged, but the most frequent response—ranked number 1 by 83% of the managers—was integrity. I believe that an emphasis on integrity will help women succeed in the workplace. This image of trustworthiness and credibility will serve us well, whether with our boards of directors, or co-workers, or the consumers we serve.

In a world where we're constantly dealing with problems that other people create for us, integrity is one area over which each of us has 100% control. Without this personal set of values to guide our actions, we are unable to make consistent decisions or to inspire confidence and trust.

The fourth common denominator that I have seen among successful women is a commitment to those who follow.

As today's leaders, we have an obligation to make an investment not only for the next quarter, but for the next century. The decisions and contributions we make affect today's world and today's children—and that is our legacy. It sometimes takes courage to make a good long term decision when today's bottom line will suffer. But that's the stewardship we owe to our children—to the girls and boys who will become the leaders of tomorrow.

It also means offering a helping hand to those just starting on the ladder of success.

About twenty years ago, a group of us formed an organization called "Executive Women in Government," which still flourishes today. Its purpose was twofold: to help younger women, who wanted to follow our footsteps into public service, with information and advice, and to provide women in policy positions with an opportunity to relate to one another across government. Such networking is still key.

It is important to remember that helping others on the path to success does not mean defining success for them. And the fifth and final challenge for all of us in being more like a woman is to not let others define success for us.

It is a tempting trap, but an unfulfilling one. If we are to grow and succeed, then we cannot let others dictate what is right for us. And neither our colleagues nor our friends can make the tough decisions for us.

In the summer of 1995, I grappled with a decision affecting my career. I was President of the American Red Cross, and wanted to campaign for my husband as he sought the presidency of the United States. Some people didn't understand. Why should I have to leave my job, they asked, to play the role of the "good wife"? While the people asking the question probably considered themselves quite "liberated," what they were really asking was, "why can't a woman be more like a man?"

My decision was to support my husband. I made the choice—to take a year's leave of absence—not because I had to, but because I wanted to. I also planned to return to the presidency of the Red Cross, regardless of the outcome of the election. If Bob had won, I guess that would have made me the first First Lady working outside the White House. And isn't that what we women have been fighting for all these years—the freedom to pursue the lives we choose? The freedom to decide how best to achieve our personal fulfillment based on our own standards, our individual goals, and what's best for our families?

And let me add, part and parcel of not letting others define success or make our decisions, is not blaming others when those decisions don't lead to the results we anticipated. Every successful person makes mistakes along the way. And they take their lumps, they learn, and they don't make the same mistakes twice.

As I was preparing to begin my duties as president of the American Red Cross, my mother reminded me that she had once served as a Red Cross volunteer during WWII. And she said, "Elizabeth, nothing I ever did made me feel so important."

And perhaps in the final analysis that is what success is all about: finding something which infuses you with a sense of mission, with a passion for your life's work; finding something that leads you to say, "Nothing I ever did made me feel so important." Here in this room, and across America, are those who've discovered that feeling through a career as a businesswoman, a volunteer, a professor, a public servant, a mother! No one can tell you where you will find that feeling . . . how you will define success . . . that's a decision we must make for ourselves.

In the fairy tales we read as children, having been rescued by the prince, the woman lives happily ever after. That was the pattern in *Cinderella*, *Snow White* and *Sleeping Beauty*.

It is high time for a new fairy tale. A fairy tale about a young girl—or even a mature woman—who isn't a princess. A woman who sees there are things that need to be changed to make life better for herself and others. A woman who's not a victim of life or circumstances, and who doesn't need a rescuer. A woman who believes in herself and knows she can succeed, and can pass that success on to others. We need a tale about a woman who motivates, inspires, manages and builds.

Thanks to you, that story is more than a fairy tale. Indeed, there are hundreds of true life stories in this room today. And thanks to many of you, there will be thousands more tomorrow.

AN AMERICA WE CAN BE SPEECH
Lancaster, Pennsylvania, April 7, 1998

Elizabeth Dole was the keynote speaker at the Lancaster County Chamber of Commerce Annual Dinner at the Hershey Resort in Hershey, Pennsylvania. This speech highlights her talents as a multitasker; she entertained her audience with funny stories drawn from her experience, while at the same time presenting the positions she has held in national government service. Dole discussed at length how and why America is ripe for a change of moral climate, especially of individual character. Author Nichola Gutgold was in the audience and heard this speech delivered live. The text was provided by Elizabeth Dole.

In the early days of the Reagan Administration, I served as Assistant to the President for Public Liaison. I was charged with rallying support for the president's agenda, and one evening, my staff and I were meeting to divide up the names of senators who had not yet taken a public stand on one of the President's legislative initiatives.

The session came to an abrupt end when I said I was going home to cook a candlelight dinner. "That's great, Elizabeth," said my deputy. "But it's only 6:00 P.M.! Isn't it a bit early for you to be going home? Don't you want to finish targeting those undecided Senators?"

"You don't understand," I said. "Tonight, I'm targeting Bob Dole." And for those of you wondering, I did get Bob's vote. And even though the candlelight dinner was successful, I never tried it out on any other Senator!

The art of persuading senators is just one lesson I have learned in my career in the nation's capital. During that career, I have been privileged to have three very distinct missions.

As Secretary of Transportation, I was charged with overseeing American's material resources—our highways, airways, and railways.

As Secretary of Labor, my priority was America's human resources—improving the skills of our work force, helping to resolve a bitter coal strike.

And at the American Red Cross, my focus is on inner resources—inspiring people to volunteer, to give of their financial resources and their blood.

And tonight, I've been asked to share with you a few of the insights I've gained about organizations and people, and a few observations about how America has changed. . . . and how we must change in the future—for in today's fast-paced world, the only constant is change.

Perhaps the biggest change I have witnessed during my career is the role of women—both in Washington—the public sector—and in the work force in the private sector. I can still vividly recall my first day of class at Harvard Law School. I was one of 24 women in a class of 550. And a male student came up to me and demanded to know what I was doing there. In what can only be described as tones of moral outrage, he said, "Elizabeth, what are you doing here? Don't you realize that there are men who would give their right arm to be in this law school—men who would use their legal education?"

That man is now a senior partner in a very prestigious Washington law firm. And every so often I tell this little story around town. I love to tell this story! And you'd be amazed at the number of my male classmates in high-powered Washington law firms who've called me to say, "Tell me I'm not the one. Tell me I didn't say that, Elizabeth!"

And I remember the day in the early 1970s when I was working at the Nixon White House as Deputy Assistant to the President for Consumer Affairs, and I hurried to the Metropolitan Club in Washington for a meeting with some Cleveland, Ohio attorneys and businessmen.

As I rushed by him, the doorman yelled "Stop! You can't go in there lady! Women are not permitted in this club!" I told him there must be some misunderstanding. My name is Elizabeth Hanford, I said. "I work at the White House and I have a meeting on the 4th floor with some business people from Cleveland."

"I'm sorry," he said. If you were Queen Elizabeth, you still couldn't go in." The meeting only took place after I sent over another staffer who may have been a man, but who had not—as I had—spent the entire week-end preparing for the meeting!

Those events occurred in the past. Today, over 40% of students entering Harvard Law School are female. The Metropolitan Club—and many others across the country—have long since opened their doors to women. And, at the Department of Labor, I met regularly with a number of Assistant Secretaries. Four of them—for Policy, Congressional Affairs, and International Affairs—were women.

And while women most certainly have not reached the millennium—particularly in failing to equal the earnings of our male counterparts and in the disturbingly low increase in the number of women in top management positions—there are other signs that women are playing key roles in the revolutionary change in America's work force. Women-owned businesses are the fastest growing segment of the U.S. small business economy. And did you realize that these women owned businesses are employing more workers than the entire Fortune 500 corporations combined?

As women enter the workforce in record numbers they bring with them unique skills—for example, dealing with needs, issues, and market forces that are often not clearly defined. Rebecca McDonald, former President of Tenneco's natural gas marketing subsidiary, points out, "Women have a higher tolerance for ambiguity because we're always responsible for tending to the emotional needs of others—which are very fluid. We learn to read between the lines and come up with creative solutions for accommodating people."

I decided from almost my first day in Washington that I would bypass the full-time practice of law, and instead seek a career in government service. Like many others of my generation, I regarded public service as a noble calling—as a chance to make a difference in the issues of our time.

Some said back then that I had "stars in my eyes" when it came to my desire to work in government. And perhaps I did. But my years as a servant of the public were everything I had hoped for and more. And that's a message I share as often as I can with America's young people.

I share it because over the years, Americans have grown increasingly disenchanted with our government. I believe many qualified people are being discouraged from entering government service. The words, "I'm from the government, and I'm here to help," are guaranteed to get laughs. And that was not the case when I started out.

In fact, at the end of the 1950s and the beginning of the '60s, when Americans were asked "How much of the time can you trust your government to do the right thing," two of every three citizens answered, "all of the time," or "most of the time." When that question is asked today, "all of the time," or "most of the time," is the response of barely one out of ten Americans.

What's behind this dramatic transformation? The federal government has become too big, too complex, too bureaucratic. Decisions once made in state legislatures, in city halls, and around kitchen tables, are now made in Washington. People feel that their government doesn't have confidence in their wisdom, therefore, they shouldn't have confidence in the government.

What we need to do, it seems, is to remember the wisdom of our country's founders, and the 10th Amendment to the Constitution: Those powers not specifically delegated to the federal government or prohibited to the states are reserved for the states and for "we the people"—you and me!

And speaking of our Founders, have you ever wondered what happened to the 56 men who signed the Declaration of Independence?

These men who invented America were not wide-eyed rabble rousers. They were soft-spoken men of means and education. They placed a greater value on liberty than security. With a firm reliance on the protection of the Divine Providence, they pledged to each other their lives, their fortunes, their sacred honor. And courageous men and women of honor have continued to sacrifice for our country throughout history.

What would these Patriots think if they could see America today? What's happened to duty, honor, and personal responsibility?

Three and four decades ago, a generation came of age in this country with expectations as innocent as they were grand. We wanted for America more freedom, more tolerance, more compassion. And there were amazing advances. We overturned legal segregation and made progress against discrimination. We have seen real gains for minorities and women. And we must never go back. Not an inch. American ingenuity transformed the way people work, learn, and communicate, in a world without walls.

Who among us would turn back the clock? Yet this country, which has come so far, has lost so much. Our sense of limitless possibility has run into a stone wall of crime, violence, drugs, illegitimacy and incivility. The deep and unsettling fear is that the nation given to us by our Founders— given to us by our parents—was a much better place than the America we are preparing to turn over to our children.

And the insult of this injury is that our intentions were good.

We wanted our schools not only to teach, but to nurture children's self esteem and solve a variety of special problems. But now, in many cases, they hardly teach at all. When we were growing up, our education system was the envy of the world. Now almost every parent who can't escape our schools is desperate to reform them.

We wanted to end the silly censorship which kept Joyce's *Ulysses* in a brown paper wrapper. But we have ended up with a pornographic culture and a society that no longer blushes.

We ached for poor children, hungry in the richness of America, and created a welfare system to help them. But when we substituted handouts for jobs, we destroyed responsibility. When welfare programs offered a choice between cash and a husband, we devalued marriage. When fatherless children took control of the streets, we lost society's linchpin: respect for the law.

We wanted to ensure that our courts were fair, our police were careful and that the innocent had a chance to be heard—regardless of personal wealth or political power. But today we have a system of crime without punishment, victims without justice, and neighborhoods without peace.

We are a good and noble people, but we have forgotten the strength of our rights depends on their limits, that the shifting sands of changing wants is no ground upon which to build a nation. We don't have to abandon our dreams, but we must not forget the values and principles that allow us the luxury of dreaming.

We want the world for our children to be a safe harbor, shielded from worry. Our parents managed that for us. We lived in homes with locks we didn't turn, on streets where we played safely till dark on long summer evenings.

But what happened to that simple gift? Children today have e-mail and Nintendo, but what they lack is the ease of living in a world without worry. Why are we not giving our children what was given to us?

There are so many complex reasons. But I believe there is one reason above all others. In seeking to make America better, we have neglected to make her good. We have been embarrassed to talk about the values that make our lives happy and safe and fulfilled. The values of those patriots—responsibility and altruism; courage and perseverance; discipline; modesty; and a willingness to work not for our own gratification, but for the joy of knowing that our children will benefit.

We must ask ourselves if in pursuing life's options, we have left behind the fundamentals.

We have campus speech codes to keep us civil. We apply harassment rules to schoolyard kisses. Drug policies have become so tied in knots we can no longer distinguish between aspirin and crack. And edicts from our courts now protect the freedom of molesters and stalkers and abusers so well that America's children and daughters and wives no longer trust society to keep them safe.

This substitution of regulation for responsibility is a kind of Puritanism for people who no longer believe in character, who no longer believe in the wisdom and goodness of the people. But we will never write enough rules. Individual and national character are what we need in this country.

I think many of us have reached a point of reflection—a kind of collective head-shaking. Are we content with what is happening on our watch? When we pass control of America to our children, will we be proud of the choices we made? Of the country those choices produced?

Are things beginning to change? I believe the answer is yes. "Do your own thing!" is giving way to "respect your parents." Family time is becoming a priority again. People are openly hungry for the inner peace that comes from faith. And countless children are going to sleep each night to the sound of a parent's voice reading from the *Book of Virtues.*

And what is true in our lives can also be true in our country.

We must choose education over social engineering. We must teach our children again the basics of math and reading and citizenship. How appalling that one in four high school seniors in the great United States of America is considered functionally illiterate! We must return discipline and parental involvement to every school. And in those cases—especially in low-income areas—where schools have failed completely, parents must be given other choices.

We must choose to return safety to our streets and moral seriousness to our war on drugs. Drug use is up 141% among teenagers in recent years. Cocaine use was up 166% in one year alone and 8th grade marijuana use has tripled. It is mainly the poor and minorities who are victimized by the drugs and the gangs that profit from them. It is often the weak and the elderly who are targeted by criminals.

As citizens of the greatest country on the face of the earth, we've got to trust ourselves and our values, not solely the government and its intentions. I believe we must direct our resources and authority back to parents and principals, policemen and pastors—men and women with the power to turn a community around, starting with a single life or a single classroom or a single street corner.

None of us can claim perfection and few can wear the mantle of hero or heroine, but each of us has the option of choosing a life of decency and self-discipline, self reliance and diligence. From time to time, we all fail our own standards, but our standards will never fail us.

Yes, our nation has been on a long and restless journey. But we have begun to rediscover the place that is our home. We can never return to the age of innocence. But we can move on to an age of rediscovery. With clear heads, open eyes and full hearts we can choose above all else those things that are most important, that will endure, that we will always see as noble.

Our future is not preordained—we must choose it. But I believe it is the American destiny to choose well.

Thank you very much and God bless you.

AMERICAN RED CROSS RESIGNATION SPEECH
Washington, D.C., January 4, 1999

On January 4, 1999, Elizabeth Dole officially announced her resignation as president of the American Red Cross in a speech widely covered in the media. In her remarks, she reviewed all that the Red Cross had accomplished under her leadership. She hinted as well at a possible political future for herself. Multitasking, she subtly suggested that if she could lead a huge organization like the Red Cross, she could also lead the country. This speech was found January 7, 1999, on http://www.cnn.com/ALLPOLITICS/stories/1999/01/04/dole/.

Good afternoon, everyone. And to those of you who are visitors, a warm welcome to the American Red Cross and a Happy New Year to each and every one of you!

Norm [Augustine], one of the highlights of my American Red Cross career has been the opportunity to work with you. Your wise counsel, encouragement and support have meant the world to me. Thank you for your outstanding board leadership and unfailing commitment to the Red Cross. And my personal heartfelt thanks for your friendship.

You know, I've spent a lot of time over the holidays thinking about the future. And I have a great feeling about this year. Some people say our country is in a crisis. But I believe that America is equal to today's challenges. I know 1999 will be a good year—for the American Red Cross and the American people—because I know the strength and goodness of those of you in this room and around the country. You stand ready to do whatever it takes—at whatever cost or sacrifice—to bring help and hope to those in need. Red Crossers are unusually committed and remarkably strong, but we are not apart from America. We are America. Our assistance is not delivered by strangers, but by neighbors.

A pin is worn by the merchant on Main Street, the retired teacher two doors down and your best friend who teaches swimming at the pool. We are the neighbors you turn to when the water's rising, and the volunteers who open the countless shelters that offer safety from the storm. We are proud professionals, volunteers and donors, united by a common goal: to touch people's lives with compassion, when nature and chance have conspired against them.

So I'd like to start out the New Year by asking you to join me in giving all of you a well-deserved pat on the back, and a big round of applause. Shall we? [Clapping begins.] This is for you. [Sustained applause.] What a team. What a great team.

And what a joy it is to begin this exciting new year with so much of our Red Cross family gathered together, either here in this historic Board of Governors Hall, or by way of satellite hookup. To those of you just getting back from winter holidays—welcome home. To those of you who worked straight through, a heartfelt "thank you" for your sacrifices.

This beautiful building, completed in 1917 in midst of the First World War, and dedicated to the heroic women of the Civil War, inspires all of us with its reminders of those who came before. This room has been used by generations of Red Crossers who met and conquered the challenges of their times, passing stewardship to us with careful and loving hands.

We each have memories of special occasions here. And I, of course, have mine.

The first time I stood with you in this room was my first day at the Red Cross, just under eight years ago. It was February 1991. I see some faces that were here that day. Do you remember? Those were challenging times.

The integrity of our Biomedical Services, the very safety of our nation's blood, was being questioned by federal authorities and in the media.

Our disaster relief fund was staring at a potential $30 million deficit. And our services to the armed forces had become a growing financial burden with an internal report recommending dismantling. The head of the United Way was soon to be removed from office, and the entire non-profit sector was braced for unprecedented public scrutiny. If that wasn't enough, we depended on the United Way for most of our outside contributions, and the United Way was dramatically reducing its support. This was no sleepy charity. It was America's largest and most-loved philanthropy. But it was struggling mightily to preserve its tradition of trust.

I told a story at our first meeting about a night in 1945, when Gen. Dwight Eisenhower was walking along the Rhine, thinking of the crossing in which he would lead the Allied Army. He met a soldier and asked him why he wasn't sleeping. The young GI, who didn't recognize the supreme commander, said, "I guess I'm just a little nervous." "So am I," said Eisenhower. "Let's walk together and, perhaps, we'll draw strength from one another."

My friends, that's just what we did.

We spent most of this decade together, you and I. And together, we have remade our world. In years to come, when our successors meet in this room, they will view the story of these years not as a conclusion but as a prologue, as the time when we set the stage for a triumphant Red Cross in the 21st Century, when we will be the non-profit pacesetter, setting a new credo of business for businesses of the heart.

But we have not been resistant to change. We have welcomed it. With real perseverance and courage, we have rebuilt antiquated programs and services, reinvigorated them for the demands of today. We have transformed our blood operations, which provide nearly half of the nation's blood supply, into a sparkling, state-of-the-art, national system that stands today as the envy of the world.

We modernized and revitalized disaster relief and completely revamped our fund-raising capacity, which enabled us to handle well the worst and most expensive disaster year in our history, with 14 simultaneous major disasters. Last year the Red Cross raised $181 million more than we raised in 1991, despite a significant reduction in United Way funding during those years. With hard work and fresh thinking, we rescued our services to the armed forces, using the latest technology to find more efficient ways to deliver them and saving millions of dollars in the process.

For the first time in our history, we re-chartered all of our chapters based on the highest standards. And we employed new technology to update and consolidate our financial management. We have never been in better financial health than we are right now, with 1998 being the best year ever.

As we have made changes in the way we do business, we have not forgotten that our people are the heart and soul of this great organization. We've created training opportunities, like the annual three-week Harvard program, to build the leadership we need, to take this $2.1 billion organization into the next century.

As we stand here today, in the last year of a decade swirling with change, we are an organization blessed with renewed vigor and strength thanks to the vision and commitment of the entire Red Cross family. We can be proud of our venerable past, sure of a noble future and certain of a grateful public.

The years I've spent at the Red Cross with you have been the most fulfilling of my career, and I thank you. I love the American Red Cross. But the Red Cross is now solid as a rock. And at this important time in our national life, I believe there may be another way for me to serve our country. The Red Cross has been a glorious mission field. But I believe there may be other duties yet to fulfill.

When I stood here on my first day eight years ago, I knew I would need to earn my place in the Red Cross family. I knew one had to be worthy, that the honor could not be conveyed by edict or as the result of a search committee's work. So I pledged to earn the badge of a Red Crosser—the pin on my lapel—by working my first year as a volunteer. And I'm glad I did, because it helped cement the bond between us.

I've learned so much since then. I stood by your side in Florida, as we braced for Hurricane Andrew, which was hurdling across the Caribbean. I've cradled a gaunt Rwandan baby in my arms. And I've sat with our men and women in uniform far from home and loved ones as they keep the peace in Bosnia. I've stood in the Somalian garden while Red Crossers operated by flashlight on a victim of that nation's bloodshed. I've seen with you the faces of American inner city youth at risk, but not yet lost. And I've struggled with you to bring life saving information across our cultural, educational and racial ramparts.

Because of these experiences and so many more, I know now that the badges we wear are never paid in full. They must be earned, again with every day, often with danger and disease, with new efforts, longer hours and more sacrifice.

I've learned that all of us are improved each day we come to work by the continuing, exhausting effort to fulfill the Red Cross mission.

I was proud eight years ago to be chosen to lead you as your president. Today, I am humble with gratitude for the opportunity to have walked among you.

So I will be leaving you. I have not made definite plans about what I will do next. I didn't feel it was right to spend the time I owed to you thinking about anything but our work together. Soon, I will begin considering new paths and there are exciting possibilities. I will choose one and pursue it with all my might. But never will I forget the friendships we have forged here, or the indestructible, heroic heart of the American Red Cross, a family of which I will forever consider myself a part.

Thank you for your support and your love. Thank you, one and all. God bless you, and God bless the American Red Cross. Thank you so very much.

FORRESTAL LECTURE, U.S. NAVAL ACADEMY
Annapolis, Maryland, April 14, 1999

In this speech, Elizabeth Dole shared her appreciation for the role of the military, both at home and abroad, as part of the popular Forrestal Lecture series.

No doubt she wanted to demonstrate what she knew about the armed forces, reminding the cadets how she had worked with the military to deliver humanitarian aid when she was president of the American Red Cross. As a woman running for president, it was important for her to establish her credibility. She pledged to support the military, mentioning that she favored increased readiness and a missile defense system. This speech was provided by Kerry Tymchuk.

Thank you, ladies and gentlemen, for that very warm welcome, and thank you Midshipman Frederick, for those wonderful words of introduction. And heartfelt thanks to Admiral Ryan for the kind invitation to be with you and to Admiral Roughead, Dean Miller, and Midshipman Nance for your efforts in making this evening possible. What a pleasure it is to be here.

It is a special honor for me to join the prestigious roster of speakers who have stood before you to deliver the Forrestal Lecture. I don't need to tell you how important James Forrestal was, first, in creating the great naval force that helped win World War II, and then, in serving as this nation's first Secretary of Defense.

But I'm not sure how much you may know, about how he came to be involved with the Navy.

When World War I broke out, Forrestal was a young man and eager to serve. He and some of his college friends from Princeton decided to volunteer. So they went down to the nearest Army barracks to sign up. But these eager recruits were turned away. They were told they had to go through channels.

Forrestal thought that was possibly too bureaucratic for him. So he and a friend went to a Marine Corps' recruiting station. Are there any Marines or future Marines here tonight?

Well, at the station, Forrestal found himself standing in a long line. Up ahead they saw another college fellow a lot like themselves. And they overheard this young man ask the Sergeant, "So, when do I receive my commission?" The Sergeant stared at him and said, "If you pass your physical—which I doubt—you'll go to boot camp in Parris Island. After a year, *if* you're very exceptional . . . you may be a corporal."

Forrestal looked over at his buddy and they both slipped out of line and left. Finally he tried for a Navy commission. In order to get it, he actually learned to fly a plane. It was the early days of naval aviation. But even then, I'm afraid he was rated "generally inept." But he stuck to it and won his wings.

These experiences may be one reason why, when Forrestal was a senior civilian official in World War II, you didn't always find him behind his desk. He visited allied forces in France in the summer of '44. He was on a ship in the Pacific to observe the landings at Iwo Jima, and later he hit the beach himself.

I think he had learned something from his early recruiting days. First, never let red tape stand in the way of your desire to serve. And second, he admired Marines for the rest of his life.

You know, James Forrestal was truly a member of what Tom Brokaw calls "The Greatest Generation"—the men and women who saw this country through two world wars and a great depression.

I was just a child listening to the radio with my mother in February 1945, while my brother John served aboard the original USS *Saratoga*-CV 3. The ship was supporting the Iwo Jima landing when it was hit, just after dusk, by Kamikaze planes. And I recall learning this news, and hoping . . . and praying that my brother and his fellow sailors would return safely. These brave men stood strong in the face of enemy aggression. Like you, they believed in duty, honor and commitment. And they lived those values, helping make this the strongest nation in the world.

Some people think we've lost those standards today. Yes, we've been let down by people we should look up to. But these past months and years I've been traveling around the nation, talking to people—hearing their concerns and what they want for this great country. And I'm glad to say I've met countless men and women who do believe in our highest values. Men like John McCain whom I truly admire. John has lived the values of this academy—duty, honor and commitment.

And for eight years I was honored to join thousands of Red Cross workers and volunteers who share these values, who're making a positive difference at home and abroad. I know that many other people from humanitarian organizations—a number of you, here tonight—share that passion for service.

But tonight I'm especially pleased to address the brigade of midshipmen: men and women who've made service and honor really count. In the middle of this demanding Academy program, you've given your time and talents to help your neighbors. I've heard about the Midshipman Action Group and how you've put in more than 16,000 hours of community service. I know you are an inspiration to the kids you've tutored and the families you've helped. Congratulations! Bravo Zulu!

Tonight, I'd also like to remember the Academy graduates who are serving on ships and stations across the world, upholding our deepest national interests and beliefs. Right now, at least a dozen members of last year's graduating class are aboard ships in the Adriatic—ensigns like Shawn Cowan, aboard the USS *Philippine Sea* . . . Jason Foster, aboard the USS *Leyte Gulf* . . . and Rachel Nagle, aboard the USS *Vella Gulf*. They are participating in our operations to save the people and restore the peace of Kosovo.

Look around you. Less than a year from now, men and women of the Class of '99 will also be serving this nation, in places and crises yet unknown. And as the years pass, all of you will be models for future midshipmen, the midshipmen of the 21st Century.

So tonight, I can't think of a more important group of people to talk to about American leadership—in peace and in war. And I can't think of a more important time.

In recent weeks, in Kosovo, we have seen the terrible consequences of unbridled aggression and ethnic hatred. For years, Serbian leader Slobodan Milosevic has carried out a systematic, violent campaign to terrorize and destroy non-Serb communities. To date, more than half a million ethnic Albanians have fled their homes for safety in nearby countries. Behind them, Milosevic's forces have burned and looted homes . . . shot opponents . . . force-marched women and children out of cities . . . and herded fathers and sons to unknown fates.

Tragically, we've seen Milosevic in action before. Seven years ago, as head of the Red Cross, I went to the Croatian-Bosnian border to inspect a transit station for refugees from the Bosnian conflict. The station was a joint Red Cross/U.N. facility, which provided care for recently released prisoners from Serbian detention camps. Hundreds had come to the station the night before my arrival. They were being treated and interviewed to assess whether the Serb camps were abiding by the Geneva Convention.

Sadly, the survivors showed all the physical evidence of months of malnourishment, deprivation and ill-treatment. Refugees reported beatings and torture; brothers and cousins shot; wives and young sisters raped.

Of course, the former Yugoslavia is not the only place we've witnessed the evils of ethnic violence. In 1994, the Red Cross and other humanitarian groups were working to help more than a million refugees from the bloody massacres in Rwanda. Camps were hastily set up in Zaire, now Congo, for survivors. I came in with an inspection team in a small propeller aircraft. From the plane's window, I saw a huge mass of people in the choking dust and heat. I also saw jeeps and trucks with our beautiful red-on-white cross—and an enormous U.S. C-141 military aircraft, unloading critical supplies.

To those who question the military's role in such rescue efforts, I'll just say—there are simply times when nobody else can do the job.

Even with our help, thousands of Rwandans would die of wounds, infection, contaminated water and disease. That day, we literally stepped over dead bodies as we went about our work.

The Red Cross and other organizations have had long experience dealing with natural disasters. But these were not natural disasters. They were caused by humans and demanded a human cure.

Some people say, should the United States really get involved in any of this? Isn't it enough that we have groups like the Red Cross to handle humanitarian concerns? Can't the United Nations and regional bodies take care of regional problems?

The answer is simple. Wherever America's national interests and our national values intersect, this nation must lead. That includes using military force when necessary.

This is a particularly appropriate time to be reflecting on that leadership. Last month, NATO—the core of freedom since World War I—opened its doors to three new members; Poland, Hungary and the Czech Republic. These three former members of the Warsaw Pact bring with them a tremendous commitment to freedom, a freedom they value and struggled to win.

But their leaders have been the first to acknowledge that they did not do it alone. It was the United States, which kept the faith, during four decades of Cold War, which led a powerful democratic alliance to keep freedom safe in Europe and elsewhere, and which inspired the struggle for human rights and liberty.

The West's thriving free markets put the lie to Marxist propaganda. Our rule of law shamed dictatorships. Our workers' real rights inspired workers' unions like Solidarity. And our respect for the life of the spirit supported religious believers everywhere, as they kept their faith despite adversity.

Some thought that fundamental change would never come. In Korea and Vietnam, we paid a high price. America's world role, its intentions, its commitments, were frequently challenged, here at home and abroad. The Soviets led campaign after campaign to discredit and undermine our leadership.

Nowadays, there's a tendency to look back and assume democracy was unstoppable. In fact, change required leaders who had the vision and courage to stay the course. As Ronald Reagan told the British House of Commons in 1982, "It may not be easy to see, but I believe we live now at a turning point. We must be staunch in our conviction that freedom is not the sole prerogative of a lucky few . . . What I am describing now is a plan and a hope for the long term—the march of freedom and democracy, which will leave Marxism-Leninism on the ash heap of history."

The pundits were horrified at Reagan's radical prediction and tough language. But within seven years, that boldness changed the world.

As U.S. Secretary of Labor, I found myself in Poland in the summer of 1989, meeting with Solidarity labor leaders. It was August and the Soviet bloc was crumbling. In Moscow, the Communist Party's "perestroika" reforms had failed to halt economic and political collapse.

That January, Hungary had voted to allow independent parties. The last Soviet troops had left Afghanistan in February, ending a disastrous ten years of military occupation. By July, floods of East Germans were pouring into Western embassies, seeking to emigrate. Just as I arrived in Warsaw, the Polish Parliament elected its first non-Communist Prime Minister in more than 40 years. Three months later, the Berlin Wall was down. The elation was incredible.

Now, ten years later, we know that the challenges of the post-Cold War era have just begun.

Today, in many of the former Soviet nations, democratic and marketplace structures remain fragile. In Europe, NATO is struggling to address the Yugoslavia conflict, while Moscow has opposed NATO's action in defiance of world outrage at Belgrade's aggression. In the Middle East, a lasting peace is still under siege. Across the world, terrorists have struck at the West and its allies—from the World Trade Center bombing in New York City, to deadly sarin-gas attacks in the subways of Tokyo. And as the bombings in Oklahoma City and our embassies in East Africa warn us, terror may strike where we may least expect it.

Meanwhile, weapons of mass destruction and the means to deliver them are proliferating around the world. North Korean, Chinese and Russian armaments and technicians are building up the stockpiles of rogue nations. Just this week, both India and Pakistan held new tests of nuclear-capable missiles, the latest steps in an escalating arms race between those countries. In North Korea, people are starving while the communist leadership pours resources into advanced missiles and, it is reported, a nuclear-weapons program.

All the new computer technologies that work for us, are also sometimes working against us. At a recent Washington Roundtable on Science and Public Policy, a defense expert pointed out that "The world is awash in equipment far superior to that used by the United Stares itself in building its own missiles . . . The missiles and nuclear weapons that were mainstays for the United States during the Cold War were designed with the help of computers less powerful than today's better desktop models."

And there are new weapons of mass disruption, which threaten our critical infrastructure: computer viruses, e-mail attacks and "Trojan Horses" that aim to disable industry and government services, and potentially, our very defenses. Remember that "Melissa" e-mail virus, which hit companies and government a few weeks ago? In case you think it was merely annoying, consider this. I've been informed that the server that provides e-mail communications for a major naval aviation depot was bombarded by 57,000 Melissa messages. The electronic barrage brought communications temporarily to a halt. What might an actual attack do?

This constellation of new technologies and global crises may tempt us to believe we are in totally uncharted waters. But I believe the lesson of history still holds true; America has always risen to its challenges, we always will. We protect our freedom best when America leads—and when that leadership is clear, credible and capable.

Clear leadership requires a steady sense of purpose. Our free society and global economy require an environment that respects liberty and individual rights. We are the world's only superpower. More important, we are the world's only superpower democracy. If we are to shape a world that is open to our values and ideals and well-being, we must accept our responsibility to lead.

What does this mean in practical terms? First and foremost, it means staying true to our fundamental values.

Two decades of American engagement have helped build a more open, more prosperous economy in China. That has benefited the Chinese people and strengthened the ties between our nations. Meanwhile, however, China's human rights situation is sharply deteriorating. It's time to press Beijing much harder for reform.

No nation benefits from closed political structures, closed markets, and closed ideas. Washington does not do China any favors when it averts official eyes from Beijing's stagnant human rights situation, or important questions of trust and national Security.

I know we and China can talk. As Secretary of Transportation, I represented the United States in tough aviation and maritime negotiations in Beijing. While I was there, I also went, with my friends Senator Pat Moynihan and Senator Pete Dominici, to attend services in a Beijing church.

We need to support, publicly, freedom of conscience and speech in China. We need to insist on free and fair access to markets and respect for intellectual property rights. And we need to stand by our friends in Taiwan. And while we reach out to China as a partner for peace, we need to shut those doors to our military secrets.

Global stability demands no less. And that brings me to the important question of credibility. Friends and adversaries alike must trust our words. Mixed messages send mixed signals. There's a high cost in lives and resources when an adversary doubts your meaning and decides to test your will.

Our society's open debates are often misinterpreted by leaders of regimes where speech is suppressed. They think dissent means a lack of determination. Well, we will always have debate and competing interests. That's the American way. But as I've learned from years of experience in international forums, that's all the more reason for the United States Commanders-in-Chief to say what they mean and to mean what they say.

Credibility counts. And if you have any question about that, look at the U.N. weapons inspections mess in Iraq or today's tragedy in Kosovo.

When tough deadlines are set and then repeatedly postponed—when the other side appears to break its agreements with impunity—when we accept half-promises, *we* send the wrong signal about our values and our will.

That's especially true when American commitments are caged in hesitation. Long experience teaches that when we've committed military forces to a rightful goal, we should use all the power necessary to achieve it. Categorical refusals to employ ground forces, or vows that the United States won't ever go it alone—this kind of thing simply encourages adversaries to shift strategies, wait it out, or attempt to break our alliances.

Some people ask, do we have a national interest in Kosovo? The answer is: we have an interest in Europe. Our leadership is needed when aggression jeopardizes that region's stability and security and threatens our deepest democratic values.

But today, we must deal with reality. In Kosovo, we are the only power capable of stopping an immense threat to peace and progress throughout that region. We and our allies should carry out that mission in the swiftest and most effective way possible.

So today, I call on President Clinton to rally our nation, strengthen our international coalitions and build up and deploy the forces necessary to win the war. To secure our objectives, Milosevic's forces must depart from Kosovo and the refugees must return safely under the protection of a NATO-led force. To accept the status quo is to risk defeat, defeat for NATO and defeat for the humanitarian—and very American—objective of preventing genocide where we can. Does that mean ground troops? If the NATO commanders and the Joint Chiefs of Staff say that ground troops are required to accomplish our goals, then my answer is yes.

That brings me to the question of capability—making sure that today and in the future, we have the tools we need to bring to the job.

Those tools include strong alliances and effective international partnerships. Our leadership in international trade and monetary organizations is essential for upholding our core economic interests and promoting worldwide economic growth. NATO, now celebrating its 50th anniversary, can be a source of security and stability, not only for Europe, but elsewhere. For instance, in 1990, when Coalition naval forces deployed to the Persian Gulf to enforce sanctions against Iraq and later, liberate Kuwait, decades of NATO exercises and interoperability stood behind their success.

America must also preserve its pre-eminent ability to deter threats and defeat aggression. Ten years ago, real budget cuts and defense restructuring were needed to move our military away from the Cold War years. That grew into a perilous 39-percent drop from defense spending levels in the mid-1980s. Today, we are seeing the results in lowered readiness, in aging hardware and in reduced morale. Military budget cuts have turned the Pentagon into a triangle. I want to build it back up.

Shortfalls have stripped units of essential equipment and spare parts. Last year only 50 percent of non-deployed ships were mission-ready. Lack of equipment grounded aircraft and reduced tank training hours.

Perhaps worse are the shortfalls in personnel. Today's Navy recruitment goals are about one-third below Cold-War levels; even so, the Service recruited some 7,000 fewer sailors than its goals last year. The Air Force is some 1,000 pilots short of its official goals. Last month, Brigadier General John Casey testified to Congress that some Army units train at only 60 percent strength. "It's like trying to train a basketball team with only four players," he said.

Meanwhile, procurement spending is so slow that the average ship, tank or aircraft will have to last some 53 years before being replaced.

Listen to a report from the Brookings Institution—which is no apologist for military spending! "First-to-fight units may have adequate resources, but other units are suffering." The authors conclude: "Left unchecked, these trends could eventually cut into our ability to sustain a vigorous one-war strategy while conducting missions in places like Bosnia."

Should we just ask adversaries to wait?

When we stripped our defenses like this after World War II, we paid the price . . . in communist expansion in Europe and Asia, and soon, in war on the Korean peninsula. Forrestal said it best, back in 1947, in his first report as Secretary of Defense; "Our quick and complete demobilization," he said, "was a testimonial to our good will rather than to our common sense."

Let's show some common sense. Let's restore basic readiness, and let's make those essential investments in the advanced weaponry and technologies we'll need in the 21st Century. And no investment could be more important than strategic defense.

It's been more than 15 years since President Reagan asked a simple question: "What if?" "What if we could live free from fear of nuclear missile attack? What if we could intercept and destroy strategic ballistic missiles? Wouldn't it be better to save lives than avenge them?" he asked.

Much has changed—but not this. The American people still have no defense against a nuclear missile.

Let me pause a minute to quote a great American statesman, the former Senate Majority Leader, Bob Dole. "The top priority of any President should be to provide for the safety of the American people. It is his greatest responsibility."

Or hers.

Congress has spoken out clearly for a renewed effort to build a national missile defense. The Clinton administration is finally, reluctantly, pursuing a program. But it continues to wait on a deployment decision.

Friends, the debate is over. Missile defense is an absolute requirement— to protect our free world—to reduce the threat of rogue nuclear powers to our people, our allies and our overseas forces. Let's gear our programs up and make the investment we need to bring an effective system into reality.

MELROSE HIGH SCHOOL SPEECH
Melrose, Massachusetts, September 22, 1999

Elizabeth Dole, as a presidential candidate, returned to Melrose High School, where she had been a student teacher four decades earlier. In this speech, Dole discusses her plan for education reform in America. She pledges to reduce costly and cumbersome governmental bureaucracy and restore decision making to state, local, and parental authorities. This speech was obtained from the "Elizabeth Dole in 2000" Web site, http://www.edole.org, accessed September 26, 1999.

Thank you very much, Emily. When I heard you were the student body president, I thought: hmmm, a female President—that sounds pretty good to me!

And my thanks to all of you for being here with me today. It is a real joy to be back at Melrose. I loved student teaching here. And I still think Melrose students and the Red Raiders are the best in the world! Congratulations on being selected by the *Boston Globe* as one of the best football teams in the league!

As I walked through the halls of the old High School earlier this afternoon, I thought about my days as a student teacher here. My classes were 11th grade history, and one of my first lesson plans dealt with the Boston Police strike of 1919.

I wanted to make history really live for my students. So I went down to the Police Department archives and spent an afternoon combing through forty years of dusty files. Lo and behold, I found the name of a surviving member of the striking force.

Well, I tracked him down in West Roxbury and recorded his memories on tape. He was such a hit with my class that they insisted he come in and tell his story in person!

I didn't choose this lesson because it was mandated by the State or by Washington, but because it brought history to life for my students. And that was something I learned from *my* best teachers.

A lot has changed since I taught here, but some things are still the same. The key to a great school is still committed, creative teachers . . . involved parents . . . and an energetic supportive principal and staff. Let me say that I am especially pleased to share this day with your principal Mr. Burke. Talk about energy! He and so many other dedicated educators are living proof that education is not just a profession, it is a passion. It is a calling. There is nothing more fundamental to the success of our democracy than the education of our children in a robust public education system.

But ladies and gentlemen, robust does not mean hefty. Take a look at this unwieldy stack of paper. These are just a few of the federal rules and regulations that afflict your school and others. In this stack is the Clinton-Gore Elementary and Secondary Education reauthorization bill. It's more than 600 pages long. I think somebody wasn't listening to the teacher about keeping his work short and to the point.

This would be a joke if our system were working—but it's no joke. This bundle of bureaucracy is a nightmare for every school administrator, teacher, and student trapped in the infrastructure it has created. In the 35 years since the Elementary and Secondary Education Act was first passed, the federal government has poured more than $100 billion dollars into an ever-growing list of programs. And, what do we have to show for it? The vast majority of these programs failed to achieve their stated goals. Per-pupil spending has more than doubled and pupil-teacher ratios have shrunk, but we have achieved no real gains in test scores and our international educational rankings have plunged into the cellar of the industrial world. By almost every reckoning, many of our schools have become less safe, more drug-infested, more troubled—while taking on more and more duties, as one non-educational mandate after another is thrust on them by the Federal Government.

An Ohio survey discovered that local school superintendents and principals are filling out an average of 182 forms a year to meet federal requirements. Across the country, in Arizona, almost half of employees of the state educational department devote their time just to managing federal programs. Writing about the problem, Arizona's crusading state school official, Lisa Graham Keegan, has a succinct solution, "Back off, Washington."

The federal government has become a truly intrusive regulatory presence sapping state authority, local control, and parental responsibility. Every hour spent on complying with regulations is time not spent helping teachers and students. Every dollar spent on overhead is a dollar that does not reach the classroom. These hundreds of pages of regulations and onerous restrictions are burdening states and school districts just when the need for innovation is greatest.

As I've traveled the country this year, I've invited people to join me in a crusade to make history. My Presidency would make the kind of history that would reverberate around the world. And I'm not talking about my gender. I'm talking about making history by applying our values to public policy. I'm talking about restoring our public schools to greatness.

We're Americans. We have brought light to every dark corner of the world. And we have the same power to brighten the deepening shadows in our classrooms—to rocket our education scores back into world leadership—by focusing on the same ideas of freedom, competition and the rights of individuals that have made us the greatest nation on earth.

America's schools will start to improve the day we throw out the tangled political priorities advocated by this administration and represented in this bill. Our children will learn again when we resolve to put kids and parents first, and the system, second. Most important, the minds of our children will soar when freedom and accountability guide our decisions, and results rather than process become the coin of the realm in American education.

Today, I want to share my philosophy for restoring our public schools to greatness. My ideas and initiatives spring from my experience as a teacher, my three decades of public service and the counsel of visionaries within and outside my Party. I am calling for a fundamental change in federal education policy. I will increase federal dollars to the classroom and reduce federal power, while increasing the power of state and local school districts. And in exchange for flexibility, there will be a performance partnership requiring clearly stated measurable goals in student achievement.

Here at Melrose, you are being asked daily to focus on the three R's— Reading, Writing and Arithmetic—we, as educators, need to also be focused on the three R's.

First, return control to states and local school districts—give them the flexibility they need, as long as they take responsibility for tough standards for student achievement.

Second, restore discipline in the classroom and respect for teachers.

Third, reinforce parents' control of their child's education—ensure a dynamic mix of excellent schools, guaranteed by the catalyst of freedom in a competitive and accountable environment.

Return, Restore and Reinforce—simply put, these are my "three R's" for the new millennium. As President, these will be my guiding principles for breaking the stranglehold the federal bureaucracy has over our children's education. Only by implementing these three R's will we ensure that our children are learning the other three R's.

First, let's talk about flexibility. Creative problem solving at the local level is all but impossible. Right now the federal government has 788 different federal education programs. These provide only 7% of the money that we spend on public schools, but they create 50% of the paperwork for teachers and administrators. This is time and money spent getting federal dollars. I want this time and money to be spent getting results—measurable progress for all our kids.

As we enter the next millennium, it is imperative that we return education freedom and accountability to our states and local school districts. We here in this room know it, our students know it, and the majority of the members of Congress—who've made education reform a priority—know it. Parts of my vision are modeled after, and incorporate, much of the "Straight A's" legislation now in Congress.

As President, I will allow states and local school districts to choose how most federal money is spent, as long as they set, measure and reach goals for student achievement. At last, schools will be responsible for student performance, not paperwork. Some schools may need more computers, some may need better teacher training, and some may need school safety improvements. The role of the federal government will be clear: to complement, not complicate. Federal funds will work to leverage positive change, not suppress it.

Next, I want to enhance the stature of our teachers. Never has it been more important for schools to expect the best from our teachers, to honor their profession, and to reward them well. We are entrusting our nation's future to these dedicated men and women.

I will insist that government listen to classroom teachers. I know from experience how valuable their insights are. Instead of criticizing our teachers, why don't we try consulting them? Who better understands the needs than a heroic 25-year teacher?

When it comes to federal teaching funds, we will keep the commitment to flexibility. Individual states will have the freedom to boost teacher excellence in the ways their communities need most. Some states may want to invest more in teacher mentoring, others in technology training, still others in recruiting science teachers or other specialists. One size does not fit all. With more flexible funding, I will make sure that states use their funds to get our best and brightest into classrooms and to raise the standards for teachers, just as they raise standards for our students.

Teachers should receive pay for performance. Every year, good teachers leave the public schools for jobs in the private sector where merit pay rewards top contributors. It's time to let creative, enthusiastic teachers know that they are a national treasure right where they are—in our classrooms.

Retaining dedicated teachers is only part of the challenge we face. The growing student population and expected teacher requirements mean that in the decade ahead, the United States will need to recruit an estimated two million NEW teachers. I will encourage states to broaden their uses of alternative teacher certification. Let's give mid-career professionals, academics, and our best college graduates a clearer path to working and excelling in our public schools.

Next point: Both students and teachers need a climate conducive to learning. Now even the best teachers can't get lessons across to students when they have to handle disorder, disobedience and threats. The best way to restore discipline and put our teachers back in charge of their classrooms is to adopt a "zero tolerance" policy for disruptive students.

Dr. Burke knows what it takes to make Melrose a community of learners. I applaud your new discipline policy, Dr. Burke—a discipline code understood by parents, teachers, and students. You don't need hundreds of pages of regulations written by Washington. You need the flexibility to guide this school.

Principals and teachers should have the authority to discipline disruptive students or to move them to an alternative school setting. Such students must not be allowed to monopolize the teacher's time and prevent their classmates from learning. And to protect the entire school community and make sure that troubled students get the help they need, we should ensure that students' disciplinary records follow them to every school they attend.

But we need to go further. Students, parents, teachers, principals, clergy, and law enforcement officials need to come together to figure out what works best in their own community. To keep our kids safe and make our schools drug-free, I support parent-approved locker and backpack searches and drug testing. For drugs and weapons, I say: there will be no place to hide. The lives and bright futures of all students depend on our watchful care, at home and at school.

Finally, I want to empower parents by re-establishing their control. Just as we should clear the way for state and local initiatives, so we should unleash the power of parental involvement and choice. Let's post school-by-school results on the Internet so that parents, aware of what's going on at the school, can be knowledgeable participants in their child's education. And we should allow competition to foster a rich smorgasbord of education choices. Whether it's opportunity scholarships for students in failing schools, or charter schools or home-schooling, we should empower parents to make choices as long as their choices get results.

I will encourage private support for public schools as well as private schools. Many public schools have established foundations that can accept charitable donations. I propose a $1,000 per-year federal tax credit for individuals who give to such educational foundations to help low income children in grades pre-K to 12. That gift, to a public or private school, could be used for books, scholarships, or other education purposes.

And to help parents pay for a child's school or college education, I would increase the contribution limits for education savings in accounts to $3,000 a year. President Clinton vetoed a similar provision last year. Let me be clear—I will fight for these Education Savings Accounts.

Ladies and gentlemen, let me sum up: While I am proposing significant change in federal policy—a shift from paperwork to performance—all of these initiatives boil down to some simple choices. We can choose to put children first or we can put the system first; we can choose to reinvent public education, or continue to support a deeply flawed system. We can choose to measure up to America's spirit—a spirit of creativity, independence and challenge—or let this heavy stack of regulations and restrictions continue to pull our public schools further down.

I'm throwing down the gauntlet—to Members of Congress, both parties—Republicans and Democrats—and to the Members of this Administration. My challenge is this—by the time America's students begin their summer vacation next year, legislation that truly reforms education should be passed and signed into law. Let's not allow American students and teachers to begin another school year under the status quo.

I can assure you this: If this President and the 106th Congress cannot reinvent public education, then President Dole and the 107th Congress will.

There is no time to waste. For more opportunities for children. For greater hope for parents. For a stronger, better America.

Let's seize the moment. I know it can be done—and so do you.

Thank you very much.

PRESIDENTIAL WITHDRAWAL SPEECH
Washington, D.C., October 20, 1999

Flanked by her husband, Elizabeth Dole stepped out of the presidential race even before she had the opportunity to make an "official" announcement of her bid, which was scheduled for November 7, 1999, in Des Moines, Iowa. In this speech, she wistfully describes the "overwhelming odds" that made her decision to withdraw inescapable. She didn't shed a tear, just spoke from the facts, but it appears from photos carried in the media that her husband was quite taken by her defeat. In the speech, she hinted that she was a long way from twilight and would be making another important contribution to American life in the future. A draft of most of this speech was provided by Kerry Tymchuk and the rest (the spelling of names and the opening paragraphs) was found March 2, 2004, on http://www.thegreenpapers.com/News/19991020-0.html.

Good morning everyone, and thank you for coming.

Nine months ago, I embarked upon a very personal exploration, one designed to help me decide whether to seek my party's presidential nomination. Wherever I've traveled, I have found audiences hungry for a different kind of leadership, one that looks beyond focus groups and tracking polls, to what is timeless and decent and true. At the same time, I have sensed a longing for community and a desire on the part of grassroots Americans to be part of something bigger than themselves. More than 30 years ago, as a young woman from Salisbury, North Carolina, I harbored similar feelings. Determined to be part of the events of my time, I embraced the idea of public service as a noble calling. It was to help rekindle in others my own sense of youthful idealism that I left the Red Cross last January.

In the months since, much has been made of the symbolism of my candidacy. I've been all but overwhelmed by women of all ages who have invested me with their hopes and dreams, and who have contributed generously of their time, talent and resources. But along with the symbolism there was also substance—the substance of ideas, and the challenge to overcome conventional or dangerous thinking. To those who question American involvement in the world, I have repeatedly said that where our national interests and our national values intersect, we must never be afraid to lead.

We must never be afraid to lead. In the aftermath of the Cold War, I have argued for a relationship with Russia. It's based on reformist policies rather than personalities. In an era when weapons of mass destruction include computer viruses as well as North Korean missiles, I have insisted on making technology our friend as well as our protector. That means proceeding with construction of a missile defense system. Closer to home, it means realizing the promise of the Internet, while denying it to pornographers and others who would deaden the souls of our young people. I'm proud of having offered an early comprehensive plan to address the farm-crisis, and insisting that our children be protected from merchants of death—whether they sell dope on a street corner, or a sawed off shotgun over-the-counter. [I'm proud of having offered] higher teacher pay for better performance, a return of discipline to the classroom with a zero tolerance policy for disruptive students, [and] reestablishment of parental control in the schools. These are just some of the educational reforms for which I have contended.

Of course, running for president is an education in itself. At times I have felt as if there are two entirely separate campaigns underway. Outside the beltway, real people by the thousands turned out to discuss their schools and health care, tax cuts and the state of our defenses. In the real America, it's more important to raise issues than to raise campaign funds. I have tried to run a nontraditional campaign rather than a traditional one, bringing countless first-time voters into the political process, as we have sought together to make history. It's confusing to many Americans who are part of my huge crowds and share my enthusiasm that this is not a measure of success.

But this is not all that I have learned. I have learned that the current political calendar favors those who get a huge start or tap into private fortunes or have a preexisting network of political supporters. Steve Forbes has unlimited resources. Governor Bush has raised over $60 million and has about $40 million on hand. Both are starting to run T.V. ads next week. Already I have attended over 70 fundraising events. My schedule through early December would have taken me to a total of 108 fundraising events across America. Even then, these rivals would enjoy a 75 or 80-to-1 cash advantage. Perhaps I could handle 2-to-1 or even 10-to-1, but not 80-to-1.

I hoped to compensate by attracting new people to the political process, by emphasizing experience and advocating substantive issues. But important as these things may be, the bottom line remains money. In fact, it's kind of a Catch 22. Inadequate funding limits the number of staff at headquarters in key states. It restricts your ability to communicate with voters. It places a ceiling on travel and travel staff. Over time, it becomes nearly impossible to sustain an effective campaign. Wherever you go, you find yourself answering questions, not so much about guns in the classroom, or China in the World Trade Organization, but [about] money in the bank and ads on the airways.

All my life, I have been accustomed to challenging the odds. But the first obligation of any candidate is to be honest, honest with herself and honest with her supporters. Last Sunday, a 5-hour flight from Seattle gave me an opportunity to do some hard thinking. I thought about the rumor I had to answer for about 2 weeks that I was dropping out and the damage it had done to my fundraising. I thought a lot, if there was any other avenue not yet explored for raising money. When I arrived home, I told Bob that this time the odds are overwhelming. It would be futile to continue, and he reluctantly agreed. Any other decision would be less than honest to an outstanding campaign team led by the very able Tom Daffron and backed by thousands of volunteers and donors whose enthusiasm gave us a powerful grass roots presence despite our limited resources.

I can never fully convey my gratitude to each of you or to the endless stream of young people, many of you who had turned away from public service but were eager to apply your energies and idealism on my behalf. God has blessed me in so many ways. Those blessings have included friends like Earl Cox and Margaret Kluttz, who led the 18-month draft Dole movement as well as my outstanding finance chair, Bonnie McElveen Hunter. Throughout, I have been able to count on my dear family, especially my precious husband, who urged me, he urged me to share my vision of a better America in the new millennium.

In the words of the poet, we shall not cease from exploration, and the end of all our exploring will be to arrive at where we started and know the place for the first time. Today marks the latest, but by no means the last chapter in a story of service that began many years ago. The road ahead beckons. To my friends, I say, take heart. We will meet again and often—in the unending struggle to realize America's promise as a land whose greatness lies, not in the power of her government, but in the freedom of her people. At the beginning of this remarkable century, Theodore Roosevelt challenged his fellow citizens to accept obligations as freedom's champion and defender. As I leave this race, never were words more apt than Teddy Roosevelt's tribute to the man or woman in the arena: "Far better it is to dare mighty things, to win glorious triumphs even though checkered by failure than to take rank with those poor spirits who neither enjoy much nor suffer much, because they live in the gray twilight that knows no victory or defeat." God willing, there are many arenas in which to fight, many ways to contribute. So while I may not be a candidate for president in 2000, I'm a long way from the twilight.

Thank you all.

One more sentence: Thank you all, every one here for your friendship, your encouragement, and above all, your willingness to dare mighty things.

God bless each and every one of you, and God Bless America.
Thank you for joining me this morning.
Thank you so much.

DUKE UNIVERSITY COMMENCEMENT SPEECH
Durham, North Carolina, May 14, 2000

Because of Elizabeth Dole's history with Duke University, this is an especially notable graduation address. It came after her bid for the presidency, and it shows her wistfulness upon withdrawing from the race. Themes from her "An America We Can Be" speech are cast in a different way. She highlights character as a solution to contemporary tabloid morality. This speech was obtained from Elizabeth Dole.

Thank you so much for that wonderful, warm welcome. I am so grateful for the honor bestowed on me today, which I will cherish for a lifetime. Thank you, Madame President, for that more than generous introduction. We're all so grateful for your strong and able leadership. Madame President—that does have a nice ring to it, doesn't it? Oh, well. When the Class of 2000 invited me to be a part of this special day, I was both touched and flattered. After all, I come before you as a recent dropout from the Electoral College! My husband likes to compare a commencement speaker to the corpse at a funeral: you don't really expect him to say anything, but you can hardly hold the ceremony without him. Well, this morning, I feel like anything but funereal.

Today is the latest, but by no means the last chapter in a story that began in room 304 of Alspaugh House in the autumn of 1954. Actually, it began a few months earlier than that, when I decided to apply to Duke, and nowhere else, because my older brother John went here. I've always put John on a pedestal, so it seemed only natural that I should want to follow in his academic footsteps. At the time, it seemed just as logical to apply for the Angier Duke Scholarship. Unfortunately, the logic escaped the scholarship committee. While I made it to the finals, I can still remember sitting in the breakfast room one morning opening mail, tears streaming down my face—and John putting things in perspective. "You shouldn't be crying," he told me. "Dad's the one who's going to have to pay the bills. If anyone around here should be crying, it's Dad."

Well, it's great to see so many old friends here in Wallace Wade Stadium. And it's an honor to share this stage with a statesman and public servant for whom I have great respect, my fellow degree recipient Ambassador Andrew Young. Both Andy and I have been around long enough to know who everyone has really come to see today—so before going any further, I want to salute the Class of 2000 and [student commencement speaker] Holly Cooper, whose words of reflection and insight in the pursuit of truth and the traditions of this great university were an inspiration to us all. I salute you. It's been quite a ride for the Class of 2000: over the last four years, you have survived Hurricanes Fran and Floyd, the Achievement Index, the departure of Wild Bill's, Y2K and the Great Snow of 2000.

For the Duke family, this millennial commencement marks a historic crossroads on the calendar. Seventy-five years have passed since President Keohane's predecessors vowed to "develop our resources, increase our wisdom, and promote human happiness." One might think a 75th anniversary would impose the heavy weight of time. On the contrary—such a day reminds us that youth, like idealism, is very much a state of mind—and that a university can never grow old so long as it nurtures the flame of innovation and curiosity.

Here we are reminded that, while knowledge is important, wisdom is essential. And the ultimate wisdom is not to be found in the tidal wave of data that saturates our airwaves, our front pages, our modems and textbooks. The poet Robert Frost put it best when he said, "What we do in college is to get over our little mindedness." It is in that same spirit that we gratefully pause to recognize instructors—in and out of the classroom—who have assisted countless Duke graduates to raise their sights and enlarge their minds.

For me—and I suspect for many of you as well—the greatest of teachers was also the first. So on this Mother's Day of happy reunions and emotional partings, of popping flashbulbs and unabashed pride, I hope you will indulge me if I take a moment to express a daughter's love and gratitude to her mother, Mary Hanford, who'll be 99 years old on May 22nd. Recently, I established a Duke scholarship in Mother's name. Although it hardly compares with the gifts she's bestowed on her loved ones, it does illustrate the debt owed by each of us to those who have gone before. Commencement Day acknowledges such debts, equaled only by the fresh obligations that the Class of 2000 will assume to all who follow in your wake.

In a larger sense, this ceremony is an act of faith—a faith renewed whenever we step forward to redeem our time through a vision of things that ought to be. We are honored today by the presence of President Jimmy Carter, Rosalynn Carter and Lady Bird Johnson. As I have traveled this country and many places around the world, I see the positive difference that President and Mrs. Carter continue to make in the lives of others. Their deep faith has been an inspiration to me personally, and an example

to countless millions. And like my own mother, Mrs. Johnson has combined tradition with trailblazing. No American has done more to introduce us to the beauties of nature, or remind us that we are all stewards
of God's creation. I cannot let this occasion pass without acknowledging
the grace, the generosity, the inspiration of two First Ladies who have always been ladies first.

Society, it has been said, is a partnership between the dead, the living,
and those yet to come. Consider the nation into which my mother was
born. At the start of the 20th century, the average life expectancy for an
American man was 46 years; for a woman, 48 years. The telegraph system—Internet of its day—strained to carry 63 million messages a year. The
Dow Jones Industrial Average passed the 100 mark in January 1906. Foreign immigrants streamed through Ellis Island—the American front
porch—at a rate of 100 per hour. Yet the Census Bureau didn't even keep
statistics on the number of Hispanics or Asian Americans.

Fast forward to the 1950s—enshrined in popular memory as a time of
hula hoops, "I Love Lucy" and political indifference. Undoubtedly, some
in this audience harbor fond recollections of an era when men wore the
pants and women wore the earrings. When surfing was an activity pursued on a board in the ocean, not with a mouse in the dorm room. My
classmates worried about pollution of the air, not the airwaves. And we
danced to Chubby Checker instead of Smashing Pumpkins.

The world has turned over many times since the class of '58 drank Coke
at the Devil's Den, partied at the Saddle Club, and exerted leadership
through White Duchy and Red Friars, groups abandoned as "elitist" in
the egalitarian '60s. To be sure, Duke in the '50s was a great research institution that sometimes felt like a finishing school. Duchesses were in-
structed to eat breakfast every day, avoid blue jeans and wear hats and
hosiery to church. Besides observing the 10:30 curfew, we were told to go
down receiving lines at every dance, and to write thank you notes to every
date and hostess.

Well, it's easy to look back and laugh at so innocent a culture. Yet if a
great university teaches us nothing else, it is to be on guard against facile
generalizations, some based on nothing more than nostalgia tinged with
condescension. I know. As a member of the so-called Silent Generation, I
can tell you we were anything but silent. Indeed, my first letter home put
my parents on notice that I intended to pursue a somewhat unconven-
tional path.

"I think it would be fascinating to learn about American government,
history in the making," I told them. This was not necessarily what they
had in mind. Truth be told, Mother had hoped that I would study home
economics—the natural prelude to marriage and a life next door in our

beloved Salisbury. Yet, like any good teacher, Mother has always been prepared to learn from her students. On receiving my letter, she consulted a professor at the University of North Carolina from our hometown. "Let her take political science," he breezily reassured her. "We need women in government. And anyway, they all get married eventually."

Even then, such attitudes were being challenged by women who refused to accept either limits or labels. Here again I find myself standing on the shoulders of giants. Florence Brinkley was a professor of English literature and dean of the Woman's College. No title, however, can begin to gauge her imprint on two generations of Duke students. Miss Brinkley's ambition was to serve, not to be. Her enemies were the slipshod and second rate.

What she gave us was beyond calculation. It was Dean Brinkley who urged me to spend a summer at Oxford University. She nurtured my interest in politics, helped me establish a campus leadership training program for women, and lent tacit support to a whole series of undergraduate reforms. By the time we were through, we'd even managed to push Saturday night curfew back to one o'clock Sunday morning. After much cajoling, I persuaded the dean that the student government and judicial board would accomplish so much more if only we scheduled our retreat at Myrtle Beach. And we did. It was great. Closer to home, I spent long hours working on an honor code, a subject which remains a perennial object of undergraduate debate. As I recall, East Campus was much more favorably inclined to the idea than West Campus. Apparently some things never change.

That's not all that bonds my generation of campus activists with today's Campus Social Board and Students Against Sweatshops. To enforce the 18th Amendment at Duke in my days, we had a semi-official watchdog; in undergraduate parlance, the Delta Patrol. Forty years later, students, faculty and parents alike are struggling to combat a culture in which alcohol and drugs co-exist with sexual violence. What a horror, especially when played out against a tabloid culture wherein celebrity trumps accomplishment, and shame seems the surest route to 15 minutes of televised notoriety.

I don't know whether age bestows wisdom. I'll settle for perspective as the next best thing. My own experience tells me that America is nothing if not a work in progress. Stop and think: in the span of a single lifetime, we have left the surface of the earth to soar into the heavens and explore distant solar systems. We've conquered diseases that once ravaged mankind. A century after the telephone redefined distance, cyberspace—a term coined by science fiction writer William Gibson in 1984—promises to transform life as we know it.

And that's just the beginning. Too rapidly for some, much too slowly for others, we have at last begun to honor promises we made to one another at the dawn of the republic. We have demolished legal and cultural barriers that formerly mocked our democratic aspirations. Indeed, we rejoice in the rich diversity of a land that resembles nothing so much as Joseph's many-colored coat. How diverse? Consider this: today's Americans buy more salsa than ketchup.

None of this happened by accident. It happened because of the Florence Brinkleys, the Jimmy and Rosalynn Carters, the Andrew Youngs, the Lady Bird Johnsons, the Bob Doles and countless others dissatisfied with the status quo. Officiating at a wedding in 1931, Justice Benjamin Cardozo spoke of "three great mysteries" in the lives of mortal beings: the mystery of birth at the beginning; the mystery of death at the end; and, greater than either, the mystery of love. Everything that is most precious in life is a form of love, he said. "Art is a form of love, if it be noble; labor is a form of love, if it be worthy; thought is a form of love, if it be inspired."

If Commencement Day is about anything, it is this mysterious love, this overarching passion for possibility that makes today's ceremony both a linking of the generations and a renewal of hope. I read not long ago that Madison Avenue is having trouble coming up with a label for those—including many in this graduating class—who are seen as the natural successors of Generation X, which in turn succeeded the Boomers, which in turn were divided between hipsters and the Me Generation.

Let me suggest an alternative: Why not dispense with labels altogether? After all, what is a label but a preconception brought to life, a marketing tool that blurs your identity and judges you by the car you drive, the jeans you wear or the CDs that you buy? In such a culture, we don't know people—we categorize them. Replacing subtlety with stereotype, we rob citizens of their most precious possession—their individuality. In any event, America needs leaders, not labels. Lest we forget: it wasn't a label that wrote the Gettysburg Address, or charged up San Juan Hill or refused to move to the back of a segregated bus in Montgomery, Alabama.

Nothing so stamps our individuality as our beliefs. Deciding what you believe is the essence of education. Acting upon those beliefs is the essence of a purposeful life. For no cynic ever built a cathedral. Growing up in small town North Carolina, I was taught that we are all sinners, and that righteousness should never be confused with self-righteousness. Religion was about doing things for people, not standing in judgment of people. Our faith taught us that service came before self. Nor was political activism frowned upon. On the contrary, think of the historic contributions made by men and women who have lived for—and, on occasion, been willing to die for—their beliefs. From John Winthrop's city upon a hill and

Dorothy Day's social gospel to the vision of racial justice so eloquently espoused by the Reverend Martin Luther King, the truest believers have been among the most powerful champions of the exploited and oppressed.

Forty years have passed since John F. Kennedy shattered, once and for all, the irrational prejudice against Catholics in the White House. Today, an equally irrational prejudice is applied by some, not only against those stigmatized as "the religious right," but against anyone primarily driven by their faith to pursue a better world. One of the glories of America is that no one tells you what to believe. At the same time, the essence of our government is self-government. That means millions of individuals acting upon their beliefs, demanding a government they can be proud of—consistent with Duke's own mission to "develop our resources, increase our wisdom, and promote human happiness."

Certainly my generation can never forget how the modern civil rights revolution unfolded on a powerful wave of Biblical teaching, African-American spirituals and a courage reminiscent of the early martyrs. Since then, believers of all stripes have regarded society's imperfections as a call to duty, not as an excuse for bitterness. Nor have they hesitated to criticize those who care more for their pockets than for their principles. After all, the cash register has yet to be invented that has a conscience. On no one does this responsibility fall more heavily than the university. It has been said that while men may be born free, they cannot be born wise; and it is the duty of the university to make the free, wise. One need look no further than the Duke Chapel—heart as well as soul of this campus—or the Durham Neighborhood Partnership to appreciate just how much a committed university can do to enhance the health, advance the learning and promote the safety of its neighbors.

Meanwhile, we are told that change is the only constant. Yet, amidst so much change, it is critically important that we cling to what is changeless—to love and honor and reverence for things seen and unseen. In this age of satellite dishes, automated tellers and 500 channels on which to watch infomercials for the Ab Flex, may I suggest that we frazzled humans have need of inspiration as well as information, and of faith to match our facts. You don't have to be a missionary to have a sense of mission. All you need is the love of which Justice Cardozo spoke.

So why, you ask, do so many current opinion makers seem leery of faith as a basis for public service? It isn't enough to say we inhabit a secular age. At the end of a century which has severely tested man's humanity, billions of people acknowledge a higher power, one who guides our conscience and raises us above the level of mere existence. Perhaps our culture is worshipping the wrong god—material wealth and professional status. In our nation's capital and in too many other places, success is often defined by the power you hold, the names in your Rolodex or the view from your office window.

Yet this is not the gold that Duke mints with every graduation. For the real gold is the kind that cannot be measured with dollar signs or weighed on a scale. Class of 2000, I'm sure I don't tell you something new when I say that life is much more than the sum total of possessions. For such things will rust away, wear away or depreciate, but your inner resources—character—must never tarnish. Whether on the floor of Congress, in the boardrooms of corporate America or in the corridors of a big city hospital, character provides both a sense of direction and a means to fulfillment. It asks not what you want to be, but who you want to be. For in the final analysis, it is your moral compass that counts far more than any bank balance, any resume and, yes, any diploma.

Character expresses itself in countless ways. To me, however, it is tested—as it is defined—through the practical application of faith. I hasten to add that faith is about nothing if not humility. In his book *Beside Still Waters: Searching for Meaning in an Age of Doubt*, Gregg Easterbrook takes pains to refute the notion that America's Founders wished to ban spiritual expression from the public square. They were products of a particular culture, he writes, a colonial society that knelt before an established church, and that all too often permitted Anglican or other sects to repress those with whom they differed.

It was this exclusionary idea—this compulsory faith—to which they took exception. They never insisted on government hostility toward faith itself. The late Joseph Cardinal Bernardin summed it up brilliantly when he declared, "to endorse a properly secular state, which has no established ties to any religious institution, does not mean we should support a secularized society, one in which faith is reduced to a purely private role." Here is a critical distinction, all the more important for a nation that at times appears so eager to celebrate our differences that we forget what, if anything, unites us.

At the start of a new millennium, nothing is more important than repairing the frayed bonds of community in America. In this era of runaway isolation—"when people all over the developed world eat, read, watch and do pretty much the same things, but isolated from others"—it is often hard to tell where life begins and entertainment leaves off. Controversies are made for and by television; politics are reduced to fodder for late-night comics. Aware of our power, we seem uncertain as to our purpose.

To its harshest critics, our nation's capital is a chamber of horrors. To many of those holding office it is a pressure cooker. To me, Washington is nothing more or less than a mirror held up to the people and the process it represents. If it is less civil than it might be, isn't that a reflection of a society coarsened by tabloid values? No doubt to many of you, Washington may seem an alien place, a city of hot air, shrill voices and manufactured controversies. Perhaps you have lost interest in today's virtual reality politics, where more and more candidates without ideas hire consultants without convictions to run campaigns without substance.

Yet this is the one luxury we cannot afford. For representative government is exactly that—representative. If politics seems irrelevant, then it falls to you to make it more relevant. If it appears lacking in civility, then your task is to help civilize it. In my eight years as president of the American Red Cross, I saw the evil that humans can inflict on one another— saw it in the dim eyes of starving children in Rwanda and in the paralyzing grief of parents in Oklahoma City. I have felt the hopelessness and despair of families who have lost everything to a tornado's brief, terrifying violence.

But I have also been uplifted by the extraordinary power of human generosity—of a kindness not legislated by any Congress or Parliament, but mandated by faith and in neighborliness and, yes, occasional saintliness. At the outset, I quoted Robert Frost, no mean educator himself, on the civilizing mission of the university. Let me conclude with some other lines from the Yankee poet. They were penned in the bleak 1930s, when hardship shadowed America and fanaticism stalked the globe. Yet they are timeless, I think, in suggesting the relationship of belief to action, and of service to success.

My object in living is to unite
My avocation and my vocation

"My object in living is to unite my avocation and my vocation." I have never heard a more eloquent summons to the purposeful life—or a more compelling argument for a faith that serves your country and your conscience. You take from this ceremony much more than a diploma. You take with you the responsibility for writing the next chapter of the American story. What we become as a nation will depend in large measure on what you become—and what you believe.

I hope you never forget those who have gone before, nor those who will come after. For Heaven and the future's sakes, don't get jaded. Don't fall victim to cynicism. Remember that life is not meant to be endured, but enjoyed. Retain your curiosity, and though you may get wrinkles, you will never grow old. Be brave. Take risks. Above all, be yourselves, for therein lies the greatest gift you can return to those who have given so much that you might join the Duke family. May love and need be one, and all your work be play for mortal stakes. Congratulations, and God bless you all. Thank you so very much.

REPUBLICAN NATIONAL CONVENTION SPEECH
Philadelphia, Pennsylvania, August 1, 2000

The 2000 Republican National Convention, held in Philadelphia, featured Elizabeth Dole as one of the Republican Party's most favored spokespeople. She approached the podium to throngs of applause and support. In this speech, she praises George W. Bush as a presidential candidate who could lead the country in the right moral direction—toward a politics of purpose. This speech was obtained by the author Nichola Gutgold from the GOP Press Department at the convention.

Thank you very much.

You have heard Condoleezza Rice speak eloquently of America's place in the world. I, too, wish to address our nation's security tonight. I speak not of military weapons, but of moral ones, of the defense of values as well as territory.

Long before there was an American dream, there was a dream of America as liberty's home and refuge. It was for this, that a million heroes fought and bled and died.

Not only to protect land on a map, much as they might cherish their home and hearth; nor to encroach on other lands or menace other peoples, or impose our way of life on anyone—but merely, heroically, to ensure freedom's survival in the hostile world.

Let us be clear; the success of freedom can never be measured in material terms alone. For one day, each of us will be held to account not for the money we made, but for the difference we made. Not for the worldly status we may have enjoyed, but for the stewardship we provided.

Freedom empowers the heart. It levels walls and shatters ceilings—including glass ceilings.

Ladies and gentlemen, in my eight years as President of the American Red Cross, I saw things that will haunt me for the rest of my life—the evil that humans can inflict on one another—saw it in the dim eyes of starving children in Somalia and in the paralyzing grief of parents in Oklahoma City.

But I have also been uplifted by the extraordinary power of the American heart—by those armies of compassion, who are willing to cross town or cross the globe to minister to those they've never met and will never see again. People who go where government cannot, and others will not, who carry our values of peace and democracy around the world, putting service before self. Such kindness and generosity are not legislated by any Congress. They arise from faith, neighborliness, and yes, occasional saintliness.

Indeed I learned long ago that you don't have to be a missionary to be filled with a sense of mission. The 20th century was America's century—not because of our power, but because of our purpose. Today, millions of Americans—of both parties and no party—are seeking a politics of purpose.

The next President of the United States must defend both America's interests and America's ideals. No one, no one understands this better than Governor George W. Bush!

In an era of rampant cynicism and indifference toward government, he is determined to bring civility to the public square and restore our pride in our leaders. Throughout his career, he has appealed to the best in people, bridging our differences rather than exploiting them.

As President, he will put an end to the smash-mouth politics of recent years and to the name-calling that tarnishes our trust and alienates so many real people whose real problems can never be solved in a focus group or soothed by a spin-doctor.

George W. Bush will be a different kind of leader! He will use words to inspire, not inflame. He will move beyond the stale labels and sterile confrontations that all too often divide the American family. And, make no mistake, there are divisions in liberty's home.

Tonight, too many of our neighbors are hurting. At a time of economic prosperity, there are too many American homes without hope—too many street corners where despair reigns—too many classrooms where children are being left behind.

Like any good conservative, Governor Bush deplores waste—above all else, wasted lives.

He will repair the frayed strands of community. And he knows that sometimes the best way to do this is through non-profits, businesses, civic and religious groups, schools and charities.

George W. Bush understands there is power—and there is a higher power. He knows there is no strength without integrity; no security apart from strong character. For these timeless values form our first line of defense. Let this be our mission and our mandate—to defend frontiers of the heart, armed with faith and steeled by conviction.

Today, America resembles nothing so much as Joseph's many-colored coat, and in our diversity lies our strength. With that strength comes a matching responsibility—to make wrong into right . . . hope into reality . . . in the old, biblical words, to "let justice roll down like waters and righteousness like a mighty stream." Here, my friends, is the standard we raise. This is the faith of our fathers and mothers, the American cause we hold sacred, our politics of purpose.

In the words of that great hymn:

America! America!
May God thy gold refine
Till all success be nobleness
And every gain divine!

May God bless us in this great endeavor.
And may God bless America.

SENATE KICKOFF ANNOUNCEMENT SPEECH
Salisbury, North Carolina, February 23, 2002

This speech officially began Elizabeth Dole's U.S. Senate race in North Carolina. In the audience were supporters and well-wishers. Her original announcement date had been September 11th, but Dole postponed her announcement because of the terrorist attacks on America. This speech shows Dole at her best; she is honest, passionate, and direct. The text was obtained February 27, 2002, from the Web site: http://www.elizabethdole.org.

Good afternoon, everybody.

Thank you for coming out today to join me for an important announcement about a big decision I have made, and a big decision the people of North Carolina will make this year. I thank you all, and especially my husband, Bob, and my mother, Mary Hanford.

With their blessing, I am formally announcing that I have decided to run for the United States Senate from the great state of North Carolina!

As you may know, an event in Salisbury was originally scheduled for September 11th, but that sad day changed the course not only of my campaign, but our nation.

Wherever I have gone in the course of my travels around this state, I have found a bipartisan desire for a different kind of politics, a positive campaign worthy of challenges we confront and the sacrifices being made in defense of American democracy. So with your permission this afternoon, I'd like to dispense with the usual format and tell you as simply as I can who I am and why I am running for the United States Senate.

I am Mary and John Hanford's daughter, raised to believe that there are no limits to individual achievement and no excuses to justify indifference. From an early age I was taught that success is measured, not in material accumulations, but in service to others. I was encouraged to join causes larger than myself, to pursue positive change through a sense of mission, and to stand up for what I believe.

I am Bob Dole's wife, blessed with the love of a great and decent man, whose quiet acts of generosity are on a par with his wartime heroism.

And I am a daughter of North Carolina, a proud Tar Heel who's always cherished my roots here in Salisbury. I have never forgotten the words of this state's greatest twentieth century writer, which I learned at Duke University. "The unity that binds us all together," wrote Thomas Wolfe, "That makes this earth a family, and all men brothers and sons of God, is love. That love can take many forms. It is the love of one human being for another, a love which cements our attachment to a place of memory, the love of work and the sense of mission which must of necessity replace purely individual ambition if that work is to be truly fulfilling."

It is that love, that sense of mission, that binding unity, which have done so much to redefine our public life since September 11th. It is in such times of testing that we take the measure of our leaders, our institutions, and ourselves. Who could have imagined, that in the process of liberating Afghanistan we would liberate ourselves as well?

In the months since September 11th, politicians in both parties have risen to the level of statesmanship. The courage of our fighting men and women has been equaled only by the character of those on the home front. In the midst of war and recession, Americans nevertheless assert their belief that our country is on the right track. Why? Because we have rediscovered the sense of mission defined by Thomas Wolfe. Because today politics has a purpose, and we all have a president to look up to in George W. Bush!

The cynics predict it's only a matter of time before we revert to business as usual. I couldn't disagree more! Too many have sacrificed too much to surrender to the lowest common denominator. This is especially true in the public arena. The people of North Carolina deserve better than name calling and finger pointing. They deserve what they demand—serious people addressing serious issues in thoughtful and creative ways, and my positive campaign will reflect that desire.

The next senator from North Carolina will face many challenges. Let me tell you where I stand on some of the issues that matter to all of us here, beginning with national defense, jobs and education.

The terrorist attacks reminded us of what is at stake in the current global war against evil. The federal government has no greater responsibility than the security of this nation, and as our president and his team move forward on many fronts, the nation's resolve will be challenged again and again.

But the American people today are proving themselves equal to the challenge, perhaps guided—and yes, inspired—by the quiet, but steady hands of the Greatest Generation that rose to this occasion six decades ago.

Today's generation has taken on a new seriousness and sense of purpose about the defense of the nation and what it stands for.

As a United States Senator, I can assure you that the courageous men and women on the front lines of this war—many trained right here in North Carolina—the Army troops from Fort Bragg, the Marines from Camp Lejeune, Cherry Point and New River, the Air Force from Pope and Seymour Johnson—will have no stronger supporter. I am filled with pride for the role this state plays in defending our freedoms!

I know some of our veterans are here with us today, and I promise you that one of my top priorities is to stand up for you and our men and women in uniform. Now, would all of you please stand up, so we can show our appreciation for your service and your sacrifice?

If our young men and women are called into harm's way, on the front lines in the war against terrorism, they must have the best equipment, the best training, and the highest morale. Ladies and gentlemen, no more food stamps! No more substandard housing! I support President Bush's call for higher pay and better benefits for our military!

Here in North Carolina, the impact of the War has been felt not only by our military bases, but in our airports, hotels, restaurants, stores and factories. The impact of September 11th on the travel and tourism industry compounded the slumping economy in textiles, apparel, and furniture.

Let's face it, folks, North Carolina's economy is going through a painful transition. There's no getting around it. We find ourselves under assault by a recession, a downturn that spares few, if any, sectors in the state's economy.

Many are hurting, and many need help. They live in the small towns, on the farms and even in the shade of those glorious buildings that rise to the sky in Charlotte and Raleigh.

The people in our manufacturing sector who have worked so hard to make this state proud, are now burdened with a disproportionate share of the economic pain. And their pain is real! As I've crisscrossed this state, I've heard from people who have either lost their jobs or are worried, about losing their jobs. They're worried about car payments, college funds, mortgages.

Are there some textile or apparel or furniture workers here today? Please stand up. I know your jobs are threatened by unfair trade practices. Trade has many benefits for our nation—I am a supporter of free and fair trade—but if we open our markets, we must insist that others do the same—we must strictly enforce the trade laws, and provide a level playing field. Thank you for standing up; I want you to know I will stand up for you, and all North Carolina workers, in the United States Senate. Putting the economy back on track will require the same kind of resolve, discipline and focus that is now being applied to the war on terrorism. To do anything less on the economic front would be a dramatic failure of leadership. The Senate should pass an economic stimulus package to help get our economy moving again, but recently the Senate leadership abandoned the bill, and walked away from the workers. I'm for extending unemployment benefits, too, but our goal should be to get people paychecks, not unemployment checks!

And we certainly should not be looking to take more out of the paychecks of those who are working. I know some in Washington think the answer to our problems is to raise taxes. They're wrong. Raising taxes in a recession and at a time of war is exactly the wrong policy. That's why I was proud to take the No New Taxes Pledge so the working families of North Carolina will never have to wonder where my vote will be when it comes to raising taxes. I will not vote to raise your taxes!

I want to help North Carolina's economy grow again by investing in our community colleges, by earning more transportation dollars for our state, by vigorously promoting information technology, by opening markets for our farmers, by enacting a tobacco buyout, by freeing entrepreneurs and small business from strangling red tape—by creating new and better jobs!

And I will not only stand up for the workers of this state, I will stand by you, literally, as I begin a series of job days around the state, working side by side with the people who form the backbone of our state's economy—on our farms, at our airports, in our factories and in our classrooms.

Would the teachers in the audience please raise your hands? I won't call on you! Now let me ask you to please stand up, so we can show our appreciation for you. Thank you. Teaching is not just a job, it's a calling, a noble endeavor. Thank you for all you do for our children. For a brief period—while I was working toward a master's degree in education and government, I had the opportunity to serve as an 11th grade history teacher. Back then in the public schools, the classroom was really a showroom—a showroom of American excellence and achievement. Needless to say, we've lost a lot of ground in the last few decades, for a variety of reasons. We need a major shift in education policy, especially from the federal level. The Federal government accounts for 6% of the money in our schools, but 50% of the regulations! Teachers tell me all the time, they'd rather spend more money and time on children than on paperwork. Every hour spent filling out forms is an hour that doesn't go to our kids; every dollar is a dollar that doesn't go to the classroom. We need results from our students, not more regulations—performance, not more paperwork! I believe education should be a national priority, but with local control. Restoring our public schools to greatness must occur at the local level. We can't run our schools by remote control from Washington, D.C. After all, what we need in Salisbury may be very different from what's needed in San Francisco, California or Sanford, North Carolina. My guiding principles are first, to restore local and parental control, with high standards. While we're putting computers in every classroom, let's put the parents back in every classroom as well!

Second, we must establish measurable goals and strict accountability; and third, restore discipline to the classroom and respect for teachers. The President's bipartisan education bill is a strong first step, but there's lots of work to make the vision, I outlined, a reality. In the Senate, you can be sure, I will stand up for teachers, parents and students!

We need to make sure that health care coverage is more affordable and more accessible to the families of North Carolina. We must strengthen Social Security and Medicare for this and future generations, and help our seniors get prescription drugs. And don't let anyone tell you differently! We need to make sure that health care coverage is more affordable and more accessible to the families of North Carolina.

We need to make sure our homes and neighborhoods are safe, and that our gun laws are stringently enforced. But at the same time, we don't need to pass new laws that infringe on the rights of the law-abiding citizens of North Carolina.

We need to protect our environment, especially here in North Carolina, where the purity of the mountain streams and the beaches of our coast are not only beautiful, but an important part of our local economy.

Ladies and gentlemen, today marks the formal launch of my campaign to succeed Jesse Helms in the United States Senate. I say "succeed" him because we'll never "replace" him. I can still hear my dad saying, "Jesse is our watchdog; a relentless watchdog for North Carolina." And Bob Dole says, "You always know where Jesse is. You don't have to look under the table. You know where he stands."

Senator Helms looms large inside the Capitol building up in Washington, leveraging his stature to get things done for North Carolina—as well as for the nation—protecting our people, our businesses, our way of life. We have become accustomed to seeing his stature manifest itself in constituent service second-to-none. I will continue Senator Helms' commitment to excellent constituent service to all North Carolinians, regardless of political affiliation.

I have been involved in public policy for thirty-five years. I believe my leadership—the ability to bring together Democrats and Republicans to achieve results—has been tested and proven, that I can bring to the table a wealth of experience for North Carolina that enables me to be effective from day one.

One of the most emotional experiences of my life was a visit to Ground Zero. As I walked on that now hallowed ground, through the wreckage of the World Trade Center, three of my life's most important experiences seemed to come together.

I thought about the men and women of the Coast Guard I once led as Secretary of Transportation, just blocks away standing watch in New York Harbor and along our coastlines, part of our homeland defense. I thought about our priority to enhance safety in all aspects of transportation—especially air safety, installing air marshals and security coordinators due to the 1980's hijackings, and how much more we must do in this new, more dangerous environment.

People who had worked for me at the Department of Labor came up to reintroduce themselves. They were working hard to clean up and make safer what remains a very dangerous work site for the rescue workers.

I talked to the Red Cross staff and volunteers, who were helping rescue workers with food, beds and dealing with the trauma of their heroic efforts through mental health counseling, a program we started during the 8 years I was Red Cross president.

The service I've been privileged to render and the people I was fortunate enough to work with and lead, never seemed more important or more relevant, than on that cold day I spent, at the devastation in lower Manhattan.

It is this service and these experiences I will draw upon if I have the honor of serving as your United States senator. But experience is not the only factor in representing our state. The values we share as North Carolinians are more important. Honesty, integrity, hard work, faith, personal responsibility—these are the values that guide me.

I also believe we must foster a culture that respects life. That respect must be afforded to the most vulnerable in our society, including the elderly, the infirm, and those not yet born. Since September 11th, we have experienced a sense of universal fraternity—love of country, love of community, love of neighbor. Ultimately, what is the source of that love? When I was serving in the White House as Assistant to the President, Ronald Reagan and I found ourselves alone in a holding room as he waited to give a major speech. I was always amazed at his inner peace and sense of direction, so I asked him how he handled the challenges of the nation's highest office.

He told me, "When I was governor of California, Elizabeth, it seemed like everyday yet another disaster was put on my desk. And I felt an urge to look behind me for someone to hand it off to. One day, I realized I was looking in the wrong direction. I looked up instead of back. I'm still looking up, Elizabeth. I couldn't go another day in this office," President Reagan said, "if I didn't know I could ask God's help and it would be given."

I couldn't agree more. With God's help, I will run a positive campaign worthy of you—the people I seek to serve.

Finally, my friends, and neighbors, we must remember a successful campaign can't happen without you. So today, I'm asking for your prayers and your vote. Thank you for being here with me today. God bless you. And God bless this Great State and this great land of the free—America.

U.S. SENATE ACCEPTANCE SPEECH
Salisbury, North Carolina, November 5, 2002

Elizabeth Dole joyfully addressed the exuberant crowd that gathered on election night in her hometown of Salisbury, North Carolina. She had just been elected the first woman from that state to hold a seat in the U.S. Senate. The theme song from the movie *Rocky III* played in the background as the crowd stomped and cheered. She pledged to work hard for all her constituents, asking especially for her opponent's supporters to give her a chance to represent them. This text was transcribed from a Real Time Internet broadcast of the speech at Web site: http://www.nbc17.com/news/1769083/detail.html, accessed November 6, 2002.

Oh, wow, what a night! I'm so proud to be a North Carolinian! I'm just as thrilled as you are! We'll never forget this night, will we?

A few moments ago, I got a call from Erskine Bowles. He congratulated me on my victory, and he was very gracious. He obviously cares very much about the people of North Carolina, and I want to say to those who voted for Erskine Bowles, give me a chance. I intend to be a senator for all of North Carolina!

Obviously, there are so many people I want to thank who worked so hard for this campaign and the thousands of contributors and supporters who have been to the rallies and encouraged others to come out and vote. Obviously, I'd like to thank every one individually, but I can't do that tonight. Let me mention a few people whom I must thank. First of all, my husband, Bob Dole. Let me tell you, he's the best surrogate any candidate could have. He wanted to get to all one hundred counties, and he got close; he did really well. He got on the phone and called the county coordinators and really spent time cheering people on. I want to thank my precious mother and my brother John, and his wife Bunny. I'll tell you, they have really been there for me—a tremendous source of support. And I think they all put a lot of miles on the cars, running up and down the highway to all of the different events across North Carolina. I think some of you heard me say—one day I was traveling and in front of me I saw a car with a bumper sticker on it that said "Dole for Senate," and I said "Why don't you pull up right beside them, so I can wave hello and thank them?" And, when we pulled up along side of them it was Bunny and John—my brother and sister in law. Oh my.

I want to thank Senator Jesse Helms. Yes. You know, Senator Helms I appreciate so much not only his support in this campaign, but the job he did in the United States Senate. I can still hear my dad saying, "Jesse is our watchdog"—a relentless watchdog for North Carolina. I remember Bob Dole saying, "You always know where Jesse is. You don't have to look under the table. You know where he stands, because he says what he means and he means what he says." I'll tell you, he's had a great constituent service for the people of North Carolina, second to none. I intend to emulate that and stand just as tall and have a really good constituent service for the people of this state. So, we'll really work hard.

There are two former senators who've worked mighty hard. Lauch Faircloth, as a senior advisor; Jim Broyhill, who's been working very, very hard. I appreciate it so very much.

Yes, indeed. Now, I certainly want to mention my wonderful chairman of the campaign, Margaret Kluttz. Margaret, I love you, you are a precious friend.

Thank you so much and God bless you.

MAIDEN SENATE SPEECH ON WORLD HUNGER
Washington, D.C., June 5, 2003

Elizabeth Dole's first major address on the floor of the U.S. Senate was delivered on National Hunger Awareness Day. This speech shows how Dole "hit the ground running," as a new senator. Eloquently, she petitioned her fellow senators to make a commitment to feeding the hungry of North Carolina and other regions across the United States and globe. She used religious language and imagery to advocate a contemporary method of "gleaning," including tax incentives and other initiatives. This speech, provided by Elizabeth Dole, demonstrates her vast experience with policy.

I would like to thank you, Mr. President, and especially Majority Whip, McConnell, and Democrat Whip, Reid, for their very kind words. And I want to thank you and other members of the leadership for their unwavering support of this freshman class. I also want to recognize Senator Frist's call for the traditional courtesies of a maiden speech to be extended to the new Senators, and to express my appreciation for his commitment to the rich history of this great institution.

Tradition has held that by waiting a respectful length of time, the senior colleagues would appreciate the humility shown by a new member of the Senate, who would use the occasion to address an issue of concern.

I come in that sense today, Mr. President, to share my thoughts on a matter that weighs heavily on my mind. Hunger is the silent enemy lurking within too many American homes. It is a tragedy I have seen firsthand and far too many times throughout my life in public service.

This is not a new issue. In 1969, while I was serving as deputy assistant to the President for Consumer Affairs, I was privileged to assist in planning the White House Conference on Food, Nutrition and Health. In opening the conference, President Nixon said, "Malnourishment is a national concern because we are a nation that cares about its people, how they feel, how they live. We care whether they are well and whether they are happy." This still rings true today.

And on National Hunger Awareness Day, I want to highlight what has become a serious problem for too many families, particularly in North Carolina.

My home state is going through a painful economic transition. Once thriving textile mills have been shuttered . . . family farms are going out of business . . . tens of thousands of workers have been laid off from their jobs. Entire areas of textile and furniture manufacturing are slowly phasing out as high-tech manufacturing and service companies become the dominant industries of the state. Many of these traditional manufacturing jobs have been in rural areas, where there are fewer jobs and residents are *already* struggling to make ends meet.

In 1999, North Carolina had the 12th lowest unemployment rate in the United States. By December 2001, the state had fallen to 46th. That same year, according to the Rural Center, North Carolina companies announced 63,222 layoffs. Our state lost more manufacturing jobs between 1997, and the year 2000, than any state except New York.

Entire communities have been uprooted by this crisis. In the town of Spruce Pine in Mitchell County, 30 percent of the town's residents lost their jobs in 2001. Ninety percent of those layoffs were in textile and furniture manufacturing.

These are real numbers and real lives from a state that is hurting. Our families are struggling . . . to find jobs . . . to pay their bills . . . and as we hear more and more often—even to put food on the table.

In fact, the unemployment trend that started in 1999, resulted in 11.1 percent of North Carolina families not always having enough food to meet their basic needs. That's according to the U.S. Department of Agriculture. And North Carolina's rate is higher than the national average.

Mr. President, this means that among North Carolina's 8.2 million residents, nearly 900,000 are dealing with hunger . . . some are hungry . . . others are on the verge.

My office was blessed recently to meet a young veteran, Michael Williams, and his family. Michael served his country for 8 years in the United States Army, before leaving to work in private industry to use the computer skills he gained in the military. He was earning a good living, but after the September 11th terrorist attacks, he and his wife Gloria felt it was time to move their two children closer to family, back home to North Carolina.

But Michael found a shortage of jobs since his return. He worked with a temp agency . . . but that job ended. It has been so hard to make ends meet that the family goes to a food bank near their Clayton, North Carolina, home twice a month . . . because with rent, utilities and other bills, there is little left to buy food.

Their story is not unlike so many others. Hard-working families are worrying each day about how to feed their children.

And if this weren't enough, our food banks are having a hard time finding food to feed these families. In some instances, financial donations have dropped off or corporations have scaled back on food donations. In other cases, there are just too many people and not enough food.

At the Food Bank of the Albemarle in Northeast North Carolina, executive director Gus Smith says more people are visiting his food bank even as donations are off by 25 percent. Gus says, "We just can't help everybody at this point and time." To try to cope, they recently moved to a four-day work week, meaning the entire staff had to take a 20 percent pay cut *just* to keep the doors open.

America's Second Harvest, a network of 216 food banks across the country, reports it saw the number of people seeking emergency hunger relief rise by 9 percent in 2001, to 23.3 million people. In any given week, it is estimated that 7 million people are served at emergency feeding sites around the country.

These numbers are troubling, indeed. No family in North Carolina or anywhere in America should have to worry about where they will find food to eat! No parent should have to tell their child, there is no money left for groceries! This is simply unacceptable! I spent most of the Congressional Easter recess going to different sites in North Carolina . . .

homeless and hunger shelters . . . food distribution sites . . . soup kitchens
. . . farms . . . even an office where I went through the process of applying for government assistance through the WIC program—Women Infants
and Children. I was also able to meet on several occasions with a group
known as the Society of St. Andrew.

This organization—like some others across the country—is doing impressive work in the area of gleaning. That's when *excess* crops that would
otherwise be thrown out are taken from farms, packing houses, and warehouses and distributed to the needy. Gleaning immediately brings to my
mind the Book of Ruth, in the Old Testament. She gleaned in the fields
so that her family could eat. You see, Mr. President, in Biblical times,
farmers were encouraged to leave crops in their fields for the poor and
for travelers. Even as far back as in Leviticus, Chapter 19, in the Old Testament, we read these words, "And thou shalt not glean thy vineyard,
neither shalt thou gather every grape of thy vineyard; thou shalt leave
them for the poor and the stranger." So gleaning was long a custom in
Biblical days . . . a command by God to help those in need.

It's a practice we should utilize much more extensively today. It's astounding that the most recent figures available indicate that approximately
96 billion pounds of good, nutritious food—including that at the farm and
retail level—is left over or thrown away. It is estimated that only 6 percent of crops are actually gleaned in North Carolina. A tomato farmer in
western North Carolina sends 20,000 pounds of tomatoes to landfills each
day during harvest season.

Mr. President, I ask unanimous consent to present an example of produce on the Senate floor. The produce can't be sold; sometimes it's under-
weight or not a perfect shape—like this sweet potato.

Other times it's simply surplus food—more than the grocery stores can
handle . . . but it's still perfectly good to eat. Imagine the expense to that
farmer in dumping 20,000 pounds of tomatoes each day during his harvest season!

And this can't be good for the environment. In fact, food is the single
largest component of our solid waste stream . . . more than yard trimmings
or even newspapers! Some of it does decompose . . . but it often takes several years. Other food just sits in landfills, literally mummified. Putting
this food to good use through gleaning will reduce the amount of waste
going to our already overburdened landfills. And I am so appreciative of
my friends at Environmental Defense for working closely with us on this
issue.

Gleaning also helps the farmer because he doesn't have to haul off or
plow under crops that don't meet exact specifications of grocery chains.

And certainly it helps the hungry by giving them not just any food, but food that is both nutritious and fresh.

The Society of St. Andrew is the only comprehensive program in North Carolina that gleans available produce, then sorts, packages, processes, transports and delivers excess food to feed the hungry. In 2001, the organization gleaned 9.7 million pounds—or 29.1 million servings of food. It only costs a penny a serving to glean and deliver this food to those in need. Even more amazing, the Society of St. Andrew does all of this with a tiny staff and an amazing 9,200 volunteers.

These are the types of innovative ideas we should be exploring. I was told by the Society of St. Andrew that $100,000 would provide at least 10 million servings of food for hungry North Carolinians. I set out to raise that money for the Society in the last few weeks, and thanks to the compassion of a number of caring individuals, companies, and organizations, we were able to surpass our goal and raise more than $180,000—enough for at least 18 million servings of food! More than ever, I believe this is a worthy effort that can be used as a model nationwide. I'm passionate about leading an effort to increase gleaning in North Carolina and across America.

The gleaning system works because of the cooperative efforts of so many groups . . . from the Society of St. Andrew and its volunteers that gather and deliver the food to the dozens of churches and humanitarian organizations that help distribute this food to the hungry.

Indeed, gleaning is, at its best, a public-private partnership. Private organizations are doing a great job with limited resources, but we must make some changes on the public side, to help them leverage their scarce dollars to feed the hungry. I have heard repeatedly that the single *biggest* concern for gleaners is transportation. The food is there. The issue is how to transport it in larger volume. I want to change the tax code to give transportation companies that volunteer trucks for gleaned food a tax incentive!

And there are other needed tax changes. Currently, only large publicly traded corporations can take tax credits for giving food to these gleaning programs. But it's not just large corporations that provide this food . . . it's the family farmers and the small businesses. Why should a farmer who gives up his perfectly good produce or the small restaurant owner who gives food to the hungry not receive the same tax benefits? The Senate has already passed legislation as part of the CARE Act that would fix this inequity. Now the House of Representatives needs to complete work on this bill!

But the answer to the hunger problem doesn't stop with gleaning. That is just part of the overall effort. There are other ways we can help, too.

This year we'll be renewing the National School Lunch and other important child nutrition programs, and there are a number of interesting components to these programs that I am interested in reviewing.

Under School Lunch, children from families with incomes at or below 130 percent of poverty are eligible for free meals. Children from families with incomes between 130 percent and 185 percent of poverty can be charged no more than 40 cents. This may seem like a nominal amount, but for a struggling family with several children, the costs add up. School administrators in North Carolina tell me they hear from parents in tears, because they don't know how to pay for their child's school meals.

The federal government now considers incomes up to 185 percent of poverty when deciding if a family is eligible for benefits under the WIC program. Shouldn't we use the same standard for school lunch? Standardizing the guidelines would even allow us to immediately certify children from WIC families for the School Lunch Program. It's time to clarify this bureaucratic situation and harmonize our federal income assistance guidelines.

The School Lunch Program is a vital component of our commitment to child nutrition, and we must do everything to maintain and strengthen its integrity so that it works for those who need it . . . and isn't viewed as a government giveaway!

There are a lot of interesting ideas being discussed, such as adjusting area eligibility guidelines in the Summer Food and other child nutrition programs, but these need to be looked at carefully, and we need to ask important questions, like how many people would be affected and what the costs would be? I've discussed many of these ideas with groups like America's Second Harvest, Bread for the World, the Food Research and Action Center and the American School Food Service Association. I look forward to the opportunity of exploring them further during reauthorization of these important programs in the Agriculture Committee, on which I am honored to serve.

But our work cannot stop within our own borders. The Food and Agriculture Organization of the United Nations says hunger affects *millions* worldwide. During my 8 years as president of the American Red Cross, I visited Somalia during the heart-wrenching famine.

In Baidoa, I came upon a little boy lying under a sack. I thought he was dead . . . but as his brother sat him up, I could see that he was severely malnourished. I asked for camel's milk to feed him, and as I raised the cup to his mouth, I put my arm around his back. The feeling of the little bones almost piercing through his flesh is something I will never forget. That is when the horror of starvation becomes real—when you can touch it.

There are many things which will haunt me the rest of my life. When 1 million Rwandans fled the bloodshed in their country, they stopped at the worst possible place—on volcanic rock in Goma, Congo. They could not dig for latrines—cholera and dysentery were rampant. They couldn't dig for graves. As I tried to help refugees, I was literally stepping over dead bodies, which were collected by the roadside and carried off, twice a day, to mass graves.

Former Senators Bob Dole and George McGovern are the architects of the Global Food Program, which has a goal of ensuring that 300 million school children overseas get at least one nutritious meal a day. The Department of Agriculture estimates that 120 million school-age children around the world are not enrolled in school, in part because of hunger or malnutrition. The majority of these children are girls. The Global Food for Education Program is now operating in 38 countries and feeding 9 million school children. I want to see this program expanded, and I plan to work on appropriations to advance that goal. Just helping a child get a good meal can make such a difference in developing countries. Feeding children entices them to come to school which allows them to learn . . . to have some hope, a future. And improved literacy helps with productivity, thereby boosting the economy.

This problem deserves national discussion. Hunger affects so many aspects of *our* society. In the spirit of that landmark conference held by the White House in 1969, I'm asking President Bush to convene a second White House conference so that the best and brightest minds can review these problems together.

I am honored to work with leaders in the battle to eradicate hunger . . . Former Congressman Tony Hall, now the United States Ambassador to the U.N. food and agricultural programs . . . and Former Congresswoman Eva Clayton, from my own state of North Carolina, now an Assistant Director-General for the U.N. Food and Agriculture Organization in Rome. Both were champions on hunger while in Congress. And there are many others . . . former Agriculture Secretary Dan Glickman . . . a leader on gleaning . . . Catherine Bertini, Under Secretary-General of the United Nations who is praised for her leadership to get food aid to those in need throughout the world . . . Congresswoman Jo Ann Emerson . . . co-chair of the Congressional Hunger Center, who carries on the legacy of her late husband Bill, who was a dear friend and a leader on this issue. And here in this body, my Chairman on the Agriculture Committee, Thad Cochran, ranking member Tom Harkin, Dick Lugar, Patrick Leahy, Pat Roberts and Gordon Smith . . . are all leaders in addressing hunger issues.

Partisan politics has no role in this fight. Hunger doesn't differentiate between Democrats and Republicans, and just as it stretches across so many ethnicities, so many areas . . . so must we.

As *Washington Post* columnist David Broder wrote yesterday, "America has some problems that defy solution. This one does not. It just needs caring people and a caring government, working together."

I get inspiration from the Bible in John, Chapter 21, when Jesus asks Peter, "Do you love me?" Peter, astounded that Jesus was asking him this question again, says, "Lord, you know everything. You know that I love you." And Jesus replies, then, "Feed my sheep." One of North Carolina's heroes, the Reverend Billy Graham, has often said that "We are not cisterns made for hoarding, we are vessels made for sharing." I look forward to working with Billy Graham in this effort.

Indeed, every religion, not just Christianity, calls on us to feed the hungry. Jewish tradition promises that feeding the hungry will not go unrewarded. Fasting is one of the pillars of faith of Islam and is a way to share the conditions of the hungry poor while purifying the spirit and humbling the flesh. Compassion or *Karuna* is one of the key virtues of Buddhism. So, you see, this issue cuts across religious lines, too.

Mr. President, I speak today on behalf of the millions of families who are vulnerable, who have no voice. For this little Sudanese girl . . . in this picture, stumbling toward a feeding station . . . and so many like her . . . I saw this picture in a newspaper some years ago, and it has been emblazoned on my mind ever since.

Anthropologist Margaret Mead once said, "Never doubt that a small group of thoughtful, committed citizens can change the world. Indeed, it is the only thing that ever has."

One of my heroes is William Wilberforce, a true man of God. An old friend, John Newton, persuaded him that his political life could be used for the service of God. He worked with a dedicated group . . . they were committed people of faith, and his life and career were centered on two goals: abolishing slavery in England and improving moral values. He knew that his commitment might cost him friends and influence, but he was determined to stand for what he believed to be right. It took 21 years, and William Wilberforce sacrificed his opportunity to serve as Prime Minister—but he was the moving force in abolishing slavery and changing the moral values of England.

Mr. President, in my lifetime, I have seen Americans split the atom, abolish Jim Crow, eliminate the scourge of polio, win the Cold War, plant our flag on the surface of the moon, map the human genetic code and belatedly recognize the talents of women, minorities, the disabled and others once relegated to the shadows.

Already, a large group of citizens have joined what I believe will become an army of volunteers and advocates. Today, I invite all of my colleagues to join me in this endeavor . . . let us recommit ourselves to the goal of eradicating hunger. Committed individuals *can* make a world of difference . . . even, I might say, a different world.

Mr. President, I ask consent that my letter to President Bush be included in the record at this point. I yield the floor.

Notes

CHAPTER 1

1. Elizabeth Dole, speech at the Republican National Convention, August 14, 1996.

2. In 1988, that was a formidable, yet very necessary task, because of the phenomenon known as the "gender gap." The gender gap stemmed from an observation that in the 1980 election, Ronald Reagan had won the presidency with men supporting him by only 8 percent more than women. But after two years of the Reagan presidency, public opinion polls and electoral results both showed that, if anything, this gap was widening. Women were becoming more opposed to Reagan's handling of the economy, foreign policy, environmental protection, and issues touching on equality of the sexes. Enlisting a powerful female Republican to speak at the convention was therefore an important strategy, and the GOP relied on Elizabeth Dole to do it.

3. The National Prayer Breakfast speech is a noteworthy event in Washington, D.C. Speakers over the years have included Rev. Billy Graham, Ronald Reagan, and Bill Clinton. To be chosen to give this speech is an honor, and it exemplifies a certain status that the speaker has achieved.

4. Aaron Zitner, "On the Campaign Trail, Two Doles Are Better than One," *Concord Monitor*, October 3, 1987.

5. Judi Hasson, "Elizabeth Takes the Floor," *USA Today*, August 15, 1996, 5A.

6. Michelle Caruso and Jere Hester, "GOP Flipping Its Liddy after Talk," *Daily News*, August 16, 1996, 26.

7. The lament is present in comments such as the one made by speech communication scholar Karlyn Kohrs Campbell, who pinpointed some of the difficulties Hillary Clinton encountered to her lawyerly style of speech. Campbell noted, "Hillary Rodham Clinton's style of public advocacy typically omits all of the discursive markers by which women publicly enact their femininity. Her tone is usually impersonal . . . her ideas unfold deductively . . . all kinds of evidence

is used. . . . She is impassioned but very rarely emotional." Karlyn Kohrs Campbell, "The Discursive Performance of Femininity: Hating Hillary," *Rhetoric and Public Affairs* 1, 1998: 1, 6.

8. For more information on the White House Project, visit the Web site at http://www.thewhitehouseproject.org/.

9. Rob Christensen, "Elizabeth Dole Series: A North Carolina Belle Blazes DC Trail: Part 1," *News and Observer* (Raleigh), October 13, 2002.

10. Ellen Goodman, "Mrs. Dole's Early Takeoff," *Washington Post*, September 19, 1987, A23.

11. Richard Cohen, "Elizabeth Dole, Wife: Her Smile Is Worth More than Her Service," *Bergen County Record* (Hackensack, N.J.), September 22, 1987, B1.

12. Ann Grimes, *Running Mates: The Making of a First Lady* (New York: William Morrow, 1990), 73–74.

13. This section was compiled from several sources, including: Bob Dole, Elizabeth Dole, Richard Norton Smith, and Kerry Tymchuk, *Unlimited Partners, Our American Story* (New York: Simon and Schuster, 1996); Richard Kozar, *Elizabeth Dole* (Philadelphia: Chelsea House Publishers, 2000); Carolyn Mulford, *Elizabeth Dole, Public Servant* (Hillside, N.J.: Enslow Publishing, 1992); Eileen Lucas, *Elizabeth Dole, a Leader in Washington* (Brookfield, Conn., The Millbrook Press, 1998).

14. Dole et al., *Unlimited Partners, Our American Story*, 77.

15. Ibid., 79.

16. The *Feminine Mystique* was published by Betty Friedan in 1963. This study began with interviews of the 1942 alumni of Smith College. Through her research, Friedan discovered that many women felt worthless because of societal pressure to live their lives through their husbands and children. Certainly, Elizabeth Dole felt the pressure of societal expectations on her, but she says she "followed her own drumbeat."

17. Helen Thorpe, "Liddy in Waiting," *George*, August 1999, 110.

18. Margie Kelley, "When I'm 64," *Harvard Law Bulletin*, Summer 2003. http://www.law.harvard.edu/alumni, accessed January 30, 2004.

19. Katie Leishman, "A Very Private Public Person," *McCall's*, April 1988, 131–35.

20. Richard Kozar, *Elizabeth Dole* (Philadelphia: Chelsea House Publishers, 2000), 58–59.

21. Dole et al., *Unlimited Partners, Our American Story*, 187.

22. Jane Ciabattari, "Five Who Could Be President," *Parade*, February 6, 1999, 6–7.

23. Sylvia Brooks, "Elizabeth Dole Says Gospel Had Daily Role," *Columbus Dispatch*, September 26, 1997, B1.

24. Betty Ford, phone interview with Nichola Gutgold, September 16, 1998.

25. Eleanor Clift and Tom Brazaitis, *Madam President: Shattering the Last Glass Ceiling* (New York: Scribner, 2000), 323.

26. Elizabeth Dole, interview with Nichola Gutgold and Molly Meijer Wertheimer, July 8, 2003.

27. Elizabeth Dole, interview with Nichola Gutgold, April 8, 1998.

28. Ibid.

29. Rob Christensen, "Elizabeth Dole Series: A North Carolina Belle Blazes DC Trail: Part 1." *News and Observer* (Raleigh), October 13, 2002.

30. Charles V. Zehren, "Convention 96/More than Just a Supportive Spouse," *Newsday*, August 15, 1996, A6.

31. Kerry Tymchuk, interview with Nichola Gutgold, September 11, 2000.

32. Richard Kozar, *Elizabeth Dole* (Philadelphia: Chelsea House Publishers, 2000), 22.

33. Helen Thorpe, "Liddy in Waiting" *George*, August 1999, 129.

34. Bob Dole, interview with Nichola Gutgold and Molly Meijer Wertheimer, December 17, 2001.

35. In one of the toasts, Dole talked about the friendship between the Polish people and the American people. She said that we share "a single soul of friendship." She also said that as friends, the people of the United States are eager to help the Polish people reach "the shores of freedom." In another toast, she compared the struggle of the Polish people today with the struggle of the American people two hundred years ago. She talked about personal sacrifices of the fifty-six men who signed the Declaration of Independence. She quoted Tom Paine in her speech: "Those who expect to reap the blessings of freedom must undergo the fatigue of supporting it." She recognized the sacrifices of the Polish people and told them that the American people are with you (toasts, Presidential Mission to Poland, November 28–December 2, 1990).

36. Kerry Tymchuk, interview with Nichola Gutgold, September 11, 2000.

37. John Sedgwick, "The Woman Behind That Unwavering Smile," *Newsweek*, August 19, 1996, 36.

38. Elizabeth Dole, interview with Nichola Gutgold and Molly Meijer Wertheimer, July 8, 2003.

39. Elizabeth Dole, interview with Nichola Gutgold, April 7, 1998.

40. Elizabeth Dole, speech at the AFL-CIO Constitutional Convention, November 13, 1989.

41. Elizabeth Dole, speech at University of Virginia commencement, May 17, 1987.

42. Ibid.

43. Ibid.

44. Elizabeth Dole, speech at *Redbook*/Mothers Against Drunk Driving event, May 9, 1997.

45. Elizabeth Dole, speech at University of Virginia commencement, May 17, 1997.

46. Ibid.

47. Ibid.

48. John F. Dickerson and Nancy Gibbs, "Elizabeth Unplugged," *Time*, May 10, 1999, http://www.time.com.

49. Sylvia Brooks, "Elizabeth Dole Says Gospel Had Daily Role," *Columbus Dispatch*, September 26, 1997, B1.

50. Beth Harpaz, *The Girls in the Van; A Reporter's Diary of the Campaign Trail* (New York: Thomas Dunne Books, 2001), 250.

51. Elizabeth Dole, interview with Nichola Gutgold, April 7, 1998.

52. Ibid.

53. Elizabeth Dole, interview with Nichola Gutgold and Molly Meijer Wertheimer, July 8, 2003.

54. Elizabeth Dole, interview with Nichola Gutgold, April 8, 1998.

55. Kerry Tymchuk, 1996 Convention speech, e-mail to Nichola Gutgold, November 11, 2000.

56. Elizabeth Dole, interview with Nichola Gutgold, April 8, 1998.

CHAPTER 2

1. "Elizabeth Dole for President" (campaign brochure, Exploratory Committee, Arlington, VA).

2. Carolyn Mulford, *Elizabeth Dole, Public Servant* (Hillside, N.J.: Enslow Publishers, 1992), 49.

3. Ibid., 48.

4. Ibid., 50.

5. Ibid., 51.

6. Ibid., 53.

7. Robert Dole, Elizabeth Dole, Richard Norton Smith, and Kerry Tymchuk, *Unlimited Partners, Our American Story* (New York: Simon and Schuster, 1996), 141; hereafter, Dole et al.

8. Mulford, *Elizabeth Dole, Public Servant*, 56.

9. Ibid., 56.

10. Dole et al., *Unlimited Partners, Our American Story*, 156.

11. Mulford, *Elizabeth Dole, Public Servant*, 59.

12. The FTC was made up of five commissioners, and no one party could have more than three members. Elizabeth Dole was a registered Independent at the time, but consumer groups felt that she had worked under a Republican president, so she was sympathetic to that line of thinking. It took her several weeks to convince consumer advocate leaders to support her and the Senate Commerce Committee to accept the presidential appointment. See Mulford, *Elizabeth Dole, Public Servant*, 59–60; Dole et al., *Unlimited Partners, Our American Story*, 146–47.

13. Mulford, *Elizabeth Dole, Public Servant*, 59–60.

14. Dole et al., *Unlimited Partners, Our American Story*, 153.

15. Ibid., 156.

16. Mulford, *Elizabeth Dole, Public Servant*, 80.

17. Dole et al., *Unlimited Partners, Our American Story*, 199.

18. Mulford, *Elizabeth Dole, Public Servant*, 82.

19. Dole et al., *Unlimited Partners, Our American Story*, 202.

20. Ibid., 222.

21. Ibid.

22. Maureen Dowd, "A Woman's Touch for the Cabinet," *Time*, January 17, 1983.

23. Dole et al., *Unlimited Partners, Our American Story*, 223.

24. Mulford, *Elizabeth Dole, Public Servant*, 85.

25. Dole et al., *Unlimited Partners, Our American Story*, 226–27.

26. Ibid., 226.

27. Ibid., 223.

28. Ibid., 224.

29. Mulford, *Elizabeth Dole, Public Servant*, 89.

30. Dole et al., *Unlimited Partners, Our American Story*, 224–25.

31. Mulford, *Elizabeth Dole, Public Servant*, 61.

32. Dole et al., *Unlimited Partners, Our American Story*, 226.

33. Steve Olson, with Dean R. Gerstein, *Alcohol in America: Taking Action to Prevent Abuse* (Washington, D.C.: National Academy Press, 1985), iii–iv.

34. Robert D. Hershey, Jr., "A Political and Bureaucratic Force," *New York Times*, August 22, 1983, B8.

35. Dole et al., *Unlimited Partners, Our American Story*, 228.

36. "Dole Defends Tough Airline Fines for Safety Violations," *Associated Press*, May 13, 1986.

37. "Dole Remaining Neutral in Battle for Air Route," *United Press International*, January 31, 1987.

38. Dole et al., *Unlimited Partners, Our American Story*, 227.

39. *MacNeil/Lehrer News Hour*, Transcript # 2548, July 3, 1985.

40. Frank T. Csongos, "Washington News," *United Press International*, November 21, 1985.

41. Dole et al., *Unlimited Partners, Our American Story*, 227.

42. Ibid., 229.

43. Mulford, *Elizabeth Dole, Public Servant*, 99.

44. Elizabeth Dole, speech at the Department of Transportation Awards Ceremony, September 16, 1987.

45. Mulford, *Elizabeth Dole, Public Servant*, 106.

46. Dole et al., *Unlimited Partners, Our American Story*, 272–73.

47. Mulford, *Elizabeth Dole, Public Servant*, 108.

48. *Hearing Before the Committee on Labor and Human Resources United States Senate* (Washington, D.C.: U.S. Government Printing Office, January 19, 1989), 35.

49. Elizabeth Dole, "Everybody Counts," Fourth Annual State of the Workforce Address, October 24, 1990.

50. Dole et al., *Unlimited Partners, Our American Story*, 274.

51. Mulford, *Elizabeth Dole, Public Servant*, 116.

52. Dole et al., *Unlimited Partners, Our American Story*, 274.

53. Richard Kozar, *Elizabeth Dole* (Philadelphia: Chelsea House Publishers, 2000), 74–75.

54. Dole et al., *Unlimited Partners, Our American Story*, 274–75.

55. Ibid., 275.

56. Mulford, *Elizabeth Dole, Public Servant*, 118.

57. Ibid., 78.

58. Dole et al., *Unlimited Partners, Our American Story*, 283.

59. Kozar, *Elizabeth Dole*, 77.

60. Mulford, *Elizabeth Dole, Public Servant*, 112.

61. Michael Verespej, "'Rip Van Osha' No Longer Sleeping," *Industry Week*, June 5, 1989, 74.

62. Wayne E. Veneman, "Labor Secretary Dole Announces Record Fine for Mine Disaster," *U.S. Newswire*, July 5, 1989.

63. Mulford, *Elizabeth Dole, Public Servant*, 110.

64. Harris Collingwood, "Uncle Sam Wades into the Mining Strike," *Business Week*, October 30, 1989, 46.

65. William Lowther, "A Bitter Deadlock," *Maclean's*, November 20, 1989, 72.

66. "Dole Intervenes in Pittston Dispute," *Coal Age*, December 1989, 14.

67. "Pittston Coal Strike Over," *Mining Journal*, January 5, 1990, 1.

68. "Pittston, UMWA Reach Settlement in Strike Negotiations, *Coal Age*, January 1990, 13.

69. Mulford, *Elizabeth Dole, Public Servant*, 111.

70. Kirk Victor, "Liddy Dole: Off the Sidelines for Good," *National Journal* 22 (1990): 3, 136.

71. Dole et al., *Unlimited Partners, Our American Story*, 275.

72. Mulford, *Elizabeth Dole, Public Servant*, 115.

73. Dole et al., *Unlimited Partners, Our American Story*, 276.

74. Peter Kilborn, "Labor Wants to Take on Job Bias in the Executive Suite," *New York Times*, July 30, 1990, A1.

75. Bob Dole continued to work on the "glass ceiling" after Elizabeth stepped down as head of DOL. He introduced the Glass Ceiling Act of 1991 into Congress, which set up a twenty-one-member commission charged with finding ways to end discrimination against women and minorities for top management positions. This act was part of a larger initiative, the Women's Equal Opportunity Act of 1991, which dealt with other issues, such as sexual harassment; see Cindy Skrycki and Frank Swoboda, "Breaking the Corporate Glass Ceiling," *Washington Post*, January 14, 1991, A9.

76. Dole et al., *Unlimited Partners, Our American Story*, 276.

77. Mulford, *Elizabeth Dole, Public Servant*, 119.

78. Johanna Schneider, "Dole Unveils Wide-Reaching Initiative to Support Women in the Skilled Trades," *U.S. Newswire*, November 23, 1990.

79. Mulford, *Elizabeth Dole, Public Servant*, 112.

80. Dole et al., *Unlimited Partners, Our American Story*, 280.

81. Mulford, *Elizabeth Dole, Public Servant*, 126.

82. Sam Walker, "Elizabeth Dole: Smashing the Glass Ceiling," *Christian Science Monitor*, August 17, 1993, 14.

83. Kozar, *Elizabeth Dole*, 80.

84. John S. Glaser, *The United Way Scandal: An Insider's Account of What Went Wrong and Why* (New York: John Wiley & Sons, 1994).

85. Paul Leavitt, "Nationline," *USA Today*, February 5, 1991, 6A.

86. Chuck Conconi, "Occasional," *Washington Post*, February 5, 1991, C3.

87. Melissa Haussman, "Can a Woman Be Elected President? Strategic Con-

siderations under Reformed Nominating and Financing Rules," *White House Studies*, Summer 2001, 1–15; http://www.findarticles.com, accessed February 25, 2004.

88. Dole et al., *Unlimited Partners, Our American Story*, 310–11.

89. "Question: Are You Concerned about the Safety of the Nation's Blood Supply?" *USA Today*, November 19, 1991, A12.

90. Kozar, *Elizabeth Dole*, 82–84.

91. Dole et al., *Unlimited Partners, Our American Story*, 290.

92. Ibid., 291.

93. Carlos Byars, "Red Cross Feels Pressure to Show Results," *Houston Chronicle*, October 10, 1997, A40.

94. Dole et al., *Unlimited Partners, Our American Story*, 311.

95. Kozar, *Elizabeth Dole*, 82–84.

96. Richard Stewart, "Teens Crossing State Line to Drink," *Houston Chronicle*, June 5, 1994, 1.

97. Frank Greve, "Hirings May Mean Elizabeth Dole Will Seek Presidency," *Houston Chronicle*, March 24, 1997, A10.

98. Frank Greve, "Elizabeth Dole Back at the Red Cross Where All Things Aren't Rosy," *Houston Chronicle*, March 9, 1997, 17.

99. "Mrs. Dole's Donations," *Washington Post*, May 8, 1996, A17.

100. Greve, "Elizabeth Dole Back at the Red Cross," March 9, 1997, 17.

101. Ibid.

CHAPTER 3

1. Elizabeth Dole, speech at National Prayer Breakfast, February 5, 1987.

2. Laurie Goodstein, "White House Seekers Wearing Faith on Sleeve and Stump," *New York Times*, August 31, 1999, A1.

3. Robert Dole, Elizabeth Dole, Richard Norton Smith, and Kerry Tymchuk, *Unlimited Partners, Our American Story* (New York: Simon and Schuster, 1996), 47; hereafter, Dole et al.

4. Elizabeth Dole, speech, *Charlotte Observer*, June 16, 1986.

5. Elizabeth Dole, "A Tradition of Trust," speech, February 4, 1991.

6. Elizabeth Dole, speech at *Redbook*/Mothers Against Drunk Driving event, May 9, 1997.

7. Dole et al., *Unlimited Partners, Our American Story*, 49.

8. Richard Kozar, *Elizabeth Dole* (Philadelphia: Chelsea House Publishers, 2000), 20.

9. Dole et al., *Unlimited Partners, Our American Story*, 78.

10. Ibid., 93.

11. Carolyn Mulford, *Elizabeth Dole, Public Servant* (Hillside, N.J.: Enslow Publishers, 1992), 79.

12. Ibid., 83; Dole et al., *Unlimited Partners, Our American Story*, 214.

13. Dole et al., *Unlimited Partners, Our American Story*, 215.

14. Ibid., 215.

15. Sylvia Brooks, "Elizabeth Dole Says Gospel Had Daily Role," *Columbus Dispatch*, September 26, 1997, B1.

16. Elizabeth Dole, "A Tradition of Trust," speech, January 4, 1999.

17. Helen Thorpe, "Liddy in Waiting," *George*, August 1999, 110.

18. Linda Hobgood, "For Such a Time as This," paper presented at National Communication Association Annual Conference, Miami, FL, November 2003.

19. Thorpe, "Liddy in Waiting," 110.

20. Dole et al., *Unlimited Partners, Our American Story*, 197.

21. Linda Hobgood, interview with Kerry Tymchuk, July 14, 2003.

22. Elizabeth Dole, speech at University of Virginia commencement, May 17, 1987.

23. Elizabeth Dole, speech at Department of Transportation Awards Ceremony, September 16, 1987.

24. Elizabeth Dole, speech at Duke University commencement, May 14, 2000.

25. Elizabeth Dole, "An America We Can Be," speech, April 7, 1998.

26. Elizabeth Dole, speech at Albion College commencement, May 4, 1991.

27. Elizabeth Dole, speech at the 1996 Republican National Convention, August 14, 1996.

28. Howard Fineman and Matthew Cooper, "Back in the Amen Corner," *Newsweek*, March 22, 1999, 33.

29. Dole et al., *Unlimited Partners, Our American Story*, 41–43.

30. Mulford, *Elizabeth Dole, Public Servant*, 88–89.

31. Ibid., 96.

32. Elizabeth Dole, speech at *Redbook*/Mothers Against Drunk Driving event, May 9, 1997.

33. Dole et al., *Unlimited Partners, Our American Story*, 274.

34. Mulford, *Elizabeth Dole, Public Servant*, 112.

35. Dole et al., *Unlimited Partners, Our American Story*, 279.

36. Elizabeth Dole, toasts for Presidential Mission to Poland, November 28–December 2, 1990.

37. Mulford, *Elizabeth Dole, Public Servant*, 113.

38. Ibid.

39. Terri J. Wallo, *Compass Readings* (Beaverton, OR: Skies American Publishing Co., 1991), 30.

40. Dole et al., *Unlimited Partners, Our American Story*, 290.

41. Ibid., 312.

42. Ibid., 316.

43. Ibid., 307.

44. *ABC News*, April 29, 1992.

45. Dole et al., *Unlimited Partners, Our American Story*, 15.

CHAPTER 4

1. Elizabeth Dole, speech to the 300 Group, London, November 15, 1989.

2. Elizabeth Dole, Economic Summit Speech for Women, May 20, 1997.

3. Cheryl Lavin, "Mrs. Dole Is No Stranger to Power; On Surface, Softer than Mrs. Clinton, but Just as Driven," *Chicago Tribune*, March 24, 1996, 1C.

4. Karlyn Kohrs Campbell, "The Discursive Performance of Femininity: Hating Hillary," *Rhetoric and Public Affairs* 5, no. 1: 1–19.

5. Matt Andrews, "Elizabeth Dole for President? Is She a Liberal Feminist in Disguise?" *Midwest Today*, Spring 1999, http://www.midtod.com/elizabethdole.phtml, accessed March 3, 2002.

6. Helen Thorpe, "Liddy in Waiting," *George*, August 1999, 110.

7. Tabitha Soren, "Elizabeth Dole's Newest Job: Wife," *USA Today*, August 4, 1996, 6.

8. Carolyn Mulford, *Elizabeth Dole, Public Servant* (Hillside, N.J.: Enslow Publishers, 1992), 77.

9. Ibid., 34.

10. Ibid., 30.

11. Ibid., 29.

12. Robert Dole, Elizabeth Dole, Richard Norton Smith, and Kerry Tymchuk, *Unlimited Partners, Our American Story* (New York: Simon and Schuster, 1996), 54; hereafter, Dole et al.

13. Ibid., 80.

14. Mulford, *Elizabeth Dole, Public Servant*, 41.

15. Elizabeth Dole, speech, *Charlotte Observer*, June 16, 1986.

16. Mulford, *Elizabeth Dole, Public Servant*, 11.

17. Ibid., 43.

18. Ibid., 44.

19. Rob Christensen, "Elizabeth Dole Series: A North Carolina Belle Blazes D.C. Trail; Part 1," *News and Observer* (Raleigh), October 13, 2002.

20. Ibid.

21. Mulford, *Elizabeth Dole, Public Servant*, 47.

22. Dole et al., *Unlimited Partners, Our American Story*, 90.

23. Thorpe, "Liddy in Waiting," 114.

24. Mulford, *Elizabeth Dole, Public Servant*, 64–65.

25. Ibid., 59.

26. August 13, 1996.

27. Mulford, *Elizabeth Dole, Public Servant*, 65.

28. Elizabeth Dole, speech at the Women's Bureau 70th Anniversary/Eve Awards Banquet, October 23, 1990.

29. Dole et al., *Unlimited Partners, Our American Story*, 139.

30. Cary O'Dell, *Women Pioneers in Television* (Jefferson, N.C.: McFarland, 1996), 119–34.

31. Dole et al., *Unlimited Partners, Our American Story*, 140.

32. Mulford, *Elizabeth Dole, Public Servant*, 54.

33. Dole et al., *Unlimited Partners, Our American Story*, 141.

34. Ibid., 141–42.

35. Mulford, *Elizabeth Dole, Public Servant*, 56.

36. Ibid., 56.

37. Ibid., 75.

38. Ibid., 62.

39. Dole et al., *Unlimited Partners, Our American Story*, 152.

40. Elizabeth Dole, interview with Nichola Gutgold and Molly Meijer Wertheimer, July 8, 2003.

41. Matt Andrews, "Elizabeth Dole for President?"

42. Dole et al., *Unlimited Partners, Our American Story*, 152.

43. Ibid., 213.

44. Ibid.

45. Mulford, *Elizabeth Dole, Public Servant*, 80.

46. Elizabeth Dole, speech at the Women's Bureau 70th Anniversary/Eve Awards Banquet, October 23, 1990.

47. Sara Fritz, "The President Tackles His 'Gender Gap,'" *U.S. News & World Report*, November 8, 1982, 52.

48. Mulford, *Elizabeth Dole, Public Servant*, 81. See, for example, Eric Gelman, "Elizabeth Dole, White House Shut Out," *U.S. News & World Report*, May 17, 1982, 27; Sara Fritz, "The President Tackles His 'Gender Gap.'"

49. Her nomination followed a study conducted by the White House that found women's support of Reagan to be about 15 percentage points less than the support he received from men; see, for example, Robert A. Kittle and Patricia A. Avery, "Behind Reagan's Trouble with Women Voters," *U.S. News & World Report*, May 31, 1982, 51.

50. "'Madame Secretary' Takes Charge," *U.S. News & World Report*, January 17, 1983, 14.

51. Dole et al., *Unlimited Partners, Our American Story*, 230.

52. Mulford, *Elizabeth Dole, Public Servant*, 90.

53. Ibid., 90–91.

54. Dole et al., *Unlimited Partners, Our American Story*, 230–31.

55. "Excepts from Bush's News Conference with Elizabeth Dole," *New York Times*, December 25, 1988, 22.

56. Elizabeth Duncan Koontz was also from Salisbury, North Carolina. Appointed to head the Women's Bureau by Richard Nixon in 1969, her primary area of interest was breaking the cycle of poverty by education and skills training for women. See Martin Weil, "Elizabeth Koontz, Former Head of Women's Bureau, Dies," *Washington Post*, January 7, 1989, 36.

57. Elizabeth Dole, speech at the Women's Bureau 70th Anniversary/Eve Awards Banquet, October 23, 1990.

58. Mulford, *Elizabeth Dole, Public Servant*, 118.

59. Carol Hymowitz and Timothy Schellhardt, "The Glass Ceiling," *Wall Street Journal*, March 27, 1986, 1.

60. Elizabeth Dole, speech at the Women's Bureau 70th Anniversary/Eve Awards Banquet, October 23, 1990.

61. Ibid.

62. Ibid.

63. Julia Lawlor, "PepsiCo, Sterling in 'Glass Ceiling' Probe," *USA Today*, October 25, 1990, 1B.

64. Mulford, *Elizabeth Dole, Public Servant*, 118.

65. Dole et al., *Unlimited Partners, Our American Story*, 276.

66. Elizabeth Dole, speech to the 300 Group, London, November 15, 1989.

67. Elizabeth Dole, speech at the Women's Bureau 70th Anniversary/Eve Awards Banquet, October 23, 1990.

68. Ibid.

69. Mulford, *Elizabeth Dole, Public Servant*, 75–76.

70. Elizabeth Dole, speech at the Women's Bureau 70th Anniversary/Eve Awards Banquet, October 23, 1990.

71. Johanna Schneider, "Dole Unveils Wide-Reaching Initiative to Support Women in the Skilled Trades," *U.S. Newswire*, November 23, 1990.

72. Mulford, *Elizabeth Dole, Public Servant*, 110.

73. Ibid.

74. Ibid., 119.

75. For a brief history of the waves of U.S. feminism, see: "Living the Legacy: The Women's Rights Movement, 1848–1998." The National Women's History Project, http://www.legacy98.org/move-hist.html, accessed February 3, 2004.

76. Dole et al., *Unlimited Partners, Our American Story*, 145.

77. Mulford, *Elizabeth Dole, Public Servant*, 75.

78. Elizabeth Dole, speech, *Charlotte Observer*, June 16, 1986.

79. Dole et al., *Unlimited Partners, Our American Story*, 145.

80. Ibid., 146.

81. Ibid., 145.

82. Ibid., 146.

83. Maureen Dowd, "A Women's Touch for the Cabinet: With Her at Transportation, the Dole's Are Moving Along," *Time*, January 17, 1983, 11.

84. Sarah Booth Conroy, "The Secretaries' Pool of Wisdom," *Washington Post*, April 22, 1983, D1.

85. Elizabeth Dole, speech at Duke University commencement, May 14, 2000.

86. Elizabeth Dole, speech at the Women's Bureau 70th Anniversary/Eve Awards Banquet, October 23, 1990.

87. Elizabeth Dole, speech at the Economic Summit for Women, May 20, 1997.

88. Executive Women in Government was formed in 1974 by a group whose members were concerned about the small percentage of women in leadership positions in the federal government. At that time, there were fewer than one hundred women in senior positions. According to their Web site, objectives of the group include "advocating the advancement of women in the social, economic, and political structures of our society and advancing women in senior leadership positions." http://www.execwomeningov.org/about_ewg/history.html, accessed July 26, 2003.

89. Elizabeth Dole, interview with Nichola Gutgold and Molly Meijer Wertheimer, July 8, 2003.

90. This heading was suggested to us by Simona Bettineschi, a sophomore student at the Pennsylvania State University, Hazleton Campus; unpublished research paper: "Is She or Isn't She: Elizabeth Dole and the Many Faces of Feminism," April 2, 2003.

91. Elizabeth Dole, interview with Nichola Gutgold and Molly Meijer Wertheimer, July 8, 2003

92. Bob Dole, interview with Nichola Gutgold and Molly Meijer Wertheimer, December 17, 2001.

93. Elizabeth Dole, speech at the Economic Summit for Women, May 20, 1997.

94. Sam Walker, "Smashing the Glass Ceiling," *Christian Science Monitor*, August 17, 1993, 14.

95. Victor Volland, "Dole Extols Virtues of Women in Speech Here: Qualities of Compassion, Tolerance, Would Be Ideal for a President, She Says," *St. Louis Post Dispatch*, November 12, 1997, C2.

96. "Racing to Support Elizabeth Dole," *Buffalo News*, January 22, 1998, 2D.

97. Cultural feminism is a view that celebrates women's special qualities, sometimes suggesting that these traits are "better" than men's qualities; see, for example, Wendy Kolmar and Frances Bartkowski, *Feminist Theory: A Reader* (Mountain View, Calif.: Mayfield Publishing, 2000). The liberal feminist approach focuses on achieving equality between men and women in the United States by removing the legal constraints that impede women's access to rights and opportunities; see, for example, Susan Gluck Mezey, *In Pursuit of Equality: Women, Public Policy, and the Federal Courts* (New York: St. Martin's Press, 1992), 2.

98. Mulford, *Elizabeth Dole, Public Servant*, 71.

99. Richard Kozar, *Elizabeth Dole* (Philadelphia: Chelsea House, 2000) 55–56.

100. Ibid., 35.

101. Ibid., 58–59.

102. Ibid., 56.

103. Laura Parker, "Transportation Secretary on the Road," *Washington Post*, September 5, 1987, A1.

104. Ibid.

105. Ibid.

106. Mulford, *Elizabeth Dole, Public Servant*, 103.

107. Bernard Weinraub, "Mrs. Dole Weighs Resigning to Join Husband's Campaign," *New York Times*, September 13, 1987, 1.

108. Ellen Goodman, "Mrs. Dole's Early Take Off," *Washington Post*, September 19, 1987, A23.

109. Stephen C. Fehr, "Elizabeth Dole's Style Winning Over Many Voters," *Kansas City Times*, October 14, 1987, B6.

110. Kozar, *Elizabeth Dole*, 71–72.

111. Fehr, "Elizabeth Dole's Style."

112. Ann Grimes, *Running Mates: The Making of a First Lady* (New York: William Morrow, 1990), 73–74.

113. Fehr, "Elizabeth Dole's Style."

114. Ibid.

115. Mulford, *Elizabeth Dole, Public Servant*, 124.

116. Kozar, *Elizabeth Dole*, 84.

117. Ibid., 85, 88–89.

118. Dole et al., *Unlimited Partners, Our American Story*, 197–98.

119. Kozar, *Elizabeth Dole*, 58.

120. Mulford, *Elizabeth Dole, Public Servant*, 1978.

121. David Lauter, "Labor Post to Go to Elizabeth Dole," *Los Angeles Times*, December 25, 1988, 1.

122. Richard Stengel, "Liddy Makes Perfect," *Time*, July 1, 1996, 30.

123. John Carlin, "She Acts Just Like a Lady, Like a Little Lady, the Little Lady: Elizabeth Dole; Bob Dole's Greatest Asset Could Have Been His Strongest Rival," *The Independent* (London), August 18, 1996, 17.

124. Mulford, *Elizabeth Dole, Public Servant*, 120.

125. Suzanne Haik Terrell, "Dole as a Role Model," *Times Picayune* (New Orleans), July 18, 1996, B6.

126. Kozar, *Elizabeth Dole*, 13.

CHAPTER 5

1. Elizabeth Dole, speech at the Republican National Convention, August 1, 2000.

2. Carolyn Barta, "Elizabeth Dole Adopts New Roles in Promoting Campaign GOP," *Dallas Morning News*, August 15, 1996, 23A.

3. Robert Dole, Elizabeth Dole, Richard Norton Smith, and Kerry Tymchuk, *Unlimited Partners, Our American Story* (New York: Simon and Schuster, 1996), 78; hereafter, Dole et al.

4. Ibid., 81.

5. Elizabeth Dole, interview with Nichola Gutgold, April 7, 1998.

6. Carolyn Mulford, *Elizabeth Dole, Public Servant* (Hillside, N.J.: Enslow Publishers, 1992), 77.

7. "Young Pro," *Newsweek*, August 30, 1976, 39.

8. Dole et al., *Unlimited Partners, Our American Story*, 171.

9. Mulford, *Elizabeth Dole, Public Servant*, 72.

10. Richard Kozar, *Elizabeth Dole* (Philadelphia: Chelsea House, 2000) 57.

11. Dole et al., *Unlimited Partners, Our American Story*, 172.

12. Mulford, *Elizabeth Dole, Public Servant*, 77.

13. Douglas E. Kneeland, "Mrs. Dole Honored," *New York Times*, September 3, 1976, 1.1.

14. Dole et al., *Unlimited Partners, Our American Story*, 172.

15. Mulford, *Elizabeth Dole, Public Servant*, 76.

16. Dole et al., *Unlimited Partners, Our American Story*, 185.

17. Kozar, *Elizabeth Dole*, 61.

18. Mulford, *Elizabeth Dole, Public Servant*, 76.

19. Ibid., 78.

20. Robert D. Hershey Jr., "A Political and Bureaucratic Force," *New York Times*, August 22, 1983, B8.

21. Phil McCombs, "Roasted! The Gridiron's Raucous Ribbing of One & All," *Washington Post*, March 26, 1984, C1.

22. Donnie Radcliffe, "Style; Washington Ways," *Washington Post*, March 27, 1984, E1.

23. Mulford, *Elizabeth Dole, Public Servant*, 94.

24. Ibid., 93.

25. Ibid.

26. Elizabeth Kastor, "The Dance of the Doles; Partners in Politics, Trying Out Steps for 1988," *Washington Post*, August 25, 1984, G1; "Bob and Elizabeth Dole," *U.S. News & World Report*, April 9, 1984, 16.

27. Julia Reed, "Running against Hurricane 'W,'" *Newsweek*, July 12, 1999, 28–29.

28. Bernard Weinraub, "Dole and Her Husband Gain Favor in Alabama," *New York Times*, July 20, 1987, A12.

29. Stephen C. Fehr, "Elizabeth Dole's Style Winning Over Many Voters," *Missouri Times* (Kansas City), October 14, 1987, B6.

30. Ibid.

31. David Johnson, "Dole Reported to Be Quitting to Aid Husband's Campaign," *New York Times*, September 14, 1987, 14.

32. Aaron Zitner, "On the Campaign Trail, Two Doles Are Better than One," *Monitor* (Concord, N.H.), October 3, 1987.

33. Anonymous, "Esquire's Woman of the Year 1988; Elizabeth Hanford Dole," *Esquire*, August, 1988, 106–7.

34. *McCall*, April 1988.

35. Zitner, "On the Campaign Trail."

36. Ellen Goodman, "A Dole on the National Ticket?" *Minneapolis Star Tribune*, April 5, 1988, 10A.

37. Marjorie Williams, "Bob and Liddy Dole, Doing the Town," *Washington Post*, 16 August 16, 1988, E1; Lawrence L. Knutson, "Dole and Dole: If Bush Calls, Who Will Answer?" *Associated Press*, August 16, 1988.

38. Eileen Putnam, "Mrs. Dole Acknowledges Gender Gap, Asks Women to Have an Open Mind," *Associated Press*, August 16, 1988.

39. Elizabeth Dole, speech at the Republican National Convention, August 15, 1988.

40. Ibid.

41. Elizabeth Dole, interview with Nichola Gutgold, April 7, 1998.

42. David Behrens, "Good Night, Liddy; Elizabeth Dole Takes Her Leave from the Corridors of Public Power," *Newsday*, November 26, 1990, 52.

43. Michelle Caruso, "Elizabeth's One Tough Missus," *Daily News*, August 14, 1996, 25.

44. Cheryl Lavin, "Mrs. Dole No Stranger to Power; On Surface Softer than Mrs. Clinton, but Just as Driven," *Chicago Tribune*, March 24, 1996, 1.

45. Elizabeth Bumiller, "Running against Hillary," *New York Times Magazine*, October 13, 1996, 37.

46. Ibid., 38.

47. Ibid., 40–41.

48. Kozar, *Elizabeth Dole*, 49.

49. Charles V. Zehren, "Convention 96/More than Supportive Spouse," *Newsday*, August 15, 1996, A6.

50. Henry Louis Gates Jr., "The Next President: Dole 2000: The GOP's Best

Hope for the White House Is an Un-Republican Named Elizabeth Dole," *New Yorker*, October 20–27, 1997, 228.

51. R. A. Dyer, "Republican National Convention; Now, the Rub Is to Sell Dole on 'Warm Fuzzies,'" *Houston Chronicle,* August 16, 1996, 18.

52. Joe Frolick, "Elizabeth Dole: 'Iron Fist in a Velvet Glove,'" *Plain-Dealer* (Cleveland, Ohio), August 16, 1996, 16A.

53. Dyer, "Republican National Convention," 18.

54. Howard Fineman, "Bring on the Baby Boomers," *Newsweek*, August 26, 1996, 18.

55. Kathleen Hall Jamieson, personal correspondence with Nichola Gutgold, May 21, 1997.

56. Dyer, "Republican National Convention," 18.

57. Ibid.

58. "Liddy's Walk: A Galvanizing Moment for TV-Conventions Debate," *Houston Chronicle*, August 16, 1996, 44.

59. Martha Brandt, "Cashing in on Letting Hillary Be Hillary," *Newsweek*, September 2, 1996, 24.

60. Robert Dvorchak, Dennis B. Roddy, James O'Toole, and John Nichols, "A Starring Role for Elizabeth Dole," *Pittsburgh Post-Gazette*, August 18, 1996, A19.

61. Cheryl Lavin, "Mrs. Dole No Stranger to Power; On Surface Softer than Mrs. Clinton, but Just as Driven," *Chicago Tribune*, March 24, 1996, 1.

62. Steve Goldstein, "Mrs. Dole a Double-Edged Asset: Convention Role Debated by the GOP," *Times Picayune*, July 23, 1996, A3.

63. John Carlin, "She Acts Like a Lady, Like a Little Lady, Like the Little Lady; Bob Dole's Greatest Asset Could Have Been His Strongest Rival," *Independent* (London), August 18, 1996, 17.

64. Gates, Jr., "The Next President: Dole 2000," 228.

65. Martin Fletcher, "Sister Frigidaire v Steel Magnolia," *The Times*, April 11, 1996.

66. Julia Malone, "First Lady Facing Tough Task at Convention," *Rocky Mountains News*, August 25, 1996, 2A.

67. Carlin, "She Acts Like a Lady," 17.

68. Victoria Pope, "An Iron Fist in a Velvet Glove," *U.S. News & World Report*, August 19, 1996, 26–27.

69. Howard Fineman, "Bring on the Baby Boomers," *Newsweek*, August 26, 1996, 18.

70. Frolick, "Elizabeth Dole: 'Iron Fist in a Velvet Glove,'" 16A.

71. Kozar, *Elizabeth Dole*, 93–95.

72. Lisa Anderson, "A Blend of Sugar and Steel: Elizabeth Dole Always the Best Running Mate," *Chicago Tribune*, August 14, 1996, A17.

73. Rose Post, *Salisbury Post*, http://www.salisburypost.com/liddy/liddydole122898.html, accessed February 2, 2004.

74. Gary Mays, "Thompson Promotes Dole for President, the Visiting Elizabeth Dole, That Is," *Wisconsin State Journal*, January 29, 1997, C1.

75. Edwin Chen, "Bob Dole a Year Later," *Newsday*, September 30, 1997, B6.

76. Thomas Galvin, "A Dole Could Still Fill a White House Role," *Daily News* (New York), November 3, 1997, 10.

77. "Elizabeth Dole Has No Plans to Run for President," *Baltimore Sun*, December 22, 1997, 2A.

78. "Never Too Soon to Start," *Newsweek*, March 9, 1998, 4.

79. "That's Madam Vice President," *The Morning Call*, November 1, 1998, B1.

80. Thomas J. Neff and James M. Citrin, *Lessons from the Top* (New York: Currency/Doubleday, 2001), 91.

81. "Periscope: The 2000 Campaign," *Newsweek*, January 18, 1999, 4.

82. Susan J. Carroll, Caroline Heldman, and Stephanie Olson, "'She Brought Only a Skirt': Gender Bias in Newspaper Coverage of Elizabeth Dole's Campaign for the Republican Nomination," unpublished paper, White House Project Conference, Washington, D.C., February 20, 2000.

83. Janine Yaglielski and Kathleen Hayden, "Bush Wins Iowa GOP Straw Poll," http://www.allpolitics.com, August 15, 1999, accessed February 22, 2004.

84. "Elizabeth Dole for President," campaign letter, September 23, 1999.

85. Alison Mitchell, "Elizabeth Dole Questions Clinton's Policies on Iraq and Serbia," *New York Times*, April 15, 1999, A26.

86. Elizabeth Dole, "Measuring Up: Restoring the Greatness of American Schools," speech, September 22, 1999.

87. Jill Zuckman, "Dole Outlines Get-Tough Approach to Improve Schools, Merit Pay for Teachers, Drug Testing for Students Urged," *Boston Globe*, September 23, 1999, A8.

88. Dan Balz, "Hoping to Be 'Part of History,'" *Washington Post*, July 15, 1999, A3.

89. Howard Fineman, "Will a Woman Ever Become President?" *Newsweek*, June 26, 2000, 20–22.

90. Mary Matalin, "Elizabeth Dole's Inability to Represent the Feminist Movement as a Presidential Candidate Because of Her Pro-Life Stance," *Hardball with Chris Matthews*, March 23, 1999.

91. Elizabeth Dole, withdrawal announcement speech, October 20, 1999.

92. "Campaign Briefing," *New York Times*, March 22, 2000, A24.

93. Elizabeth Dole, speech at the Republican National Convention, August 1, 2000.

94. Ibid.

95. David S. Broder, "N.C. Candidates Forced into a Holding Pattern," *Washington Post*, April 28, 2002, A4.

96. "Dole Plan," campaign brochure.

97. Amy Frazier, "Dole Welcomed with Down-Home Dinner," http://www.elizabethdole.org, accessed April 3, 2002.

98. Mary Brewer Brown, interview by Nichola Gutgold and Molly Meijer Wertheimer, July 8, 2003.

99. Elizabeth Dole, speech, U.S. Senate Candidacy Kickoff, February 23, 2002.

100. Dana Damico and David Rice, "Bowles, Dole Get Endorsements from Famous People as Race Draws to Close," http://www.journalnow.com, accessed February 21, 2004; see also, *Winston-Salem Journal*, November 2, 2002, 1.

101. Elizabeth Dole, acceptance speech to the U.S. Senate, November 7, 2002.

102. Dole et al., *Unlimited Partners, Our American Story*, 81.

CHAPTER 6

1. "A long way from the twilight" is a phrase Elizabeth Dole used when she withdrew from the presidential race on October 20, 1999. The full sentence is, "While I might not be a candidate for the presidency in 2000, I am a long way from the twilight."

2. Elizabeth Dole, speech at Duke University, May 14, 2000.

3. Michelle Caruso, "Elizabeth's One Tough Missus," *Daily News*, August 14, 1996, 25.

4. Lisa Anderson, "A Blend of Sugar and Steel: Elizabeth Dole Always the Best Running Mate," *Chicago Tribune*, August 14, 1996, 17.

5. Not since 1964, when Margaret Chase Smith announced her bid for the presidency, did a Republican woman attempt to win the presidency.

6. Elizabeth Bumiller, "Running against Hillary," *New York Times Magazine*, October 13, 1996, 37.

7. Eleanor Clift and Tom Brazaitis, *Madam President Breaking the Last Glass Ceiling* (New York: Scribner, 2000), 160.

8. Elizabeth Dole, presidential withdrawal speech, October 22, 1999.

9. Clift and Brazaitis, *Madam President*, 43.

10. Elizabeth Dole, speech at the Economic Summit for Women, May 20, 1997.

11. Dole has won many more awards than we have included.

12. In her "America We Can Be" speech, Elizabeth Dole spoke for a renewal of patriotic values. She presented this speech before the terrorist attacks of September 11, 2001.

13. Irwin Speizer, "Elizabeth Dole Series—Big Changes at the Red Cross," *News Observer* (Raleigh, N.C.), March 25, 2003, http://www.newsobserver.com/front/story/1815620p1815248c/html, accessed February 6, 2004.

14. Elizabeth Dole, "A Tradition of Trust," speech, February 4, 1991.

15. Elizabeth Dole, Prayer Breakfast speech, February 5, 1987.

16. From an article that appeared in the *Salisbury Post*, January 16, 2004, http://www.salisburypost.townnews.com/articles/2004/01/16/editorials/16-01edit_hanford.txt, accessed February 20, 2004.

17. Elizabeth Dole, Prayer Breakfast speech, February 5, 1987.

18. Elizabeth Dole, "A Tradition of Trust," speech, February 4, 1991.

19. Carolyn Mulford, *Elizabeth Dole, Public Servant* (Hillside, N.J.: Enslow Publishers, 1992), 59.

20. Bob Dole, interview with Nichola Gutgold and Molly Meijer Wertheimer, December 17, 2001.

21. Mark Lorando, "Keynotes," *Times-Picayune* (New Orleans), August 15, 1996, A4.

22. Henry Louis Gates Jr., "The Next President: Dole 2000: The GOP's Best Hope for the White House Is an Un-Republican Named Elizabeth Dole," *New Yorker*, October 20–27, 1997, 228.

23. Elizabeth Dole, speech, Senate Campaign Kickoff, February 23, 2002.

24. Elizabeth Dole, maiden Senate speech, June 5, 2003.

25. Elizabeth Dole, interview with Nichola Gutgold, April 7, 1998.

26. Lorando, "Keynotes," A4.

27. Bob Dole, interview with Nichola Gutgold and Molly Meijer Wertheimer, December 17, 2001.

28. Clift and Brazaitis, *Madam President,* 320.

29. Judi Hesson, "Elizabeth Dole Takes the Floor," *USA Today*, August 15, 1996, A5.

30. Katherine Q. Seelye, "On the Trail, Dole's Wife Seeks Votes of Women," *New York Times*, October 5, 1996, A10.

31. Elizabeth Dole, speech at Duke University, May 14, 2000.

Bibliography

PRIMARY SOURCES

Interviews

Brown Brewer, Mary. Interview with Nichola Gutgold and Molly Wertheimer, July 8, 2003, Washington, D.C.

Dole, Elizabeth Hanford. Interview with Nichola Gutgold, April 8, 1998, Hershey, Pa.

———. Interview with Nichola Gutgold and Molly Wertheimer, July 8, 2003, Washington, D.C.

Dole, Robert. Interview with Nichola Gutgold and Molly Wertheimer, December 17, 2001, Washington, D.C.

Ford, Betty. Phone Interview with Nichola Gutgold, September 16, 1998.

Tymchuk, Kerry. Interview with Nichola Gutgold, September 11, 2000, Beaverton, Ore.

Personal Correspondence

Jamieson, Kathleen Hall. Personal correspondence with Nichola Gutgold, May 21, 1997.

Tymchuk, Kerry. E-mail correspondence with Nichola Gutgold, November 11, 2000.

SECONDARY SOURCES

Articles

Alexander, Paul. "Vice Can Be Nice." *Mirabella*, September 2000, 66–69.

Anderson, Lisa. "A Blend of Sugar and Steel: Elizabeth Dole Always the Best Running Mate." *Chicago Tribune*, August 14, 1996, A17.

Babcock, Charles. "Elizabeth Dole's Fine Line between Charity, Politics; Red Cross, Presidential Camp Share Major Donors." *Washington Post,* May 2, 1996, A1.

Balz, Dan. "Hoping to Be 'Part of History.'" *Washington Post,* July 15, 1999, A3.

Barta, Carolyn. "Dole Adopts New Role in Promoting Campaign GOP." *Dallas Morning News,* August 15, 1996.

Behrens, David. "Good Night, Liddy; Elizabeth Dole Takes Her Leave from the Corridors of Public Power." *Newsday,* November 26, 1990, 52.

Bisbee, Dana. "Elizabeth Dole at Crossroads." *Boston Herald,* April 13, 1995, 29.

Blyth, Myrna. "One Smart Lady." *Ladies Home Journal,* August 1999, 44.

Bomann, Mieke H. "Newspaper Reporting on Women Candidates Differs from That of Men." *Times Union,* October 22, 2000, A5.

Brandt, Martha. "Cashing in on Letting Hillary Be Hillary." *Newsweek,* September 2, 1996, 24.

Broder, David S. "N.C. Candidates Forced into a Holding Pattern." *Washington Post,* April 28, A4.

Brooks, Jeanne F. "Elizabeth Dole Talk Blends Humor and Insights." *San Diego Union-Tribune,* September 26, 1997, B1.

Brooks, Sylvia. "Elizabeth Dole Says Gospel Had Daily Role." *Columbus Dispatch,* September 26, 1997, B1.

Bumiller, Elizabeth. "Running against Hillary." *New York Times Magazine,* October 13, 1996, 37–41.

Byars, Carlos. "Red Cross Feels Pressure to Show Result; Elizabeth Dole Talks from Club Here." *Houston Chronicle,* October 10, 1997, A40.

Carlin, John. "She Acts Just Like a Lady, Like a Little Lady, the Little Lady: Elizabeth Dole; Bob Dole's Greatest Asset Could Have Been His Strongest Rival." *Independent* (London), August 18, 1996, 17.

Caruso, Michelle. "Elizabeth's One Tough Missus." *New York Daily News,* August 14, 1996, 25.

Caruso, Michelle, and Jere Hester. "GOP Flipping Its Liddy after Talk." *New York Daily News,* August 16, 1996, 26.

Chen, Edwin. "Bob Dole a Year Later." *Newsday,* September 30, 1997, B6.

Christensen, Rob. "Elizabeth Dole Series: A North Carolina Belle Blazes DC Trail: Part 1." *News and Observer* (Raleigh, N.C.), October 13, 2002.

Ciabattari, Jane. "Five Who Could Be President." *Parade,* February 6, 1999, 6–7.

Cohen, Richard. "Elizabeth Dole, Wife: Her Smile Is Worth More than Her Service." *Bergen County Record* (Hackensack, N.J.), September 22, 1987, B1.

Collingwood, Harris. "Uncle Sam Wades into the Mining Strike." *Business Week,* October 30, 1989, 46.

Collins, Gail. "Taking the 'Help' Out of Helpmate." *New York Times,* May 18, 1999, A 22.

Conroy, Sarah Booth. "The Secretaries' Pool of Wisdom." *Washington Post,* April 22, 1983, D1.

Consoni, Chuck. "Occasional." *Washington Post,* February 5, 1991, C3.

Conway, Ann. "Dole Offers Words About Wisdom." *Los Angeles Times,* June 2, 1997, E1.

Csongos, Frank T. "Washington New." *United Press International,* November 21, 1985.

Cuniberti, Betty. "Dole's Decision on Why She's Quitting to Hit the Campaign Trail." *Los Angeles Times,* September 18, 1987, D10.

Damico, Dana, and David Rice. "Bowles, Dole Get Endorsements from Famous People as Race Draws to Close." *Winston-Salem Journal,* 2 November 2002. http://www.journalnow.com, accessed February 22, 2004.

Dickerson, John F., and Nancy Gibbs. "Elizabeth Unplugged." *Time,* May 10, 1999. http://www.time.com, accessed February 22, 2004.

Dobbin, Muriel. "Elizabeth Dole Under Scrutiny." *Sacramento Bee,* February 10, 1996, A 14.

"Dole Defends Tough Airline Fines for Safety Violations." *Associated Press,* May 13, 1986.

"Dole Drops Out; Her Poor Showing Wasn't Just a Money Problem." *Pittsburgh Post-Gazette,* October 22, 1999, A22.

"Dole Remains Neutral in Battle for Air Route." *United Press International,* January 31, 1987.

Dowd, Maureen. "A Women's Touch for the Cabinet: With Her at Transportation, the Doles Are Rolling Along." *New York Times,* January 17, 1983, 11.

Dubenport, Ellen. "Careful Packaging Is Turning Viewers Off: Her Words Soften Even TV Anchors." *St. Petersburg Times* (Fla.), August 15, 1996, 8A.

Dvorchak, Robert, Dennis B. Roddy, James O'Toole, and John Nichols. "A Starring Role for Elizabeth Dole." *Pittsburgh Post-Gazette,* August 18, 1996, A19.

Dyer, R.A. "Republican National Convention: Now, the Rub Is to Sell Dole on 'Warm Fuzzies.'" *Houston Chronicle,* August 16, 1996, 18.

"Elizabeth Dole Not Planning White House Bid." *Baltimore Sun,* December 22, 1997, 2A.

"Excerpts from Bush's News Conference with Elizabeth Dole." *New York Times,* December 25, 1988, 22.

Fehr, Stephen C. "Elizabeth Dole's Style Winning Over Many Voters." *Missouri Times* (Kansas City), October 14, 1987, B6.

Fields, Suzanne. "Is the Country Ready for a High Octane First Lady?" *Washington Times,* December 4, 1995, 40.

Fineman, Howard. "Bring on the Baby Boomers." *Newsweek,* August 26, 1996, 18.

———. "Will a Woman Ever Become President?" *Newsweek,* June 26, 2000, 20–22.

Fineman, Howard, and Matthew Cooper. "Back in the Amen Corner." *Newsweek,* March 22, 1999, 33.

Fletcher, Martin. "Sister Frigidaire vs. Steel Magnolia." *The Times* (London), April 11, 1996.

"Flight 847: Aviation Security; Flight 847: The Crew's Story; Political Fallout." *MacNeil/Lehrer News Hour,* Transcript #2548, July 3, 1985.

Fournier, Ron. "Dole Leaving Red Cross, Eyeing White House." *Morning Call* (Allentown, Pa.), January 5, 1999, A3.

Fritz, Sara. "The President Tackles His 'Gender Gap.'" *U.S. News & World Report,* November 8, 1982, 52.

Frolick, Joe. "Elizabeth Dole: 'Iron Fist in a Velvet Glove.'" *Plain-Dealer* (Cleveland, Ohio), August 16, 1996, 16A.

Galvin, Thomas. "A Dole Could Still Fill A White House Role." *New York Daily News,* November 3, 1997, 10.

Gates, Henry Louis, Jr. "The Next President: Dole 2000: The GOP's Best Hope for the White House Is an Un-Republican Named Elizabeth Dole." *New Yorker* 73, no. 32 (October 20–27, 1997): 228.

Gelman, Eric. "Elizabeth Dole, White House Shut Out." *U.S. News & World Report,* May 17, 1982, 27.

"Gender Isn't the Only Gap." *Newsweek,* May 17, 1999, 6.

Gibbs, Nancy. "What Dole Is Doing Wrong." *Time,* February 5, 1996, 22.

Goldstein, Steve. "Mrs. Dole a Double Edged Asset: Convention Role Debated by GOP." *Times-Picayune* (New Orleans), July 23, 1996, A3.

Goodman, Ellen. "Mrs. Dole's Early Take Off." *Washington Post,* September 19, 1987, A23.

———. "A Dole on the National Ticket?" *Minneapolis Star Tribune,* April 5, 1988, 10A.

———. "Gender-Neutral Dollar Eliminated Only Woman Running for President." *Morning Call* (Allentown, Pa.), October 26, 1999, A15.

Goodstein, Laurie. "White House Seekers Wear Faith on Sleeve and Stump." *New York Times,* August 31, 1999, A1.

"GOP Eyes the Other Dole." *Altoona Mirror* (Altoona, Pa.), May 10, 1998, B1.

Greenberg, Brigitte. "Dole Pushes Gun Control in Commencement Speech." *Standard Speaker* (Hazleton, Pa.), May 25, 1999, 2.

Greve, Frank. "Elizabeth Dole Back at the Red Cross Where All Things Aren't Rosy." *Houston Chronicle,* March 24, 1997, A10.

———. "Hirings May Mean Elizabeth Dole Will Seek Presidency." *Houston Chronicle,* March 24, 1997, A 10.

Haik, Terrell Susan. "Dole as a Role Model." *Times Picayune* (New Orleans), July 18, 1996, B6.

Hasson, Judi. "Elizabeth Dole Takes the Floor." *USA Today,* August 15, 1996, A5.

Haussman, Melissa. "Can a Woman Be Elected President? Strategic Considerations under Reformed Nominating and Financing Rules." *White House Studies,* Summer 2001, 1–15. http://www.findarticles.com, accessed February 25, 2004.

"Hearing Before the Committee on Labor and Human Resources: Elizabeth Hanford Dole of Kansas, to Be Secretary of Labor, U.S. Department of Labor." *U.S. Government Printing Office,* Washington D.C., January 1989.

Hershey, Robert D., Jr. "A Political and Bureaucratic Force." *New York Times,* August 22, 1983, B8.

Hymowitz, Carol, and Timothy Schellhardt. "The Glass Ceiling." *Wall Street Journal,* March 27, 1986, 1.

Johnson, David. "Dole Reported to Be Quitting to Aid Husband's Campaign." *New York Times,* September 14, 1987, 14.

Kelly, Margie. "When I'm 64." *Harvard Law Bulletin,* Summer 2003. http://www.law.harvard.edu/alumni, accessed January 30, 2004.

Kenny, Sack. "Exit Mrs. Dole Drums, and None Too Soon." *New Hampshire Sunday News*, October 24, 1999, editorial page.

Kirchofer, Tom. "Dole's Education Platform Urges Locker, Backpack Searches." *Daily Collegian* (State College, Pa.), September 23, 1999, 10.

Kittle, Robert A., and Patricia A. Avery. "Behind Reagan's Trouble with Women Voters." *U.S. News & World Report*, May 31, 1982, 51.

Knutson, Lawrence L. "The Senator Gets a Letter from His Wife." *Associated Press*, May 27, 1986.

———. "If Bush Calls, Who Will Answer?" *Associated Press*, August 16, 1988.

Koehl, Carla, and Sarah Van Boven. "Campaign '96 All that Glitters." *Newsweek*, August 26, 1996, 6.

Kosora, Weston. "The Relentless Mrs. Dole." *Newsweek*, February 5, 1996, 30.

Kramer, Michael. "Liddy without Tears, Money Was Part of It, but the Real Reason Her Campaign Tanked Was that Dole Was a Candidate without Substance." *New York Daily News*, October 24, 1999, 47.

Lauter, David. "Labor Post to Go to Elizabeth Dole." *Los Angeles Times*, December 25, 1988, part 1, column 5.

Lavin, Cheryl. "Mrs. Dole Is No Stranger to Power; On Surface, Softer than Mrs. Clinton, but Just as Driven." *Chicago Tribune*, March 24, 1996, C1.

Lawlor, Julia. "PepsiCo, Sterling in 'Glass Ceiling' Probe." *USA Today*, October 25, 1990, 1B.

Leishman, Katie. "A Very Private Public Person." *McCalls*, April 1988, 131–35.

Leonard, Mary. "Liddy's Way." *Boston Sun*, May 9, 1999, A2.

"Liddy's Walk: A Galvanizing Moment for TV-Conventions Debate." *Houston Chronicle*, August 16, 1996, 44.

"A Life of Grace and Kindness." *Salisbury Post*, January 16, 2004. http://www.salisburypost.townnews.com/articles/2004/01/16/editorials/16-01edit_hanford.txt, accessed February 20, 2004.

"Living the Legacy: The Women's Rights Movement, 1848–1998." National Women's History Project, http://www.legacy98.org/move-hist.html, accessed February 3, 2004.

Lorando, Mark. "Keynotes." *Times-Picayune* (New Orleans), August 15, 1996, A.

Lowther, William. "A Bitter Deadlock." *Maclean's*, November 20, 1989, 72.

"'Madame Secretary' Takes Charge." *U.S News & World Report*, January 17, 1983, 14.

Malone, Julia. "First Lady Facing Tough Task at Convention." *Rocky Mountains News*, August 25, 1996, 2A.

Mannies, Jo. "Hillary Clinton, Elizabeth Dole Reach Stand off in Public." *Post Dispatch*, July 14, 1996, 9A.

Mays, Gary. "Thompson Promotes Dole for President: The Visiting Elizabeth Dole, That Is." *Wisconsin State Journal*, January 29, 1997, 1C.

McCombs, Phil. "Roasted! The Gridiron Raucous Ribbing of One and All." *Washington Post*, March 26, 1984, C1.

McKee, Victoria. "The Woman Who Never Says Never." *London Times*, November 12, 1990, features.

Mitchell, Alison. "Elizabeth Dole Questions Clinton's Policies on Iraq and Serbia." *New York Times*, April 15, 1999, A26.

"Mrs. Dole a Double-Edged Asset: Convention Role Debated by the GOP." *Times Picayune* (New Orleans), July 23, 1996, A3.

"Mrs. Dole's Donations." *Washington Post*, May 8, 1996, A17.

Nowell, Paul. "Not Quite Candidate Dole Revels in Hometown Rally." *Morning Call* (Allentown, Pa.), March 11, 1999, A9.

Orin, Deborah. "Will We Have a Woman VP?" *New York Post*, February 8, 2000, 26.

"An Overview 1920–2003." Women's Bureau, U.S. Department of Labor, Washington, D.C. http://www.dol.gov/wb/info_about_wb/interwb.htm, accessed January 30, 2004.

Parker, Laura. "Transportation Secretary on the Road: With Spotlight on Department, Dole Campaigns for Husband." *Washington Post*, September 5, 1987. A1.

———. "The Dilemma of Liddy Dole." *Washington Post*, October 1, 1987.

"Pittston Coal Strike Over." *Mining Journal*, January 5, 1990, 1.

"Pittston, UMWA Reach Settlement in Strike Negotiations." *Coal Age*, January 1990, 13.

Podhoretz, John. "Elizabeth Dole's Painful Lesson—You Need Confidence and a Genuine Message to Win the White House." *New York Post*, October 22, 1999, 29.

Polman, Dick. "Female Faces in the 2000 Race." *Philadelphia Inquirer*, April 12, 1998, E4.

Pope, Victoria. "An Iron Fist in a Velvet Glove." *US News and World Report*, August 19, 1996, 26–27.

Powell, Michael. "The Right Wing and a Prayer." *Washington Post*, August 4, 1999, C1.

"Question: Are You Concerned about the Safety of the Nation's Blood Supply?" *USA Today*, November 19, 1991, A12.

"Racing to Support Elizabeth Dole." *Buffalo News*, January 22, 1998, 2D.

Radcliffe, Donnie. "Style, Washington Ways." *Washington Post*, March 27, 1984, E1.

"Red Cross Wonder Woman?" *Business Week*, January 25, 1999, 81.

Reed, Julia. "Running against Hurricane 'W.'" *Newsweek*, July 12, 1999, 28–29.

Rush, George, and Joanna Molloy. "Books Finds Bad Blood in Mrs. Dole's Red Cross." *New York Daily News*, October 10, 1996, 14.

Saroyan, Strawberry. "Can a Woman Win the White House?" *George*, February 1999, 94.

Sauer, Mark. "Despite Rumors, the First Lady Will Play Central Role in Chicago." *San Diego Union Tribune*, August 27, 1996, A1.

Schemo, Diana Jean. "Curiosity in Dole Exceeds Support." *New York Times*, October 7, 1999, A28.

Schneider, Johanna. "Dole Unveils Wide-Reaching Initiative to Support Women in the Skilled Trades." *U.S. Newswire*, November 23, 1990.

Sedgwick, John. "The Woman Behind that Unwavering Smile." *Newsweek*, August 19, 1996, 36.

Seelye, Katherine Q. "On the Trail, Dole's Wife Seeks Votes of Women." *New York Times,* October 5, 1996, A10.

Skrycki, Cindy, and Frank Swoboda. "Breaking the Corporate Glass Ceiling." *Washington Post,* January 14, 1991, A9.

Smith, Bruce. "Elizabeth Dole Pledges to Rebuild US Military Might." *Morning Call* (Allentown, Pa.), September 28, 1999, A4.

Sobieraj, Sandra. "Dole Ends Bid to Be First Female President." *Morning Call* (Allentown, Pa.), October 21, 1999, A1.

"A Softer Look, A Strong Appeal." *Newsweek,* August 30, 1999, 4.

Soren, Tabitha. "Elizabeth Dole's Newest Job: Wife." *USA Weekend,* August 4, 1996, 6.

Stengel, Richard. "Liddy Makes Perfect." *Time,* July 1, 1996.

Stewart, Richard. "Teens Crossing State Line to Drink." *Houston Chronicle,* June 5, 1994, 1.

"Successful Initiative for Breaking the Glass Ceiling to Upward Mobility for Minorities and Women." Paper prepared for the Glass Ceiling Commission Conference, New York. http://www.ilr.cornell.edu, accessed February 23, 2004.

Talbot, Margaret. "Here Come the Wives." *New York Times,* March 14, 1999, 15.

Thorpe, Helen. "Liddy in Waiting." *George,* August 1999, 110.

Tucker, Cynthia. "Will the Real Elizabeth Dole Please Stand Up?" *Denver Post,* April 27, 1996, B7.

Veneman, Wayne E. "Labor Secretary Dole Announces Record Fine for Mine Disaster." *U.S. Newswire,* July 5, 1989.

Verespej, Michael. "'Rip Van Osha' No Longer Sleeping." *Industry Week,* June 5, 1989, 74.

Victor, Kirk. "Liddy Dole: Off the Sidelines for Good." *National Journal* 22, no. 3 (January 20, 1990): 136.

Volland, Victor. "Dole Extols Virtues of Women in Speech Here: Qualities of Compassion, Tolerance, Would Be Ideal for a President, She Says." *St. Louis Post Dispatch,* November 12, 1997, C2.

Walker, Sam. "Smashing the Glass Ceiling." *Christian Science Monitor,* August 17, 1993, 14.

Wallo, Terri J. "Elizabeth Dole Provides Impetus for Gulf Crisis Fund." *Compass Readings,* May 1991, 20–31.

Weil, Martin. "Elizabeth Koontz, Former Head of Women's Bureau, Dies." *Washington Post,* January 7, 1989, 36.

Weinraub, Bernard. "Dole and Her Husband Gain Favor in Alabama." *New York Times,* July 20, 1987, A12.

———. "Mrs. Dole Weighs Resigning to Join Husband's Campaign." *New York Times,* September 13, 1987, A1.

———. "Mrs. Dole to Seek a More Meaningful Role in Race." *New York Times,* January 13, 1988, D26.

Wilkie, Dana. "Not a Lot of Female GOP Candidates." *San Diego Union-Tribune,* October 5, 1997, A3.

Will, George. "Cast of Characters Line Up to Campaign for Presidency." *Morning Call* (Allentown, Pa.), January 6, 1999, A13.

Williams, Marjorie. "Bob and Liddy Dole, Doing the Town: On the Run with a Well-Oiled Political Act." *The Washington Post*, August 16, 1988, E1.

Yaglielski, Janine, and Kathleen Hayden. "Bush Wins Iowa GOP Straw Poll." August 15, 1999. http://www.allpolitics.com, accessed February 22, 2004.

"Young Pro." *Newsweek*, August 30, 1976, 39.

Zehren, Charles V. "Convention '96/More than Just a Supportive Spouse." *Newsday*, August 15, 1996, A06.

Zitner, Aaron. "On the Campaign Trail, Two Doles Are Better than One." *Concord Monitor*, October 3, 1987.

Zuckman, Jill. "Dole Outlines Get-Tough Approach to Improve Schools, Merit Pay for Teachers, Drug Testing for Students Urged." *Boston Globe*, September 23, 1999, A8.

Books

Clift, Eleanor, and Tom Brazaitis. *Madame President: Shattering the Glass Ceiling.* New York: Scribner, 2000.

Glaser, John S. *The United Way Scandal: An Insider's Account of What Went Wrong and Why.* New York: John Wiley & Sons, 1994.

Grimes, Ann. *Running Mates: The Making of a First Lady.* New York: William Morrow, 1990.

Harpaz, Beth. *The Girls in the Van: A Reporter's Diary of the Campaign Trail.* New York: Thomas Dunne Books, 2001.

Kolmar, Wendy K., and Frances Bartkowski. *Feminist Theory: A Reader.* Mountain View, Calif.: Mayfield Publishing Company, 1999.

Mazey, Susan Gluck. *In Pursuit of Equality: Women, Public Policy, and the Federal Courts.* New York: St. Martin's Press, 1992.

Neff, Thomas, and James M. Citrin. *Lessons from the Top: The 50 Most Successful Business Leaders in America—and What You Can Learn from Them.* New York: Currency/Doubleday, 2001.

O'Dell, Cary. *Women Pioneers in Television.* Jefferson, N.C.: McFarland Press, 1996.

Olson, Steve, with Dean R. Gerstein. *Alcohol in America: Taking Action to Prevent Abuse.* Washington, D.C.: National Academy Press, 1985.

Pamplin, Robert B. Jr., and Gary K. Eisler. "Elizabeth Dole," in *American Heroes: Their Lives, Their Values, Their Beliefs.* Farmington Hills, Mich.: Thorndike Press, 1995.

White, Jane. *A Few Good Women: Breaking the Barriers of Management.* New York: Prentice-Hall, 1992.

Campaign Materials

"Elizabeth Dole for President." Brochure produced by the Elizabeth Dole for President Exploratory Committee, P.O. Box 98132, Washington, D.C. 20077.

"Elizabeth Dole for President." Campaign letter, September 23, 1999.

Newscasts

Jennings, Peter. *ABC News.* 6:15 p.m., September 15, 1987.

Selected Biography

Dole, Bob, and Elizabeth Dole, with Richard Norton Smith and Kerry Tymchuk. *Unlimited Partners: Our American Story.* New York: Simon and Schuster, 1996.

Kozar, Richard. *Elizabeth Dole.* Philadelphia: Chelsea House Publishers, 2000.

Lucas, Ellen. *Elizabeth Dole: A Leader in Washington.* Brookfield, Conn.: The Millbrook Press, 1998.

Mulford, Carolyn. *Elizabeth Dole: Public Servant.* Hillside, N.J.: Enslow Publishers, Inc., 1992.

Thesis and Critical Studies

Bettineschi, Simona. "'Is She or Isn't She': Elizabeth Dole and the Many Faces of Feminism." Research paper presented at Research Fair, Pennsylvania State University, Hazleton Campus, April 2, 2003.

Campbell, Karlyn Kohrs. "The Discursive Performance of Hating Hillary." *Rhetoric and Public Affairs* 1, no. 1 (1998): 1–17.

———. "Shadowboxing with the Stereotypes: The Press, the Public and the Candidate's Wives." Research Paper R-9, Harvard University, John F. Kennedy School of Government, July 1993.

Carroll, Susan J., Caroline Heldman, and Stephanie Olson. "'She Brought Only a Skirt': Gender Bias in Newspaper Coverage of Elizabeth Dole's Campaign for the Republican Nomination." Paper presented at the White House Project Press Conference on Women's Leadership, Washington, D.C., 2001. http://www.thewhitehouseproject.org, accessed February 11, 2004.

Gutgold, Nichola. "The Rhetoric of Elizabeth Dole: Managing Rhetorical Roles 1987–1999." Dissertation, Pennsylvania State University, December 1999.

———. "Managing Rhetorical Roles: Elizabeth Dole from Spouse to Candidate 1996–1999." *Women and Language,* Spring 2001, 29–38.

Hobgood, Linda. "For Such a Time: The Candidacies of Elizabeth Dole." Paper presented at the National Communication Association Convention, Miami, November 22, 2003.

Index

About the Authors

MOLLY MEIJER WERTHEIMER is Associate Professor of Speech Communication and Women's Studies at Penn State, Hazleton.

NICHOLA D. GUTGOLD is Assistant Professor of Communication Arts and Sciences at Penn State, Berks-Lehigh Valley.